MULTINATIONALS AND
EAST ASIAN INTEGRATION

MULTINATIONALS AND EAST ASIAN INTEGRATION

Edited by

Wendy Dobson and
Chia Siow Yue

INTERNATIONAL DEVELOPMENT RESEARCH CENTRE, CANADA
AND
INSTITUTE OF SOUTHEAST ASIAN STUDIES, SINGAPORE

Published jointly by the
International Development Research Centre (www.idrc.ca)
PO Box 8500, Ottawa, ON, Canada K1G 3H9
(for exclusive distribution in Canada, the United States, and Europe)
ISBN 0-88936-806-6
and the
Institute of Southeast Asian Studies (www.iseas.ac.sg)
Heng Mui Keng Terrace, Pasir Panjang, Singapore 119596, Republic of Singapore
(for exclusive distribution in Australia, New Zealand, and throughout Asia)
ISBN 981-3055-60-X
ISSN 0218-2114

Canadian Cataloguing in Publication Data

Main entry under title:
Multinationals and East Asian integration

Co-published by the Institute of Southeast Asian Studies.

Includes bibliographical references.

ISBN 0-88936-806-6

1. International business enterprises — East Asia.
2. East Asia — Economic conditions.
I. Dobson, Wendy.
II. Chia, Siow Yue.
III. International Development Research Centre (Canada).
IV. Institute of Southeast Asian Studies (Singapore).

HD2755.5M84 1997   338.8'88159   C97-980159-1

A microfiche edition is available.

CONTENTS

PART III. CROSSING BORDERS

TABLES AND FIGURES

PREFACE

This project originated in an interest, as the title implies, in the role of firms in East Asia's dynamic growth and regional integration. Three questions motivated the research: What are the links between trade and investment at the level of the firm? How should we understand the contribution of these linkages, rather than intergovernmental trade agreements, to the apparent rapid integration of the East Asian region? Do Asian investors (or investors of any particular nationality) have special influence that might lead to a regional bloc?

These should be straightforward questions to answer, but statistics on firm-level activities are almost nonexistent unless gathered by primary research. The editors were fortunate to assemble a dedicated team of East Asian economists interested in actual observation of multinational affiliates and internationalizing East Asian firms. The project fit the objectives of the International Development Research Centre's (IDRC's) regional integration program, and generous support was provided. IDRC also wished to ensure the knowledge obtained in the project would be made available to researchers in transition economies. As a result, Vietnamese and Chinese researchers participated in two project workshops held in Singapore in 1994 and 1995.

Surveys of 241 firms in the eight economies listed below constituted the main research activity in 1993–94. Primary data collection was very time consuming and difficult because of the reluctance of firms to grant interviews or complete questionnaires and because of the scarcity of data available to local managers. Many were able to provide only interval data for one point in time. We are very grateful to those managers who participated in our surveys. Participating researchers were also creative and persistent, in one case enlisting a spouse to make a personal contact.

We have taken care to distinguish different levels of analysis, including aggregate trade and foreign direct investment (FDI) flows at the country and regional levels, and trade flows within and among firms of several nationalities in several industries.

Our conceptual framework emphasizes the importance of relative factor endowments as determinants of the linkage between trade and investment. In this study, most of the manufacturing industries attracting FDI inflows are global industries, such as electronics, that produce differentiated products. Multinational firms are adept at slicing up the value chain and allocating, through FDI, segments to locations with differing comparative advantages. While national industrial structures appear on the surface to be quite similar, below that level of analysis is a plethora of intrafirm networks within which complementary trade and FDI links are very apparent. Intermediate goods are produced in one location; shipped to other locations in the region, where further value is added; and assembled into differentiated and homogeneous final goods. These networks, in turn, are linked into global networks in these industries. In the electronics industry, we estimate that at least 55% of intraregional trade is also intrafirm.

These firm-level linkages have several implications for regional integration. First, FDI and associated trade flows have a positive sum impact on host economies. Everyone gains from the division of labour according to evolving locational characteristics of host economies. Second, governments position their economies to take advantage of such division of labour by influencing the cost and availability of inputs and access to customers. They should rely more on framework policies such as prudent macroeconomic policies and open trade and investment policies including open domestic markets. These are preferable to direct interventions such as trade-related investment measures. Third, the growing similarity of national industrial structures in East Asia, while promoting growth, is also producing vulnerability. More than half of East Asia's exports were destined for outside the region as recently as 1994 (WTO 1996); thus, cyclical and, possibly, structural vulnerabilities to such factors as currency appreciation and slowdown in world demand for these exports should be anticipated.

Several terms used in this study require clarification at the outset. The first is *East Asia*. We included eight host economies: Guangdong province (China), Hong Kong, Indonesia, Malaysia, the Philippines, Singapore, Taiwan, and Thailand. South Korea is not included because until recently it was not a major host. More recent arrivals like Vietnam are not included for the same reason and because of the lack of complete statistics. Throughout the study, we refer to our subjects as "economies," which is a common practice, although at times we use the generic term *country studies*. In addition, we define the companies that are our subjects as international, multinational, and global firms. By *multinational* and *global*, we mean large firms with operations in several economies, including those outside East Asia. *International* firms refers to multinational enterprises and global firms, as well as small and medium-sized enterprises (SMEs) that originate within the region and have more modest cross-border investments."

Finally, although this study was made possible by IDRC and the Institute of Southeast Asian Studies, the findings and views expressed are those of the authors alone.

Wendy Dobson
Chia Siow Yue
January 1997

ACKNOWLEDGMENTS

This project was made possible by the financial support of Canada's International Development Research Centre (IDRC) and the generous cooperation of the Institute of Southeast Asian Studies (ISEAS) in Singapore. We acknowledge, in particular, the initiatives of Chan Heng Chee, then ISEAS Director, and of W.R. Spence, Director of the IDRC Regional Office in Singapore, who provided insightful advice as the project got under way. Special thanks are also due to Eric Ramstetter, Professor of Economics, Kansai University, for his invaluable and generous efforts as a participant researcher and for his knowledge and connections, which were responsible for a valuable database from the Australian National University.

Although they are in no way responsible for the final product, valuable critical advice came from T.J. Chen, whose cooperation augmented the country surveys; and Leonard Cheng, George Abonyi, Dennis Encarnation, William E. James, Mohamed Ariff, Shigeki Tejima, and Dennis Tachiki, who read and commented on various drafts or participated in project workshops, or both.

Finally, the project logistics alone would have overcome the editors but for the expert assistance of Y.L. Lee, Executive Secretary, ISEAS, and Vivien Choy, Administrative Coordinator, Centre for International Business, University of Toronto.

We gratefully acknowledge the expert and dedicated research of Birgitta Weitz, Stephanie Leblond, and Walid Hejazi. Extensive editorial assistance was also provided by Birgitta Weitz. We are indebted to Bill Carman, Managing Editor, IDRC Books, for his role in bringing this volume to publication.

Part I

INTRODUCTION

Chapter 1

EAST ASIAN INTEGRATION

Synergies Between Firm Strategies
and Government Policies

Wendy Dobson

A frequently cited corollary of East Asia's remarkable economic dynamism is that its economies are rapidly and spontaneously integrating with one another. Although many of the reasons for such integration, and its consequences, have been extensively studied, the cross-border activities of firms have not.

How do firms influence East Asian integration?[1] International firms[2] create linkages across borders in their search for profitable opportunities through trade, foreign direct investment (FDI), technology contracts, and other arrangements that provide flexibility needed to adjust to change and uncertainty in increasingly competitive factor and product markets. Change and uncertainty are generated in markets by such factors as technological advance, exchange rate volatility, and governments' policies and regulations affecting market access and production costs. Host governments in East Asia encourage FDI inflows to augment domestic savings, to promote technological transfer to accelerate economic development, and to obtain access to international markets for their exports.

The purpose of this study is to examine the trade and investment activities of international firms in selected manufacturing industries in eight East Asian economies — those of China (Guangdong province), Hong Kong, Indonesia, Malaysia, the Philippines, Singapore, Taiwan, and Thailand — to cast light on their impact on regional economic linkages. How is their production organized, particularly with respect to their traded activities? How much trade is intrafirm? intraindustry? Do these patterns differ by corporate nationality (that is, home country of investor), by location, by industry, and by the age of the enterprise or its size? What do these patterns imply about countries' trade policies and about the intraregional intensity of trade and investment ties compared with those with the rest of the world? Do international firms' independence and their growing importance in global production[3] discipline governments' domestic policy freedom? Research questions based on these initial questions are posed in the final section of this chapter.

---

[1] Economic integration is the process by which barriers to flows of goods, services, and capital are reduced, allowing the freer play of market forces. This process, which can be spontaneous or induced by trade liberalization agreements among governments, has been described as "shallow" integration. It is distinguished from "deep" integration, which is seen to occur when governments alter domestic policies to harmonize policies or converge with the economic performance of their partners.

[2] *International firms* refers to multinational enterprises (MNEs), which locate parts of their operations in different countries; multidomestic firms, which replicate operations in multiple countries; and small and medium-sized enterprises (SMEs), which produce on a smaller scale across borders.

[3] The World Bank (1995) and the United Nations Committee on Trade and Development (UNCTAD 1994) estimate that world sales of foreign affiliates of MNEs may now exceed the world's total exports.

This topic implies several levels of analysis: the regional level, the level of individual economies, and the firm level in particular industries. The overview in this chapter relates regional integration and firm behaviour. In the next section, I review studies of the determinants of regional integration, to establish whether trade and investment ties are becoming more intensive within the region than with the rest of the world. The third section shifts the focus to firms and governments and suggests possible "synergies" between their respective strategies. In studying firms' role in integration in this study, we focus on the value-chain activities of affiliates and their associated intrafirm trade, rather than on the more traditional measure, intraindustry trade (IIT). Firms' production and trade in host economies are influenced by such well-known determinants as location, industry, corporate nationality of the parent, and affiliates' age and size. Host governments' public policies aimed at attracting or influencing the value-added activities of international firms are prominent locational determinants.

In the final section, research methodology, study design, and research questions are presented. Unique data sources were used for this study, including eight firm-level surveys conducted in 1994 by the authors in the eight East Asian economies, which are significant recipients of FDI inflows.[4] The firm-level surveys were carried out in the electronics, textile and garment, auto, and chemical industries, which are the recipients of much of the inflows of manufacturing-related FDI and account for a significant share of trade. Taken together, these industries accounted for nearly half of world merchandise trade in 1994 and 60% of Asian exports (WTO 1996). Patterns of intrafirm trade in these industries, holding location constant, are analyzed in the eight country chapters; in Chapter 10, the firm is held constant in an analysis of the cross-border activities of six electronics firms.

Regional integration

The traditional determinants of integration among a group of economies are gravity (proximity and size of respective economies); growth rates of the economies; policies (creation of preferential trade ties, reduction of barriers to trade, and host-country policies to influence direct investment); and firms (the activities of firms, measured traditionally through IIT).

The role of policies has received extensive study because of concerns that the world may be organizing into regional trading blocs. Successive multilateral trade negotiations in the postwar period, progress toward currency convertibility, and dramatic improvements in international communications and transportation have reduced barriers to international business and facilitated flows of trade and investment. Intraregional trading arrangements in the European Union (EU) and those in the North American Free Trade Agreement (NAFTA) have raised concerns that regional trading blocs are forming.[5] Economists generally view bloc formation as a negative development. They believe that, whether through formal institutional arrangements or through more spontaneous market-driven developments, blocs will yield a lower level of world welfare than would a fully open and multilateral trading system.[6]

---

[4] The Republic of Korea is not included because it has not until recently been an important destination for FDI. Although Korean firms have become significant outward investors in the region, few agreed to participate in our surveys.

[5] Regional integration can be either market or policy driven. East Asian integration has occurred in the absence of a formal institutional framework, whereas integration in Europe and North America has occurred with formal trade agreements. The term *bloc* generally refers to arrangements among partners in an institutional framework in which policies toward nonpartners become more restrictive or exclusive.

[6] The issue has stimulated heated debate. This debate is summarized in Federal Reserve Bank of Kansas City (1991). Paul Krugman, on one side, took the position that, in theory, free-trade zones are undesirable because they divert trade from low-cost to high-cost suppliers. In practice, however, free-trade zones increase market size and are therefore likely to be trade promoting because of their contribution to productive efficiency and competitiveness. Fred Bergsten took the opposite position — that moving to free-trade zones was bad, both in theory and in practice. He argued that, too often, institutionalized free-trade zones may have the implicit goal of diverting trade and that a free-trade zone in the Western hemisphere would divert trade from low-cost producers around the world.

In East Asia, trade flows have been growing rapidly for the past two decades. Intraregional trade increased in the 1980s, as it had earlier in North America and the European Economic Community. If the increased intensity of these trade flows is simply the result of growth and development, rather than of preferential arrangements negotiated by governments, then fears of an evolving trading bloc are overblown. Measures of integration, summarized below, show that East Asia is closely tied into the world trading system. Only very recent evidence suggests that ties within the region are becoming more intensive than those with the rest of the world.

Historically, preferential trading arrangements have not played much of a role in the integration of East Asian economies. Such arrangements have existed in the Association of Southeast Asian Nations (ASEAN) since 1977, yet in 20 years the intra-ASEAN share of ASEAN's total trade has barely increased: from 17.1% in 1970 to 18.3% in 1992 (Hill 1995). Indeed, the fastest trade growth within the region has been the growth of trade with China since 1979, and this has occurred in the absence of formal trade-liberalization agreements. Such trends toward spontaneous regional integration result from progressive outward orientation of individual economies' trade and investment policies and unilateral liberalization of goods and capital markets. Governments have also moved aside to facilitate the creation of "subregional economic zones" of economic cooperation, most notably the SIJORI growth triangle (Singapore; the Malaysian state of Johore; and Batam Island in Riau, Indonesia) and the South China Economic Zone (including Guangdong province of China and Hong Kong). In both cases, governments have recognized that economic complementarities between available cheap labour and land in some parts of the subregion and capital available in Singapore and Hong Kong, respectively, could contribute to higher rates of regional growth and development than would otherwise have been possible.

Since the early 1990s, however, governments have been moving toward more formalized preferential arrangements. In January 1992, ASEAN heads of state adopted the Common Effective Preferential Tariff (CEPT) agreement, which will lead to the establishment of the ASEAN Free Trade Area (AFTA). In September 1992, a modest institutional framework was created for the Asia–Pacific Economic Cooperation (APEC) forum as a vehicle for regional economic cooperation. Since November 1994, when the Bogor Declaration was signed by APEC leaders at a summit meeting in Indonesia, a framework has existed in which free trade will be pursued in the group during the next two decades.

Measures of integration

Has intraregional trade increased more rapidly than would be predicted in a systematic framework measuring a normal level of trade? Gravity models shed light on the question, using distance and economic-size variables to explain bilateral flows among countries in a group. If there were nothing to the notion of trading blocs, gravity variables would absorb most of the explanatory power. Frankel (1993) found some evidence of a special regional effect, with a drop in the bias in the first half of the 1980s and a slight increase in the second half implying that intraregional trade cannot be entirely explained by proximity and size.[7]

Historical gravity models show a steady decline in the regional bias of East Asian trade in all but the last 5 years (Petri 1993). Gravity coefficients have fallen steadily in the postwar period. This is true for most individual East Asian economies as well.[8]

The traditional measure of integration has been indices of IIT (for example, Grubel and Lloyd 1975; Belassa 1986). This measure is usually applied to economies with similar structures and income levels. IIT indices measure the extent to which an economy's imports in an industrial category approximate its exports in the same category; in other words, the index measures trade in

---

[7] None of these results was statistically significant, though.

[8] This is with the exception of China, where the decline has been rapid, and the Philippines, where there has been an increase. Both these changes have political explanations.

differentiated products. IIT has formed the basis for an increasing amount of trade in world manufactures for the past three decades. Indeed, formal trading arrangements in Europe were facilitated by rising IIT, which afforded opportunities for specialization in differentiated products and continued trade among partner economies.

Several studies of the Asia–Pacific region have identified similarities in per capita incomes, relative factor endowments, geographic proximity, common borders, and participation in regional trading arrangements as determinants of IIT (Fukusaku 1992; Dobson 1993; Drysdale and Garnaut 1993; Saxonhouse 1993). Indices for 1970, 1980, and 1990 for 15 Asia–Pacific economies — the 8 economies in this study, the 3 NAFTA economies, Australia, New Zealand, India and Japan — reveal a general pattern of rising IIT. Intra-East Asian trade-intensity indices declined, however, during the same period (Drysdale and Garnaut 1993). Taken together, these measures indicate that much remains to be done within the ASEAN countries (excluding Singapore) to liberalize the structure of protection of final consumption goods, intermediate products, and basic raw materials (Flatters and Harris 1995).

Simpler measures of trade intensity and ratios of evolving intraregional trade flows indicate that ties with the rest of the world continue to dominate the region's trade (Petri 1993). Integration can also be measured by estimating the ratio of extraregional exports and imports relative to a country's gross national product (GNP) (Lawrence 1991).[9] By this measure, extraregional trade is very important to Japan and Southeast Asia. The importance of extraregional trade means that no region is in a position to sever or significantly curtail its trade ties with the rest of the world by forming closed blocs.

Japan-centred integration?

Some analysts have focused on the political economic question of whether Japan has tried to influence its neighbours' trade toward itself. Successive waves of outward investment from Japan have flowed to the United States, Europe, and more recently East Asia. Although the East Asian share of these flows has been small, the size of investment inflows relative to the sizes of host economies has been significant. Inflows since the mid-1980s have increased the stock of Japanese investment such that it now approximates the US share in many economies.

A single economic theory explaining these surges of outward FDI is lacking (Graham and Krugman 1993), but some assert, rightly or wrongly, that Japan is pursuing a political strategy to become the centre of a potentially self-sustaining Asian economic system (Fallows 1994). Measured purely by trade shares, evidence of a "triangular" trading relationship among these economies existed in the 1986–92 period (Table 1.1). In Table 1.1, the share of each economy's manufacturing exports is presented as a ratio of its import shares with Japan, the United States, Europe, and ASEAN-9 (the eight study economies plus Korea). Typically, ratios with Japan are less than one — an economy's exports to Japan as shares of total exports are about one-third the size of its import shares from Japan. The ratios for the United States are the reverse: exports shares are two to five times larger than import shares. Europe's are closer to parity, while the ratios among the ASEAN-9 economies show Indonesia, Taiwan, and Singapore to be the most export dependent. In effect, Japan's East Asian neighbours depend on it for imports and on the United States and Europe for export markets.

More sophisticated analysis using gravity models does not find evidence that Japan is diverting trade toward itself, however. Although trade between Japan and other Asian countries increased substantially in the late 1980s, the intraregional bias did not (as measured by introducing a dummy variable for trade with Japan [Frankel 1993]). The trend in bilateral trade between Japan and its neighbours can be explained readily as a natural outcome of the overall growth of Japanese trade, the emphasis in the structure of Japanese production on machinery and other intermediate and capital goods, and the growth levels attained in other Asian economies.

---

[9] This measure simply looks at a country's dependence on world trade. It could easily be refined to look at a country's dependence on a region. Furthermore, it would be useful to have a time series of these ratios to see what is happening to this dependence, however defined.

Table 1.1. Ratios of manufacturing export to import shares:
East Asian economies and the triad.

Host economy	Japan	United States	Europe	ASEAN-9[a]
China				
1986	0.35	2.00	0.65	1.65
1989	0.63	2.00	1.00	0.94
1992	0.65	2.20	1.33	0.77
Hong Kong				
1986	0.18	5.25	1.75	0.35
1989	0.35	4.13	2.00	0.47
1992	0.28	4.00	1.90	0.63
Indonesia				
1986	0.81	1.36	0.84	1.40
1989	1.19	1.00	0.94	1.12
1992	0.68	1.14	0.95	1.19
Malaysia				
1986	0.35	1.30	1.19	0.94
1989	0.30	1.39	1.46	1.13
1992	0.29	1.35	1.31	1.18
Philippines				
1986	0.48	1.67	1.50	0.73
1989	0.56	2.18	1.40	0.75
1992	0.58	2.24	1.33	0.64
Singapore				
1986	0.33	1.33	0.71	1.16
1989	0.33	1.21	0.93	1.19
1992	0.30	1.17	1.07	1.08
Taiwan				
1986	0.23	2.13	0.79	1.75
1989	0.32	1.61	1.00	2.10
1992	0.31	1.45	1.38	1.29
Thailand				
1986	0.31	1.57	1.06	1.09
1989	0.37	2.18	1.21	0.80
1992	0.45	2.00	1.20	0.81

Source: Annex Tables 1.A1 and 1.A2.
[a] The eight study economies plus Korea.

Firms, governments, and regional integration

International firms contribute to integration because their cross-border investments in affiliates and their joint ventures and strategic alliances are trade promoting.[10] MNE affiliates are more trade oriented than local firms, and the relationship between trade and their investments in local affiliates is increasingly complementary. Historically, the major foreign investors in East Asia have been Japanese and American firms (Table 1.2). Since 1980, however, Taiwanese and Korean firms and, more recently, firms from Southeast Asia have become more significant sources of investment flows

---

[10] Empirical studies of links between trade and investment have focused on the impact on home economies of outward investment by MNEs (Bergsten et al. 1978) and on the impact of FDI on host economies (Reuber 1973). Others have sought to determine whether trade and FDI are substitutes or complements (Lipsey and Weiss 1981, 1984). Increasingly, however, attention has turned to assessing the impacts of production-location decisions on trade flows of host countries. Recent work suggests that trade and FDI are complements: host-country exports are generally positively affected when FDI flows into a subsidiary that produces downstream products, production complements, or demand substitutes (Petri 1995).

Table 1.2. Stocks of FDI by host and source economy, 1980 and 1992 shares of host economies' totals.

Host economy	United States	Japan	East Asia[a]	Others
China				
1986	16.8	10.7	61.7	10.8
1991	10.1	12.5	66.2	11.2
Hong Kong				
1984	53.7	21.0	2.1[b]	23.2
1994	26.8	33.5	12.0	27.7
Indonesia				
1980	4.7	37.5	13.7	44.1
1992	4.3	20.7	22.9	52.1
Malaysia				
1986	10.3	25.7	23.7	40.3
1993	10.6	32.3	29.4	27.7
Philippines				
1980	54.6	16.8	5.4	23.2
1992	47.4	21.0	10.3	21.3
Singapore				
1980	22.5	11.7	19.6	46.2
1992	17.0	23.3	11.8	47.9
Taiwan				
1980	35.0	18.6	30.3	16.1
1992	27.2	29.0	19.8	24.0
Thailand				
1980	35.6	28.9	17.5	18.0
1992	17.3	34.0	31.8	16.9

Source: China, Ministry of Foreign Economic Relations and Trade (MOFERT); APEC Economic Committee (1995); national sources for Hong Kong, Malaysia, and Singapore.

Note: Chinese data are utilized cumulative inflows; Malaysian data are actual fixed assets; Philippines data are cumulative foreign-equity investments since 1970; Singapore data represent year-end values of foreign direct investments; Thai data consist of equity inflows, net of repatriated investments, plus net intercompany loans outstanding since 1970. Data for Hong Kong, Malaysia, and Singapore are for manufacturing only. Data for Indonesia and Taiwan are cumulative approved inflows since 1967 and 1952, respectively.

[a] East Asia includes China, four newly industrialized economies (Hong Kong, Singapore, Taiwan, and Korea), and four ASEAN economies (Indonesia, Malaysia, the Philippines, and Thailand).

[b] For Hong Kong, East Asia includes only Singapore and China.

in China, Indonesia, Malaysia, Thailand, and the Philippines.[11] European investors are also entering the region in increasing numbers; they are included in the Other category in Table 1.2, which accounts for significant shares of FDI stock in Singapore and Indonesia. Although the industrial distribution of FDI favours nonmanufacturing (with large stocks in natural resources, trading activities in the case of the Japanese, and more recently services), manufacturing-related FDI is concentrated in the electronics and electrical, textile and garment, chemical, and auto industries, which constitute the focus of this study.

Economic theory linking trade and FDI is only in the early stages of development. Until recently, explanations of international trade were developed in isolation from those explaining FDI. "New trade" theorists have refined traditional trade theory, based on the principle of comparative advantage, with the application of industrial organization models that incorporate assumptions of imperfect competition, differentiated products, and returns to scale.

---

[11] FDI flows are measured by East Asian governments as either intended (but not necessarily realized) investments or actual investments. In Table 1.2, FDI data are reported on a notification basis by Malaysia, Indonesia, and China and as actual investments in the other economies.

Theories about why firms internationalize, that is, engage in international production through FDI rather than carrying on international business through market transactions such as trade, is a very general one. It is based on the organizational theories of Coase (1937) and Williamson (1975) and adaptations by Dunning (1988) in which MNEs produce abroad to reduce transactions costs. They also gain economic and strategic advantage by exploiting their distinctive proprietary assets in several markets. They choose to do so within the firm (by "internalizing"), rather than through the market (by exporting or licencing their technologies or through a variety of arrangements such as strategic alliances), because of the perceived efficiencies of protecting those assets from imitation and because markets and alliances are imperfect ways to transfer newer or more advanced technologies.

MNEs locate affiliates or plants in cross-border locations for several reasons: factor cost or supply (such as low-cost labour or plentiful natural resources); the existence of a large or rapidly growing market; public policies, such as fiscal incentives, financial inducements, tariffs, availability of infrastructure, and political stability; and strategic factors, such as the desire to preempt entry by rivals or to secure access to local technologies, skills, etc. (Safarian 1993).

Attempts to link trade and investment are of two kinds. One is based on the product cycle framework, of which two variants have been applied to analysis of the East Asian experience. Vernon's (1966) model described the product cycle behaviour of innovating firms in industrialized countries. Kojima (1978), following Akamatsu (1962), described the behaviour of imitating firms in Japan and other developing countries.

Vernon's (1966) model begins with a product innovation by an oligopolistic firm that, once it achieves dominance in its home market, starts exporting. As costs rise and imitators appear, the producer would invest abroad in locations with lower comparative costs. Krugman (1979) showed that the innovator could retain its trade advantage by carrying on constant innovation (rather than a single innovation). Akamatsu (1962) and Kojima (1978) described the "catching-up product cycle thesis," according to which a follower country first imports a product of superior quality. As domestic demand for the product increases, it is produced domestically. After a learning process, often fostered by trade protection, costs are sufficiently reduced and quality is sufficiently improved to export the product. FDI plays a role insofar as it assists the learning process. Akamatsu had earlier adapted this framework to his "flying geese" model of diversification and industrial upgrading (in this case the sequencing was from one industry to another, rather than from imports to domestic production to exports). In this process, the leading country invests in the follower country in industries in which the leading country encounters comparative cost disadvantage relative to the follower. In this way, FDI accelerates the economic development of the follower country.

These frameworks describe both product and industry "cycles," although some authors have argued that one of the main implications — that entire industries are relocated — is not empirically supported (Bernard and Ravenhill 1995). Kojima (1995) expanded the industry-level of analysis, noting that as domestic industries mature and exports peak, outward FDI occurs, both to secure the lower cost intermediate goods needed to retain comparative advantage and to maintain market share through local sales or re-exporting. Others explain Japan's economic restructuring in the postwar period as a continuous process of interindustry upgrading to ever higher value-added manufacturing in Japan (Ozawa and Hine 1993). Still others have modified these concepts to incorporate foreign companies investing in and transferring technology to follower economies to target production of labour-intensive consumer durables and nondurables for export markets. When export competitiveness eventually declines as relative costs change, specialization shifts toward the export of capital goods (APEC Economic Committee 1995a). Japanese companies are also seen to be using differences in technical expertise and labour costs to establish a global division of labour based on sophistication of products: the Japanese parent company, for example, produces high-speed copiers, the European subsidiary produces medium-speed copiers, and the Chinese subsidiary produces low-speed copiers (JETRO 1995).

The other attempt at a unified theory is based on the extension of the new trade theory to incorporate FDI (Helpman and Krugman 1985). In this model, the firm's activities are broken down into goods and services of declining capital intensity and increasing labour intensity, including headquarters services, differentiated goods, and homogeneous goods. Transportation costs and trade barriers are ignored. Under the assumptions of the new trade theory noted earlier, increasing returns to scale promote concentration of the firm's activities, and choices as to location of FDI are determined by factor price differentials.

The greater the differences among countries in factor endowments, the more likely is a firm producing differentiated products at home to invest abroad to exploit factor price differentials. The model implies that the trade that results is likely to be exports of head office products (capital-intensive and differentiated goods and services), which are exchanged for finished versions of differentiated and homgeneous goods produced by affiliates in foreign locations. Another implication of the model is that FDI will generate complementary intrafirm trade.

In this study, we apply a framework based on comparative costs to explain linkages between trade and FDI. We assume that firms, regardless of nationality, respond to changing comparative costs in the home and host economies in much the way envisaged by both approaches discussed above.

We further assume that firms allocate foreign production in value-added segments by "slicing up the value chain" (Krugman 1995) and relocating firms and business segments as the comparative advantage of a location for investment changes. Sociologists, looking for explanations of Asian industrialization, have also analyzed value-chain segments, which they call "commodity chains," as organizational determinants of national economic performance (for example, Gereffi and Korzeniewicz 1994; Gereffi 1996).

Using the "segment" as the unit of analysis, we do not expect that entire industries will relocate but expect that industry **segments** will. Firms in the assembly-based industries, be they multinationals or international firms of more recent vintage, link these value-added activities into production networks as ways to increase international competitiveness. Faced with intensifying competition because of such factors as deregulation, falling trade barriers, and increasing capital mobility, these firms seek production efficiencies by unbundling value-added activities that were previously vertically integrated within a single location or production unit. Locational factors, particularly factor endowments and government policies, are determinants of where those activities will be allocated.

Value-added activities with price sensitivity, standard technologies, and low entry barriers will be located — and relocated — to sites with comparative advantage in, for example, low-cost labour or plentiful natural resources. Services or products that embody recent innovations or are capital or technology intensive with high entry barriers will be allocated to sites with comparative advantage in skilled labour, low-cost communications, and infrastructure. Production networks are created by these cross-border trade linkages, either within a firm or among cooperating firms, because the many intermediate goods in the assembly-based industries that are the focus of this study must be shipped from where they are produced to other locations (with different comparative advantage) where further value is added in the form of finishing, testing, assembly, or marketing. (Domestic linkages are also created, but because of the regional-integration focus of this study, they are of less interest.) This unbundling is facilitated by firm-specific capabilities in microelectronics and information technology to coordinate production and trade of the many components to be assembled into the final product.

We link the firms' activities to economy-wide restructuring through our view of the importance of host governments' policies as locational determinants. Of course, the direction of causation is two way: the activities of foreign firms also affect the industrial structures of host economies. Our focus, however, is primarily on the impacts sought by governments; hence, we regard host-government policies as locational effects.

Governments have been notably successful in marshalling inputs through industrial upgrading — a willingness, perhaps unique to follower economies, to restructure entire industries (and, more recently, value-added activities within industries) in line with the shifting comparative advantage of the host economy. They have also been successful in creating new sources of comparative advantage in the form of supplies of more advanced skills, and more sophisticated infrastructure.

We inquire into the impact of home-country effects (of different corporate nationality) on MNEs' investment and trade behaviour, asking whether Japanese MNEs behave significantly differently from US or other firms. We examine, as well, whether firms in the same industry behave the same way regardless of home country and location; that is, are there industry effects? Finally, because multinational behaviour may be influenced by both a firm's age and its national origins (Vernon 1972, 1994), these dimensions become a necessary part of our analysis. We ask whether the age of the affiliate in the host economy (vintage) or its size influences its trade and investment behaviour.

In the sections that follow, I first review the literature on these questions and then present our study questions and research design.

Location effects: countries and comparative advantage

Explanations advanced for the high and sustained growth rates achieved in East Asian economies have generated heated debate. Rapid factor accumulation is a major explanation (Young 1994), aided by openness to trade and foreign investment, avoidance of large price distortions, sound macroeconomic polices, and government interventions that were conditional on performance (World Bank 1993).

Often overlooked, however, is the fact that despite the common characteristic of "miracle" growth performance, these economies are also economically, culturally, and politically diverse. Measures of this diversity, which is difficult to capture in a simple way, will reflect factor accumulation, common to all these economies, and differentiation among them according to productivity-enhanced growth. Productivity growth is achieved through advances in efficiency in the use of factors of production, the introduction of new technologies (including managerial innovations), and better quality skills and can be measured by such indicators as an economy's annual research and development (R&D) expenditures, openness to FDI as a source of technical transfer, imports from Organisation for Economic Co-operation and Development economies (because such imports will embody more advanced technologies than are available locally), and education as an indicator of absorptive capacity.

Indicators of this kind have been developed by Coe et al. (1994) and, when applied to the economies in this study (Fig. 1.1), help to illustrate the diversity within the group.[12] When the economies are ranked by per capita income, measured on a purchasing power parity (PPP) basis, a "hierarchy" becomes apparent. Singapore ranks highest on the productivity indicators, followed by Hong Kong and Taiwan. Both Hong Kong's and Taiwan's indicators reflect differential policy influences: Hong Kong lacks Singapore's large government expenditures on R&D (relying exclusively on market forces), while the Taiwanese government, until recently, has restricted FDI inflows. Interestingly, whereas Malaysia's indicators resemble those in Hong Kong, Malaysia's low GERD ratio (gross expenditures on R&D as a percentage of GNP) resembles that in Thailand. Thailand and Indonesia share relatively low educational levels for the group, in contrast to the Philippines. With the exception of that indicator, however, the indicators of the Philippines are among the lowest in the group.

---

[12] The indicators in Figure 1.1 are as follows:
 ❖ GERD ratio: R&D expenditure/GDP (WEF 1995);
 ❖ FDI/GDP: FDI stock in US dollars as a ratio of GDP in US dollars (APEC Economic Committee 1995a);
 ❖ Foreign R&D capital stock: stock of OECD countries' technical knowledge embodied in imports from OECD countries (Coe et al. 1994); and
 ❖ Education: secondary-school enrollment rate as percentage of population of secondary-school age (Coe et al. 1994).

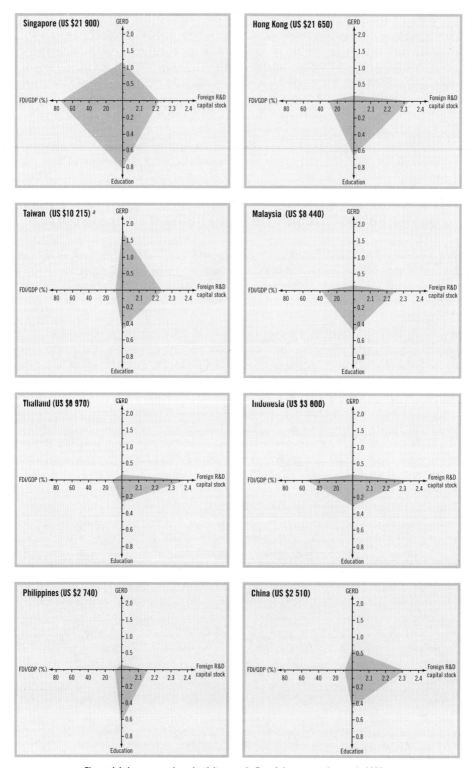

Figure 1.1. Incomes and productivity growth: East Asian economies, early 1990s.
Source: Coe et al. (1994); Asian Development Bank (1996); World Bank (1996); World Economic Forum (1996).
Note: Per capita income on the basis of purchasing power parity (1994) is given in parentheses.
[a] Taiwan income in current US$.

Thus, although the indicators overlap in some ways, they suggest three "levels" in the group, which are suggested most consistently by the per capita income indicators: Singapore, Hong Kong, and Taiwan are the closest to being productivity driven and enjoy five-figure per capita incomes. They are followed by Malaysia and Thailand, which continue to rely heavily on factor (particularly investment) accumulation and enjoy per capita incomes in the US$7 000–8 000 range. Figure 1.1 illustrates the difficulties of generalizations, but indicators suggest that Indonesia, the Philippines, and China rely on factor accumulation, which is also reflected in per capita incomes in the US$2 000–4 000 range.

Such diversity has allowed a division of labour that is well understood by business and government in the region and is significant in this study because of the ways both players have taken advantage of it in pursuing their respective objectives. Governments seek to raise living standards and meet welfare objectives through high economic growth rates. East Asian governments have also sought to upgrade their industrial structures by encouraging continuous introduction of new, more advanced, higher value-added industries and destruction or relocation to follower economies of mature standard-technology industries with waning competitiveness. As upgrading occurs, a country's industrial structure evolves toward higher-productivity, higher-wage industries and industry segments, and its comparative advantage (and therefore its trade pattern) changes through time.

In most East Asian economies, MNEs are seen to be sources of growth because they supply additional savings and transfer technology and develop new skills, as well as other managerial assets such as international marketing networks. These inputs contribute to the objectives of industrialization and international competitiveness. Host economies enjoy the social benefits of higher employment rates, more diversification of employment opportunities, greater acquisition of new skills, and higher incomes than would otherwise have been the case. Most have also been careful to encourage firms to develop an export orientation relatively early, to begin to meet market tests of the success of development policies.

During the past 30 years, trade policies have changed from encouraging import substitution to encouraging exports. Hong Kong and Singapore have pursued export-led growth with free trade; Singapore has actively encouraged the inflow of multinationals, so much so that its industrial structure is dominated by foreign firms. MNEs now account for a large share of manufacturing production and an even larger share of manufactured exports. In contrast, Taiwan practiced import substitution for a considerable period within an overall policy of export-led growth and restricted FDI inflows until recently. Small local firms have proliferated in Taiwan and Hong Kong, resulting in a highly decentralized industrial structure. Among the economies of Indonesia, Malaysia, the Philippines, and Thailand, the promotion of FDI inflows has been accompanied by the development of local private conglomerates and large state-owned enterprises.

Policies towards FDI have been liberalized to improve administrative frameworks, introduce and improve investment incentives, and relax ownership and performance requirements. Administrative frameworks have simplified screening and approval procedures and established "one-stop" investment centres in response to demands for transparency in regulations and administrative procedures and for speedier processing of approvals, which can be crucial to time-sensitive investments in electronics.

Governments increasingly resort to fiscal and other incentives to attract FDI (Table 1.3), despite several studies showing that incentives have little impact on location decisions and are unnecessary for attracting FDI already headed for the region. Investment diversion to specific countries represents resource misallocation and "beggar-thy-neighbour" policies. Some argue that the welfare effects of such incentives depend on whether they protect and promote inefficient activities or facilitate dynamic comparative advantage by promoting skills development and encouraging local SMEs to become component suppliers to multinationals.

Governments also impose ownership restrictions and performance requirements on FDI to protect domestic enterprises and to exact maximum benefits from foreign firms. These measures include

Table 1.3. Use of fiscal incentives in East Asia.

	Countries offering incentives in early 1990s (*n*)	Range of incentives (changes between mid-1980s and 1990s)		Countries that offer incentives (changes between mid-1980s and 1990)	
		More	Less	More	Less
Sample size (*n*)	17	10		10	
Type of incentive					
Exemptions from import duties	13	X			X
Reduction of standard corporate tax rate		X		=	=
Tax holidays		X		X	
Specific deductions on gross earnings for income-tax purposes	12	X		X	
Accelerated depreciation			X		X
Duty drawbacks	8	X		X	
Investment–reinvestment allowance		=	=	X	
Deductions from social-security contributions		X		X	

Source: UNCTAD (1995).
Note: X, more incentives were offered, or more countries offered incentives; =, no change.

restrictions on the share of foreign equity in an investment, on land ownership, on participation in strategic sectors, and on remittances; licencing requirements; limits on royalties and fees; local-content rules; and requirements to employ local personnel, to export, to balance trade, to transfer technology, and to transfer price administration.

The combined use of these policies imposes a huge and unnecessary resource loss on some economies, distorts business decisions, and may not maximize efficiency and competitiveness. Import restrictions and local-content requirements in the auto industry in the economies in this study, for example, have led to suboptimal plant scales, sourcing of high-cost local inputs, and higher prices for consumers.

Many of the policy restrictions on FDI violate World Trade Organization (WTO) principles of right of establishment, national treatment, and unconditional most-favoured-nation (MFN) treatment. The Uruguay Round trade-related investment measures (TRIMS) agreement requires developing countries to phase out local-content measures and trade-balancing requirements within 5 years because they are inconsistent with General Agreement on Tariffs and Trade (GATT) principles on national treatment. Foreign-exchange-balancing restrictions and domestic-sales requirements are also considered inconsistent with GATT regulations on quantitative restrictions. Yet governments are reluctant to act unilaterally or multilaterally to remove tax incentives, restrictions, and performance requirements beyond the TRIMS agreement, as manifested in the weak provisions of this agreement and of the Nonbinding Investment Principles adopted by the APEC governments in 1994.

In summary, the rapid growth of trade and investment ties in East Asia has been facilitated by the economic diversity of host economies, the appearance of new competitors, and the willingness of governments to modify policy and to encourage industrial restructuring to exploit changing market conditions. But it is the firms searching for profitable opportunities through trade and investment that have driven the integration process.

Firms, corporate nationality, and organizational attributes

Firms

International firms exploit national and regional diversity to promote their own competitive advantage within their industry. Building on the traditional concept of comparative advantage, Porter (1986) developed the "diamond" model of determinants of a firm's competitive advantage to augment the traditional measure of relative factor abundance with such factors as market size, existence of suppliers and buyers in the industry, industry structure, and rivalry within the industry.

Several of the industries in this study — consumer and industrial electronics, computers, autos, and chemicals — are global industries in which firms organize their activities and operations across a number of economies to promote competitive advantage. A firm's position in one country affects its position in others. These are industries that are also characterized by significant barriers to entry, differentiated products, high levels of IIT, and strategic behaviour.[13]

Global firms are able to integrate and manage their activities across borders. Indeed, their global activities would not be sustainable without these capabilities. They link operations in countries with differing locational advantages (which include host-government incentives). Affiliates are organized to carry out value-added activities in various locations to preserve or enhance competitive advantage. Each of these activities must add value for the buyer. Downstream sales and marketing activities are likely to be located close to buyers in local markets (hence the increase in related service activities in the region as incomes have risen). Upstream production and operations, as well as related support activities, will be located where they best promote the firm's global competitive advantage.

Understanding the links between trade and investment requires understanding the firms' basic strategic choices made to achieve competitive advantage over their rivals:

❖ By pursuing cost advantages in ways that ensure that the buyer gets value comparable to that provided by rivals but at lower cost;

❖ By pursuing a differentiation strategy in which it carries out its activities in a "unique" way that differentiates the product from those of rivals and allows the supplier to command a premium price for its unique brand; or

❖ By focusing either on even lower priced products or on segments or products that require highly specialized technologies and command high prices to offset low-cost competition, thus concentrating in ways that buyers value.

Porter (1990) pointed out that several strategies will be found in any particular industry.

It is popularly assumed that most foreign firms in the industries in this study pursue some variation of a low-cost strategy in East Asia (for example, APEC Economic Committee 1995a), such as defensive investments to reduce costs and so preserve or enhance global competitive advantage. Although this is true of many companies, reality is more complicated and interesting. Each strategic choice has benefits and risks; indeed, all three strategies can be seen in firms' activities in the region. The low-cost strategy is, of course, the most straightforward. The producer aims to undersell rivals with the same products by reducing production and transactions costs, locating near low-cost factor supplies, or achieving significant economies of scale.

Differentiation strategies depend on a firm's ability to reconfigure the value chain or identify sources of uniqueness in the way it links or locates segments; to coordinate; and to learn. Timing of the introduction and evolution of the strategy can be crucial to its uniqueness. Differentiators face

---

[13] Multidomestic industries are those in which firms compete in several countries but on a country-by-country basis; the international industry is a collection of domestic industries. Such patterns are found in such service industries as retailing, distribution, and insurance. Although these services (or goods) are not heavily traded — rather, the goal is to serve the local market — MNEs exploit their intangible assets, such as brand names or marketing and management skills; therefore, competition is intense.

several other risks: the strategy may be too broad; it may also be too costly, in part, because of its breadth and because it is costly to produce (requiring coordination); and it is always vulnerable to imitation.

The success of a focus strategy is also determined by a firm's ability to identify differences among particular segments and to concentrate on only one or a few in ways that produce unique products compared with those available from less focused firms. The advantages of such a strategy are that the firm can take advantage of economies of scale or of customer loyalty, which may even be global, but in a narrow set of activities. The risks, like those for the differentiator, are that the firm may encounter competition in the selected segments from firms that are broader based. Imitators are a threat, as are substitution and rapid technological change. This discussion illustrates the importance of firm strategy in understanding production and the links between trade and FDI at the firm level. Much of the literature assumes that these linkages are influenced by corporate nationality, that is, the behaviour of corporations from different countries in which the corporations maintain their headquarters. I explore this issue in the next subsection.

Corporate nationality

Concerns about the strategic behaviour of Japanese firms and the Japanese government, leading to Japan-centred integration and impediments to market access in the region by non-Japanese firms, originate in concerns that Japanese business groups replicate abroad the exclusionary behaviour they display in Japan.

Are there systematic differences in trade and FDI behaviour of Japanese, Western, and non-Japanese Asian firms? Like Western MNEs, Japanese multinationals have managed the product cycle in ways that serve their global strategies. These strategies are characterized by goals of corporate survival to meet employment commitments, as well as by constant technological upgrading to meet fierce domestic and global competition (Rapp 1995). FDI plays a key role in these strategies, and controlling technology transfer is fundamental to their success. Unlike many Western firms, which have tended to close down low value-added production when it becomes uncompetitive, Japanese producers have used FDI to maintain export competitiveness for goods for which global demand still exists, for example, through the use of offshore export platforms that produce goods for export to third countries. Offshore production has also been used to source relatively low-cost imports to the home country, a common practice among Western firms.

Studies of organizational behaviour provide related insights into how corporate nationality might influence trade and FDI linkages. The home business environment, in which management decisions to expand operations abroad are made, may influence choices about products, markets, and modes of operation. This phenomenon is known as path dependence. Attributes of the organization in the home environment can become locked in through decisions about asset configuration and organizational structure (Bartlett and Ghoshal 1989). Such arguments suggest that firms will transfer ownership advantages to foreign production. Thus, it could be expected that Japanese investors will transfer the vertical *keiretsu*, particularly in autos and electronics, because it is a source of competitive advantage (Gittelman and Graham 1994).

Inquiries into variation in firms' behaviour by corporate nationality in East Asian markets, using firm-level data, are scarce. Those available are of two kinds: those that use standard theoretical approaches and aggregate data and those that focus on the behaviour of Japanese firms. The standard approaches fail to find large differences in behaviour by corporate ownership *per se;* the existence of ownership advantages is a more important explanatory variable. Among firms operating in Thailand, for instance, foreign-owned firms generally tended to be trade dependent. Japanese MNEs in Thailand had higher capital intensity per employee than other MNEs and were more foreign-labour dependent than US or European MNEs but less so than developing-country MNEs (Ramstetter 1994c).

Another study of Japanese firms in Thailand estimated the direct and indirect[14] trade effects of Japanese direct investment (Petri 1992). Although Japanese affiliates accounted for much of Thailand's exports in the 1986–90 period, they tended to create a trade deficit with Japan and trade surpluses with third countries. Not only were the indirect effects of investments in Japanese-affiliates firms positive, but also, once the investment phase was complete, indirect trade effects more than off-set firms' direct trade deficits.

The literature on Japanese corporate behaviour includes Japanese studies asserting that Japanese multinationals are different or unique. Some studies assert that Japanese direct investment tended to take minority-ownership positions in joint ventures involving the general trading companies in ways that enhanced trade more than did American investments (Kojima 1978, 1990), but more recent contradictory empirical evidence has undermined this hypothesis. Other studies accept variants of the general argument that characteristics of Japanese economic and industrial organization differ from Western laissez-faire organization (Tyson 1992; Bergsten and Noland 1993b).

Evidence to support these contentions is mostly anecdotal, but views are evolving toward one of Japanese production networks in East Asia as more inclusive as they gain international experience (studies in Doherty 1995). Such a view accords with broader approaches to the evolution of business enterprises that see all as subject to intense competitive pressures and uncertainty in all industrialized economies, including Japan (Westney 1996).

Organizational attributes

The foregoing discussion raises the question of whether organizational attributes may be a relevant variable in firms' cross-border behaviour. Comparisons of patterns of intrafirm trade by US and Japanese affiliates in East Asia, using firm-level data, failed to find marked differences by corporate nationality in performance in the same industries in different locations (Encarnation 1992; Dobson 1993). Dobson (1993) found evidence, however, that US electronics firms were reshaping their operations into networks involving contractual relationships with suppliers (many of them Japanese firms); at the same time, Japanese producers were responding to local governments' incentive programs to open their supply chains to local suppliers. Singapore's Local Industry Upgrading Programme (LIUP) is one example of a local incentive to force open sourcing programs to include local suppliers. Malaysia's subcontract-exchange scheme is another. In other words, organizational structures of producers from different backgrounds may be converging in response to competitive forces (industry effects) and local incentives (location effects). Another outcome, however, of this internationalization of the vertical *keiretsu* is that Japanese firms responding to pressures to source locally find the cost advantages of vertical groups realized in Japan are undermined abroad (Westney 1996).

Although the main unit of analysis in this study is the MNE and its affiliates, a number of different business organizations exist in East Asia, most of them characterized by networks of firms. *Network* is a term that applies to MNE affiliates among which locational division of labour occurs; it also applies to Asian business groups in which linkages are based on personal relationships.

The defining characteristic of ownership and production structures of Korean, Japanese, and Chinese business systems[15] is that they are relationship-based networks. In Japan, major business groups link networks of firms by cross-shareholdings. The groups also span industrial sectors and develop strong vertical linkages with firms within each sector, which in turn rely heavily on stable, long-term subcontracting relationships with small independent supplier firms. Employees expect guaranteed employment until retirement and regular salary increments as they gain experience. This system allows for investment in human capital; these investments, plus involvement of employees in decision-making, contribute to low employee turnover and often-intense loyalty to the firm's objectives.

---

[14] That is, displacement by affiliates of sales or procurement from local and third-country firms.
[15] This discussion draws on Orrú et al. (1991) and Biggart and Hamilton (1993).

Korean *chaebol* consist of business groups owned by families. These groups developed in the 1960s and 1970s, during Korea's industrialization push, and benefited from favourable government policies, including low-cost loans targeting the steel, ship-building, and other heavy industries and the chemical industries. Most *chaebol* are huge conglomerates and involve highly centralized managerial control. They are also vertically integrated, which makes them dominant in their industrial sectors. As a result, they tend to segment the Korean economy, in contrast to the integrating role commonly attributed to the *keiretsu* in the Japanese economy.

The Chinese family firm is another important form of business organization in the region. While these firms are controlled by a few individuals, capital tends to come from family and friends acting as silent partners. Production takes place in networks of firms, all of which tend to be small or medium sized. Members in the networks tend to be independent firms, however, that choose to divide components production among themselves and jointly produce finished products, rather than entering into subcontracting relationships.

These networks are explained by linkages between governments and firms that favour monopolistic behaviour, as in the *chaebol*, and by the fact that efficiency can be achieved by working in groups based on trust and relationships to overcome the uncertainties that exist when markets are fragmented or in the absence of commonly agreed "rules of the game," such as legal frameworks. Just as in the Western MNEs, where uncertainty is reduced by internalizing transactions, so in business networks market imperfections and uncertainties can be overcome better within the group than by acting alone. Our interest is in how these organizations might change as they internationalize. Available evidence suggests vintage and size play a role in these changes.

Vintage and size

Traditionally, global firms get started in the domestic market by solving a local problem or exploiting a local opportunity. To do this, they develop learning capabilities and proprietary advantages that they can then build on in international markets. Acer, Giant, Mitac, and other Taiwanese firms are examples of East Asian firms that began as original equipment manufacturer (OEM) suppliers and developed their own brands that are being marketed and increasingly produced internationally. Development of the managerial, marketing, and other capabilities required to operate as a global firm takes time. In Thailand, the initial trade impact of direct investment was negative, but once the investment phase was complete the trade impact became positive overall (Petri 1992). Dobson (1993) found that both American and Japanese affiliates relied more heavily on parents and the home market for key components during the initial stages of investment than they did once the investment had been made. In the electronics industry, she also found that both relied heavily on Japanese suppliers in the absence of local or other international sources.

Recent evidence of Taiwan firms venturing abroad provides insights into the behaviour of those East Asian investors. Most Taiwanese investors in manufacturing tend to be small and medium-sized firms whose intangible assets are their abilities to conduct small-scale, flexible production, which they are able to do because of support from an efficient home-country production network (Chen 1995b). These firms invest abroad to escape unanticipated increases in production costs at home and have done so without much market research. Because such firms lack financial and managerial resources, the founder may move to the offshore location, taking the firm's proprietary assets and leaving a minor operation, if any, in Taiwan. Although the firms maintain close connections to Taiwan's domestic production network at first, because the margin of competitive advantage relative to local firms in host economies is so thin, they "localize" quickly to survive by increasing local sales and procurement and then diversifying into new areas of production to take advantage of local demand. It remains to be seen whether such firms, as they gain in size and experience, remain localized or become more sophisticated international firms.

Summary

In summary, this overview shows how existing studies have incorporated aggregate data on trade and FDI to explain integration; others have studied the development process; still others, the MNE. In the chapters that follow, we will use aggregate and firm-level data on FDI and trade to throw light on how firm strategies affect East Asian integration. Firms respond to locational factors, including government policies, and allocate value-chain segments in different locations to take advantage of complementarities that they can exploit through intrafirm trade and IIT within evolving production networks. In this sense, location matters. We will also examine the role of corporate nationality. The evidence reviewed above suggests that as a differentiator of trade and investment patterns, corporate nationality is not particularly important, but it may influence production patterns because of differing modes of ownership and production in which relational ties can exclude outsiders, such as western MNEs. Yet, vintage and size effects can be important here because as firms gain international experience and respond to competitive pressures by imitating competitors' successful behaviour, patterns of production and trade might be expected to converge. Finally, we will examine industry effects to determine whether and why trade and FDI might be complementary. These are some of the central questions in the country studies that follow.

Study design and organization

Eight country studies are presented in this volume. These studies were prepared by researchers who conducted firm-level surveys in eight East Asian economies that have received significant FDI inflows. Studies of the three leading economies — those of Singapore, Taiwan, and Hong Kong — are followed by studies of Guangdong province (China) and the ASEAN-4 economies — Thailand, Malaysia, the Philippines, and Indonesia.

Each country study uses three main data sources. One is primary survey data of individual firms in industries characterized by significant foreign ownership in many of the countries in the study. Each researcher identified the universe of firms in each industry and selected 30–40 firms, both local and foreign, to be surveyed. The number was determined by time and financial resources available for the study. Standardized interview protocols were then sent to each firm, with follow-up by telephone and personal interviews. Because of the small sample sizes, researchers focused on firms of Japanese, US, and East Asian origins, although local and European firms were not systematically excluded. The second data source was the Australian National University (ANU) International Economic Database, which consists of United Nations trade statistics subjected to special measures to increase their internal consistency and accuracy. These data are used to summarize recent trends in intraregional trade in the industries surveyed. The third data source was national statistics on particular aspects of trade and on stocks of host economies' inward FDI.

Each study summarizes the economic and policy characteristics of the economy, as well as overall patterns of trade and investment. The centrepiece of each is analysis of procurement and sales data from the surveys. In Table 1.4, the industries studied and the geographic location of firms surveyed are summarized, as are the shares of industry sales represented by the surveyed firms. In five economies, these firms represent a significant share of total sales.

A total of 241 firms were surveyed in the eight economies. The industrial distribution of the firms was as follows: electronics, 155; autos, 22; textiles and garments, 50; chemicals, 11; and other industries, 3. By corporate nationality, the distribution was Japanese, 34%; US, 17%; newly industrialized economies (NIEs), 20% — many of these being Hong Kong firms in China; local firms, 14%; and other, 20%. Surveys gathered data on sales and procurement within firms and groups, as well as information on sources and uses of capital and production efficiency. In three studies, complete data were obtained; in the others, firms were only willing to release interval data.

Table 1.4. Geographical and industrial distribution of surveyed firms.

Economy	Number of firms	Share of total	Industry	Number of foreign firms	Share of industry sales
China	30	13	Electronics	15	NA
			Textiles	15	NA
Hong Kong	33	9	Electronics	14	14.0
			Textiles	4	
			Leather goods	2	7.0
			Plastic goods	1	
Indonesia	36	15	Electronics	8	NA
			Automobiles[a]	5	NA
			Textiles and garments	15	NA
Malaysia	28	12	Electronics	18	41.0
			Automobiles	10	25.0
Philippines	23	9	Electronics	11	25.0
			Textiles and garments	12	10.0
Singapore	29	13	Electronics	29	20.0
Taiwan	42	17	Electronics	31	36.0
			Chemicals	11	8.5
Thailand	29	12	Electronics	23	76.0
			Automobiles	6	14.0

Source: Authors' surveys.

Note: NA, not available.

[a] Because automobile dealers received separate questionaires for sedans and for commercial vehicles, the number of "firms" (that is, the number of questionnaires) increased to eight in the survey in Chapter 9.

To study the links between trade and FDI flows among the economies in which affiliates are located, empirical data on intrafirm trade, IIT, and intraregional trade are analyzed in each of the country chapters. To provide an overall flavour of intraregional trade in the industries in this study, trade intensities[16] are presented in Tables 1.5–1.8 for each of the eight economies with Japan, the United States, Europe, and the group as a whole for 1986, 1989, and 1992.[17] Reasons for these trends will be sought in subsequent chapters. Trade intensity varies by industry. Highest intraregional intensities appear, in declining significance, in the office- and computing-machinery (OCM, Table 1.6), chemicals (Table 1.8), and textiles and garments (T/G, Table 1.7) industries. Trade between partners is often twice to three times (or more) as large as what would be expected on the basis of these countries' shares in world trade. In the electronics industry (Table 1.5), however, intensities are highest in trade outside the region — with the EU and Japan (with the exception of China and Indonesia, for which intraregional intensities are strongest but declining). Trade intensities in OCM for Thailand, Taiwan, and Singapore are also extraregional — with the United States. Similarly, in T/G, the Philippines', Hong Kong's, and Malaysia's intensities are also highest with the United States.

Trends during the short period of observation are mixed. In electronics, extraregional trade (with the EU) is rising in three cases, falling in two, and unchanged in the cases of Singapore and Taiwan. In OCM, intraregional intensity shows no trend; intensities with the United States are declining, whereas Thailand's intense relationship with Japan is rising. In T/G, the intraregional intensities are

---

[16] Trade intensity is a measure of the trade between pairs or groups of countries relative to their shares of world trade. The intensity index (I_{ij}) is calculated as follows:

$$I_{ij} = \frac{X_{ij}/X_i}{M_j/(M_W - M_i)}$$

where X_{ij} is country i's exports to country j; X_i is country i's exports; M_j is country j's imports; M_W is world imports; and M_i is country i's imports.

[17] Autos are not included because of data problems.

Table 1.5. Electronic machinery (including parts and appliances: ISIC 383):
trade-intensity coefficients for eight East Asian economies.

	Japan	United States	Europe	ASEAN-8[a]
China				
1986	0.81	0.34	0.80	7.24
1989	0.98	1.04	1.59	4.01
1992	1.47	1.14	2.05	3.06
Hong Kong				
1986	0.71	1.67	2.94	0.53
1989	0.76	1.24	2.66	0.63
1992	0.41	0.92	2.04	1.05
Indonesia				
1986	0.07	0.03	0.77	7.86
1989	2.90	1.00	1.93	1.93
1992	1.94	1.79	2.80	1.42
Malaysia				
1986	3.07	1.81	2.82	2.16
1989	2.07	1.78	2.36	2.21
1992	2.21	1.67	2.49	2.06
Philippines				
1986	2.93	1.47	3.72	2.93
1989	1.75	2.21	2.71	1.58
1992	6.25	2.23	2.41	1.00
Singapore				
1986	1.57	1.41	2.51	2.43
1989	1.63	1.24	2.67	1.97
1992	1.71	1.01	2.16	1.96
Taiwan				
1986	2.48	2.01	2.32	1.36
1989	2.77	1.72	2.51	1.48
1992	2.45	1.58	2.66	1.77
Thailand				
1986	0.49	1.22	1.48	5.11
1989	2.57	2.12	2.38	1.70
1992	3.83	1.76	2.47	1.80

Source: ANU (1995).
Note: ISIC, International Standard Industrial Classification.
[a] The eight study economies.

declining or unchanged for all but Taiwan, where it is rising. In chemicals, intensities decline in five economies, rise in two, and are unchanged in one.

One of the clearest patterns is Thailand's and Indonesia's trade with Japan, where intensities increase in all industries (for Indonesia, in all industries but OCM). In contrast, Hong Kong's, Singapore's, and Taiwan's intensities are largely unchanged. The Philippines' and Malaysia's are mixed, as are China's (with rising intensities in electronics and OCM).

Research questions

The studies in Chapters 2–9 analyze both aggregate trade and FDI flows, as well as firm-level surveys. These chapters examine several questions. The first set of questions relates to how firms exploit location. We expect to see MNEs, which are increasingly adept at manipulating segments of the value chain, allocating segments to regional locations with appropriate comparative advantage, as is suggested in Table 1.9. We expect to see high value-added segments in Singapore, Taiwan, and Hong Kong; lower value-added activities in the other economies; and migration of these activities from one economy to another as location variables change.

Table 1.6. Office and computing machinery (ISIC 3825):
trade-intensity coefficients for eight East Asian economies.

	Japan	United States	Europe	ASEAN-8[a]
China				
1986	0.44	0.14	0.18	17.31
1989	0.83	0.59	0.51	11.24
1992	0.63	1.04	0.55	7.35
Hong Kong				
1986	1.01	2.24	0.94	1.76
1989	0.79	1.72	0.88	2.86
1992	1.62	1.02	0.58	4.48
Indonesia				
1986	1.06	0.00	0.00	8.69
1989	0.09	0.06	0.62	11.72
1992	0.19	0.19	0.42	12.13
Malaysia				
1986	0.83	1.47	0.67	8.42
1989	2.20	1.47	0.19	8.48
1992	1.36	1.21	0.51	6.95
Philippines				
1986	0.10	0.46	0.00	19.48
1989	0.64	0.30	0.16	2.05
1992	1.02	0.58	0.77	7.74
Singapore				
1986	0.17	2.77	0.64	1.78
1989	0.55	2.15	0.69	2.12
1992	0.80	1.72	0.98	1.84
Taiwan				
1986	1.74	2.29	0.85	1.05
1989	0.80	1.67	1.22	1.32
1992	0.46	1.60	1.30	1.23
Thailand				
1986	2.06	2.85	0.31	1.84
1989	1.87	1.53	0.52	6.55
1992	2.74	1.19	0.50	6.38

Source: ANU (1995).
Note: ISIC, International Standard Industrial Classification.
[a] The eight study economies.

This dynamic should help to explain why, for example, MNEs use Singapore and Hong Kong as locations of key support activities such as management of regional operations, finance, and procurement. In the case of Singapore, the government has levered off Singapore's strategic location in Southeast Asia and targeted supply of low-cost communications infrastructure and highly skilled labour that will enhance the efficiency of such business segments. Market forces, path dependence, and proximity to China have contributed to Hong Kong's strategic position.

In the ASEAN-4 countries, firms can be expected to exploit locational advantages such as low-cost labour and infrastructure. What we would like to know more about are the kinds of value-added activities located in a particular economy, why they are there, and how these activities link with other firms' activities or other activities of the firm. Do all foreign multinationals in consumer electronics produce the same components and engage in the same segments of activities in the value chain in Malaysia, for example?

The second set of research questions relates to whether trade and investment behaviour of investing firms differs by corporate nationality when industry and location effects are controlled. The international firm's competitive behaviour within its industry will be revealed through its trade, as

Table 1.7. Textile and garments (ISIC 321 + 322):
trade-intensity coefficients for eight East Asian economies.

	Japan	United States	Europe	ASEAN-8[a]
China				
1986	2.20	0.90	0.62	4.43
1989	1.81	0.82	0.60	3.72
1992	2.07	0.83	0.58	2.92
Hong Kong				
1986	0.79	1.81	1.14	0.36
1989	0.53	1.57	0.94	0.31
1992	0.31	1.44	0.73	0.24
Indonesia				
1986	0.72	1.93	0.82	3.54
1989	0.85	1.80	1.49	1.67
1992	1.01	0.99	1.29	2.38
Malaysia				
1986	0.95	2.26	1.29	1.66
1989	0.71	2.27	1.48	1.23
1992	0.73	2.02	1.38	1.51
Philippines				
1986	1.03	2.35	1.64	0.83
1989	0.49	3.01	1.42	0.28
1992	0.63	2.88	1.14	0.72
Singapore				
1986	0.24	1.95	0.52	2.27
1989	0.17	1.77	0.75	1.89
1992	0.22	1.58	0.83	1.65
Taiwan				
1986	2.00	1.79	0.48	2.63
1989	1.28	1.49	0.39	2.56
1992	0.93	1.42	0.37	3.29
Thailand				
1986	0.85	1.03	1.81	1.31
1989	1.11	0.98	1.39	0.93
1992	1.35	1.21	1.08	0.67

Source: ANU (1995).
Note: ISIC, International Standard Industrial Classification.
[a] The eight study economies.

measured by procurement and sales both within the firm and outside. A particularly interesting dimension of this issue is the large proportion (20%) of investing firms from the Asian economies themselves that are included in our surveys. Do these firms provide a "new" model of investor? How are investing firms from the Asian economies evolving as players in the region? Thus, a related study objective is to compare their strategies with those of other international firms because the former are both young and small. Do they locate production abroad simply because of rising costs at home? If this is the case, will they grow into international firms (producing more trade and integration in the region) if they lack the managerial abilities to configure and coordinate their activities? Do they have particular advantages from solving a problem in the home market that they use as a lever to enter foreign markets (that is, are they exercising some kind of first-mover advantage)? Another related issue is how these firms from different home environments adjust their organizations to achieve their international production objectives.

The third set of research questions is about firms' impact on regional integration. We expect to see that regional integration is positively influenced by the intrafirm trade and investment within international firms. Allocation and coordination in the region should lead to increasing intrafirm

Table 1.8. Chemicals (ISIC 351 + 352): trade-intensity coefficients for eight East Asian economies.

	Japan	United States	Europe	ASEAN-8[a]
China				
1986	2.61	1.00	1.48	2.25
1989	2.53	0.82	1.23	1.77
1992	1.89	0.99	1.13	1.75
Hong Kong				
1986	2.36	1.91	0.31	1.98
1989	0.42	0.24	0.06	0.49
1992	0.23	0.16	0.08	0.52
Indonesia				
1986	0.51	0.60	0.65	2.41
1989	1.11	0.31	0.59	2.25
1992	1.14	0.44	0.41	1.78
Malaysia				
1986	1.82	1.08	0.69	2.44
1989	1.62	0.78	0.43	2.16
1992	2.15	0.35	0.40	2.50
Philippines				
1986	1.81	0.86	0.18	1.18
1989	1.44	0.82	0.32	1.65
1992	1.68	0.76	0.24	1.59
Singapore				
1986	1.09	0.82	0.23	3.06
1989	0.98	0.72	0.28	2.26
1992	0.73	1.12	0.36	2.06
Taiwan				
1986	2.23	1.20	0.31	1.73
1989	1.99	0.83	0.28	1.63
1992	0.83	0.72	0.33	2.19
Thailand				
1986	1.63	0.21	0.31	2.71
1989	1.49	0.40	0.25	1.80
1992	2.14	0.48	0.23	1.78

Source: ANU (1995).
Note: ISIC, International Standard Industrial Classification.
[a] The eight study economies.

Table 1.9. Harnessing diversity: locational characteristics and the allocation of business segments in East Asian manufacturing.

Host economy's comparative advantage	Firm's value-added activity		
	Low	Medium	High
Innovation driven	• Sales and service	• High value-added components production	• R&D activities • Head offices, hub activities
Investment driven	• Sales and service	• Medium value-added components production • Assembly and testing	• Design and development • Head offices, hub activities
Factor driven	• Low value-added components production • Assembly • Sales and service		

Note: R&D, research and development.

trade and a greater density of intraregional linkages. Interfirm and firm–government cooperation to reduce costs and risks associated with higher value-added activities, such as R&D, can also be expected to contribute to intraregional linkages.

The results of the country studies are synthesized in the third and final part of the volume in two ways: first, in Chapter 10 the firm is the analytical focus and MNEs' cross-border activities are traced and analyzed. Firms included in this chapter were selected on the basis that they appeared in several country studies.

The final chapter presents the results of the study and draws conclusions based on the three main research questions. Some of the main themes and conclusions are as follows:

1. Regional integration is influenced by international firms in two ways. First, it is enhanced by NIE producers based in the region who invest defensively in other regional locations and by multinational firms' (or their local affiliates') investments in components, intermediate products, and services that are shipped around the region, both to add value and to reach final customers. Second, regional integration can be reduced by firms from outside the region whose trade is outside the region. Although the relative magnitudes of these offsetting trends are difficult to estimate, the positive influence of investments from within the region is growing.

2. The region's diversity is "harnessed" by governments intent on industrial upgrading and by MNEs whose objectives are served by exploiting locational differences. Governments, MNEs, and East Asian firms act strategically.

3. Firms exploit the region's diversity by slicing up the value chain and allocating and reallocating value-added activities — rather than entire industries — according to a location's comparative advantage.

4. Similar industries are locating in the region through FDI, but different locations attract different value-added segments, creating the potential for a positive-sum game in which everyone gains. This conclusion implies the desirability of reevaluating a widespread perception of a negative-sum game that underlies the competition among governments for FDI inflows.

5. Differences in corporate nationality influence production, but location and industry effects dominate corporate nationality as determinants of trade patterns.

6. Intrafirm trade is growing fast; because such trade and investment are complementary, coherence should be sought in trade and investment policies, and governments should cooperate in removing obstacles to intraregional trade and investment flows.

Annex:
Table 1.A1. Destination of manufactured exports from
eight East Asian economies.

	Shares of exporter's total manufactured exports (%)			
	Japan	United States	Europe	ASEAN-9[a]
China				
1986	11	18	13	43
1989	12	20	14	44
1992	11	22	16	43
Hong Kong				
1986	4	42	21	17
1989	6	33	20	27
1992	5	28	19	37
Indonesia				
1986	27	19	16	28
1989	31	14	16	28
1992	17	16	21	31
Malaysia				
1986	8	26	19	29
1989	8	25	19	35
1992	8	23	17	40
Philippines				
1986	12	35	24	19
1989	14	37	21	15
1992	15	38	20	18
Singapore				
1986	8	24	10	36
1989	8	23	13	37
1992	7	21	15	39
Taiwan				
1986	10	49	11	14
1989	12	37	15	21
1992	11	32	18	27
Thailand				
1986	10	22	18	25
1989	13	24	17	20
1992	15	24	18	22

Source: ANU (1995).
[a] The eight study economies plus Korea.

Annex:
Table 1.A2. Sources of manufactured imports by
eight East Asian economies.

	Shares of importer's total manufactured imports (%)			
	Japan	United States	Europe	ASEAN-9[a]
China				
1986	31	9	20	26
1989	19	10	14	47
1992	17	10	12	56
Hong Kong				
1986	22	8	12	49
1989	17	8	10	57
1992	18	7	10	59
Indonesia				
1986	33	14	19	20
1989	26	14	17	25
1992	25	14	22	26
Malaysia				
1986	23	20	16	31
1989	27	18	13	31
1992	28	17	13	34
Philippines				
1986	25	21	16	26
1989	25	17	15	20
1992	26	17	15	28
Singapore				
1986	24	18	14	31
1989	24	19	14	31
1992	23	18	14	36
Taiwan				
1986	42	23	14	8
1989	38	23	15	10
1992	36	22	13	21
Thailand				
1986	32	14	17	23
1989	35	11	14	25
1992	33	12	15	27

Source: ANU (1995).
[a] The eight study economies plus Korea.

Part II

COUNTRY STUDIES

Chapter 2

SINGAPORE

Advanced Production Base and Smart Hub
of the Electronics Industry

Chia Siow Yue

The study of the relationship between trade and foreign direct investment (FDI) in Singapore in this chapter addresses four issues. First, what makes Singapore such an attractive investment location for foreign multinationals? Second, where does Singapore stand in the value chain of international companies, and how is this affected by the government's strategic planning? Third, how extensive is the linkage between FDI and trade, and does the nationality of firms affect corporate behaviour with regard to trade orientation and intrafirm trade? Fourth, how is regional trade and investment integration in East Asia affected by Singapore's role as a manufacturing base and regional hub?

This chapter adopts two levels of analysis. At the aggregate level, the study traces the transition of Singapore from a traditional entrepôt to a manufacturing base and eventual regional hub, the role of foreign multinational enterprises (MNEs) in manufacturing and their trade behaviour, and the role of Singapore's trade in manufactures in regional integration. At industry and firm levels, the study examines the FDI–trade nexus further, focusing on the Singapore electronics industry. The choice of electronics was based on two considerations. Internationally, electronics is one of the world's most globalized industries, with electronics MNEs having established offshore production plants and activities around the world. Corporate strategies to split production processes and distribute value-chain activities into different locations and to engage in offshore production and procurement have helped electronics MNEs to reduce costs and remain competitive, and they have contributed to the growth of intraindustry and intrafirm trade. Successful globalization requires coordination of the geographically dispersed activities, however, and this emphasis on coordination has contributed to the growth of regional-headquarters (RHQ) activities. In Singapore, electronics was found to be the largest manufacturing industry, and electronics products and components were found to account for about half of Singapore's domestic exports of manufactures and a growing part of its entrepôt trade. This study of the industry's trade and investment patterns was based on data drawn from the census of industrial production (published and unpublished tabulations), Singapore Economic Development Board (EDB) reports, media reports, and a questionnaire survey and interviews with a sample of manufacturing firms and regional operational headquarters.

From entrepôt to manufacturing base and hub

Singapore is a small city-state in Southeast Asia. It is one of the most internationally oriented and integrated economies in the world, with total merchandise and service trade running at more than triple its gross national product and inward FDI stock ranking among the largest in the developing world. The high trade orientation reflects a small resource base and market, as well as Singapore's entrepôt role and free-trade policy. The high FDI penetration reflects Singapore's role as a manufacturing base for foreign multinationals and as a financial, transportation, logistics, and trading hub.

The city-state has served as a regional entrepôt since the early 19th century. The initial advantages of a natural, deep harbour, a strategic location astride shipping plying between East Asia and Europe and the free-port policy of the British colonial administration were reinforced by the development of transportation, commercial, and financial infrastructure and facilities and by the accumulation of expertise in trade and finance. The entrepôt function was largely one of importing Western manufactures for redistribution in the region and collecting the region's primary commodities for marketing to the West. The performance of this function led to the growth of ancillary storage and warehousing, shipping, and banking services. Singapore's intermediary role facilitated trade flows and reduced transaction costs for buyers and sellers. Since the early 1950s, however, the entrepôt's growth has been constrained by the efforts of neighbouring countries to develop their own ports and to engage in direct marketing of their primary products and in import-substituting industrialization.

Singapore embarked on industrialization in 1960 to reduce dependence on entrepôt activities. Import substitution was pursued in the initial years because of the difficulties in exporting that faced the infant industrial economy and the prospect of a relatively large market resulting from unification with Malaysia. Unification was short lived, and political independence for the small city-state, in August 1965, necessitated a drastic change in economic strategy. Export manufacturing became imperative, and courting foreign multinationals was perceived as essential in view of the weak domestic technological base and the long lead-time needed to transform domestic entrepôt traders and small-scale entrepreneurs into a dynamic industrial entrepreneurial class able to compete in the global market. Various measures and infrastructural and skills-development efforts gave Singapore a reputation as a highly attractive and competitive manufacturing base for foreign MNEs in search of low-cost export platforms. By the late 1970s, Singapore had become a major world production centre for electronic products and components. Sustained, rapid economic growth, ensuing labour shortage, and rising costs eroded Singapore's competitive advantage as a low-wage manufacturing base and necessitated a shift in industrial structure toward high-tech manufacturing and high value-added services. Policies were launched in the late 1970s and early 1980s to promote industrial restructuring, but the implementation process was interrupted by the 1985 recession.

The postrecession economic strategy, initially outlined in a report of the Singapore Economic Committee (1986) and subsequently elaborated on in the Strategic Economic Plan (Singapore Economic Planning Committee 1991) called for the promotion and development of Singapore as a total business centre and the development of high-tech and high value-added manufacturing and services as twin engines of growth and strategic responses to the changing external and domestic economic environments. Externally, the globalization trend was accelerating as multinationals distributed different activities to different locations according to the competitive advantage of each. Domestically, Singapore as a production base was increasingly constrained by the lack of natural resources and a small labour pool, technological base, and domestic market. With its strong infrastructural foundation and rapid development of skills and information technology, Singapore was seen to have the capabilities needed to go beyond manufacturing to other parts of the business value chain, such as research, product development and design, process engineering, international marketing and distribution, and operational-headquarters (OHQ) functions (EDB 1994a).

The Strategic Economic Plan outlined two strategic elements: developing highly specialized niches and upgrading the low-productivity domestic sector. The approach followed Michael Porter's cluster framework to achieve competitiveness (Porter 1986). Close consultations with the private sector led to the identification of 13 clusters in manufacturing and services. The cluster plans identified global and regional trends in technology, industry, business, and competitiveness and evaluated Singapore's advantages and core capabilities. The government established a Cluster Development Fund of S$1 billion to promote strategic projects in manufacturing and services. Strategies for the manufacturing and service sectors were grouped under Manufacturing 2000 and International Business Hub 2000 programs, respectively.

The Manufacturing 2000 program affirms the importance of manufacturing for Singapore and aimed at maintaining the sector's share of gross domestic product (GDP) at no less than 25%. Value-chain analysis is used to identify gaps in existing industry clusters and to formulate initiatives and strategies to close them. The continuing emphasis on Singapore as a manufacturing base reflects the recognition, through value-chain analysis, that modern manufacturing and services are complementary.

The International Business Hub 2000 advocates a parallel strategy (to that of manufacturing) to develop Singapore as a global city and a hub for business and finance, logistics and distribution, and communications and information. The hub strategy for Singapore was based on the observation that key economic activities, such as finance, shipping, air transport, telecommunications, and information functions, are increasingly concentrated in a few strategic centres around the world, each one acting as a hub to service its extended "hinterland" and link it to the world. Singapore sought to secure the first-mover advantage by planning far ahead, organizing itself as a world-class team and investing in human resources (education, training, and industrial relations) and infrastructure (airport, seaport, telecommunications network, and financial and industrial facilities), to obtain a lead on the competition. The Singapore hub's value added is its ability to offer first-class products and services and its reputation for quality, reliability, and excellence.

Apart from providing world-class hardware and software, the Singapore hub needed to attract international business, including regional OHQs and international traders. Tax incentives were introduced to improve Singapore's locational attractions. Singapore is already host to some 4000 multinational corporations, and many of them already have divisions performing various RHQ functions. Reasons cited for the choice of Singapore as regional OHQ among firms interviewed for this study include strategic geographical location; excellent transport and communications infrastructure, logistics, and financial services; political stability, a conducive environment for business, and a good living environment for executives; availability of good-quality human resources and the widespread use of English; the strong supportive role of government institutions, such as Singapore Economic Development Board (EDB) and Singapore Trade Development Board (TDB), and minimal transactions costs of investment, trade, and immigration procedures; and generous tax incentives.

The hub strategy also calls for building good relations with regional countries through political diplomacy, outward investment, and joint ventures to combine the competitive strengths of Singapore and its partners to attract international investors. This view has led to Singapore-government initiatives to establish growth triangles and overseas industrial parks. The SIJORI growth triangle is a partnership arrangement between Singapore, Johore (in Malaysia), and Riau (in Indonesia) that combines the competitive strengths of the three areas to make the subregion more attractive to regional and international investors. More specifically, it links the infrastructure, capital, and expertise of Singapore with the natural and labour resources of Johore and Riau. As part of this regionalization strategy, Singapore has also established industrial parks in Suzhou and Wuxi (China), Bangalore (India), and Vietnam, combining Singapore's capital resources and expertise in industrial-infrastructure development and management with local availability of land and labour resources.

Trade in manufactures and the role of FDI

The question of how closely the Singapore economy is integrated with other East Asian economies through trade and investment is examined in this section.

Trade in manufactures

Official national and international published statistics on Singapore's merchandise trade omit the extensive Singapore–Indonesia trade and hence underestimate the extent of Singapore's trade ties with the other economies in the Association of Southeast Asian Nations (ASEAN) and with the broader East Asian region. Attempts by some researchers to fill the gap with data from Indonesian official sources have not resolved the problem because Indonesian trade statistics, based on a different reporting system, do not provide adequate coverage of the entrepôt-trade component.

Singapore's entrepôt role remained a significant integrating factor in 1986–93, accounting for nearly 40% of Singapore's total exports of manufactures. Table 2.1 presents Singapore's trade in manufactures and shows how it is distributed among imports, exports, domestic exports, and entrepôt exports by destination and sourcing (data are based on official trade data and exclude trade with Indonesia). Total trade with the East Asian economies is growing; the region's trade share rose from 46% in 1986 to 53% in 1993, and the upward trend is evident for imports, exports, domestic exports, and entrepôt exports. In East Asia, trade ties are strongest with the ASEAN group (particularly Malaysia) and with Japan.

Singapore depends on the United States–European Community (US–EC) market for its domestic exports, but it is becoming more dependent on East Asia (particularly Japan and Malaysia) for imports. It is also more dependent on East Asia for entrepôt exports than for domestic exports. More imports are sourced from East Asia than from the United States and Europe combined. East Asia's share rose to 62% by 1993, but the US–EC share had dropped to less than 33% by then. Economies in the ASEAN group, particularly Malaysia, are the fastest-growing import suppliers, but Japan continues to account for more than 25% of manufactures. On the export side, the East Asian market (accounting for 43% of exports in 1993) has overtaken the US–EC market (which fell to 41% by 1993). The rising East Asian share is more evident in domestic exports (accounting for 36% of exports by 1993).

A triangular trade pattern is evident in trade with the United States and Japan; Japan is a major supplier of manufactures, and the United States is a major market. This pattern is found in several countries in the region and has added another dimension to the US–Japan trade conflict. If Japanese investments in East Asia result in host countries importing more capital goods and components from Japan and exporting more final manufactures to the United States, then the US trade deficit with Japan could be replicated in a growing number of East Asian countries. For Singapore, Japan supplied more than 25% of its manufactured imports but absorbed less than 6% of its domestic exports, whereas the United States supplied 18% of Singapore's manufactured imports and absorbed 32% of its domestic exports. Sourcing from Japan is associated with the competitiveness (price, quality, and service) of Japanese capital goods, whereas the low level of exports to Japan is associated with Japan's nontariff barriers, including its internal distribution system. However, as demonstrated by the industry- and firm-level analyses in later sections of this chapter, FDI and corporate strategies also play a part.

Inward FDI in manufacturing

Singapore remains a large net recipient of FDI flows, although its outward FDI has been growing rapidly in recent years. In 1992, its inward FDI stock stood at S$56.7 billion, more than three times its outward FDI stock of S$17.7 billion. This imbalance is more pronounced for manufacturing, which had inward FDI of S$20.9 billion and outward FDI of only S$3.8 billion. Although East Asian investment flows, small as they may be, are increasing, those from the United States and Europe are declining.

Even so, the stock of inward FDI has had a significant effect. Singapore has harnessed the technological, managerial, and marketing resources of foreign MNEs to transform the traditional entrepôt economy into an export–manufacturing economy and to further engage the MNEs in moving Singapore up the product-, process-, and functional-value chains, that is, progressing from products

Table 2.1. Total imports and exports of manufactures (SITC 5–8).

Year	World	Asia-8[a]	Japan	China	NIEs-3[b]	Hong Kong	South Korea	Taiwan	ASEAN-3[c]	Malaysia	Philippines	Thailand	United States	European Community	Rest of the world
Total trade (S$ millions)															
1986	65 943	30 290	11 856	1 322	6 753	2 601	1 513	2 639	10 359	7 893	531	1 935	17 337	9 524	8 791
1989	136 626	64 397	23 491	2 333	15 606	5 581	4 034	5 991	22 967	17 130	1 336	4 501	34 213	20 727	17 289
1991	162 451	81 806	28 006	2 581	19 034	7 611	4 372	7 051	32 185	24 317	1 184	6 684	35 534	24 619	20 492
1992	172 320	84 211	28 393	3 063	20 872	8 852	4 232	7 788	31 882	22 309	1 411	8 163	38 376	27 054	22 679
1993	205 787	109 097	34 787	4 078	26 369	11 200	6 021	9 148	43 863	31 744	2 380	9 739	43 426	29 408	23 856
Imports (S$ millions)[d]															
1986	36 527	20 363	10 554	764	4 338	1 185	1 167	1 986	4 706	3 385	275	1 047	7 316	5 658	3 191
1989	72 848	40 716	19 909	1 386	9 425	2 555	2 783	4 087	9 997	7 792	473	1 732	15 111	10 700	6 321
1991	87 526	51 782	23 601	1 788	10 471	3 196	2 896	4 379	15 922	12 492	396	3 034	16 427	12 019	7 298
1992	91 943	53 168	23 904	2 006	10 499	3 396	2 691	4 411	16 759	12 645	426	3 688	17 624	12 985	8 166
1993	110 959	68 450	29 113	2 520	13 134	4 061	3 883	5 190	23 683	17 984	716	4 983	20 270	14 063	8 176
Exports (S$ millions)															
1986	29 415	9 927	1 302	558	2 414	1 416	347	652	5 652	4 508	256	888	10 021	3 866	5 601
1989	63 778	23 681	3 583	947	6 182	3 026	1 251	1 904	12 969	9 338	862	2 769	19 102	10 027	10 968
1991	74 925	30 024	4 405	793	8 563	4 414	1 476	2 673	16 263	11 825	788	3 650	19 107	12 600	13 194
1992	80 377	31 043	4 490	1 057	10 373	5 456	1 540	3 377	15 123	9 664	985	4 475	20 752	14 069	14 513
1993	94 827	40 648	5 674	1 558	13 235	7 139	2 137	3 958	20 181	13 760	1 664	4 757	23 155	15 344	15 680
Domestic exports (S$ millions)															
1986	18 204	4 206	888	360	1 260	654	195	411	1 699	1 213	111	374	8 777	2 780	2 441
1989	39 129	11 017	2 452	560	3 537	1 702	699	1 136	4 468	2 729	334	1 406	15 948	7 474	4 690
1991	46 029	14 558	3 060	370	4 623	2 318	798	1 507	6 506	4 261	380	1 865	15 992	9 551	5 928
1992	49 937	15 696	3 048	438	5 675	2 946	871	1 858	6 534	3 765	423	2 346	17 142	11 531	5 569
1993	57 978	20 655	4 035	791	7 205	3 891	1 229	2 085	8 625	5 737	746	2 142	18 789	11 596	6 938
Entrepôt exports (S$ millions)															
1986	11 212	5 721	415	198	1 155	762	152	241	3 954	3 295	145	513	1 186	1 087	3 160
1989	24 648	12 664	1 131	387	2 644	1 324	552	768	8 501	6 609	529	1 363	3 154	2 553	6 278
1991	28 897	15 466	1 345	423	3 940	2 096	678	1 166	9 757	7 564	408	1 785	3 115	3 049	7 266
1992	30 440	15 348	1 441	619	4 698	2 510	669	1 518	8 590	5 899	563	2 129	3 610	2 538	8 944
1993	36 850	19 992	1 640	767	6 030	3 248	909	1 873	11 556	8 023	919	2 614	4 366	3 749	8 743
Domestic exports/total exports (% distribution)															
1986	61.89	42.37	68.17	64.51	52.17	46.18	56.19	63.06	30.06	26.91	43.39	42.17	87.58	71.89	43.58
1989	61.35	46.52	68.43	59.11	57.22	56.24	55.85	59.68	34.45	29.22	38.71	50.77	83.49	74.54	42.76
1991	61.43	48.49	69.46	46.64	53.99	52.52	54.08	56.37	40.00	36.03	48.20	51.10	83.70	75.80	44.93
1992	62.13	50.56	67.90	41.44	54.71	54.00	56.54	55.04	43.20	38.96	42.97	52.42	82.60	81.96	38.37
1993	61.14	50.82	71.10	50.76	54.44	54.50	57.50	52.67	42.74	41.69	44.80	45.04	81.15	75.57	44.24

(continued)

Table 2.1 concluded.

Year	World	Asia-8[a]	Japan	China	NIEs-3[b]	Hong Kong	South Korea	Taiwan	ASEAN-3[c]	Malaysia	Philippines	Thailand	United States	European Community	Rest of the world
Total trade (% distribution)															
1986	100.00	45.93	17.98	2.01	10.24	3.54	2.29	4.00	15.71	11.97	0.80	2.93	26.29	14.44	13.33
1989	100.00	47.13	17.19	1.71	11.42	4.08	2.95	4.38	16.81	12.54	0.98	3.29	25.04	15.17	12.65
1991	100.00	50.36	17.24	1.59	11.72	4.68	2.69	4.34	19.81	14.97	0.73	4.11	21.87	15.15	12.61
1992	100.00	48.87	16.48	1.78	12.11	5.14	2.46	4.52	18.50	12.95	0.82	4.74	22.27	15.70	13.16
1993	100.00	53.01	16.90	1.98	12.81	5.44	2.93	4.45	21.32	15.43	1.16	4.73	21.10	14.29	11.59
Imports (% distribution)															
1986	100.00	55.75	28.89	2.09	11.88	3.24	3.19	5.44	12.88	9.27	0.75	2.87	20.03	15.49	8.74
1989	100.00	55.89	27.33	1.90	12.94	3.51	3.82	5.61	13.72	10.70	0.65	2.38	20.74	14.69	8.68
1991	100.00	59.16	26.97	2.04	11.96	3.65	3.31	5.00	18.19	14.27	0.45	3.47	18.77	13.73	8.34
1992	100.00	57.83	26.00	2.18	11.42	3.69	2.93	4.80	18.23	13.75	0.46	4.01	19.17	14.12	8.88
1993	100.00	61.69	26.24	2.27	11.84	3.66	3.50	4.68	21.34	16.21	0.65	4.49	18.27	12.67	7.37
Exports (% distribution)															
1986	100.00	33.75	4.43	1.90	8.21	4.81	1.18	2.22	19.22	15.33	0.87	3.02	34.07	13.14	19.04
1989	100.00	37.13	5.62	1.49	9.69	4.75	1.96	2.99	20.34	14.64	1.35	4.34	29.95	15.72	17.20
1991	100.00	40.07	5.88	1.06	11.43	5.89	1.97	3.57	21.71	15.78	1.05	4.87	25.50	16.82	17.61
1992	100.00	38.62	5.59	1.32	12.91	6.75	1.92	4.20	18.82	12.02	1.22	5.57	25.82	17.50	18.06
1993	100.00	42.86	5.98	1.64	13.96	7.53	2.25	4.17	21.28	14.51	1.75	5.02	24.42	16.18	16.54
Domestic exports (% distribution)															
1986	100.00	23.11	4.88	1.98	6.92	3.59	1.07	2.26	9.33	6.67	0.61	2.06	48.22	15.27	13.41
1989	100.00	28.16	6.27	1.43	9.04	4.35	1.79	2.90	11.42	6.97	0.85	3.59	40.76	19.10	11.99
1991	100.00	31.63	6.65	0.80	10.04	5.04	1.73	3.27	14.13	9.26	0.82	4.05	34.74	20.75	12.88
1992	100.00	31.43	6.10	0.88	11.37	5.90	1.74	3.72	13.08	7.54	0.85	4.70	34.33	23.09	11.15
1993	100.00	35.63	6.96	1.36	12.43	6.71	2.12	3.60	14.88	9.90	1.29	3.70	32.41	20.00	11.97
Entrepôt exports (% distribution)															
1986	100.00	51.03	3.70	1.77	10.30	6.80	1.35	2.15	35.26	29.39	1.29	4.58	10.58	9.69	28.18
1989	100.00	51.38	4.59	1.57	10.73	5.37	2.24	3.11	34.49	26.81	2.14	5.53	12.80	10.36	25.47
1991	100.00	53.52	4.66	1.46	13.64	7.25	2.35	4.04	33.77	26.18	1.41	6.18	10.78	10.55	25.15
1992	100.00	50.42	4.73	2.03	15.43	8.25	2.20	4.99	28.22	19.38	1.85	6.99	11.86	8.34	29.38
1993	100.00	54.25	4.45	2.08	16.36	8.82	2.47	5.08	31.36	21.77	2.49	7.09	11.85	10.17	23.73

Source: TDB (n.d.).
Note: SITC, Standard Industrial Trade Classification.
[a] Asia-8, China, Hong Kong, Japan, Malaysia, the Philippines, South Korea, Taiwan, and Thailand.
[b] NIEs-3, Hong Kong, South Korea, and Taiwan.
[c] ASEAN-3, Malaysia, the Philippines, and Thailand.

in which technology is mature to more advanced products at earlier phases of the product cycle, adopting capital-intensive and automated production processes, and moving beyond manufacturing into both upstream and downstream activities of design, research, product development, procurement, marketing, and regional coordination.

Singapore has consistently been rated by various international business surveys as one of the most attractive investment locations in the world. In addition to the general attractions listed earlier for Singapore as a regional OHQ is the liberal FDI policy on investments in manufacturing. Apart from the lack of xenophobia, a result of Singapore's history and geography, there is the pragmatic recognition that leapfrogging into export manufacturing requires foreign MNEs that can augment Singapore's scarce technological, managerial, and marketing resources and expertise. Recognizing Singapore's lack of locational advantages in natural resources and market, efforts to attract FDI eschewed import protection and focused on providing efficient infrastructure and industrial facilities; efficient bureaucracy and a well-established institutional and legal framework; a trained and disciplined work force; and generous fiscal incentives with minimal ownership restrictions and performance requirements. Despite labour shortages and rising costs, Singapore remains highly attractive to foreign investors, which is evident from the continuing uptrend in FDI inflows. Singapore offers low investment risks, high productivity, and extensive linkages with the region.

FDI inflows have shifted progressively from labour-intensive activities to projects with higher value added and higher technological content, due to a growing number of foreign MNEs establishing world-class plants with highly automated operations. By 1989, the manufacturing FDI stock (Table 2.2) showed a heavy concentration in electronics (36%), followed by chemical products (21%), petroleum products (11%), machinery (11%), and transport equipment (8%). Data on investment commitments show FDI flowing increasingly into the electrical and electronic and chemical industries in the past decade.

Measured by inward FDI in manufacturing, Singapore is less integrated with East Asia than with the United States and Europe (Table 2.3). Of the stock of inward FDI in 1992, US–European investors accounted for 63%, whereas Japanese investors accounted for less than 33%. Japan's share of the total stock rose sharply in 1986–92, however, triggered by the dramatic appreciation in the yen in 1986. Inward investment from the rest of East Asia was very limited. These patterns also reflect the combination of ownership advantages of investors from the industrialized countries (consisting of sophisticated technology and marketing channels and expertise) and Singapore's locational

Table 2.2. Stock of inward foreign investment in the manufacturing sector, 1989.

Industry	Amount (S$ millions)	Distribution (%)
Total manufacturing	19 841.9	100.00
Electronic products, components	7 158.2	36.08
Chemicals, chemical products	4 162.3	20.98
Petroleum, petroleum products	2 218.9	11.18
Machinery	2 175.5	10.96
Transport equipment	1 645.3	8.29
Instrumentation, photographic and optical goods	570.7	2.88
Fabricated metal products	546.7	2.76
Food, beverages, tobacco	389.3	1.96
Other manufacturing	325.5	1.64
Rubber, plastic products	234.2	1.18
Paper, paper products, printing, publishing	174.8	0.88
Textiles, garments, leather	135.0	0.68
Basic metals	58.2	0.29
Wood, wood products, including furniture	47.3	0.24

Source: Government of Singapore (n.d.a).

**Table 2.3. Invesment in gross fixed assets in manufacturing
by country of origin.**

Source	Actual cumulative investment	
	1986	1992
	Amount in (S$ millions)	
Total	20 924	39 168
Local	6 804	10604
Foreign	14 120	28 565
United States	5 137	9 678
Japan	3 369	9 093
Europe	4 595	8 331
EC	4 295	7 805
United Kingdom	1 867	2 860
Netherlands	1 674	3 367
Germany	274	666
France	183	563
Other EC	296	350
Sweden	139	101
Switzerland	106	261
Other Europe	55	164
Other countries	1 019	1 463
	Distribution (%)	
Foreign	100.00	100.00
United States	36.38	33.88
Japan	23.86	31.83
Europe	32.54	29.17
EC	30.42	27.32
United Kingdom	13.22	10.01
Netherlands	11.86	11.79
Germany	1.94	2.33
France	1.30	1.97
Other EC	2.10	1.23
Sweden	0.98	0.35
Switzerland	0.75	0.91
Other Europe	0.39	0.57
Other countries	7.22	5.12

Source: EDB (1994c).
Note: EC, European Community.

advantages of cost-effective manufacturing and strategic logistical base. In contrast, East Asian investors lack such ownership advantages, and Singapore, in turn, offers no locational advantage to such investors seeking lower labour costs than those available at their home bases. In fact, Singapore's outward investments in the less advanced economies of Southeast Asia and China have been driven by the same push and pull forces as those facing investors from other Asian newly industrialized economies (NIEs).

The significance of foreign investment penetration in the Singapore economy is clear from Table 2.4. Data from the industrial census for 1992 show that 60% of the equity capital in Singapore's manufacturing sector was of foreign origin. Of the 31 industries with an International Standard Industrial Classification (ISIC) at the three-digit level, only 3 had foreign-equity ratios of less than 10%. In the two largest industries (electronics and petroleum refineries), accounting for more than half of manufacturing output, the foreign-equity ratios were 88% and 93%, respectively.

Table 2.4. Export sales and imported materials in the manufacturing sector, 1992.

Industry (by 3-digit ISIC code)		Establishment (*n*)	Distribution (%)		
			Foreign equity	% of sales exported	% of materials imported
Total manufacturing		3 917	61	60	71
351	Industrial chemicals	74	93	63	49
353–4	Petroleum products	18	93	31	99
384	Electronics	247	88	81	66
361–2	Pottery, china, glass	12	88	40	89
369	Nonmetallic mineral products	27	86	31	79
383	Electrical machinery	149	83	58	60
352	Paints and other chemicals	97	80	78	66
386	Instruments, optical goods	60	74	90	76
314	Tobacco products	3	68	47	71
332	Furniture and fixtures	135	53	40	51
382	Machinery	464	49	63	60
321	Textiles	64	49	39	70
381	Fabricated metal products	528	47	28	70
341	Paper and paper products	100	43	34	71
364	Cement	5	43	5	99
311–2	Food	293	42	52	76
357	Plastic products	295	36	21	54
356	Rubber products	25	30	4	64
355	Gum processing	3	27	71	81
372	Nonferrous metals	20	25	45	71
313	Beverage	14	21	30	39
365	Structural cement	33	19	3	32
390	Other manufacturing industries	155	18	54	28
385	Transport equipment	246	18	58	72
322	Garments	347	15	80	67
342	Printing and publishing	361	14	23	68
331	Wood and wood products	74	12	43	82
371	Iron and steel	15	10	24	62
323	Leather and leather products	20	8	26	67
324	Footwear	27	7	46	71
363	Structural clay products	6	0	0	82

Source: EDB (1994a).
Note: ISIC, International Standard Industrial Classification.

The FDI–trade linkage

FDI in Singapore is trade creating. In 1992, the manufacturing sector not only had a high foreign-equity ratio but also was highly trade oriented (Table 2.4; 71% of material inputs were imported, 60% of sales were exported). Interindustry differentials in trade orientation were also large. At one end were petroleum products and cement, for example, in which import ratios were as high as 99%; in 20 other industries, the ratios were more than 65%. These high ratios reflect the lack of backward linkages because of the lack of natural resources and low vertical integration of industries. Upstream processing industries, in which import ratios were even higher, included instruments and optical goods (90%) and other highly export-oriented industries, such as electronics, nonindustrial chemicals, instruments and optical goods, and garments. The high export ratios reflect Singapore's limited domestic market and its role as an export production platform for MNEs. Industries with low export ratios tend to be those producing intermediate products, some of which are absorbed by domestic downstream industries, and those in publishing and printing and beverages, in which lack of proximity to customers and bulkiness discourage exports.

The high level of export orientation of Singapore's manufacturing sector is strongly linked to the level of foreign ownership and the export orientation of foreign firms. In 1992, foreign-equity capital accounted directly for 74% of the manufacturing sector's exports. Wholly foreign-owned firms alone accounted for 75% of direct export sales, whereas wholly locally-owned firms contributed a mere 8%. The US–European and Japanese MNEs accounted for 77% of direct exports. Export ratios averaged 71% in wholly foreign-owned firms and only 32% in wholly locally-owned firms (joint ventures fell in between).[1] Local firms' low export ratios reflect the greater difficulties of small and medium-sized enterprises (SMEs) in exporting, as well as their role as suppliers of parts and components for the Singapore-based foreign MNEs.[2]

The correlation between export ratios and foreign-equity ratios among the 31 industries was not very strong, with a correlation coefficient of 0.38. Although most of the large export-oriented industries had high foreign-equity participation, two notable exceptions were the garments industry, in which the foreign-equity ratio was only 15% and the export ratio was 80%, and the transport equipment industry (largely shipyards), in which the ratios were 18% and 58%, respectively. Singapore's modern export-oriented garment industry was founded in the 1960s by investors from Hong Kong and Taiwan seeking to escape their home countries' export quotas under the Multifibre Arrangement; the industry became indigenized when these investors subsequently took up Singapore citizenship. The foundation of the export-oriented shipyards was laid in the 1970s, when the former British naval dockyards were converted to state-owned enterprises, which were subsequently listed on the local stock exchange.

Export sales of Singapore's manufacturing industries depend mostly on US firms and the US market. In 1992, firms with majority US capital accounted for 45% of total direct exports by the manufacturing sector, whereas the US market accounted for 37% of the manufacturing sector's direct export sales. Firms with majority Japanese capital accounted for 19% of total direct exports, whereas the Japanese market accounted for only 7% of the manufacturing sector's direct export sales. Firms with majority EC capital accounted for 13% of total direct exports, whereas the EC market accounted for 21% of the manufacturing sector's direct export sales. The linkage between foreign firms and sales to home countries for the electronics industry is taken up in the next section.

Singapore's electronics industry

Singapore is a major manufacturing and trading centre in the region for electronic products, components and parts, and supporting services. This section considers Singapore's position in the industry value chain, including production, technology development, procurement, marketing and sales, and RHQ functions.

Electronics trade

Data generated from the International Economic Database of the Australian National University (ANU) show that, among the eight economies in this study, Singapore ranked first as an exporter of office and computing machinery (ISIC 3825) and electrical machinery (ISIC 383) and second only to Hong Kong as an importer. As illustrated, this dominant position can be accounted for by large domestic production and entrepôt trade.

Singapore's national trade data (excluding trade with Indonesia) illustrate the composition of domestic exports and re-exports and the product composition in its total exports. In 1992, Singapore's total trade in electronics reached S$74.3 billion, with imports of S$30.8 billion and exports of S$43.5 billion, of which re-exports accounted for 26.5% (Table 2.5). The largest categories

---

[1] Among foreign firms (100% and majority foreign equity), US firms had the highest export ratio (84.5%), followed by Japanese firms (61.6%). The lower export ratio of EC firms (49.7%) was in part due to their concentration in petroleum refining, an industry that is a crucial supplier of Singapore's domestic needs for petroleum products.

[2] It should be noted that the export ratios of local firms were no lower than those of local firms in many East Asian economies.

Table 2.5. Trade in electronic products and components, 1992.

Product	Imports Value (S$ millions)	Imports Share (%)	Exports Value (S$ millions)	Exports Share (%)	Domestic exports Value (S$ millions)	Domestic exports Share (%)	Re-exports Value (S$ millions)	Re-exports Share (%)	Export–import balance (S$ millions)	Domestic exports/total exports (%)
Total	30 800.8	100.00	43 455.5	100.00	31 941.3	100.00	11 514.2	100.00	12 654.7	73.50
Industrial electronics	10 165.5	33.00	22 095.7	50.85	18 641.0	58.36	3 454.8	30.00	11 930.2	84.36
Disk drives	1 448.4	4.70	9 913.3	22.81	8 979.2	28.11	934.1	8.11	8 465.0	90.58
Computers and subassemblies	5 688.0	18.47	7 612.0	17.52	6 528.3	20.44	1 083.7	9.41	1 924.0	85.76
Telecommunications equipment	1 299.9	4.22	1 330.6	3.06	670.1	2.10	660.5	5.74	30.8	50.36
Others	1 729.3	5.61	3 239.8	7.46	2 463.4	7.71	776.4	6.74	1 510.5	76.04
Consumer electronics	7 234.2	23.49	10 455.2	24.06	5 716.3	17.90	4 738.9	41.16	3 221.0	54.67
Colour TV sets	1 009.6	3.28	2 120.6	4.88	1 207.1	3.78	913.5	7.93	1 111.0	56.92
Radio-cassette recorders	721.5	2.34	1 350.4	3.11	806.1	2.52	544.3	4.73	628.9	59.70
TV receivers and subassemblies	1 324.3	4.30	1 665.8	3.83	1 278.4	4.00	387.4	3.36	341.5	76.74
Other radio-broadcast receivers	388.7	1.26	1 046.5	2.41	647.8	2.03	398.7	3.46	657.9	61.90
Videocassette recorders	925.9	3.01	1 398.7	3.22	669.7	2.10	729.0	6.33	472.9	47.88
Others	2 864.2	9.30	2 873.1	6.61	1 107.1	3.47	1 766.0	15.34	8.9	38.53
Electronic components	13 401.1	43.51	10 904.6	25.09	7 584.1	23.74	3 320.5	28.84	(2 496.5)	69.55
Integrated circuits	7 095.5	23.04	6 871.1	15.81	4 822.4	15.10	2 048.7	17.79	(224.4)	70.18
Colour picture tubes	480.6	1.56	655.8	1.51	568.1	1.78	87.7	0.76	175.2	86.63
Capacitors	887.5	2.88	502.2	1.16	358.0	1.12	144.2	1.25	(385.3)	71.28
Resistors	407.3	1.32	187.8	0.43	124.2	0.39	63.6	0.55	(219.5)	66.13
Other	4 530.2	14.71	2 687.8	6.19	1 711.4	5.36	976.3	8.48	(1 842.5)	63.68

Source: TDB (1992).
Note: TV, television.

of domestic exports were disk drives, computers and subassemblies, integrated circuits (ICs), television (TV) receivers and subassemblies, and colour TV sets. Re-exports were concentrated in ICs, computers and subassemblies, disk drives, colour TV sets, radios and videocassette recorders (VCRs), and telecommunications equipment.

Singapore's domestic exports of electronics still depend on US–EC markets, which absorbed 64.1% of such exports in 1992. East Asia accounted for 26.3%, but Japan's share was only 5.1% (Table 2.6). The very small Japanese share is noteworthy in view of the extensive presence of Japanese electronics firms in Singapore and may be attributed to both Japan's import barriers and the corporate strategies of Japanese electronics firms in Singapore (this is elaborated on later).

Export destinations showed variations according to product lines, and these were associated with ownership of firms in the different industry sectors and products. The United States and Europe were the major markets for industrial electronics, consumer electronics, and ICs. The US market absorbed more than half of Singapore's domestic exports of disk drives, nearly half of its exports of computers and subassemblies and TV receivers and subassemblies, and more than one-quarter of its exports of radio-broadcast receivers and ICs. The US affiliates in Singapore dominated the disk drive and computers and subassemblies. The EC market absorbed nearly half of Singapore's domestic exports of telecommunications equipment and VCRs and more than one-quarter of its exports of disk drives, computers and subassemblies, colour TV sets, and other radio-broadcast receivers. Japan's market share was small for most electronic products and components, significant only in sound equipment (microphones, loudspeakers, and amplifiers) and in electronic-display devices. Leading Japanese consumer-electronics firms, such as Sony, Nippon Electric Company Ltd (NEC), Japanese Victor Corporation (JVC), Matsushita Electrical Industrial Co. (MEI), Toshiba, and Hitachi, were the main producers of consumer-electronics products and electronic-display devices in Singapore, but they did not necessarily export them back to their home country.

ASEAN and the Asian NIEs provided large markets for Singapore's domestic exports of electronic components, particularly Malaysia, indicating the increasingly integrated production pattern in East Asia and Singapore's role in the value chain. The ASEAN region (particularly Malaysia) was the main market for passive electronic components, whereas the Asian NIEs (particularly Hong Kong and Taiwan) provided major markets for ICs and colour-picture tubes.

Electronics production

The electronics industry dominates Singapore's manufacturing sector, and foreign investment was found to dominate the electronics industry. In 1994, the industry recorded S$49.3 billion in output and S$13.4 billion in value added, the latter accounting for 42% of the manufacturing sector's value added and more than 10% of GDP. Employment in the industry was 123 400, which accounted for 34% of total manufacturing employment and more than 7% of national employment. The industry was made up of both large and small original-equipment-manufacturer (OEM) suppliers and vendors, producing and supplying a wide range of final products, subassemblies, and parts and components for both industrial and consumer markets. The industry is characterized by the dominance of foreign MNEs, concentration in industrial electronics and electronic components, strong export orientation, rapid restructuring, and relocating of labour-intensive processes and lower-end product lines to neighbouring countries.

Foreign investment and local enterprise

Singapore did not benefit from early waves of FDI into East Asia because these were destined more for South Korea and Taiwan and were motivated by investors' desire to locate behind trade barriers designed to stimulate import-substituting production. Singapore did, however, become a major recipient of later FDI flows, motivated by maturing product cycles, globalization strategies, and exchange-rate realignments.

Table 2.6. Domestic exports of electronic products and components by destination, 1992.

Product	World total (S$ millions)	Asia-8[a]	Japan	China	NIEs-3[b]	Hong Kong	South Korea	Taiwan	ASEAN-3[c]	Malaysia	Philippines	Thailand	United States	European Community	Canada	Rest of the world
Total	31941.3	26.33	5.12	0.23	10.57	5.11	1.48	3.97	10.42	6.08	0.46	3.88	39.80	24.25	0.86	8.77
Industrial electronics	18641.0	14.95	3.69	0.09	6.46	2.42	1.27	2.76	4.71	1.12	0.19	3.39	49.38	29.11	0.87	5.69
Disk drives	8979.2	12.00	2.97	0.03	8.41	2.63	1.29	4.50	0.58	0.12	0.08	0.39	56.00	27.24	0.38	4.39
Computers and subassemblies	6528.3	18.27	3.75	0.14	3.17	1.89	0.35	0.93	11.21	2.24	0.17	8.80	48.42	25.31	1.55	6.45
Telecommunications equipment	670.1	18.91	4.34	0.41	8.11	6.99	0.15	0.97	6.05	2.66	2.12	1.27	21.27	46.50	1.83	11.48
Others	2463.4	15.81	6.00	0.06	7.59	1.84	3.98	1.77	2.15	1.41	0.15	0.60	35.43	41.26	0.63	6.87
Consumer electronics	5716.3	28.09	5.02	0.40	10.17	7.54	0.76	1.86	12.51	7.58	0.26	4.67	27.58	25.01	1.80	17.52
Colour TV sets	1207.1	17.45	0.66	0.02	9.65	7.97	0.40	1.28	7.12	0.23	0.32	6.56	16.23	29.58	2.30	34.45
Radio cassette recorders	806.1	22.58	10.90	0.27	7.82	6.27	0.11	1.43	3.60	2.59	0.05	0.97	23.68	21.43	2.93	29.38
TV receivers and subassemblies	1278.4	35.58	2.78	1.42	3.80	1.32	1.36	1.12	27.58	18.44	0.49	8.65	47.10	7.99	1.48	7.84
Other radio-broadcast receivers	647.8	9.98	3.59	0.00	4.21	3.02	0.26	0.93	2.18	1.38	0.07	0.73	31.56	35.33	2.24	20.89
Videocassette recorders	669.7	25.02	0.06	0.00	23.47	19.95	0.00	3.53	1.49	0.35	0.03	1.11	23.83	46.68	1.71	2.76
Others	1107.1	47.53	11.92	0.21	15.23	10.33	1.69	3.22	20.17	14.69	0.31	5.16	20.18	23.12	0.62	8.56
Electronic components	7584.1	52.98	8.69	0.43	20.97	9.89	2.53	8.55	22.89	17.15	1.27	4.47	25.46	11.72	0.11	9.73
Integrated circuits	4822.4	39.90	9.89	0.08	22.28	11.55	2.11	8.62	7.66	5.55	0.25	1.86	35.95	12.35	0.04	11.76
Colour picture tubes	568.1	83.60	10.53	4.44	25.31	2.45	1.90	20.97	43.31	31.30	2.10	9.91	0.05	5.87	0.00	10.49
Capacitors	358.0	72.63	1.50	0.21	18.00	15.78	0.13	2.09	52.92	34.65	5.25	13.02	3.39	18.21	0.05	5.71
Resistors	124.2	69.50	0.86	0.00	5.45	2.24	1.06	2.15	63.19	45.39	4.45	13.36	11.98	9.61	0.13	8.78
Others	1711.4	74.35	6.79	0.14	17.58	7.02	4.53	6.03	49.84	39.46	2.80	7.58	9.94	10.69	0.36	4.66

Source: TDB (1992).

Note: ASEAN, Association of Southeast Asian Nations; NIE, newly industrialized economy; TV, television.

[a] Asia-8, China, Hong Kong, Japan, Malaysia, the Philippines, South Korea, Taiwan, and Thailand.

[b] NIEs-3, Hong Kong, South Korea, and Taiwan.

[c] ASEAN-3, Malaysia, the Philippines, and Thailand.

The first influx of foreign MNEs, which established Singapore's electronics industry, occurred in the late 1960s. Singapore's locational advantages were the ready availability of trainable low-wage labour and stable industrial relations, well-developed industrial parks, and transportation and telecommunications infrastructure, which facilitated early startups and just-in-time manufacturing. There was also strong government support intended to train human resources, promote local supporting industries, provide attractive investment incentives, and actively promote investment through EDB, including an investment mission to the United States in 1967. The push factors came from US firms seeking offshore production with maturing product cycles and needing to offset rising domestic labour costs to remain internationally competitive; the relocation of labour-intensive processes, such as semiconductor assembly was facilitated by sections 806.30 and 807.00 of the US tariff schedule, which impose import tariffs only on the value added of the imports and exempt the input content of US origin. The influx of American investments in electronics in Singapore from 1968 on was led by semiconductor MNEs engaged in assembly and testing of simple ICs for re-export. FDI by US electronic firms was soon followed by that of Europeans and Japanese. Investments in semiconductor assembly were followed by investments in consumer electronics as Singapore's attractions as an export platform became better known.

The FDI inflows were disrupted by the global recession of the mid-1970s, which led to an industry shakeout. With economic recovery, a new wave of FDI followed, this time led by investments in electronic components and advanced consumer electronics. Japanese investors were more prominent, reflecting the more aggressive outward FDI by Japanese corporations responding to internationalization of the Japanese economy and rising costs. Japanese investments in Singapore were primarily for exports to third-country markets, particularly as Japanese affiliates in South Korea and Taiwan increasingly faced trade restrictions in the US and European markets.

The Singapore economy went into recession again in the mid-1980s. The postrecession wave of FDI in electronics was led by US MNEs in industrial electronics, particularly disk drives and other computer peripherals, computer systems, and ICs, reflecting the globalization of the US electronics industry. Singapore's early cost advantage had eroded, however, and its future competitiveness depended increasingly on the skills levels and productivity of its work force and its excellent infrastructure.

Foreign investments accounted for 88% of the total foreign equity in the industry in 1992 (Table 2.7). The FDI penetration was highest in consumer and industrial electronics and lowest in electronic components. In consumer and industrial electronics, well-established international brand names and the technological superiority of foreign MNEs were strong barriers to the entry of local firms. Foreign ownership was almost 100% in consumer electronics and in the industrial-electronics subsectors of computers and data-processing equipment, disk drives, and office machinery and equipment; foreign dominance in communications equipment was less strong because of a large state-owned enterprise. In electronic components, foreign equity was dominant in semiconductors and capacitors, but in resistors and printed circuit boards (PCBs) with electronic parts, local ownership was dominant, with a proliferation of local firms undertaking contract manufacturing and acting as suppliers for the foreign MNEs. Major US firms included Conner Peripherals, Maxtor Peripherals, Western Digital, Seagate, and Micropolis in disk drives; Hewlett-Packard (HP) and Digital Equipment Company in computer peripherals; American Telephone & Telegraph Co. (AT&T) and Motorola in communications equipment; CTS Corp. in resistors; and Compaq and Digital in PCBs with electronic parts. Major European firms included Olivetti and Siemens in computer peripheral equipment, Philips and Thomson in TV sets and subassemblies, and Philips in audio–video (AV) combination equipment.

It took more than a decade before a large base of local supporting industries emerged to complement the large base of foreign MNEs operating in the Singapore electronics industry. Initially, the development of local supporting industries was left completely to market forces. However, MNEs were reluctant to source locally because local suppliers were uncompetitive in quality and reliability, and, in the absence of local-content performance requirements, they chose to source from imports.

Table 2.7. Electronics industry, 1992.

Industry (by 5-digit ISIC code)	Establishment (n)	Employment (n)	Total sales (S$ millions)	Net value added (S$ millions)	Establishment (%)	Employment (%)	Total sales (%)	Net value added (%)	% of foreign capital	% of sales exported	% of materials imported (%)
Total	247	122 562	32 379	6 166	100.00	100.00	100.00	100.00	88	81	66
Industrial electronics	63	52 654	15 918	3 137	25.51	42.96	43.0	50.88			
38411 Computers and data-processing equipment	15	3 033	2 286	317	6.07	2.47	2.5	5.14	96	92	63
38412 Disk drives	15	28 695	8 285	1 421	6.07	23.41	23.4	23.04	99	93	70
38413 Computer peripheral equipment	20	11 012	3 590	860	8.10	8.58	9.0	13.95	87	90	64
38414 Office machinery and equipment	4	1 971	335	94	1.62	1.61	1.6	1.52	99	91	57
38415 Communications equipment	9	7 943	1 422	446	3.64	6.48	6.5	7.24	68	71	51
Consumer electronics	20	20 978	5 010	731	8.10	17.12	17.1	11.85			
38422 TV sets and subassemblies	5	5 307	1 588	97	2.02	4.33	4.3	1.57	100	90	62
38423 Microphones, loudspeakers, amplifiers	4	3 072	333	104	1.62	2.51	2.5	1.68	100	63	40
38426 Audio–video combination equipment	11	12 599	3 090	530	4.45	10.28	10.3	8.60	97	80	49
Electronic components	129	38 507	8 737	1 865	52.2	31.42	31.4	30.25			
38441/3/9 Semiconductor devices	26	14 746	4 252	739	10.53	12.03	12.0	11.99	84	88	94
38461 Capacitors	8	3 474	468	163	3.24	2.83	2.8	2.65	86	70	93
38462 Resistors	6	846	61	22	2.43	0.69	0.7	0.36	38	75	73
38463 Printed circuit boards without electronic parts	22	5 389	680	212	8.91	4.40	4.4	3.44	51	38	74
38464 Printed circuit boards with electronic parts	67	14 052	3 276	728	27.13	11.47	11.5	11.81	43	69	58
Other electronic products and components	35	10 423	2 715	433	14.17	8.50	8.5	7.02	85	46	54

Source: EDB (1994a).

Note: ISIC, International Standard Industrial Classification; TV, television

Subsequent active technical and financial support from EDB and other government agencies improved the technical capability and financial strengths of local SMEs, and a core of local suppliers emerged to provide critical components and services to support the manufacture of disk drives, computers, colour TVs, VCRs, instrumentation, and other precision engineering products.

A notable scheme was implemented in 1986, the Local Industry Upgrading Programme (LIUP), whereby specific MNEs and large local companies are linked to local suppliers, providing focused assistance to improve their operational efficiency and develop their technical capabilities. LIUP initially focused on operational upgrading for vendors to improve the quality and reliability of their products but has progressed to collaborations in product and process development. By 1994, LIUP had 32 partners and 180 local vendors. Many local enterprises have since developed niche products and services in their own right and become OEM manufacturers and contractors. A few local enterprises have also become global in scale. The best known is Creative Technology, which is listed on National Association of Securities Dealers Automated Quotations (NASDAQ), as well as the Singapore Stock Exchange. By adopting a niche approach, Creative Technology has become a world leader in multimedia applications, and its success has been emulated by Aztech, another Singapore firm. Together, Creative Technology and Aztech dominate the world supply of sound cards.

The FDI–trade linkage

Table 2.7 shows the high trade orientation of the electronics industry, with an average export ratio (export to total sales) of 81% and an average import ratio (imports to total material inputs) of 66% in 1992. Export orientation varied with product sectors, being highest in industrial electronics and lowest in electronic components, ranging from more than 90% for computers and data-processing equipment, disk drives, and office machinery and equipment to less than 40% for PCBs. Product segments with a stronger foreign-equity presence tended to be more export oriented, with a correlation coefficient of 0.47 between foreign-equity ratios and export ratios. Import dependence showed no correlation with foreign ownership. It was highest in upstream components and lowest in downstream consumer and industrial products. The upstream end of the electronics industry depended heavily on overseas supplies of raw materials, but the downstream end of the industry could increasingly source parts and components from domestic production.

Tables 2.8 and 2.9 show the FDI–trade linkage of the 247 electronics establishments covered by the 1992 census of industrial production. A number of characteristics of FDI in the electronics industry at this time may be noted.

First, the industry was dominated by wholly foreign-owned firms, 108 of them compared with 45 joint ventures. This reflected MNE preference for full ownership control in technology-intensive and export-oriented industries, as well as Singapore's complete lack of foreign-equity restrictions.

Second, the foreign firms were mainly from Japan (49), the United States (48), and Europe (20). Firms with majority capital from the Asian NIEs were singularly absent, with only two firms from Hong Kong and one from Taiwan; the data do not reveal the prevalence of minority-equity participation by investors from these NIEs. Japanese and US firms dominated different sectors of the industry, with Japanese firms in consumer electronics and US firms in industrial electronics; this mirrored the strengths of Japanese and US electronic giants in different niches at the global level. By contrast, local firms were concentrated in the less scale-, capital-, and technology-intensive PCB sector.

Third, most of the industry's exports were undertaken by foreign firms. The US firms accounted for 65% of the industry's exports, followed by Japanese firms (17%) and European firms (12%), whereas Singapore firms accounted for a mere 5%. Foreign firms were much more export oriented than local firms. Of the 128 foreign firms, nearly half exported at least 90% of sales, and only 7 did not export at all. In contrast, of the 119 local firms, nearly half did not export at all, and only

Table 2.8. Electronics industry: sales destination by ownership, 1992.

	Establish-ment (n)	Foreign equity (%)	Total sales (%)	Domestic sales (%)	Direct exports (%)	Distribution of total sales (%)													
						Asia-8[a]	Japan	China	NIEs-3[b]	Hong Kong	Korea	Taiwan	ASEAN-3[c]	Indonesia	Malaysia	Philip-pines	United States	Europe	Rest of the world
Dominant ownership																			
Total	247	87.9	100.00	18.74	81.26	15.81	4.45	1.84	4.38	2.32	0.43	1.63	5.13	0.20	3.04	1.90	38.46	20.61	6.38
Singapore	119	14.1	100.00	47.54	52.46	14.04	0.68	1.04	3.58	0.85	0.15	2.58	8.75	0.83	6.99	0.34	17.70	15.92	4.79
Japan	49	98.2	100.00	35.12	64.88	26.34	11.19	2.45	4.89	2.82	0.38	1.69	7.82	0.47	5.79	1.55	16.13	11.28	11.13
United States	48	99.7	100.00	9.71	90.29	12.75	2.93	2.08	3.97	1.98	0.41	1.59	3.77	0.01	1.41	2.35	54.65	19.23	3.66
Europe	20	99.8	100.00	13.82	86.18	12.81	2.21	0.06	6.11	4.13	0.82	1.15	4.43	0.15	3.41	0.38	13.07	48.17	12.13
Other	11	78.6	100.00	25.91	74.09	11.07	0.05	0.01	2.79	2.41	0.02	0.37	8.24	2.19	4.14	1.90	12.50	37.00	13.48
Distribution (%)																			
Total	100.00	—	100.00	100.00	100.00	100.00	100.00	100.00	100.00	100.00	100.00	100.00	100.00	100.00	100.00	100.00	100.00	100.00	100.00
Singapore	48.18	—	7.81	19.81	5.04	6.94	1.19	4.39	6.38	2.85	2.75	12.35	13.31	32.36	17.97	3.85	3.59	6.03	5.86
Japan	19.84	—	21.76	40.79	17.38	36.27	54.68	28.97	24.30	26.47	19.30	22.53	33.14	51.38	41.52	17.80	9.13	11.91	37.94
United States	19.43	—	58.59	30.35	65.10	47.25	38.49	66.25	53.19	50.00	56.02	56.99	42.98	2.53	27.11	72.61	83.26	54.66	33.59
Europe	8.10	—	11.34	8.36	12.03	9.19	5.63	0.39	15.82	20.17	21.89	8.03	9.78	8.25	12.72	5.23	3.85	26.50	21.56
Others	4.45	—	0.50	0.69	0.46	0.35	0.01	0.00	0.32	0.52	0.02	0.11	0.80	5.50	0.68	0.50	0.16	0.90	1.05

Source: EDB (1994a).
Note: ASEAN, Association of Southeast Asian Nations; NIE, newly industrialized economy.
[a] Asia-8, China, Hong Kong, Japan, Malaysia, the Philippines, South Korea, Taiwan, and Thailand.
[b] NIEs-3, Hong Kong, South Korea, and Taiwan.
[c] ASEAN-3, Malaysia, the Philippines, and Thailand.

Table 2.9. Electronics industry: distribution of establishments by equity, export sales, and home-country sales, 1992.

	Establishment (n)						Distribution (%)					
	Total	Japan	United States	Europe	Other foreign	Local	Total	Japan	United States	Europe	Other foreign	Local
Foreign equity (%)												
100	108	43	44	16	5	94	43.7	87.8	91.7	80.0	45.5	79.0
>50	19	6	4	4	6	25	7.7	12.2	8.3	20.0	54.5	21.0
<50	26	0	0	0	0	0	10.5	0.0	0.0	0.0	0.0	0.0
0	94	0	0	0	0	0	38.1	0.0	0.0	0.0	0.0	0.0
Total	247	49	48	20	11	119	100.0	100.0	100.0	100.0	100.0	100.0
Export sales (%)												
90–100	70	14	30	11	3	12	28.3	28.6	62.5	55.0	27.3	10.1
67–90	42	10	6	5	4	17	17.0	20.4	12.5	25.0	36.4	14.3
33–67	41	16	7	1	1	16	16.6	32.7	14.6	5.0	9.1	13.4
1–33	30	6	3	1	3	17	12.1	12.2	6.3	5.0	27.3	14.3
0	64	3	2	0	0	57	25.9	6.1	4.2	0.0	0.0	47.9
Total	247	49	48	20	11	119	100.0	100.0	100.0	100.0	100.0	100.0
Exported sales to home country (%)												
90–100	15	3	9	3	0		6.1	6.1	18.8	15.0	0.0	
67–90	9	2	6	1	0		3.6	4.1	12.5	5.0	0.0	
33–67	14	2	8	4	0		5.7	4.1	16.7	20.0	0.0	
1–33	43	27	7	5	5		17.4	55.1	14.6	25.0	45.5	
0	46	15	18	0	6		18.6	30.6	37.5	0.0	54.5	
Total	247	49	48	20	11		100.0	100.0	100.0	100.0	100.0	

Source: EDB (1994a).

12 exported more than 90% of sales. A large number of the local firms were SMEs serving the Singapore-based foreign MNEs through OEM and provision of parts and components.

Fourth, of the industrialized country investors, US firms were the most export oriented, with an export ratio of 90%, followed by European firms, with 86%, whereas Japanese firms had a much lower export ratio of 65%. Among the 48 US firms, 30 exported more than 90% of production, and only 2 did not export at all. Among the 49 Japanese firms, 14 exported more than 90% of production and 3 did not export. The Singapore firms had the lowest export ratio, 52%, but this was much higher than the average export ratio of Singapore firms for the whole manufacturing sector.

Fifth, US firms tended to export more to their home country than the Japanese firms. The share of total sales destined for the home market was 55% for US, 11% for Japanese, and 48% for European firms. Individual-firm performance showed that most of the 48 US firms shipped at least 33% of sales back to the United States, with 9 shipping more than 90%. In contrast, most of the 49 Japanese firms shipped less than 33% of sales to Japan. The major markets for Japanese firms were local (35%). The US firms, on the other hand, sold to the home market and Europe. The data clearly demonstrate differences in US and Japanese corporate strategies for offshore production, the former to supply the home and third-country markets, the latter to supply largely the host and third-country markets.

Sixth, the electronics industry's exports to the United States were overwhelmingly undertaken by US firms (83%), whereas exports to Japan were undertaken by both Japanese (55%) and US firms (38%). Exports to Europe were led by US firms, followed by the European and Japanese ones.

Firm-level survey

A firm-level survey was carried out between October 1994 and April 1995 to study the determinants of intrafirm trade links by eliciting information on the procurement and sales pattern of electronics manufacturing firms by nationality. A questionnaire common to the eight economies in this research project was used. The sampling frame was derived from three main sources: Singapore 1000 (a directory of 1 000 industrial firms, by a private publisher), the directory of electronics manufacturers published by SEDB, and the directory of electronics trade published by the Singapore Trade Development Board. Efforts were made to choose a representative sample by size, ownership nationality, vintage (year of establishment), and product lines. About 200 firms were identified; questionnaires were mailed and followed up by fax and telephone with requests for individual interviews. Thirty-four firms responded, but some refused to complete portions of the questionnaire they regarded as sensitive. Of the 34 respondent firms, 18 were producing electronic components, 8 were in industrial electronics, 3 were in consumer electronics, and 5 were OHQs. The sample consisted of 29 wholly foreign-owned affiliates, 4 wholly local firms, and 1 joint venture. By nationality, 14 firms were Japanese; 14, US; 2, European; 1, Taiwanese; and 4, local. By vintage, some of the US and Japanese firms had been manufacturing in Singapore for more than 20 years and belonged to the first cohort that invested in Singapore in the late 1960s and early 1970s. Others of more recent vintage included the OHQs. By product line, Japanese firms were more heavily represented in AV equipment and components, and US firms were more heavily represented in computers, disk drives, and components. The firms ranged from the very large, with several thousand workers, to those with fewer than 100 workers. The five OHQs surveyed are analyzed in the next section. The focus of this section is the 29 manufacturing firms, which represented 12% of all electronic firms in the 1992 industrial census and 20% of total sales in 1994. As several respondents chose not to disclose data on levels of sales and purchases, it was possible only to tabulate frequency distributions of percentage shares.

Sales destinations and channels are presented in Table 2.10. Consistent with the industrial census data, the survey found the 29 respondent firms to be highly export oriented. All firms exported, with 15 having export ratios of more than 90% (including some with 100%), and only 1 firm exported less than 33% of production. There were no notable differences in export orientation

Table 2.10. Surveyed firms in electronics by investing country and destination of sales.

Nationality (% sales)	Surveyed firms (*n*)				
	Exported	Intrafirm	To parent	Interaffiliate	Home country
Japan	12	12	12	12	12
>90	5	7	2	4	2
67–90	2	0	0	0	0
33–67	5	1	0	1	0
<33	0	3	6	2	9
0	0	0	2	3	1
Unknown	0	1	2	2	0
United States	12	12	12	12	12
>90	7	5	2	0	2
67–90	1	3	2	0	3
33–67	3	1	3	3	2
<33	1	1	0	2	0
0	0	0	2	4	2
Unknown	0	2	3	3	3
Europe	2	2	2	2	2
>90	1	0	0	0	1
67–90	1	1	1	0	0
33–67	0	0	0	0	0
<33	0	1	1	1	1
0	0	0	0	1	0
Unknown	0	0	0	0	0
Singapore	3	3	3	3	3
>90	2	0	0	0	0
67–90	1	0	0	0	0
33–67	0	0	0	0	0
<33	0	1	1	1	2
0	0	1	1	1	1
Unknown	0	1	1	1	0
Total	29	29	29	29	29
>90	15	12	4	4	4
67–90	5	3	2	0	3
33–67	8	2	3	4	2
<33	1	6	8	6	12
0	0	1	5	8	4
Unknown	0	5	7	7	4

Source: Interviews and questionnaires.

between firms of different nationalities. The three local firms were as export oriented as the foreign firms; this was not representative because it contradicts the census evidence. Export orientation was not correlated with years in operation or with firm size (employment). However, there was some correlation with product lines: computer and disk-drive firms were much more export oriented than firms producing components. Export orientation was also lower among foreign firms that had multiple affiliates in Singapore because local interaffiliate sales reduced the export propensity of some affiliates.

The firm-level survey provided insights into intrafirm trade not available from industrial-census data. There was evidence of a high level of intrafirm sales. Of the 29 firms, 23 reported intrafirm-sales activities, but 5 did not disclose such information. For 12 of the firms, intrafirm sales accounted for more than 90% of total sales, and for another 3 firms it accounted for more than 65%. Sales to parent companies were reported by 17 firms, whereas interaffiliate sales were reported by 14. Intrafirm sales (sales to parent and interaffiliate sales) were common to Japanese and US firms. In addition, US firms confirmed the aggregate data, which showed a stronger tendency to export back to the home country. Where OHQs existed in Singapore to coordinate the sales activities of affiliates and where local affiliates were required to export through the OHQ, the local affiliates' direct sales to parents were reduced and local and interaffiliate sales rose. OEM production and contract manufacturing were common. Firms produced parts and components for themselves, as well as for their competitors, to take advantage of economies of scale and better use of specialized know-how.

The most important market for electronics was the United States (Table 2.11), with 13 firms reporting it as the lead destination, followed by 7 firms reporting Malaysia as the lead destination. Only three firms reported Japan as the lead destination, and another firm ranked Japan as the second largest market. All US firms that reported export destinations gave the United States as the lead destination. For Japanese firms, four reported Malaysia as the lead destination, and an equal number (three) reported Japan and the United States as lead destinations. Apart from the United States and Japan, other lead destinations for the exports of the electronic firms were the EC and Hong Kong.

The firm-level survey confirmed the difference in investment motivation for US and Japanese firms: whereas US overseas investment and production were aimed largely at serving the US market, Japanese overseas investment and production were targeted at non-Japanese markets. Thus, despite extensive Japanese manufacturing investments in Singapore, exports of manufactures to Japan remained negligible compared with exports to the United States. To the extent that Japanese offshore plants were selling more widely in the East Asian economies than US offshore plants, the Japanese reinforced the role of Japan in integrating the East Asian economies with Japan through the investment process and in supplying industrial goods to its East Asian neighbours.

Tables 2.12 and 2.13 present sourcing of raw materials and components for the firms surveyed. The data confirm that electronic firms in Singapore depended heavily on foreign sources of materials and components. All firms reported dependence on import sourcing, and 24 of the 29 respondent firms reported importing more than 67% of materials and components. Import dependence showed some correlation with product lines: the correlation was higher for firms producing components than for firms producing final products because raw materials had to be sourced from imports, whereas components were increasingly sourced from the many foreign and local suppliers and vendors based in Singapore. Nonetheless, the high level of import sourcing meant that the electronics industry was still not very vertically integrated, and despite the efforts by the government to develop local suppliers and vendors, import sourcing remained dominant. The inability of local suppliers to meet the strict technical standards and the Japanese tradition of sourcing from long-term suppliers were additional factors preventing more local sourcing. Japanese and US firms showed no notable difference in the degree of import sourcing.

Intrafirm sourcing was important. Of respondent firms, eight sourced more than 90% intrafirm, and only five sourced completely at arm's length. Intrafirm sourcing was more important for Japanese than for US firms but was unimportant for European and Singapore firms. Sourcing from parents was more common than from other affiliates. All firms sourced from the home country, with seven of the firms sourcing more than 67% from the home base. Japanese firms sourced a higher percentage from the home country than did US firms.

Japan was the lead supplier of raw materials and components. Of the surveyed firms, 25 imported from Japan, with 14 of these firms reporting Japan as the lead supplier and 9 reporting Japan as second-most important supplier. The United States was the second most important source of materials and components, followed by Malaysia and the EC. Hong Kong and Taiwan were also suppliers. Only a small number of firms reported sourcing from Indonesia, the Philippines, and Thailand.

Import sourcing was related to the nationality of the firm. Japanese firms tended to import from Japan; US firms, from the United States. Of the 11 surveyed Japanese firms, 8 ranked Japan as the lead supplier, and the other 3 ranked Japan as second. The US firms, however, sourced equally from the United States and Japan, with five firms indicating the United States and five indicating Japan as lead supplier.

Table 2.11. Surveyed firms in electronics by investing country and ranked importance of export markets.

Nationality	Surveyed firms (n)												
	Japan	United States	Indonesia	Malaysia	Philippines	Thailand	Hong Kong	South Korea	Taiwan	China	European Community	Canada	Other
Japan	12	12	12	12	12	12	12	12	12	12	12	12	12
Rank 1	3	3	0	4	0	0	1	0	0	0	1	0	0
Rank 2	1	2	0	1	0	1	0	0	1	0	2	0	2
Rank 3	2	2	0	0	0	1	3	0	0	1	2	0	0
Rank 4 and over	5	0	2	2	2	3	2	1	3	1	4	2	4
No export	1	5	10	5	10	7	6	11	8	10	3	10	6
Unknown	0	0	0	0	0	0	0	0	0	0	0	0	0
United States	12	12	12	12	12	12	12	12	12	12	12	12	12
Rank 1	0	8	0	1	0	0	1	0	1	0	0	0	0
Rank 2	0	0	0	1	0	0	1	0	1	0	4	0	0
Rank 3	2	0	0	1	0	0	1	2	1	0	1	0	0
Rank 4 and over	1	0	0	2	1	0	2	1	0	2	0	3	2
No export	8	3	10	6	9	10	6	8	8	9	6	8	9
Unknown	1	1	2	1	2	2	1	1	1	1	1	1	1
Europe	2	2	2	2	2	2	2	2	2	2	2	2	2
Rank 1	0	0	0	1	0	0	0	0	0	0	1	0	0
Rank 2	0	1	0	0	0	0	0	0	0	1	0	0	0
Rank 3	1	0	1	0	0	0	0	0	0	0	0	0	0
Rank 4 and over	0	1	0	0	0	0	0	0	1	0	0	0	1
No export	1	0	1	1	2	2	2	2	1	1	1	2	1
Unknown	0	0	0	0	0	0	0	0	0	0	0	0	0
Singapore	3	3	3	3	3	3	3	3	3	3	3	3	3
Rank 1	0	2	0	1	0	0	0	0	0	0	0	0	0
Rank 2	0	0	0	0	0	0	0	0	0	0	3	0	0
Rank 3	1	0	0	0	0	0	2	0	0	0	0	0	0
Rank 4 and over	0	1	0	1	0	0	0	0	0	1	0	1	0
No export	2	0	3	1	3	3	1	3	3	2	0	2	3
Unknown	0	0	0	0	0	0	0	0	0	0	0	0	0
Total	29	29	29	29	29	29	29	29	29	29	29	29	29
Rank 1	3	13	0	7	0	0	2	0	1	0	2	0	0
Rank 2	1	3	0	2	0	1	1	0	2	1	9	0	2
Rank 3	6	2	1	1	0	1	6	2	1	1	3	0	0
Rank 4 and over	6	2	2	5	3	3	4	2	4	4	4	6	7
No export	12	8	24	13	24	22	15	24	20	22	10	22	19
Unknown	1	1	2	1	2	2	1	1	1	1	1	1	1

Source: Interviews and questionnaires.

Table 2.12. Surveyed firms in electronics by investing country
and sourcing of materials and components.

Nationality (% sourcing)	Surveyed firms (*n*)				
	Imported	Intrafirm	From parent	Interaffiliate	Home country
Japan	12	12	12	12	12
>90	7	6	2	1	6
67–90	1	1	2	0	0
33–67	3	1	1	1	3
<33	0	1	2	3	2
0	0	0	2	4	0
Unknown	1	3	3	3	1
United States	12	12	12	12	12
>90	6	2	0	0	0
67–90	4	0	0	2	1
33–67	1	3	2	2	3
<33	0	3	5	2	6
0	0	1	2	3	0
Unknown	1	3	3	3	2
Europe	2	2	2	2	2
>90	1	0	0	0	1
67–90	0	0	0	0	0
33–67	0	0	0	0	0
<33	1	1	1	2	1
0	0	1	1	0	0
Unknown	0	0	0	0	0
Singapore	3	3	3	3	3
>90	1	0	0	0	0
67–90	2	0	0	0	0
33–67	0	0	0	0	0
<33	0	0	0	1	3
0	0	3	3	2	0
Unknown	0	0	0	0	0
Total	29	29	29	29	29
>90	15	8	2	1	7
67–90	7	1	2	2	1
33–67	4	4	3	4	6
<33	1	5	8	8	12
0	0	5	8	8	3
Unknown	2	6	6	6	0

Source: Interviews and questionnaires.

The asymmetrical behaviour of Japanese subsidiaries in Singapore, with sales targeted at non-Japanese markets while sourcing from Japan, helped to explain the triangular trade pattern and trade imbalance observed in macro- and industry-level data. However, the procurement pattern of Japanese subsidiaries may be changing. The rapid growth of foreign investments in the electronics industry in the economies of East Asia, first in the Asian NIEs, then in Malaysia and Thailand and spreading to China, Indonesia, the Philippines, and Vietnam, will accelerate the trend toward sourcing from a wider group of countries. Also, the sharp rise in the yen since 1993 has been pressuring Japanese corporations to try to source outside Japan and inducing Japanese component suppliers to locate offshore; the latter trend, however, will change the location of sourcing, not the nationality. Many electronics firms in Singapore, both foreign and local, are caught in an exchange-rate squeeze because their raw materials and components are sourced from Japan and hence yen denominated, but their products are exported to the United States and denominated in a rapidly depreciating currency.

Table 2.13. Surveyed firms in electronics by investing country and ranked importance of materials and components markets.

Nationality	Surveyed firms (n)												
	Japan	United States	Indonesia	Malaysia	Philippines	Thailand	Hong Kong	South Korea	Taiwan	China	European Community	Canada	Other
Japan	12	12	12	12	12	12	12	12	12	12	12	12	12
Rank 1	8	1	0	1	0	0	1	0	0	0	0	0	1
Rank 2	3	0	0	2	0	0	0	0	2	0	1	0	0
Rank 3	0	0	0	3	1	0	3	0	0	0	0	0	0
Rank 4 and over	0	0	1	0	1	2	2	1	1	0	1	1	1
No import	0	10	10	5	9	9	5	10	8	11	9	10	9
Unknown	1	1	1	1	1	1	1	1	1	1	1	1	1
United States	12	12	12	12	12	12	12	12	12	12	12	12	12
Rank 1	5	5	0	0	0	0	0	0	0	0	0	0	0
Rank 2	4	4	0	1	0	0	0	0	0	0	1	0	0
Rank 3	0	1	0	2	0	1	1	1	1	0	2	0	0
Rank 4 and over	1	0	0	3	1	1	2	3	4	1	3	2	5
No import	0	0	10	4	9	8	7	6	5	9	4	8	5
Unknown	2	2	2	2	2	2	2	2	2	2	2	2	2
Europe	2	2	2	2	2	2	2	2	2	2	2	2	2
Rank 1	0	0	0	1	0	0	0	0	0	0	0	0	0
Rank 2	1	0	0	0	0	0	0	0	0	1	2	0	0
Rank 3	1	1	0	0	0	0	0	0	1	0	0	0	0
Rank 4 and over	0	0	0	0	0	0	0	0	1	1	0	0	0
No import	0	1	2	1	2	2	2	2	0	0	0	2	2
Unknown	0	0	0	0	0	0	0	0	0	0	0	0	0
Singapore	3	3	3	3	3	3	3	3	3	3	3	3	3
Rank 1	1	0	0	1	0	0	0	0	0	0	0	0	0
Rank 2	1	1	0	0	0	0	0	1	0	0	0	0	0
Rank 3	0	0	0	0	0	0	1	0	1	0	1	0	0
Rank 4 and over	0	2	0	0	0	0	1	0	2	1	1	0	1
No import	1	0	3	2	3	3	1	2	0	2	1	3	2
Unknown	0	0	0	0	0	0	0	0	0	0	0	0	0
Total	29	29	29	29	29	29	29	29	29	29	29	29	29
Rank 1	14	6	0	3	0	0	1	0	0	0	0	0	1
Rank 2	9	5	0	3	0	0	0	1	2	1	4	0	0
Rank 3	1	2	0	5	1	1	5	1	3	0	3	0	0
Rank 4 and over	1	2	1	3	2	3	5	4	8	3	5	3	7
No import	1	11	25	12	23	22	15	20	13	22	14	23	18
Unknown	3	3	3	3	3	3	3	3	3	3	3	3	3

Source: Interviews and questionnaires.

They are thus keen to reduce sourcing from Japan and increase sourcing from Singapore and other countries in the region.

Apart from trade linkages, the survey respondents also reported strong technical linkages with their parent companies. This is not surprising for wholly foreign-owned firms and firms using relatively advanced technology. An increasing number of firms are upgrading operations and introducing designing, research and development (R&D), and other front-end activities into their Singapore operations. Several electronics giants have designated Singapore for the production of critical components and key modules and given their Singapore plants the monopoly for the design and production of specific product lines. Firms are generally dependent on the home country and the parent for machinery and equipment. However, some firms reported designing some of their own machinery and equipment. Several of the electronics giants have entered into cooperative training programs with EDB and cooperative research schemes with the local universities and research institutes.

Localization of senior personnel has been proceeding faster in the US than in the Japanese firms. Most of the senior management of companies surveyed were completely non-US, with positions filled by Singaporeans and other Asians. For the Japanese firms, however, top management was invariably Japanese. With the growth of multiplants and sales offices in the Southeast Asian region, many firms have incorporated regional training into their activities.

Production structure, upgrading, and relocation

Among the three sectors of the electronics industry, 52% of the electronics manufacturing firms in 1992 were in electronic components; 26%, in industrial electronics; and 20% in consumer electronics. However, industrial electronics dominated output and sales, whereas consumer electronics accounted for the smallest share. The industry has undergone considerable product, process, and functional upgrading along the value chain since its establishment in the late 1960s.

The industrial electronics sector accounted, in 1992, for more than 50% of the industry's exports, 50% of its output, and 43% of its employment. The sector's output is dominated by disk drives, although the production capacity of computers and communications equipment has expanded rapidly since 1992. Many companies have introduced product- and process-development capabilities.

In recent years, Singapore has produced half the world's output of computer hard disk drives, an industry characterized by steep entry barriers arising from economies of scale and demanding engineering requirements, because product reliability is critically important to competitiveness. EDB has actively courted foreign MNEs to establish the disk-drive industry. Singapore's competitive edge has been the large base of precision-engineering skills and its nimbleness in establishing production facilities. Singapore's share of the world disk-drive market has fallen from the peak of 60% to about 45% in recent years as intense global competition and falling profit margins have led US MNEs, such as Seagate, to relocate production capacity to lower-cost locations in Malaysia and Thailand, which have become major exporters of disk drives. Other disk-drive firms are upgrading through automation to maintain cost competitiveness, introducing new products with higher memory capacity, and undertaking product-development activities. Western Digital mass produces disk drives in Singapore, with disk media from the United States, magnets from Japan, surface-mount assemblies from Singapore, and PCBs from the NIEs. International Business Machines Corp. (IBM) has established a disk-drive plant with advanced automation to produce high-capacity, high-performance disk drives in its first major manufacturing investment in Southeast Asia. MEI established a highly automated disk-drive plant and is the primary volume-contract manufacturer for Quantum, the largest noncaptive supplier of rigid disk drives in the world.

Singapore is moving rapidly into production of computer systems with leading US firms, such as Apple Computer and Compaq, assembling personal computers (PCs). Apple Computer established in Singapore its first Macintosh design centre outside the United States to design Macintosh products for Asia and the global market. Compaq has doubled its capacity for portable and desktop computers for the Asia–Pacific and global markets, as well as that of PCB assemblies for Compaq's other plants. In 1993, the Singapore operation accounted for about one-third of Compaq's total global production. The Singapore operation also has a full range of capabilities and coordinates regional manufacturing and product-design activities for its portable computers. HP's Singapore operation was given the worldwide exclusive right to produce hand-held personal-productivity devices, such as calculators, palmtop computers, electronic organizers, and personal digital assistants.

In communications equipment, US telecommunications giants, such as Motorola and AT&T, are tapping Singapore's strengths in communications technology to manufacture and develop sophisticated telecommunications equipment. Motorola invested S$150 million to expand its paging operations in Singapore and built a new PCB plant and innovation centre housing the Asia–Pacific regional OHQ. In addition, AT&T's R&D unit in Singapore was accorded the prestigious Bell Laboratories status, the first such R&D unit outside the United States to be given such recognition; the unit has the full charter to develop cordless telephones, answering machines, and home-security systems. Nokia set up its Asia–Pacific regional OHQ in Singapore; the company also has a technical support centre for cellular phones and systems.

The electronic-components sector produces semiconductors, passive components, including PCBs, and display devices. In 1992, the sector accounted for 35% of industry output and 40% of industry employment. The sector is dominated by semiconductors and PCBs. Restructuring through automation and relocation of lower value-added semiconductors, such as light-emitting diodes (LEDs) and diodes to neighbouring countries, has been taking place. The semiconductor industry developed fully integrated capabilities incorporating IC design, wafer fabrication, automated assembly, and testing activities. For example, Siemens invested S$200 million in a new plant to upgrade its application-specific ICs, back-end assembly, and test operations. However, Singapore is behind South Korea in wafer fabrication, and EDB is undertaking co-investments in what is perceived to be a critical gap in the industry cluster. Tech Semiconductor was established as a joint venture between Texas Instruments, HP, Canon, and EDB. Three other wafer fabrication plants are currently in operation, one operated by SGS–Thomson and two operated by government-backed Chartered Semiconductor, with nine more in the pipeline, representing a planned investment of nearly US$20 billion. The world's leading chip makers, such as Intel, NEC, Toshiba, and Samsung, are being courted to establish additional plants in Singapore.

In the PCB sector, Singapore emerged as a leading manufacturing centre for surface-mount-technology (SMT) contracts as the contract PCB assemblers invested heavily in SMT and relocated conventional through-hole operations to neighbouring countries. The PCB assembly plants also offer turnkey services, from design and development and component sourcing to final-product testing and engineering support. The display-devices sector is dominated by Japanese consumer-electronics giants. Hitachi and Sony are producing TV colour-picture tubes in highly automated plants. Sony has chosen Singapore as its regional manufacturing base for critical components and key modules. Its Singapore plant is the first outside Japan to produce high value-added components, such as optical and magnetic devices for AV equipment, and to undertake highly automated manufacturing; it supplies 40% of the world output of compact-disk (CD) pickup mechanisms.

The consumer-electronics sector accounted for 15% of industry output and 17% of industry employment in 1992. To remain competitive, companies introduced automated manufacturing and product-design and -development centres in their Singapore operations. For example, SGS–Thomson was producing colour TV sets in Singapore with ICs from Singapore and picture tubes and some electronic components from Japan and other NIEs; it has since phased out its production of TVs in Singapore and invested S$80 million to increase its output of silicon wafers. Philips, which first began operations in Singapore in the 1950s with a transistor-radio assembly plant, has grown and restructured to include the entire process of product development from concept and design to manufacturing, including relocation of the Philips Audio Group headquarters to Singapore and a new operation to produce key modules used in CD players and CD–read-only-memory (CD–ROM) drives. The sector has moved into AV combination equipment and components, such as optical pickups for CD players and magnetic cylinders for VCRs.

In summary, rapid technological change and shortening product cycles, intensified international and regional competition, and severe labour shortages have pressured the Singapore electronics industry to undergo rapid structural change and upgrading. Corporate responses have been in two directions: new investments in process and product upgrading of Singapore operations into automated manufacturing, higher-end products, product design, and R&D to upgrade; and relocation of labour-intensive operations and mature and lower-priced product lines to neighbouring countries.

International procurement offices and regional OHQs

The value chain in Singapore's electronics industry extends beyond manufacturing to regional coordination and procurement activities. With the rapid growth of the electronics industry in the region, Singapore has become an important international trading hub for electronics. Increasingly, foreign MNEs are establishing affiliates in Singapore to function as international procurement offices (IPOs) to source components and parts from the region for their worldwide manufacturing needs and to establish OHQs to coordinate their various activities in the Asia–Pacific region and provide support services. Singapore is playing a further integrative role in East Asia through such procurement and RHQ activities.

Singapore's role as a procurement centre was boosted when the sharp appreciation in the yen in 1985–86 triggered an outward flow of FDI as Japanese OEMs sought to source offshore. Data from the Singapore Trade Development Board show that, by 1992, there were about 100 approved IPOs based in Singapore, buying S$7 billion worth of products and services, mostly in electronics. Nearly half the IPO purchases were sourced from Singapore itself, followed by Japan (14.1%), Malaysia (9.7%), Taiwan (8.2%), the United States (6.6%), Thailand (4.4%), Hong Kong (3.5%), and South Korea (3.2%). Nearly 80% of the sales were destined for Singapore itself; the rest were mainly for the United States (20%), Europe (14%), Thailand (7%), Malaysia (6%), and Japan (5%). Further appreciation of the yen since 1993 has triggered more offshore sourcing by Japanese manufacturers, and electronics downstream producers in the region are switching sourcing from Japan to other countries. The small and medium-sized component suppliers in Japan are increasingly seeking offshore production through FDI to remain cost competitive and to be able to continue supplying their traditional customers.

The East Asian economies have grown rapidly in the past two decades, and many international companies are seeking to establish regional OHQs to better serve this market and to coordinate the activities of their regional subsidiaries and affiliates. The regional OHQ provides a wide range of services to subsidiaries in the region, including business planning and coordination, treasury and risk management, sourcing of raw materials and components, marketing and sales promotion, personnel management and human-resource development, technical support, and R&D.

Singapore and Hong Kong are increasingly functioning as regional operational and business headquarters. The two city-states enjoy a number of advantages by playing this role. First, both cities are strategically located in the heart of East Asia and function as free-trade areas, the world's busiest ports, and transportation, telecommunications, and information hubs. Second, both cities have conducive business environments with political and social stability and harmonious industrial relations. Their governments are pro-business and efficient, with only few incidences of corruption. The regulatory framework is not too intrusive for business. Western legal and accounting systems are well established, and English is the language of administration and business. Third, both cities have favourable tax regimes. Hong Kong's corporate income-tax rate is only 16.5%. Singapore's has been lowered to 27%, and the liberal application of tax incentives has reduced the effective tax rate. Fourth, both are financial centres and impose no controls on capital flows and foreign-exchange transactions.

The two city-states complement and compete with each other. Many MNEs have OHQs in both, to better cover the entire Asia–Pacific region. Since the late 1970s, Hong Kong has served as the gateway to China, and Singapore has traditionally played that role in Southeast Asia. The Hong Kong authorities, however, are somewhat concerned that some MNEs may relocate their regional OHQs to Singapore as the July 1997 deadline draws nearer, when Hong Kong reverts to Chinese sovereignty and its business environment becomes less certain. Singapore, on the other hand, sees its regional OHQ role in Southeast Asia increasingly challenged by neighbouring governments keen to induce MNEs to establish OHQ activities.

To induce MNEs to locate their regional OHQs in Singapore, EDB introduced the OHQ tax incentive in 1986, providing a 10% concessionary tax rate to improve Singapore's competitive edge vis-à-vis Hong Kong. The OHQ tax incentive is awarded to companies that can contribute significantly to the development of the service sector and economy and have a long-term commitment to Singapore. Companies awarded the OHQ status have substantial business activities and sizable networks of companies in the Asia–Pacific region. They engage in a wide range of activities, including business development, marketing, R&D, technical support, training, management information systems, and procurement. Often these activities develop as a result of the MNEs' favourable manufacturing experience in Singapore and growing business opportunities in the region. By 1994, more than 50 OHQs, including several in electronics, had been granted the tax incentive. These approved OHQs had business spending totaling more than S$1.3 billion in that year.

Singapore is the OHQ for East Asia for many electronics MNEs, although the growing importance of China as a supplier of and market for electronic products and components and the impending return of Hong Kong to Chinese sovereignty have motivated some MNEs to set up separate OHQs to cover China–Hong Kong. Interviews were conducted with five electronics OHQs: MEI and Sony from Japan, Compaq and Digital from the United States, and Acer from Taiwan. The Japanese and US MNEs are electronics giants and global companies with extensive international networks, whereas Acer is the largest electronics firm in Taiwan, with an increasingly global orientation. Some OHQs have a wider scope of activities than others, but all include marketing and sales activities as crucial. Except for Acer, the other four MNEs also have manufacturing operations in Singapore.

Matsushita Electric Industrial Co.

The MEI group has 150 operations outside Japan. Three regional OHQs cover North America, Europe, and Asia, and a small office covers Latin America. The Asian OHQ is based in Singapore, but in 1994 a separate regional OHQ was established to cover China–Hong Kong. In Singapore, the MEI group established eight manufacturing operations between 1977 and 1987, which are engaged in various product lines. It was stressed in the interviews, however, that interaffiliate sales were not given preferential treatment over arm's-length transactions, and sister affiliates competed with unrelated firms to be vendors. The Singapore OHQ (Asia MEI Singapore [AMS]) was officially established in 1989, taking over the functions of a previously established Singapore sales operation. The functions of AMS cover administration, support services (corporate planning, information research, communications, human-resource development, productivity enhancement, and logistics), and sales. AMS handles domestic sales in Singapore, regional sales for products under the Panasonic name, and development of regional markets. All consumer products produced in Asian operations (outside Japan) under the Panasonic brand name are exported through the Singapore OHQ and destined mainly for the Asian region, including Singapore and Japan. Subsidiaries producing components and non-Panasonic products handle their own marketing and sales. The OHQ does not perform a centralized IPO function, and each manufacturing subsidiary sources its own inputs. The explanation given was that it was more efficient for each manufacturing operation to handle its own varied and unique procurement needs. The OHQ provides some financing for the subsidiaries within its geographical area.

Sony

Like MEI, Sony's global offshore operations are divided into three regions: Europe (including Eastern Europe), North America, and Pan-Asia, which includes the Middle East, Africa, and Oceania. Sales operations in Asia are divided into three subregions, with the Singapore office covering Southeast Asia, Oceania, and Africa, the Hong Kong office covering China and Hong Kong, and the Dubai office covering the Middle East and India. Sony first started operations in Singapore in 1973 with a sales and marketing outfit. By 1995, this had grown into six subsidiaries, with one OHQ, two manufacturing operations, one sales operation, and two support operations. The Singapore OHQ (Sony Singapore [SONIS]) was established in 1987; its forerunner was a procurement and export clearing house established in 1982. SONIS has three functional areas: corporate support, engineering and manufacturing (including IPO), and sales and marketing. The corporate support group strengthens the cohesion of the Sony group of companies and affiliates through support in corporate planning, logistics, financing, accounting, trade and legal services, human-resource development, and external relations. The engineering and manufacturing group has a well-developed manufacturing and procurement strategy. It exports worldwide the finished products and components of Sony factories while overseeing procurement activities (acquiring and testing for quality, raw materials, and ready-made parts from vendors). SONIS purchases products and components from manufacturing plants and vendors for worldwide export. Sony practices a different procurement strategy from that of MEI, believing in the benefits of centralized procurement. The IPO division performs the functions of the quality control of vendors and procurement. In procurement, the target is to raise the share of non-Japanese vendors to 30%. The rising yen is encouraging localization of procurement. The IPO handles only the quality control of components; quality control of OEM products is done at the factories and is the responsibility of the OEM. SONIS has a list of about 500 vendors, mainly from Singapore and Malaysia, but also from China, Hong Kong, Indonesia, Japan, Korea, and Thailand, from which it sources key components and parts for video and audio products, colour TVs, and display devices. More than one-third of all Sony products are produced by manufacturing operations in Southeast Asia. The OHQ is closely linked not only with other Sony companies in Singapore, but also with operations in Malaysia, Thailand, and elsewhere in the Asia–Pacific region. For product marketing and engineering, SONIS covers the whole of Pan-Asia. Its sales and service network stretches from Korea in the north to the Pacific Islands in the south and Arabia and Africa in the west.

Compaq

Compaq has regional OHQs covering Canada, Latin America, Europe (including the Middle East and Africa), Japan, and the Asia–Pacific region. Compaq has only four manufacturing plants outside the United States, based in Brazil, Scotland, Singapore, and China (Shenzhen). The Brazilian plant serves mainly Latin America; the Scottish plant serves mainly Europe. The Singapore plant was established in 1987; the Shenzhen plant, in 1994. In Asia, Compaq has sales subsidiaries in Singapore, Hong Kong, Japan, Malaysia, Taiwan, and Thailand. The Singapore OHQ was established in 1991 but only received OHQ-tax-incentive status in February 1995. Its Asia–Pacific coverage extends from China in the north to Australia and New Zealand in the south and to South Asia in the west. The Singapore OHQ provides services in strategic planning, treasury, information management, accounts, business consolidation, human-resource development, legal, engineering systems, marketing, and logistics. It has no procurement function apart from buying and selling on behalf of Compaq factories and sales offices. Its sales destinations are mainly in East Asia. Its supplies come from Compaq's factories in the United States, as well as offshore plants.

Digital

In addition to having manufacturing operations, Digital has supply centres in Singapore, Hong Kong, Tokyo, and Sydney, engineering centres in India and Australia, and IPOs in Singapore, Japan, Korea, and Taiwan. The products of these manufacturing operations are sold through the Digital parent, manufacturing subsidiaries for further processing, sales subsidiaries located in various countries, representative distributorship arrangements, and value-added resellers. The Singapore OHQ was established in early 1994. Its geographical coverage includes Japan, China, the Asian NIEs, Southeast Asia, India, Australia, and New Zealand. The functions of the Singapore OHQ are those of a management centre for sales and services, which includes strategic planning and operations, financial control, engineering and manufacturing, and sales. As a sales destination for finished products, Japan is the biggest market, whereas the sourcing is mainly done from the United States and Taiwan.

Acer

Acer started in Taiwan in 1976 as a small supplier of micro-based products and peripherals. Since then, the Acer group has grown into a major computer, peripherals, and components supplier and has become a recognized brand name in the PC world. Acer has a joint venture with Texas Instruments in a wafer-fabrication plant; the facility produces 4 Mb dynamic random-access memory (DRAM) in Taiwan, expanding into 16 Mb DRAM in 1995. Apart from having Acer brand-name products, Acer is also a major OEM supplier. Acer has no manufacturing operations in Singapore but has plants producing peripheral monitors in Penang. Taiwan remains the main manufacturing base, and there are plans to expand to Suzhou in China and Subic Bay in the Philippines. Acer has more than 70 branch offices worldwide and a global distribution network covering more than 100 countries. The Singapore OHQ was established in 1991 and was awarded OHQ-tax-incentive status in 1993. The reasons for the choice of the Singapore location included the need to maintain a presence in Southeast Asia and the Chinese cultural influence in Singapore. The functions of the Singapore OHQ are marketing and sales, logistics, technical services, finance, and some R&D. The major source of supply is PCs from its Taiwan manufacturing plants. The major markets are Indonesia and Malaysia, followed by Hong Kong, Japan, and Thailand.

Conclusion

Although Singapore is a small city-state, its extensive trade and investment activities have enabled it to become a strategic centre providing key economic services to its Southeast Asian hinterland, thereby contributing to East Asian integration. Historically, Singapore functioned as the entrepôt of Southeast Asia. In the post-1950 era, this role was increasingly constrained by the growth of competitive ports and policies of neighbouring countries to engage in direct trade in primary commodities. Singapore's pursuit of industrialization after 1960 further downgraded its economic contribution as an entrepôt.

Singapore's industrialization has been characterized by the dominant participation of MNEs from Japan, the United States, and Europe and by its high trade orientation. The two features are closely interrelated. The dominance of US and EC investors and of those countries as markets for Singapore's manufactures has diluted Singapore's integration with East Asia.

However, regional integration has been progressing rapidly along other dimensions. First, Singapore's entrepôt role underwent a revival and transformation. In 1994, entrepôt exports accounted for 40% of Singapore's total exports, of which trade in manufactures accounted for 87%. East Asian economies accounted for 60% of the entrepôt exports of manufactures (including electronics), with nearly half to Malaysia and most of the rest to Hong Kong, Japan, Taiwan, and Thailand.

Second, MNEs in electronics are increasingly distributing different parts of the value chain (production processes and product lines) among East Asian countries in response to the product cycle and improved investment environments in these countries. Japanese MNEs are increasingly active in this process for reasons outlined in this study. Singapore is also participating in this process, with foreign MNEs in the electronics industry relocating lower-end production to neighbouring countries, pushed by industrial restructuring, labour shortages, and rising costs in Singapore. Singapore firms are also investing in neighbouring countries in response to cost and factor-supply differentials and with the active encouragement of the Singapore government. The growing investment integration has contributed to the growth of intrafirm, intraindustry, and intraregional trade in parts, components, and final products.

Third, Singapore's role in regional integration is being encouraged by liberalization measures in Indonesia, Malaysia, the Philippines, and Thailand and in the Indochina states of Cambodia, Laos, and Vietnam. Singapore is a leading trading partner and investor in many of these countries. Trade and investment integration has grown with investment cooperation in the ASEAN growth triangle, encompassing Indonesia, Malaysia, and Singapore, and with trade and investment cooperation under the ASEAN Free Trade Area.

Fourth, Singapore is a regional hub. It competes with Hong Kong as a regional financial centre, a transportation, telecommunications, and information hub, an entrepôt, a procurement and distribution centre, and regional and business headquarters. Hong Kong has the locational advantage to serve as the hub of northeast Asia, particularly as a gateway and service hub for southeast China, whereas Singapore has the locational advantage in Southeast Asia.

Hong Kong's role as a hub for China has grown dramatically with the opening of China and its phenomenal economic growth since the early 1980s. China will factor increasingly in Hong Kong's growth as the huge Chinese economy continues on its dynamic expansion path and as Hong Kong reverts to Chinese sovereignty in July 1997. Uncertainties regarding the business climate of post-1997 Hong Kong may diminish its prospects for international business and will likely enhance Singapore's position as a regional hub. However, Singapore's hub role will not go unchallenged, because governments in several East Asian countries are rapidly building up infrastructure and promoting financial centres and RHQ functions with attractive investment incentives. The Singapore government is rising to the challenge of opportunities and competition through a set of strategic responses under its Strategic Economic Plan.

Chapter 3

TAIWAN

A Solid Manufacturing Base and
Emerging Regional Source of Investment

Tu Jenn-hwa

As early as the 1950s, the Taiwanese government encouraged foreign direct investment (FDI) as a source of foreign savings and technology. The 1954 *Statute for Investment by Foreign Nationals* and the 1955 *Statute for Investment by Overseas Chinese* allowed tax holidays and other incentives to attract FDI, but the impact was limited because of Taiwan's political uncertainty. Major economic reforms, such as setting up the Kaohsiung Export-Processing Zone in 1966, attracted substantial amounts of FDI. However, these inflows were subject to a cautious approval procedure and were restricted mainly to the manufacturing sector until the mid-1980s. Of course, the purpose of a strict approval procedure was to ensure that FDI inflows were "productive" and did not threaten domestic firms. In the early 1990s, a "negative" list was adopted that continued to restrict FDI in parts of the service sector, such as the construction industry.[1]

Though seemingly not as interventionist as the Korean government, Taiwan's government has attempted to stimulate economic development through various industrial policies. The 1960 *Statute for the Encouragement of Investment*, subsequently revised several times to enlarge its coverage and its popular 5-year tax holiday scheme, was transformed in 1991 into the new *Statute for Upgrading Industries* to encourage particular production activities, such as research and development (R&D) and pollution prevention (rather than specify some qualified industrial categories). Foreign firms are now accorded the same treatment as national firms in the application of this statute.

In addition to tax incentives, several public institutions have been created to conduct R&D. Shinchu Industrial Technology Research Institute (ITRI), established in 1974, has been widely considered a success. Thousands of ITRI researchers in electronics, telecommunications, machinery, chemical engineering, and natural resources have developed hundreds of patents, many of them issued by developed countries. ITRI's impact includes technology transfers to private firms, and the establishment of spin-off firms in the Shinchu Science Park (the Silicon Valley of Taiwan), and plans are under way to apply the model in the city of Tainan in southern Taiwan.

Roughly half of Taiwan's R&D expenditures come from the government. The National Science Council and the Ministry of Economic Affairs have financed R&D through many science and technology projects in the public and private sectors. R&D activities in 10 strategic industries are heavily subsidized by the government, especially in the electronics and information industry.[2]

---

[1] The recent Plan for Developing Taiwan as an Asia–Pacific Regional Operations Center may abolish this regulation in the future.

[2] The 10 strategic industries are telecommunications, information, semiconductors, consumer electronics, precision machinery and automation, aerospace, materials, specialized chemicals and pharmaceuticals, medical care and health, and antipollution.

In early 1995, an ambitious plan to make Taiwan an Asia–Pacific regional operations centre was approved. Following Hong Kong and Singapore, Taiwan aims to become a regional hub for international businesses that want to develop their East Asian business presence, particularly in the greater China area. Under this plan, a large-scale reform of various laws and regulations is under way. Much of the regulation on movements of personnel, capital, goods, services, and information will be removed. In response to the expected removal of restrictions, FDI inflows have increased substantially. Strategic alliances and joint ventures between local and foreign firms have been encouraged and assisted by the government to facilitate the building of a manufacturing centre — one of the six centres in the plan.[3]

A wide range of existing studies have shown an interest in factors influencing FDI inflows to Taiwan, as well as in their impact on the domestic economy. Riedel (1975), Tsai (1991), Tu (1990), and Tu and Schive (1996) examined the determinants of FDI, using aggregate data. Others studied the impacts: Riedel (1975) and Wu et al. (1980) drew comparisons of the behaviour of foreign and domestic firms. Chou (1980) and Liu et al. (1985) investigated the impacts of US and Japanese firms, respectively. Schive (1990) explored technology, employment, and export effects of FDI inflows and analyzed FDI outflows in 1959–85. Tu (1990) used an econometric model to study the investment and employment effects. Both Schive and Tu concluded that despite the statistically significant effects of FDI, the economic effects have been mild.

After 1985, when FDI outflows from Taiwan began to grow, several studies examined the impact on home and host economies. Chen and Chung (1993) were concerned about the effect of FDI outflows to China. Chen (1995b) extensively studied the impacts of Taiwanese FDI on host Southeast Asian economies and found that, lacking monopolistic advantages, Taiwanese firms localize rapidly, helping the host economies form efficient production networks and contributing to technology transfer and the growth of trade and employment.

Although the literature is extensive, few studies have analyzed firm-level activity, using primary data. No previous study has examined the implications of firms' behaviour on Taiwan's integration into the region. The purpose of this study is to fill this gap. Following the overall conceptual framework for this study, which is summarized below, aggregate trends in manufacturing trade and FDI, both inflows and outflows, are analyzed to provide a picture of the industrial composition of Taiwan's trade and FDI. The results of a survey of 45 firms in the electronics and chemical industries are then reported and analyzed. In the final section, I summarize my conclusions.

Conceptual framework

Several conceptual frameworks widely used in the international literature (and discussed in greater detail in Chapter 1 of this volume) are helpful in analyzing the focus of interest in this study: the reasons why firms locate production abroad and the operational patterns of firms change as they internationalize. These frameworks include Dunning's ownership–location–internalization (OLI) paradigm (Dunning 1993) and Porter's (1986) value-chain analysis. Dunning's OLI paradigm is helpful in focusing on the specific proprietary advantages of a firm to explain why firms from a particular home country locate in a particular host economy. Porter's value-chain analysis helps to explain the adjustment behaviour of individual foreign firms as they constantly seek the opportunity to increase their competitive advantage over rivals in an industry. These analytical frameworks are used in discussing the adjustment process of the sample firms in this study.

In general, the appreciation of the Taiwan dollar, rising labour costs, and labour shortage are key determinants of Taiwan's locational advantages during 1986–88. During that time, Taiwan was transformed from a net FDI receiver into a net FDI investor. Value-chain analysis helps to clarify the ways in which foreign firms' operation patterns in Taiwan have evolved, especially when one is explaining how firms adjust to the new economic environment.

---

[3] The six centres are in manufacturing, sea and air transportation, telecommunications, finance, and media.

Trade, FDI, and regional links

Manufacturing exports accounted for more than 95% of Taiwan's total exports in 1992, but their growth has been slowing, and their composition has changed. These changes have been driven by two main factors: rapid appreciation of the Taiwan dollar (40% in nominal terms) during 1986–88, which substantially curtailed the competitiveness of Taiwanese exports; and the impact of outward FDI, after the drastic currency appreciation. The large amount of FDI outflows have relocated manufacturing from Taiwan to other Asian economies.

The increasingly important role of the electrical and related informatics industries in Taiwan's manufactured exports is clear (Table 3.1). Office and computing and electrical machinery together accounted for nearly 33% of manufactured exports in 1992, up from 20% as recently as 1986. The United States and other Asian economies were the major export markets. Although the United States accounted for more than half of the exports in electronics and informatics in 1986, it was replaced as the main destination by 1992 by the Asia-9 economies (the eight study economies plus Korea). Indeed, Taiwan's exports in these industries and in the textiles and industrial-chemicals industries have grown much faster than its total manufactured exports. This growth is largely accounted for by the presence of Taiwanese investors in Asia-9, who import intermediate and capital goods from the home economy. The strong US and Asia-9 presences are also evident in the auto industry (in contrast to the lagging presence there of Japan and Europe).

On the import side (Table 3.2), Taiwan's import dependence clearly increased in 1986–92, from 48% of the value of exports to 74%. However, electronics and informatics components accounted for only 25% of imports. Industrial chemicals and autos were much more import dependent (indeed, the value of imports exceeded that of exports in each year). Japan played a major role as supplier, although less than the Asia-9 economies did, in most industries.

Tables 3.1 and 3.2 together show clear patterns of trade and FDI links in the electrical-machinery and office-computing industries, in which foreign firms are major investors in Taiwan, and in the industrial-chemicals industry, in which Taiwan is a major investor in the Asia-9 economies. Taiwan's exports to Asia-9 economies increased much faster than its total exports. During 1986–92, exports to Asia-9 increased 225%, making these economies Taiwan's leading export destination (total export share of 38%).

Areas that received large amounts of Taiwanese FDI increased their imports from Taiwan much faster than the others. For example, Taiwan's exports to the ASEAN-4 (Indonesia, Malaysia, the Philippines, and Thailand) increased 448% during 1986–92, four times the rate of total export growth. Exports to Hong Kong and China grew 311%.[4]

Inward FDI has never accounted for a significant share of total investment in Taiwan, although it has grown steadily over the last several decades[5] and peaked in 1989–90 (Table 3.3). The average annual inward FDI for the last decade was about US$1.5 billion.[6] Although the stock of US investment dominated any other investor in 1980, the US stock dropped to 15% of the total by 1992, while Japan's share rose to 29%; the European share was only 11%. On average, US and European investment per case (both US$4.7 million) exceeded Japanese investments (US$3.0 million).

Dunning's OLI framework helps to explain several of these points. First, the US and European FDI inflows represent relatively strong ownership advantages, particularly in patented technologies; thus, they are more capital and technology intensive. These investors came to Taiwan mainly to expand their markets. Only in the information industry, it seems, have US firms used Taiwan as a

---

[4] No data exist specifically for China. About 90% of the trade between Taiwan and Hong Kong uses Hong Kong as an entrepôt for China. Therefore, it is reasonable to assume Hong Kong data combine those for Hong Kong and China.

[5] FDI averaged less than 10% of total investment in Taiwan, except in 1958, when it totaled 10%.

[6] Over the past decade, the realized rates of inward FDI have averaged 50–85%. Because the Central Bank of China (in Taiwan) does not publish the realized figures by home countries and industrial distribution, only approved data are presented here.

Table 3.1. Taiwan's manufactured exports by selected ISIC category, year, and partner.

Industry	Year	World totals (US$ millions)	Share of world totals (%)								
			Japan	Hong Kong and China	Singapore	Korea	ASEAN-4[a]	Asia-9[b]	United States	European Community	Other
All manufacturing	1986	38 243	10	7	2	1	3	23	49	11	17
	1989	64 544	12	11	3	2	5	33	37	15	15
	1992	78 563	11	14	4	2	8	39	32	18	11
Textiles	1986	3 208	9	35	7	2	7	60	11	7	22
	1989	5 670	8	34	7	3	12	64	7	6	23
	1992	7 325	5	43	5	3	16	72	8	5	15
Industrial chemicals	1986	1 156	21	15	4	4	18	62	17	5	16
	1989	2 596	20	30	3	3	13	69	11	5	15
	1992	3 796	7	37	4	2	21	71	10	7	12
Office and computing equipment	1986	2 213	5	2	2	0	1	10	55	22	13
	1989	5 357	3	3	2	1	2	11	40	32	17
	1992	11 586	2	3	3	1	2	11	41	33	15
Electrical machinery	1986	5 787	6	9	4	1	2	22	54	15	9
	1989	12 169	10	10	5	2	4	31	39	18	12
	1992	13 803	9	15	6	3	8	41	32	18	9
Motor vehicles and parts	1986	619	6	1	2	0	2	11	61	4	24
	1989	1 078	12	2	2	0	3	19	46	10	25
	1992	829	13	7	2	1	5	28	47	10	15
Other industries	1986	25 260	11	4	1	1	2	19	54	10	17
	1989	37 674	15	7	2	1	5	30	42	14	14
	1992	41 224	15	10	2	1	7	35	36	17	12

Source: ANU (1995).
Note: ISIC, International Standard Industrial Classification.
[a] ASEAN-4, Indonesia, Malaysia, the Philippines, and Thailand.
[b] Asia-9, the eight study economies plus Korea.

Table 3.2. Taiwan's manufactured imports by selected ISIC category, year, and partner.

Industry	Year	World totals (US$ millions)	Share of world totals (%)								
			Japan	Hong Kong and China	Singapore	Korea	ASEAN-4[a]	Asia-9[b]	United States	European Community	Other
All manufacturing	1986	18 373	43	2	2	2	3	52	23	14	11
	1989	41 999	38	2	2	3	3	48	23	15	14
	1992	57 859	36	7	6	4	4	57	22	13	8
Textiles	1986	650	43	7	0	7	2	59	9	10	22
	1989	1 148	32	8	0	8	3	51	9	13	27
	1992	1 704	32	11	5	12	6	66	6	12	16
Industrial chemicals	1986	2 864	32	0	1	1	1	35	31	21	13
	1989	5 472	29	1	1	1	2	34	33	17	16
	1992	5 615	33	4	4	7	2	50	29	14	7
Office and computing equipment	1986	641	54	2	6	1	0	63	29	4	1
	1989	1 311	44	3	10	1	5	63	31	3	3
	1992	2 272	28	9	19	1	8	65	27	5	3
Electrical machinery	1986	3 246	56	3	3	3	3	68	21	10	1
	1989	7 429	53	5	3	5	3	69	22	7	2
	1992	11 862	44	9	9	5	4	71	21	7	1
Motor vehicles and parts	1986	638	57	0	0	1	0	58	5	31	6
	1989	2 911	29	0	0	2	0	31	24	38	7
	1992	4 814	38	0	1	3	0	42	36	18	4
Other industries	1986	10 334	40	2	2	1	4	49	23	13	15
	1989	23 728	36	2	2	2	4	46	21	14	19
	1992	31 592	34	7	5	3	5	54	19	15	12

Source: ANU (1995).
Note: ISIC, International Standard Industrial Classification; NIE, newly industrialized economy.
[a] ASEAN-4 Indonesia, Malaysia, the Philippines, and Thailand.
[b] Asia-9, the eight study economies plus Korea.

Table 3.3. Approved inward direct investment to Taiwan.

Distribution by source

Year	Total Amount (US$ millions)	Case (n)	Japan Amount (US$ millions)	Case (n)	United States Amount (US$ millions)	Case (n)	Europe Amount (US$ millions)	Case (n)	Others Amount (US$ millions)	Case (n)
1952–85	5159.8	3471	1182.2	1082	1931.6	641	550.7	124	1495.3	1624
1986	770.4	286	255.9	91	146.9	66	134.8	23	232.8	106
1987	1418.8	480	432.2	213	446.5	93	214.3	38	325.8	136
1988	1182.5	527	444.9	218	160.8	85	97.6	65	479.2	159
1989	2418.3	547	667.6	237	380.9	73	314.6	59	1055.2	178
1990	2301.9	461	838.9	184	581.3	77	282.7	49	599.0	151
1991	1778.4	389	535.2	142	612.1	68	165.5	43	465.6	136
1992	1461.4	411	421.1	120	220.4	85	165.0	44	654.9	162
1993	1213.5	323	278.0	89	235.1	67	214.5	40	485.9	127
1994	1630.7	389	395.8	117	326.8	66	244.9	43	663.2	163
1995/96	1006.2	177	185.4	58	282.8	41	141.3	16	396.7	62
1986–95/96	15182.1	3990	4455.0	1469	3393.6	721	1975.2	420	5358.3	1380

Distribution by industry

Year	Electronics and electrical Amount (US$ millions)	Case (n)	Chemicals Amount (US$ millions)	Case (n)	Services Amount (US$ millions)	Case (n)	Trade Amount (US$ millions)	Case (n)	Banking and insurance Amount (US$ millions)	Case (n)	Others Amount (US$ millions)	Case (n)
1952–85	1520.8	547	773.3	324	595.8	229	24.4	175	231.7	57	2013.8	2139
1986	231.7	69	139.9	27	45.5	51	4.8	28	80.3	3	268.2	108
1987	311.4	85	171.6	44	310.8	98	40.7	73	15.1	3	503.2	177
1988	237.3	37	104.2	25	177.1	121	109.7	207	52.1	2	502.1	135
1989	391.0	31	520.0	22	312.1	93	222.1	222	150.1	33	823.0	146
1990	377.0	41	506.7	21	167.7	82	284.1	195	315.2	19	651.2	103
1991	570.1	43	201.0	18	136.3	85	231.8	174	122.1	7	517.1	62
1992	323.3	46	106.5	7	250.9	81	221.5	181	196.4	26	362.8	70
1993	226.7	34	107.7	6	105.0	55	139.7	90	100.9	8	533.5	130
1994	296.1	38	189.6	13	112.2	58	134.2	96	168.6	16	730.0	168
1995/96	191.3	22	212.5	8	93.1	27	86.4	55	99.1	8	323.8	57
1986–95/96	3221.9	446	2259.7	191	1710.7	751	1475.0	1321	1299.9	125	5214.9	1156

Source: MOEA, Investment Commission (1995b).
Note: The realized rates of inward FDI in 1987–94 are as follows: 50%, 81%, 66%, 58%, 71%, 60%, 76%, and 84%; because the industrial distribution of the realized data is not available, approval figures are offered here.

major part in their international production network, because of Taiwan's strength in producing personal computers and peripheral products. In contrast, Japanese FDI contains a large portion of defensive FDI, to find lower-cost production locations after the appreciation of the yen. These firms tend to be less capital intensive. Moreover, many Japanese firms fully use their information network in this region; thus, their average scale is smaller than that of US and European firms. The fact that Taiwan received less inward FDI than other Southeast Asian countries has much to do with its locational advantage. One factor is that labour and land costs are relatively high in Taiwan; another is that Taiwan's local technology and market competition are relatively strong. In addition, the size of the local market is small and intellectual property rights may not be adequately protected, both factors making FDI destined for Taiwan relatively conservative and cautious.

The industrial distribution of FDI inflows is dominated by the electrical and electronics industry, which accounted for 21% of the total in the last decade. The chemical industry ranked second (15%), followed by services (11%), trade (10%), and banking and insurance (9%). This pattern reveals Taiwan's locational advantage. The Taiwanese economy has had little low-cost labour since the early 1980s and lacks natural resources and a large market but is equipped with relatively developed electrical- and electronics-production networks and technologies, so Taiwan naturally becomes a good choice for many middle-level, capital- and technology-intensive electrical and electronics investments. The booming FDI inflows in the service sectors are due to the realization of combined advantages in ownership and internalization of foreign firms, which were previously distorted by policy restrictions.

To understand fully the impact of direct investment on Taiwan's trade patterns and regional integration, Taiwan's outward investment must be considered. During 1986–88, labour shortages, wage increases, labour disputes, land-cost increases, and environmental protection together formed tremendous pressure on labour-intensive, low-profit-margin firms to move outward. Meanwhile, Southeast Asian countries, particularly Indonesia, Malaysia, and Thailand, were seriously promoting inward FDI through trade and investment liberalization and tax incentives. A wave of defensive outward FDI from Taiwan thus inevitably occurred. However, many high-tech and large firms also invested in the United States to obtain up-to-date technology, market information, and marketing channels.

By 1995–96, Taiwanese investors had accumulated by far the largest stocks of FDI in North America, which was followed by Southeast Asia as a destination (Table 3.4). The industrial distribution of outward FDI also differs from that of inward FDI. Banking and insurance account for 27% of the total; electrical and electronics, 16%; chemicals, 11%; and the service sector as a whole, more than 40%.

However, these figures underestimate actual outward FDI flows, particularly to Southeast Asia. Also, China is excluded from Table 3.4 because the statistics for China are not systematically compiled and are thus shown independently in Table 3.5. Approvals data from the five Southeast Asian countries — ASEAN-4 plus Vietnam — indicate that the stock of Taiwanese FDI totaled US$20 billion in 1986–94, which is almost 10 times more than the corresponding amount reported in Table 3.4 (US$2.5 billion). Although the average realized rate of FDI in Southeast Asia was about 30%, many Taiwanese investors, for various reasons, simply did not apply for approval. Therefore, it is believed that Taiwanese direct investment in Southeast Asia is several times higher than recorded totals. This underestimation bias tends to favour the banking and insurance industry, where investors must receive formal approval.

Outward investment to China was substantial after 1986. The Chinese government statistics (not shown here) indicate approved Taiwanese investment already reached US$100 million in 1986. Because of strict regulation of such flows, Taiwanese investment flowing to China, except that by stock-listing firms, either did not apply for approval or underreported to the Taiwanese government. Thus, the approved total for 1991–95/96 (US$5.1 billion; Table 3.5) also seriously underestimated the actual investment. Statistics released by China show that a total of US$15 billion in inward FDI from Taiwan was approved during 1986–93. Therefore, Taiwanese investments in both Southeast Asia and China are actually several times larger than those in the United States.

The industrial distribution of Taiwanese investment in China (Table 3.5) is more evenly allocated in various manufacturing sectors, with electrical and electronics taking the lead (15%) and followed by food and beverage (12%), plastics (11%), basic metals (8%), precision instruments (7%), chemicals (7%), nonmetallic minerals (6%), and textiles (6%). The purpose of Taiwan's FDI in Southeast Asia and China differs from that of its FDI in the United States. Most Taiwanese investments in Southeast Asia and China are labour-intensive, or defensive, investments resulting from the changed comparative advantage in the region and the emerging locational advantage of these countries. The more even industrial distribution in China suggests that this huge market has attracted

Table 3.4. Approved outward direct investment from Taiwan.

Distribution by destination

Year	Total Amount (US$ millions)	Total Case (n)	Hong Kong Amount (US$ millions)	Hong Kong Case (n)	Southeast Asia Amount (US$ millions)	Southeast Asia Case (n)	North America Amount (US$ millions)	North America Case (n)	Europe Amount (US$ millions)	Europe Case (n)	Others Amount (US$ millions)	Others Case (n)
1952–85	214.9	218	8.1	12	54.1	72	123.9	74	4.3	5	24.5	55
1986	56.9	32	0.3	1	7.7	4	46.7	20	0.2	1	2.0	6
1987	102.8	45	1.3	3	14.8	16	80.3	23	0.2	1	6.2	2
1988	218.7	110	8.1	9	52.7	30	130.3	44	12.1	15	15.5	12
1989	931.0	153	10.4	5	276.9	62	624.4	65	2.3	7	17.0	14
1990	1 552.2	315	33.1	27	519.8	109	838.7	137	96.2	21	64.4	21
1991	1 656.0	364	199.6	49	707.2	100	659.0	154	60.3	28	29.9	33
1992	887.3	300	54.4	53	300.3	72	449.4	100	45.9	36	37.3	39
1993	1 660.9	326	161.9	79	364.2	72	740.1	115	255.9	27	138.8	33
1994	1 616.8	324	127.3	47	297.0	84	988.3	129	22.2	21	182.0	43
1995/96	757.3	145	71.1	22	189.6	35	414.4	48	37.4	10	44.8	30
1986–95/96	9 439.9	2 114	667.5	295	2 730.2	584	4 971.6	835	532.7	167	537.9	233

Distribution by industry

Year	Electronics and electrical Amount (US$ millions)	Electronics and electrical Case (n)	Chemicals Amount (US$ millions)	Chemicals Case (n)	Services Amount (US$ millions)	Services Case (n)	Trade Amount (US$ millions)	Trade Case (n)	Banking and insurance Amount (US$ millions)	Banking and insurance Case (n)	Others Amount (US$ millions)	Others Case (n)
1952–85	67.0	38	43.3	12	9.0	9	14.6	39	1.1	1	79.9	119
1986	25.3	5	0.5	1	2.7	4	0.3	2	15.3	4	12.8	16
1987	39.6	9	9.1	5	9.0	11	4.3	8	0.0	0	40.8	12
1988	39.5	25	28.4	3	111.6	41	15.9	21	4.0	1	19.3	19
1989	121.9	56	414.9	9	54.4	14	10.7	26	172.4	11	156.7	37
1990	423.9	90	77.9	7	43.2	14	61.8	81	498.5	35	446.9	88
1991	209.3	85	67.4	17	246.6	21	84.3	134	403.7	28	644.7	79
1992	131.2	57	71.0	12	48.4	15	141.9	120	305.4	27	189.4	69
1993	104.2	54	310.3	6	67.0	21	137.8	66	451.8	60	589.8	119
1994	289.6	58	24.0	12	89.4	19	205.3	45	449.8	46	558.7	144
1995/96	119.7	30	52.9	6	18.6	10	65.7	18	268.5	17	231.9	64
1986–95/96	1 504.2	469	1 056.4	78	690.9	170	728.0	521	2 569.4	229	2 891.0	647

Source: MOEA, Investment Commission (1995a).
Note: Outward direct investment to China is excluded from this table; *Southeast Asia* refers to five countries: Indonesia, Malaysia, the Philippines, Thailand, and Vietnam.

Taiwanese investments enjoying relatively more ownership advantages in a market that has the same language and culture.

In summary, outward approved FDI flows have surpassed inward FDI flows in almost every year since 1991 (US$1.89 billion versus US$1.78 billion), although balance-of-payments data revealing actual flow figures show that Taiwan became a net outward investor in 1988 (US$4.1 billion versus US$0.96 billion). Taking unreported FDI into consideration, one may conclude that Taiwan became a net outward investor no later than 1987. According to the host-country approval data, Taiwan's total outward FDI flows into East Asia reached about US$35 billion in 1986–93, whereas those into the rest of the world only amounted to about US$6 billion. Even the more conservative balance-of-payments statistics show that, in 1987–94, outward FDI (US$25.6 billion) exceeded inward FDI by US$16.5 billion.

Table 3.5. Approved direct investment to Mainland China from Taiwan.

Year	Electronics and electrical		Food and beverages		Plastic products		Precision instruments		Basic metals and products	
	Amount (US$ millions)	Case (*n*)	Amount (US$ millions)	Case (*n*)	Amount (US$ millions)	Case (*n*)	Amount (US$ millions)	Case (*n*)	Amount (US$ millions)	Case (*n*)
1991	31.6	42	19.3	19	22.5	40	4.0	14	9.3	13
1992	34.6	31	46.4	27	45.0	42	18.0	28	10.7	21
1993	445.0	1190	324.6	791	375.9	1008	286.5	1181	256.5	776
1994	157.0	148	145.8	73	73.3	82	44.2	80	90.3	79
1995/96	106.4	43	55.3	22	46.6	13	20.0	14	29.4	27
1991–95/96	774.6	1454	591.4	932	563.3	1185	372.7	1317	396.2	916

Year	Chemicals		Nonmetallic minerals		Textiles		Others		Total	
	Amount (US$ millions)	Case (*n*)	Amount (US$ millions)	Case (*n*)	Amount (US$ millions)	Case (*n*)	Amount (US$ millions)	Case (*n*)	Amount (US$ millions)	Case (*n*)
1991	3.0	9	5.7	12	13.6	5	65.2	83	174.2	237
1992	12.8	17	4.5	9	23.3	19	51.7	70	247.0	264
1993	186.2	607	185.4	413	178.6	468	929.7	2895	3168.4	9329
1994	89.3	82	82.6	37	41.9	40	237.8	313	962.2	934
1995/96	74.5	18	44.4	15	31.6	8	179.1	111	587.3	271
1991–95/96	365.8	733	322.6	486	289.0	540	1463.5	3472	5139.1	11035

Source: MOEA, Investment Commission (1995a).
Note: More than 8000 cases illegally invested in China were allowed to apply for government approval in 1993, making the figures for 1993 abnormally high.

Large outflows to Southeast Asian countries are in part the result of the Taiwanese government's "Going-Southward" policy, adopted in 1994, which persuaded firms to diversify investment to Southeast Asia. Judged by the approval data for 1994 and the first half of 1995, this campaign exerted some effects. The People's Republic of China successfully offered special tax incentives to Taiwanese investors, which partly account for the significant investment flows to China since 1994 (US$1.55 billion).

The trade analysis in this section shows that electrical machinery and industrial chemicals rank high in both imports and exports, meaning intraindustry trade is now significant for Taiwan. Indeed, Taiwan has come to perform the role of a major processor. Industry upgrading has occurred through changes in industrial components and quality. For example, by 1995, Taiwan's sales of semiconductors, which reached US$4.4 billion (making Taiwan the world's fourth largest supplier), and monitors, which reached US$7.3 billion (making Taiwan the world's largest supplier), outperformed those of most other traditional electronics producers. Japan and the United States are the major sources of FDI, but their investments, though welcome, have not been substantial. In addition, Taiwan has become an important outward investor since the 1980s, mainly in China and Southeast Asia for defensive reasons and in the United States for aggressive reasons.

The firm-level survey

The initial research plan was to investigate three industries: electronics, chemicals, and motor vehicles and parts. Eventually, 45 valid cases were obtained, including 31 electronics firms (plus 1 local firm for comparison), 11 chemical firms, and 2 motorcycle-part firms. The analysis focuses, therefore, on electronics and chemicals — two prosperous industries. The electronics sample is distributed between consumer electronics, with 8 firms, and industrial electronics, with 23 firms, of which 8 belong to the information industry.[7] The firms produced consumer products, such as TV sets, air

---

[7] Some of the surveyed firms are difficult to classify because they produce both kinds of products. As a result, the classification here is based on my judgments regarding their principal products.

conditioners, telephone-answering machines, remote-control devices, microphones, speakers, and videocassette recorders (VCRs); and industrial products, including semiconductors and integrated circuits (ICs), circuit boards, copy machines, personal computers, liquid-crystal displays, switching regulators, and telecommunications filters and oscillators.

Among the chemical firms, seven were industrial (producing resins, lubricating oil, detergents, dyes, and polymer products) and four were pharmaceutical. As a result, we have a reasonably balanced sample distribution in these industries.

Can the survey data represent the whole of foreign firms' behaviour? I do have confidence in the data, particularly those for the electronics industry, because the sample included firms from all the sectors in Taiwan's industrial-electronics cluster. Furthermore, the top six foreign electronics firms are in this data set. Total sales of the 31 firms (US$4.3 billion) accounted for 36% of total sales (US$12.1 billion) of all foreign electronics firms (257 firms) that responded to the government's 1992 annual operation survey of foreign firms.

In the chemicals industry, 11 firms accounted for 6.2% of the 177 foreign chemical firms in the government's 1992 survey, but their total sales (US$1.0 billion) accounted for 8.5% of those of the 177 firms (US$12.1 billion). The reason that chemical firms tended to be more reluctant to participate in the survey may be the industry's oligopolistic market structure: fewer firms are willing to reveal operational information.

The sample includes 21 Japanese, 11 US, and 10 Other firms. Among 31 electronics firms, 17 were from Japan, 9 from the United States, and 5 from Other areas (France, Hong Kong, and the Netherlands). Among the 11 chemical firms, 4 were from Japan; 2, from the United States; and 5, from Other areas (Australia, the Netherlands, and Switzerland). Among 8 consumer-electronics firms, 7 were from Japan, 1 was from Other area, and none was from the United States (US firms have withdrawn from this sector). Among 8 information firms, 4 were from the United States, 3 were from Other areas, and only 1 was from Japan, indicating US strength in this sector.

The ages of the firms, measured by years of establishment, ranged from 5 to 32 years, with a relatively high average of 20.6 years. The difference between the industries was small, with electronics firms averaging 20 years and chemical firms averaging 21.5 years. The mode was in the 20- to 30-year interval, with 17 electronics and 5 chemical firms distributed in it. On average, Japanese sample firms were older, with 23.4 years of establishment. US firms were relatively young, with 16.3 years, whereas Other firms were in between, with 19.6 years of establishment.

Among 42 sample firms, 39 had production facilities; 21 had assembly facilities; and 26 conducted marketing activities. That is, half of the sample firms did not assemble products in Taiwan. Industrial-electronics and chemical firms simply produced parts or chemical materials; thus no assembly process was required. However, this still reflects the fact that higher wages drove many labour-intensive assembly activities out of Taiwan. Note that 16 firms did not conduct marketing (differing markedly from local firms); furthermore, 11 out of these 16 did not do assembly, indicating that they were each a purely intermediate part of a large international production network. Quite a few firms revealed that their parent companies had set up procurement and marketing centres in Hong Kong and then dealt with all the sourcing and marketing activities of the groups. Therefore, the subsidiaries in Taiwan purchased all imported inputs from, and sold all exports to, the centre in Hong Kong. Such an operational model is particularly popular among large Japanese firms. Indeed, among the 16 firms with no marketing activity, 10 were Japanese; 4, US; and 2 from Other areas.

With respect to patterns of ownership, 21 firms (50% of the sample) were wholly foreign owned; 19 firms (45%) were majority foreign owned; only 1 firm was minority foreign owned; and 1 firm was equally owned by foreign and local investors. However, ownership patterns differed markedly between the electronics and chemical industries. Electronics foreign firms tended to prefer 100% ownership: of the electronics firms, 20 (65%) adopted this form, but only 1 chemical firm (9%) did. Nine chemical firms (82%) were majority owned. This may have something to do with the industry's oligopolistic market structure, in which foreign investors need local partners to compete locally, something that is hardly necessary in a competitive market such as that for electronics.

Of the sample firms, 74% had local senior managers; 10% hired equal numbers of local and foreign senior managers. Among those that hired foreign managers, six were Japanese and one was US. The average length of establishment of these seven firms was 20 years, which was similar to the total average, indicating that this tendency seemed not to be related to the age of the subsidiary.

Half the firms were sole subsidiaries in Taiwan, whereas 40% had parents with one to three other subsidiaries located in Taiwan. Four firms' parents owned more than four other subsidiaries. No significant difference by industry was evident. Japanese firms held 25 other local subsidiaries; firms of Other areas held another 25; US firms held only 3, indicating that US firms had not built a network in Taiwan. However, the reason may simply have been one of firm registration. For tax and other reasons, Japanese firms tended to register several independent subsidiaries, whereas the US firms liked to keep several large departments or plants in one firm.

Most sample firms had very close relationships with their parents: 23 firms (57% of the total) had high exchange of technical information with their parents, that is to say parents constantly instructed subsidiaries in necessary techniques; 14 firms (33%) had medium exchange of technical information with their parents, that is, parents had technical cooperation contracts with their subsidiaries; however, 4 firms (10%) had no technical relationship with their parents.

The electronics and chemical firms differed in some ways in this matter. Although 65% of the electronics firms had close technical relationships (high and medium exchange of techniques) with their parents, less than 40% of chemical firms did. A probable reason for this is that relatively more production technology is embodied in fixed capital in the chemical industry than in electronics. Japanese firms maintained closer technical relationships with their parents. Of the Japanese firms, 73% maintained close technical relationships with their parents, whereas only 45% of US firms and 33% of Other firms did. Because many Japanese investments were defensive, the ownership advantage may not have been as strong as in the case of US or European firms; thus continuous instruction could have strengthened this advantage.

Parents' market control[8]

Only 6 firms (14%) were subject to strict parents' control (more than 50% of sales), and 4 of these had other subsidiaries in Taiwan, implying that they may have been restricted to selling to the other local subsidiaries. Twenty-six firms (62%) essentially enjoyed full sales freedom; and for 10 firms (24%), parents played a major role in controlling the local market.

The situation for the home market is quite different. Fifteen firms (36%) were subject to parents' strict control. This ratio was higher for Japanese subsidiaries: 10 firms (45%). This may have been a result of geographic proximity. In the world market, the subsidiaries were under even stronger restrictions: 20 firms (48%) were subject to parents' strong intervention. The ratio for Japanese electronics subsidiaries was 52% (11 firms) and as high as 67% (6 firms) for other (non-Japanese) electronics firms. This seems to indicate that Japanese and other electronics firms had very clear production and marketing networks in the world market; thus the sales management of overseas subsidiaries had to be subject to the parents' control. Further study is required.

Intraregional investment

Among the 42 firms in the sample, 62% had made other equity investments in Southeast Asia and China after 1986. This ratio was higher in electronics (68%) than in chemicals (45%). Japanese firms had a strong propensity to make such a move, especially in electronics. Indeed, 82% of Japanese electronics firms and 44% of US firms had made intraregional investments. Almost all consumer-electronics firms (7 out of 8) had done so. The significant difference between the US and Japanese

---

[8] Parents' *market control* refers to the extent of sales made by subsidiaries that require the parent's approval. For the local market, parents' control was very limited.

firms may have been due to industrial or geographical factors: that is to say, Japanese firms understood the area better.

Sales

The sample firms were, in general, large firms. The 1992 average sales were US$119 million, about twice the average sales of all the foreign electronics and chemical firms (US$45 million) responding to the government survey. However, the size variation of the sample firms was also large. The average sales of the larger 21 firms, US$218 million, were roughly 10 times those of the smaller 21 firms, US$22.4 million. The standard deviation was as high as US$159 million. On average, sample firms in the electronics industry were larger. Their average sales, US$128 million, were about 40% higher than those of the chemical firms (US$93 million). The largest electronics firm had sales of US$724 million in 1992, whereas the smallest firm had sales of merely US$7 million — a difference of a factor of more than 100. The largest chemical firm had sales of US$465 million, and the smallest chemical firm had sales of only US$6 million — a difference of a factor of 76.

The sales of 29 sample firms (74% of the 39 that answered) had increased or been maintained during 1986–92. Only 10 firms (26%) had decreased sales. Eight of these 10 firms had not increased their local capital investment, whereas all the others had increased it during this period. Moreover, four of these regressive firms had other regional investments in China, Malaysia, and Vietnam, indicating that they had probably transferred their production to other, less-developed economies.

Trade-investment linkage and operational performance

Export ratios

In recent years, the export ratio of foreign firms has been more and more like that of the domestic firms. According to the government survey, foreign electronics firms' export ratio was 59% in 1991 and 52% in 1992, which did not significantly differ from the ratio for the whole electronics industry (54% in 1991). Moreover, foreign chemical firms' export ratio was 24% in both years, almost the same as that of the whole chemical industry (23% in 1991).

Among the foreign firms in my study, the chemical firms' export ratio was 12% in 1992, only half that for all foreign chemical firms. However, the export ratio of the sample electronics firms (65%) was higher than that for all foreign electronics firms (52%). An important factor explaining the high export ratio of the sample electronics firms is that the sample includes eight large-scale information firms, which had an aggregate export ratio as high as 80% in 1992. If these eight firms are excluded, the aggregate export ratio decreases to 53%, which is essentially the same as that for foreign electronics firms.

The export ratio for the US electronics firms (64%) was only slightly higher than that for Japanese firms (61%). The other electronics firms in the sample had a higher export ratio (80%) because they included two very large information firms. Another related factor is whether the parents have conducted other intraregional FDI, that is, to Southeast Asia and China. The aggregate export ratio for the 21 electronics firms with intraregional FDI of this type was 81% in 1992, whereas that of the other 10 was only 43%. This indicates that intraregional FDI is positively correlated with exports. However, this phenomenon does not occur in the chemical industry, probably because the extent of vertical integration in this industry, particularly in pharmaceuticals, is lower.

Sales destinations

Most surveyed firms sold to the local market — nearly 50% of their overall sales — implying that foreign firms in Taiwan used Taiwan as a production base for the equally important local and non-local markets (Tables 3.6 and 3.7). About 25% went to the home country, and nearly 30% went to

Table 3.6. Intrafirm trade in the electronics industry, 1992.

Sales behaviour of foreign affiliates

	Japan (n = 17)		United States (n = 9)		Others (n = 5)		All foreign (n = 31)		Local (n = 1)		Total (n = 32)	
	Amount (US$ millions)	Share (%)	Amount (US$ millions)	Share (%)	Amount (US$ millions)	Share (%)	Amount (US$ millions)	Share (%)	Amount (US$ millions)	Share (%)	Amount (US$ millions)	Share (%)
Local economy (of which intrafirm, %)	600 (2)	40	393 (0)	36	452 (19)	32	1 445 (7)	36	59.8 (100)	13	1 504.8 (11)	34
Home economy (of which intrafirm, %)	303 (91)	20	530 (94)	48	427 (100)	30	1 260 (95)	31	NA (NA)	NA	1 260.0 (95)	28
Third country (of which intrafirm, %)	612 (49)	40	172 (76)	16	540 (78)	38	1 324 (64)	33	393.6 (100)	87	1 717.6 (72)	38
Total (of which intrafirm, %)	1 515 (39)	100	1 095 (57)	100	1 419 (66)	100	4 029 (53)	100	453.4 (100)	100	4 482.4 (58)	100

Procurement behaviour of foreign affiliates

	Japan (n = 17)		United States (n = 7)		Others (n = 3)		All foreign (n = 27)		Local (n = 1)		Total	
	Amount (US$ millions)	Share (%)	Amount (US$ millions)	Share (%)	Amount (US$ millions)	Share (%)	Amount (US$ millions)	Share (%)	Amount (US$ millions)	Share (%)	Amount (US$ millions)	Share (%)
Local economy (of which intrafirm, %)	409 (NA)	46	180 (NA)	34	159 (NA)	24	748 (10)	36	NA (NA)	NA	NA (NA)	NA
Home economy (of which intrafirm, %)	387 (63)	44	279 (84)	53	208 (97)	32	874 (78)	42	NA (NA)	NA	NA (NA)	NA
Third country (of which intrafirm, %)	93 (17)	10	68 (49)	13	288 (59)	44	449 (49)	22	NA (NA)	NA	NA (NA)	NA
Total (of which intrafirm, %)	889 (29)	100	527 (63)	100	655 (57)	100	2 071 (47)	100	NA (NA)	NA	NA (NA)	NA

Source: Compiled from interview data.
Note: NA, not available.

third countries. A difference by industry was evident. In the chemical industry, about 90% of the sales were local. In electronics, the three destinations were equally important, though information firms had a higher share going back to the home market. The sales distribution followed naturally from the pattern of market demand. Large information firms sold larger shares to the home country, through intrafirm channels. One reason for this is that their parents were downstream users; another reason is that their Taiwanese subsidiaries nominally sold products to the parents, which then resold these products to other firms, in either the home or third-country markets. In either case, the products were shipped to other destinations. This behaviour was popular among large US and Japanese electronics firms so as to practice transfer pricing and to realize tax efficiencies.

For example, a large US firm that produced semiconductors and telecom filters and oscillators in Taiwan and conducted R&D there sourced chips from a Central American subsidiary, which in turn sourced silicon from the US parent. The Taiwanese affiliate's filters and oscillators were shipped to Singapore and then back to the United States for production of the final telecom products at still

Table 3.7. Intrafirm trade in the chemical industry, 1992.

	Sales behaviour of foreign affiliates							
	Japan (n = 4)		United States (n = 2)		Others (n = 5)		All foreign (n = 11)	
	Amount (US$ millions)	Share (%)	Amount (US$ millions)	Share (%)	Amount (US$ millions)	Share (%)	Amount (US$ millions)	Share (%)
Local economy	159.5	85	575.7	100	161.8	64	897.0	88
(of which intrafirm, %)	(20)		(100)		(48)		(76)	
Home economy	2.2	1	0.0	0	46.0	18	48.2	5
(of which intrafirm, %)	(100)		(0)		(97)		(97)	
Third country	26.3	14	0.0	0	44.8	18	71.1	7
(of which intrafirm, %)	(73)		(0)		(34)		(48)	
Total	188.0	100	575.7	100	252.6	100	1 016.3	100
(of which intrafirm, %)	(28)		(100)		(54)		(75)	

	Procurement behaviour of foreign affiliates							
	Japan (n = 4)		United States (n = 2)		Others (n = 5)		All foreign (n = 11)	
	Amount (US$ millions)	Share (%)	Amount (US$ millions)	Share (%)	Amount (US$ millions)	Share (%)	Amount (US$ millions)	Share (%)
Local economy	34.3	47	0.7	19	74.5	61	109.5	55
(of which intrafirm, %)	(NA)		(NA)		(NA)		(NA)	
Home economy	23.6	33	3.0	81	1.3	1	27.9	14
(of which intrafirm, %)	(64)		(100)		(100)		(70)	
Third country	14.7	20	0.0	0	45.8	38	60.5	31
(of which intrafirm, %)	(44)		(0)		(4)		(14)	
Total	72.6	100	3.7	100	121.6	100	197.9	100
(of which intrafirm, %)	(30)		(81)		(3)		(14)	

Source: Compiled from interview data.
Note: NA, not available.

other subsidiaries. Another Taiwanese plant packaged semiconductor chips from the parent and other subsidiaries and then shipped the ICs to the parent and to a European subsidiary. However, the accounts simply showed that all sales of the Taiwanese subsidiary were shipped to the US parent.

This multinational enterprise (MNE) had also invested elsewhere in East Asia, including China. Its Chinese subsidiaries produced telecom components and parts, semiconductors, and batteries; they developed without upstream and downstream linkages with subsidiaries in Taiwan. Some equipment from the Chinese subsidiaries was formally used in Taiwanese subsidiaries, however, and Taiwanese management provided assistance in setting up the Chinese plants and in employee training. Clearly, this MNE practiced horizontal division of labour between China and Taiwan and vertical integration with its subsidiaries in the United States, Central America, Europe, and other parts of Southeast Asia. Singapore was a particularly important base for the firm because of its strategic location, allowing it to penetrate Southeast Asian markets, and its efficient infrastructure and business-support facilities.

US electronics firms relied more heavily on the home market (although the ratios were decreasing through time) than did Japanese and Other firms, which sent only 20% and 30%, respectively, to home markets in 1992 (Table 3.6). Excluding three large-scale US information firms from the sample, I found that the export ratio, to the home market, for the US electronics firms dropped to the same level as that of the other electronics firms. However, US electronics firms then became heavily reliant on the local market (67%) and only lightly exported to third countries (13% versus 40% for the Japanese electronics firms).

The marketing pattern for the information industry differed from that of traditional electronics substantially in relying more heavily on the home market. In traditional electronics, the regional familiarity and the way some large Japanese firms operated their sales through their Hong Kong centres (to realize lower tax and information costs) may have contributed to the difference in sales patterns by corporate nationality.

One may suspect that when a subsidiary is newly set up, it is quite natural that this firm relies more on its home market because of its familiarity. To examine this hypothesis, I separated Japanese electronics firms into two groups: one with more than 23 years of establishment (the average for all Japanese sample firms), or 12 firms; and a second group with fewer than 23 years, or 5 firms. The results are very clear. The younger firms relied on the home market for 47% of sales, whereas the older ones sent only 16% to the home market in 1992. This test is sensitive for American firms because the sample contains only nine firms. Similar results were obtained when the sales average was based on the sales ratio, rather than the sales value, of each firm. Because the age of the US electronics firms averaged only 15 years, whereas that of Japanese firms averaged 23 years, the vintage effect should at least partially explain the different reliance on the home market.

Intraregional investment seemed to increase foreign firms' sales to home countries. Those foreign firms with other intraregional investment exported 40% back to the home markets in 1992; and those without such investment exported only 20% back to their home markets. When information firms were excluded, however, the firms with other intraregional investment exported almost as much (22%) back to the home countries as did those without such investments. This was also the case for export ratios to third countries, but the ratios converged from the opposite direction. This finding implies that Taiwan has become an important production base for intermediate products, particularly for the information industry, with final assembly located in the large end-user markets.

Intrafirm sales

Intrafirm sales, that is, sales through parents or other subsidiaries of the same parents, have been found to be a major characteristic of trade in this study. As a whole, the ratio of intrafirm sales to total sales was 57% in 1992. However, this ratio had decreased from 66% in 1986 to 64% in 1989.

Several observations are in order. First, the electronics and chemical firms differed significantly (Tables 3.6 and 3.7). The aggregate intrafirm sales ratio was 53% for electronics and 75% for chemicals in 1992. Earlier, in 1986, the ratio was 61% for electronics and 78% for chemicals. The difference by industry may have been a result of industrial structure. If the chemical industry's market structure was oligopolistic, and firms produced differentiated products, intrafirm trade, as a form of internalization, may have decreased transaction costs more than in the electronics industry.

Second, the intrafirm sales ratio was higher if the parent conducted other FDI in Southeast Asia after 1986. The aggregate intrafirm sales ratio was 69% for the 26 firms with other regional FDI and only 47% for the other 15 firms in 1992. This situation was found in both electronics and chemicals. This means regional investment was positively correlated with intrafirm sales. Intraregional investments mainly take two forms: vertical integration and horizontal specialization. Vertical integration separates production into several processes and allocates various processes to different locations according to individual comparative advantages. Thus, intrafirm trade naturally occurs to integrate upstream and downstream production. Although it is less likely that horizontal specialization will use upstream products as inputs, it is common to observe firms acting as the local agents for other firms in the group that engage in similar activities. As a result, regional investment can naturally increase intrafirm trade.

Third, the extent of intrafirm sales was positively correlated with the scale of the firm. Of larger firms with sales of more than US$100 million, 16 had an average intrafirm sales ratio of 61%, much higher than that for the other 24 firms (46%). Firm scale was correlated to some extent with the parent size and the ability to conduct other regional FDI.

Fourth, the aggregate intrafirm sales ratio for eight information firms, at 78%, was substantially higher than that for noninformation firms, at 35% in 1992. This implies that foreign information firms, with larger scale, had stronger production and marketing networks.

Fifth, the aggregate intrafirm sales ratio for US firms (72% in 1992) was higher than that for Japanese firms (40%) and Other firms (64%). Earlier, in 1986, the gap between US firms and Other firms had been even larger, with US firms with 88%, Japanese firms with 49% and Other firms with 64%. This was probably because the US firms included four large information firms, and the European firms also contained two very large information firms. Furthermore, the trade pattern of foreign firms in Taiwan was different from that of Taiwanese subsidiaries in Southeast Asia. According to Chen (1995b), the sales ratio for Taiwanese subsidiaries coming back to Taiwan is very low (10%), although it is usually through intrafirm trade.

Procurement behaviour

According to the survey data, electronics firms, in 1992, sourced 44% of the raw materials and components from their home countries, 33% from the host market (Taiwan), and 23% from third countries (Table 3.6). This finding is not significantly different from that for the Taiwanese subsidiaries in Southeast Asia, which procured around 38% from the host economies, 40% from home, and about 20% from other areas (Chen 1995b). Japanese firms sourced heavily from both the host (46%) and home (44%) markets: US firms relied most on the home country (65%) and less on the host economy (19%). Other firms sourced more from third countries (44%) and least from the host country (24%). Data from 1986 (not shown) reveal that electronics firms sourced 49% from the home countries, 36% from the host country, and 15% from third countries. In other words, they had slightly decreased sourcing from both the home countries and the local markets and increased sourcing from third countries. This trend is particularly obvious for US firms. They had formerly sourced 95% from the home country and only about 2% each from the local market and the third countries.

Regional investment made only a little difference. Firms with other regional investment procured more from their home countries (58%) than those without (50%) and less (12%) from third countries than those without such investment (17%). This comparison clarifies one thing, that is, other intraregional investments did not make Taiwan import components from these new firms.

Intrafirm trade was also important in procurement behaviour. Of total inputs for sample firms as a whole, 43% were sourced through intrafirm trade in 1992. The intrafirm sourcing ratio was particularly high for the home market (78%), medium for third-country markets (45%), and very limited for the host market.[9]

In electronics, intrafirm sourcing in 1992 was highest for US firms (63%), less so for Other firms (57%), and relatively low for Japanese firms (29%). Both US and Japanese firms had decreased intrafirm sourcing. US firms formerly sourced through this channel in 1986 as much as 74%; the Japanese, 36%. Therefore, it seems that facing a continuously tougher economic situation in Taiwan, both US and Japanese firms reacted by decreasing procurement from home countries and increasing procurement from the local market and third countries. At the same time, these firms decreased the aggregate extent of intrafirm sourcing. They were forced to source outside their familiar environment to obtain cheaper raw materials and components.

However, if we divide the electronics firms into two groups, according to whether they conducted intraregional investment during 1986–92, we find an important difference. Firms with regional investment (14 firms) had an aggregate intrafirm sourcing ratio of 57% in 1992, much

---

[9] Unfortunately, the questionnaire did not include a question concerning local procurement, making the ratio of local sourcing unavailable. However, only very limited local sourcing occurred on an intrafirm basis. Therefore, the total intrafirm sourcing ratio may be slightly underestimated.

higher than that (35%) of firms without this type of investment (9 firms). Furthermore, the firms with regional investment had a lower aggregate intrafirm sourcing ratio (45%) in 1986, contrary to the general trend. This seems to imply that regional investment, which creates a regional production network, makes intrafirm sourcing advantageous for a firm; thus the extent of intrafirm sourcing will increase.

Employment

Although the aggregate sales of the sample firms increased by 80% during 1986–89 and further increased by 23% during 1989–92, the number of employees was kept to 38 000 to overcome the rapidly rising labour cost. However, the composition of employees was changing, with the direct labour ratio declining from 76% in 1986 to 72% in 1992. Electronics firms were more labour intensive, with 74% direct labour in 1992, whereas chemical firms had only 45% direct labour. Japanese firms were more labour intensive, with 81% direct labour in 1992, much higher than the US firms' 62%.

Capital intensity

Capital intensity can be roughly measured by fixed-capital depreciation per direct labour. Data revealed that depreciation per person increased dramatically from US$2 600 in 1986 to US$5 500 in 1989, then to US$7 100 in 1992, indicating that foreign firms used increasing capital intensity to adjust to the changing environments.

Japanese firms were least capital intensive in 1986, with depreciation per person of US$1 600, which was much less than that of US firms (US$3 700) and Other firms (US$4 100). In 1992, however, by depreciating US$5 800 per person, Japanese firms had surpassed US firms, which depreciated only US$4 800 per person. Amazingly, however, Other firms (mainly European) depreciated US$12 700 per person in 1992, rising from US$4 100 in 1986. One local computer firm depreciated US$9 200 per person, much higher than for both Japanese and North American firms but still lower than for Other firms.

A notable phenomenon is that the depreciation patterns differed significantly between firms that conducted intraregional direct investment during 1986–92 and those that did not. The depreciation per person for the former (17 firms) was US$2 600 in 1986, US$5 400 in 1989, and US$6 300 in 1992, whereas for the latter (11 firms), the corresponding values were US$4 200, US$7 700, and US$12 700. This seems to indicate that the less capital-intensive firms conducted intraregional investment during 1986–92 but that they turned out to be competitive with a lower depreciation. This is consistent with the observation that vertical integration and horizontal division of labour usually increase the competitiveness of a firm; thus the firm can compete with lower capital intensity.

Operational performance

Although it is usually difficult to gather production-cost data from foreign firms, this study, after repeated attempts, obtained cost data, including labour (direct and indirect), interest, depreciation, materials, and others, for 34 firms. If we treat sales value as production value, then the ratio of production cost to sales can be used to roughly measure operational performance.

The operational performance of the sample firms was good, with the production cost–sales ratios ranging between 0.7 and 0.8. More specifically, the ratio was 0.73 in 1986, deteriorated to 0.77 in 1989, and recovered slightly to 0.76 in 1992. The ratios for chemical firms ranged between 0.64 and 0.72, which was lower than that for electronics firms (between 0.77 and 0.79). This may reflect the fact that chemical firms enjoyed some monopolistic rents, rather than that they performed better than electronics firms.

For 15 firms that conducted intraregional investment during 1986–92, the production cost–sales ratios were 0.73, 0.75, and 0.74 for 1986, 1989, and 1992, respectively, whereas for firms that did not

Table 3.8. Growth cost/benefit (GCB) ratios for the sample firms.[a]

	Total cost		Labour cost		Depreciation cost [b]		Materials cost	
	1986–89	1989–92	1986–89	1989–92	1986–89	1989–92	1986–89	1989–92
All foreign firms (n = 34)	1.21	1.01	0.97	1.16	1.02	2.20	1.41	1.03
Electronics firms (n = 25)	1.15	1.26	0.81	1.34	1.15	1.81	1.39	1.18
Japan (n = 13)	0.79	1.16	1.16	2.22	1.40	6.72	0.80	0.30
United States (n = 8)	1.39	2.21	0.53	3.51	0.73	−4.64	2.50	3.44
Others (n = 4)	1.31	1.05	0.62	0.80	0.99	1.69	1.48	1.14
Chemical firms (n = 9)	1.45	0.44	2.20	0.81	0.56	2.58	1.27	0.17
Firms with intraregional investment (n = 20)	1.01	0.57	0.67	0.25	0.94	−0.28	1.34	0.88
Firms without intraregional investment (n = 14)	1.44	0.68	1.28	0.93	1.33	1.93	1.51	0.54

Source: Compiled from interview data.

[a] The GCB ratio is defined as follows: GCB = cost growth rate/sales growth rate. Therefore, a value larger than unity implies that costs are growing faster than sales.

[b] Only 29 firms supplied information regarding depreciation cost; hence the sum of itemized costs does not equal total cost. The depreciation cost of US firms and firms with intraregional investment declined in 1992 relative to 1989; this explains the negative GCB ratios for 1989–92.

conduct this type of investment, the ratios were 0.72, 0.82, and 0.81. This comparison clearly reveals the effects of intraregional investment. Through intraregional division of labour and vertical integration, the foreign firms in Taiwan were able to keep production cost–sales ratios low. Those firms that could not make the same move, even with a slightly better starting point, suffered deteriorating operational performance.

One way to investigate the factors that influenced the deteriorating production cost–sales ratios is to check the itemized cost performance. Defining the ratio of itemized cost growth rate to sales growth rate as the growth cost/benefit (GCB) ratio, we should be able to determine how well firms control those production factors. Table 3.8 shows that sample firms (all foreign) could not control total cost well during 1986–89 (GCB ratio > 1) but then improved in 1989–92. The efficiency improvement occurred basically in the use of materials. Labour-cost control deteriorated, and what is worse, so did the depreciation cost (or fixed capital), which can be to some extent explained because part of the fixed capital should be treated as investment, rather than as inputs.

Several detailed observations deserve note. First, no clear differential performance occurred between electronics and chemical firms. Electronics firms performed better than chemical ones during 1986–89, but this situation was reversed during 1989–92. Second, in electronics, Japanese firms performed much better than US firms, particularly in materials cost, which was the main production cost. It has been mentioned that several large Japanese firms set up procurement centres in Hong Kong to minimize input costs and take orders for regional subsidiaries. This way of organizing the value chain may have contributed to the outstanding materials-cost control of the Japanese firms in Taiwan.

Conclusion

Changing comparative advantage in East Asia in the 1980s redefined the role of Taiwan in the multinational, multiprocess production network. Taiwan's pattern of inward FDI changed substantially, and Taiwan emerged as a net foreign investor, particularly in Southeast Asia and China. Following a large-scale outward intraregional investment wave in 1986–92, Taiwan's two-way trade with the region also increased dramatically. Aggregate statistics show that the countries that received most of Taiwan's FDI increased two-way trade the most, in both exports and imports. These data clearly indicate that FDI was an engine of trade. Therefore, regional investment played an important role in the regional-integration process in East Asia.

A microstudy was conducted. Forty-two firms in the electronics and chemical industries were used to examine foreign firms' changing operations in Taiwan. Foreign firms had adjusted themselves to competitive pressures by increasing capital intensity, conducting other intraregional investment, decreasing reliance on the home market, lowering intrafirm sales, and lowering intrafirm procurement. At first glance, the US firms seemed to act quite differently from the Japanese and Other firms. When the results were controlled for the industrial and vintage differences, however, much of the national difference disappeared. The minor differences that remained may be explained by the geographic proximity of Japanese firms to the same country. Therefore, within an industry, foreign firms can be expected to behave in similar ways.

Because foreign firms react to changing global competition by reducing reliance on the home market and intrafirm trade, this will increase the contacts of foreign firms with the local and neighbouring regional economies, thus increasing regional integration. Other regional investments, at the same time as raising the export ratio and intrafirm trade of the existing foreign firms, substantially stimulate the originally nonexistent intrafirm trade within the region and promote regional integration. These trends imply that, for East Asian integration, market forces will automatically bring about its realization. The implications for governments are that they should reduce the obstacles to intraregional investment flows and trade to facilitate this process. A freer international economic environment will help both foreign and local firms to adjust to the new situation, switching to more capital and technology intensive production methods and eventually to faster economic growth.

Chapter 4

HONG KONG

Foreign Direct Investment and Trade Linkages in Manufacturing

Edward K.Y. Chen and
Teresa Y.C. Wong

Firm-level studies of trade-investment linkages in Hong Kong and the ways foreign investors in Hong Kong organize their business activities are remarkably scarce, as are attempts to analyze the networking behaviour of Hong Kong firms. This study is one of the first attempts to undertake an economic analysis of how foreign investors in the Hong Kong manufacturing sector network their business activities.

The existing international literature on trade and foreign direct investment (FDI) linkages contains numerous studies of related subjects, including studies by Katseli (1992), United Nations (1993), and Pauly (1995) on trade and FDI linkages; by Petri (1994) on the role of public policy and international linkages; by Dunning and Cantwell (1987), Dunning (1993), Lipsey (1993), and Ramstetter (1993a) on intrafirm trade and interdependence; and by Casson et al. (1986) and Dobson (1993) on the determinants and consequences of interfirm trade.

In studies of Hong Kong, some attention has been given to US investment in Hong Kong's service sector (Leventhal 1989), but none has been given to the industrial sector. In her attempt to find out why there are so many US entrepreneurs in Hong Kong and why these entrepreneurs are successful, Leventhal interviewed 30 US companies in the Hong Kong service sector. She took a sociological approach to the analysis of the problem and used a different definition of network than we do in this study. To Leventhal, network refers to relationships, such as those of an advisory network, a peer-group network, and the ties with the home country when a business has started in Hong Kong. She deliberately left out hardware types of production networking and did not look at intrafirm business ties and linkages.

Other studies have been conducted from sociological management perspectives, hypothesizing a significant correlation between cultural values and business networks. Redding and Tam (1991) argued that Chinese firms in Hong Kong tended to be smaller than foreign firms and that the difference in size would increase, mainly because of cultural differences between foreign and local firms. The Chinese network is highly familial. It lacks concern for other companies, and its management is highly suspicious of outsiders. Because the Chinese business network tends to perceive itself as insecure and vulnerable, innovations to benefit firm development are often discouraged. Wong (1992) compared the effects of cultural values on business networks in Hong Kong and Singapore, based on views similar to those of Redding. Wong argued that the network development of Chinese firms is unique and is sustained by Chinese cultural values and traditions. Wong predicted that when values change, the traditional networks will collapse and more "open" network restructuring will occur after the infiltration of Western culture and concepts.

The studies edited by Hamilton (1991) compared the ways Asians create and expand their businesses in the major societies in East and Southeast Asia. These studies also analyzed networking in Asia from a macro perspective, asking which factor — the government, the economy, or culture — is the most important cause of Asian capitalism.

Our study fills in some gaps at the firm level left by other studies taking noneconomic perspectives, and it contributes to a better understanding of adjustments to rapid structural change that characterizes Hong Kong's recent economic growth. In this study, we investigate the following issues:

- ❖ Trade-investment linkages and intraregional trade in the Hong Kong manufacturing sector at the macro level;

- ❖ Different forms of trade-investment linkages (intrafirm and interfirm) at the firm level;

- ❖ Major activities of networking among firms (supply of capital goods and technology, sourcing of intermediate products, and the export of intermediate and final products) and variations in these patterns resulting from changes in industrial sector and product line, firm size, and home country of the investing firm;

- ❖ Significance of networking in Hong Kong manufacturing;

- ❖ Reasons for networking; and

- ❖ Theoretical implications of Hong Kong's experience for the Dunning (1992) paradigm of the determinants of firm decisions to locate production abroad.

The study builds on two mutually supportive levels of analysis: the aggregate and firm-level analyses. The aggregate analysis examines Hong Kong's dynamic investment and trade relationships with the East Asian region in the past 10 years. We also point out some of the significant distortions in Hong Kong's official trade statistics, which result from the huge volume of outward processing activities between Hong Kong and China, and suggest a simple method of adjustment. In the firm-level analysis, we report the results of a survey and their implications for the interpretation of the aggregate data. We then discuss the different forms and activities of networking. We focus finally on the theoretical implications of our empirical findings and discuss some policy implications for the region as a whole.

Hong Kong's trade and investment in the Asia–Pacific region

Inflows of FDI in Hong Kong's manufacturing sector have increased rapidly since the mid-1980s (Table 4.1). The average annual growth rate during 1986–92 was about 10.9% and concentrated in the electronics and textiles and garment industries. In recent years, FDI in electronics has diversified rapidly, branching out into different product lines, mainly in the manufacture of computer products and accessories; telecommunications; audio and visual products; and electronic toys and games.

Japan, the United States, and China are the three major investing countries, each having a particular area of interest. By 1992, US investors had accumulated a 53% share of FDI in the electronics industry, and Japanese investors' stock in the electrical industry had reached 46%. By 1990, however, the total US share had been overtaken by Japan. In that year, the US, Japanese, and Chinese stocks in the textiles and apparel industry were relatively evenly distributed.

Foreign capital has played a prominent role in the development of Hong Kong manufacturing in the past decade. One of foreign capital's main effects has been trade creation, mainly through intrafirm trade. Several reasons may be cited for this strong FDI–trade linkage. First, more and more foreign affiliates in Hong Kong are serving as regional headquarters (RHQs) and international procurement offices (IPOs), or both, in the East Asian region. As an RHQ or an IPO, the foreign affiliate in Hong Kong provides a wide range of services to its subsidiaries throughout the region. These include business planning and coordination, sourcing of raw materials and components, research and development (R&D), technical support, financing, marketing, sales promotion, regional training and

Table 4.1. Foreign direct investment in Hong Kong's manufacturing industries by selected ISIC categories, year, and partner.

Industry	Year	World totals (US$ millions)	United States	Japan	Germany	United Kingdom	China	The Netherlands	NIEs	ASEAN-4[a]	Other
All manufacturing	1986	2 509	41	21	2	6	15	4	1	2	8
	1989	3 809	31	29	2	7	11	4	2	2	12
	1992	4 816	27	33	2	5	11	5	2	—	15
Electronics	1986	857	56	23	—	—	—	5	—	—	16
	1989	859	58	23	—	—	—	7	—	—	12
	1992	1 081	53	29	—	—	—	10	—	—	8
Electrical	1986	190	7	33	12	11	6	—	—	—	31
	1989	365	22	52	7	11	4	—	—	—	4
	1992	383	40	46	6	2	3	—	—	—	3
Textiles and apparel	1986	218	38	19	3	14	16	—	—	—	10
	1989	302	21	23	2	15	23	—	—	—	16
	1992	384	11	24	2	16	8	—	—	—	39
Other	1986	1 244	33	17	2	8	27	5	—	—	8
	1989	2 283	24	28	2	8	15	4	—	—	19
	1992	2 968	18	35	2	6	16	4	—	—	19

Source: Government of Hong Kong (n.d.c).

Note: *Foreign company* is defined as one with at least 25% of its paid-up capital of foreign origin; *foreign investment* is defined as fixed assets at cost before depreciation plus working capital; ISIC, International Standard Industrial Classification; NIE, newly industrialized economy; —, negligible.

[a] ASEAN-4, Indonesia, Malaysia, the Philippines, and Thailand.

personnel management, and fund and risk management. Accordingly, these activities are likely to create extensive trade-and-servicing linkages between Hong Kong and other parts of the region (Wong and Kwong 1994). According to a 1992 government survey, as many as 605 companies in Hong Kong were identified as RHQs (Government of Hong Kong 1994). Of these 605 RHQs, 75% were established during 1980–91. The United States led with 255 RHQs, followed by the United Kingdom and Japan. In addition, more than 40% of these RHQs were in manufacturing industries.

Second, just like the manufacturing sectors in other newly industrialized economies (NIEs), Hong Kong's manufacturing sector has been restructuring rapidly, with many firms assuming new roles as the operational centres for other affiliates in the region. As operational centres, business networks branch out from Hong Kong to all parts of the region, especially to South China. Accordingly, a considerable part of the networking activities, especially sourcing, procurement, exporting, and re-exporting, generates intrafirm trade.

Third, a significant proportion of FDI attracted to Hong Kong is from investors seeking low-cost labour for component outsourcing. If such motivations are underlying investors' activities, FDI is export promoting (United Nations 1993). The foreign investors subcontract relatively simple production processes to China or other lower-wage countries in the region, or both, and export raw materials and intermediate products to these countries. The semifinished products are either exported back to Hong Kong for final assembly and marketing or shipped directly to a third country.

A number of studies in the literature have focused on a taxonomy to describe how different types of FDI could be related to trade directly or indirectly. The United Nations (1993), for example, classified FDI as being of five major types:

❖ Labour seeking (trade promotion in the case of export-oriented FDI in small host economies);

❖ Resource extracting (trade promoting);

❖ Component outsourcing (trade promoting);

❖ Horizontal investment in differentiated products (trade promoting); and

❖ Services-related investment (trade promoting).

In the past, FDI in Hong Kong manufacturing was labour seeking and export oriented and therefore trade promoting at that stage. More recently, however, Hong Kong has not only attracted substantial service-related foreign investment but also manufactured foreign investment of a special kind. This kind of nonlabour-seeking, export-oriented manufacturing investment is aimed at using Hong Kong as an operations centre responsible for group management and sourcing. This new kind of manufacturing investment is perhaps the most trade promoting of all.

To verify this observation, Hong Kong trade intensities are presented in Tables 4.2–4.4. The shares of Hong Kong's imports from the region increased from 72% in 1986 to 77% in 1992; those from China alone increased from 29% to 38% during the same period. The shares of Hong Kong's re-exports to the region declined from 55% in 1986 to 44% in 1992. This decline is largely explained by increases in direct trade conducted between China and other economies, such as South Korea and Taiwan, making the role of Hong Kong as a conduit less important. Hong Kong also has particularly close trading relationships with its three Asian neighbours, China, Japan, and Taiwan. These economies also have significant two-way FDI flows with Hong Kong. Subcontracting and outward processing activities have been flourishing among the four economies. Hong Kong's close trading relationship with these economies must to a certain extent be related to their investment flows.

Hong Kong also has particularly high trade dependence on the region in textile products. In 1992, the share of textile imports from the region was 89%, and the shares of exports and re-exports to the region were 77% and 63%, respectively. In the region, China was Hong Kong's dominant trading partner in textiles, followed by the other NIEs. In 1992, the Chinese market absorbed 44% and 63% of Hong Kong's exported and re-exported textile manufactures.

Table 4.2. Hong Kong's exports of manufactures by selected ISIC category, year, and trading partner.

Industry	Year	World totals (US$ millions)	Shares of world totals (%)							
			Japan	Singapore	Taiwan and Korea	ASEAN-4 [a]	China	United States	European Community	Other
All manufacturing	1986	19 306	4	2	1	2	11	42	21	17
	1989	28 128	6	3	3	3	19	33	20	13
	1992	29 275	5	5	3	4	25	28	19	11
Textiles	1986	1 413	1	5	2	11	33	11	9	28
	1989	2 172	2	5	2	14	36	9	6	26
	1992	2 250	1	4	1	13	44	9	4	24
Apparel	1986	6 662	5	0	0	0	1	52	27	15
	1989	9 169	7	0	0	0	2	48	29	14
	1992	9 928	4	0	1	0	4	48	31	12
Electrical machinery	1986	3 013	2	2	3	2	15	45	19	12
	1989	4 503	3	3	5	3	29	29	19	9
	1992	4 404	1	9	6	4	40	19	14	7
Other	1986	8 218	4	2	2	2	14	39	19	18
	1989	12 284	7	4	4	3	24	27	17	14
	1992	12 693	7	6	5	4	34	19	13	12

Source: ANU (1995).
Note: ISIC, International Standard Industrial Classification.
[a] ASEAN-4, Indonesia, Malaysia, the Philippines, and Thailand.

Table 4.3. Hong Kong's imports of manufactures by selected ISIC category, year, and trading partner.

Industry	Year	World totals (US$ millions)	Shares of world totals (%)							
			Japan	Singapore	Taiwan and Korea	ASEAN-4 [a]	China	United States	European Community	Other
All manufacturing	1986	32 057	22	4	14	3	29	8	12	8
	1989	67 122	17	4	14	3	35	8	10	9
	1992	117 158	18	4	14	3	38	7	10	6
Textiles	1986	5 934	16	0	27	1	46	1	4	5
	1989	10 091	10	0	29	2	48	2	4	5
	1992	14 653	9	0	34	3	43	2	4	5
Apparel	1986	2 134	3	0	4	1	83	1	7	1
	1989	5 014	2	0	2	1	85	1	7	2
	1992	9 154	1	0	2	1	89	1	5	1
Electrical machinery	1986	4 749	38	5	18	5	16	10	7	0
	1989	12 148	27	5	17	6	28	10	5	1
	1992	21 454	28	7	14	5	31	9	4	2
Other	1986	19 240	22	5	10	3	20	11	17	12
	1989	39 869	18	5	12	3	28	10	13	11
	1992	71 897	19	5	12	3	32	8	13	8

Source: ANU (1995).
Note: ISIC, International Standard Industrial Classification.
[a] ASEAN-4, Indonesia, Malaysia, the Philippines, and Thailand.

Table 4.4. Hong Kong's re-exports of manufactures by selected ISIC category, year, and trading partner.

Industry	Year	World totals (US$ millions)	Shares of world totals (%)							
			Japan	Singapore	Taiwan and Korea	ASEAN-4 [a]	China	United States	European Community	Other
All manufacturing	1986	16 461	5	4	9	5	32	17	7	21
	1989	40 048	6	3	8	4	29	22	13	15
	1992	82 950	5	2	4	3	30	23	16	17
Textiles	1986	3 062	4	2	10	6	52	2	2	22
	1989	5 452	4	2	10	7	55	2	3	17
	1992	8 752	2	1	6	5	63	2	3	18
Apparel	1986	2 030	7	1	1	1	3	46	13	28
	1989	4 780	16	1	2	1	2	35	16	27
	1992	10 089	14	1	1	1	3	28	25	27
Electrical machinery	1986	4 565	3	5	12	2	28	25	14	11
	1989	11 156	3	5	11	3	20	29	17	12
	1992	22 939	4	3	2	3	18	29	21	20
Other	1986	6 804	6	5	9	8	34	10	3	25
	1989	18 660	6	3	7	5	34	20	13	12
	1992	41 170	4	2	5	3	36	23	14	13

Source: Government of Hong Kong (n.d.a).
Note: ISIC, nternational Standard Industrial Classification.
[a] ASEAN-4, Indonesia, Malaysia, the Philippines, and Thailand.

Of Hong Kong's apparel, 93% was also imported from the region in 1992, of which 89% came from China (Table 4.3). The United States and the European Community (EC) were the most important export markets, whereas the importance of the Japanese market for re-exports had been increasing.

Imports of electrical and electronic products from the region (Table 4.3), originating in China, Japan, and the other NIEs, increased slightly. But re-exports of such products to the region declined (Table 4.4) for reasons similar to those explaining the decline of Hong Kong's overall re-exports to the region. Although the share of re-exports to China also declined, the value of re-exports was still significant. The decline of China as Hong Kong's major re-export market for electrical and electronic products was to some extent cyclical because China regained its importance in 1993–94.

Official trade statistics suggest that China is Hong Kong's most important trading partner and therefore a source of potential economic volatility. However, because of the importance of outward processing in the Hong Kong–China trade, the extent of Hong Kong's dependence on China may be overestimated. In consequence, Hong Kong's geographical pattern of trade will change significantly when Hong Kong's trade is adjusted for outward-processing trade with China.

Table 4.5 presents the results of a government survey of imports from and exports to China for outward processing (Government of Hong Kong n.d.a). A substantial proportion of Hong Kong's trade with China involved outward processing in China — more than 70% of domestic exports to China, more than 60% of imports from China, and more than 70% of re-exports of Chinese origin (except to China). When trade with China is thus adjusted (eliminating the distortions caused by outward processing), it is substantially smaller than the reported trade figures.

Many scholars are concerned that outward processing simply measures products being transported back and forth and is devoid of value-added activity. Table 4.6 shows adjusted manufacturing trade. After adjustment, Hong Kong's re-exports are 15% less than the reported figures for 1991 and 1992. The importance of Hong Kong as an entrepôt has therefore been overstated in the official trade figures.

We also attempted to recalculate the shares of Hong Kong's major trading partners in manufacturing to understand the true trading relationship of Hong Kong with the region. Table 4.6 demonstrates that adjustment significantly alters these market shares. The shares of Asia as a whole (without China) and individual Asian countries (except for China) in Hong Kong's manufacturing trade increase, implying that the trade intensity between Hong Kong and the region has been underestimated and that the one between Hong Kong and China has been overestimated. Furthermore, it is generally believed that, since the mid-1980s, Hong Kong has become less trade dependent on the United States and more so on China. We now see that the changes have been exaggerated: statistics after adjustment indicate that Hong Kong is more dependent on the United States and less dependent on China than the official statistics show.

FDI–trade linkages in Hong Kong manufacturing: survey results

Firms carry out intrafirm trade for two reasons. First, it is more efficient to do business within firms. Second, multinational enterprises (MNEs) internalize intermediate-product markets across borders, through intrafirm trade (Dunning 1993). It is also important to note here that network formation is a corporate strategy involving internationalization of activities that is designed to integrate production both vertically and horizontally.

Conceptually, the increasing importance and changing pattern of inter- and intrafirm investment and trade relationships can be explained in terms of the value chain (Porter 1986, 1990), which describes different stages of production, including core activities, such as R&D, production, marketing, delivery, and provision of after-sale services, as well as supporting activities, such as procurement of inputs, technology, human resources, and other infrastructure, like management and finance. It is called a value chain because each activity in the chain adds value for the buyer. The length of the

Table 4.5. Trade involving outward processing in China.

	Total trade with China (US$ millions)	Estimated proportion of trade involving outward processing in China (%)	Adjusted trade with China (US$ millions)	Adjusted trade as percentage of unadjusted trade (%)
Total exports to China				
1989	18 596	53.0	8 740	47
1990	20 054	58.8	8 270	41
1991	26 324	55.5	11 722	45
1992	34 680	52.4	16 489	48
1993	42 863	47.9	22 322	52
Domestic exports to China				
1989	5 395	76.0	1 295	24
1990	5 911	79.0	1 241	21
1991	6 763	76.5	1 589	23
1992	7 636	74.6	1 940	25
1993	7 823	74.0	2 034	26
Re-exports to China				
1989	13 201	43.6	7 445	56
1990	14 143	50.3	7 029	50
1991	19 561	48.2	10 133	52
1992	27 044	46.2	14 549	54
1993	35 040	42.1	20 288	58
Imports from China				
1989	25 050	58.1	10 496	42
1990	30 090	61.8	11 494	32
1991	37 414	67.6	12 122	32
1992	45 145	72.1	12 595	28
1993	51 284	73.8	13 436	26
Re-exports of Chinese origin (other than to China)				
1989	NA	NA	NA	NA
1990	NA	NA	NA	NA
1991	38 317	74.1	9 924	26
1992	49 081	78.3	10 651	22
1993	57 867	80.8	11 110	19

Source: Government of Hong Kong (n.d.d).
Note: NA, not available.

chain varies with individual industries and products and changes over time in accordance with changing technology and techniques of production.

To maximize a firm's competitive advantage over its rivals, it must decide on the extent to which it will distribute value-added activities among its affiliates. Sometimes, a firm also subcontracts some activities to other firms or engages in some cooperative effort with other firms. A multinational firm therefore has two major decisions to make. One is configuration: selecting the geographic location of an activity in the value chain to serve the interests of the firm in competing against its rivals. The other is coordination: the management of intrafirm linkages to minimize transaction costs. The behaviour of many of our sample firms can be explained in this framework.

Methodology and the sample

The fieldwork for the firm-level study took place between July 1994 and February 1995. A total of 33 interviews were conducted, 21 of them with foreign firms. Because local firms also network their business activities, they are used as a control variable in this survey. The results are presented in

Table 4.6. Hong Kong's adjusted imports, exports, and re-exports of manufactures by selected ISIC category, year, and partner.

| Industry | Year | World totals (US$ millions) | Share of world totals (%) | | | | | | | |
			Japan	Singapore	Taiwan and Korea	ASEAN-4[b]	China	United States	European Community	Other
Imports											
All manufacturing	1989	62 188	18	3	15	3	35	7	10	9
	1992	109 561	19	3	15	3	39	7	9	5
Adjusted manufacturing[a]	1989	47 632	24	3	20	4	22	10	13	4
	1992	77 011	22	3	21	5	16	9	13	11
Exports											
All manufacturing	1989	67 453	6	3	6	3	25	27	16	14
	1992	111 369	5	3	4	3	29	27	17	12
Adjusted manufacturing[a]	1989	57 597	7	3	7	4	15	31	19	14
	1989	93 197	6	3	5	4	18	32	20	12
Re-exports											
All manufacturing	1989	40 048	6	3	8	4	29	22	13	15
	1992	82 950	5	2	5	3	30	23	16	16
Adjusted manufacturing[a]	1989	34 292	7	4	9	5	22	26	15	12
	1992	70 456	6	3	6	4	21	27	19	14

Source: Authors' compilations.

Note: ISIC, International Standard Industrial Classification. Manufacturing includes chemicals and related products (SIC 5); manufactured goods classified mainly by material (ISIC 6); machinery and transport equipment (ISIC 7); and miscellaneous manufactured articles (ISIC 8).

[a] Adjusted imports = manufacturing imports − imports from China related to outward processing; adjusted exports = manufacturing exports − exports to China related to outward processing; adjusted re-exports = manufacturing re-exports − re-exports to China related to outward processing.

[b] ASEAN-4, Indonesia, Malaysia, the Philippines, and Thailand.

Table 4.7. Sample firms by investment source.

Industry and investment source	Surveyed firms (*n*)
ISIC 382–387: Electrical and electronic products [a]	18
Foreign firms	14
US firms	3
Japanese firms	8
Local firms	4
ISIC 320–322, 325–329: Garments and textiles[b]	9
Foreign firms	4
US firms	3
Local firms	5
ISIC 323: Leather manufactures[c]	5
Foreign firms	2
US firms	1
Local firms	3
ISIC 356: Plastic products[d]	1
Foreign firms	1
Local firms	0
Total	33
Foreign firms	21
Local firms	12

Source: Survey results.
Note: ISIC, International Standard Industrial Classification.
[a] ISIC codes for electrical and electronic products: 382, office, accounting, and computing machinery; 383, radio, television, and communication equipment and apparatus; 384, electronic parts and components; 385, electrical appliances and housewares and electronic toys; and 386–387, machinery.
[b] ISIC codes for garments and textiles: 325–329, manufacture of textiles (including knitting); and 320–322, wearing apparel except footwear and knitwear.
[c] ISIC code for leather manufactures: 323, manufacture of leather and leather products, except footwear and wearing apparel.
[d] ISIC code for plastic products: 356, plastic products.

Tables 4.7–4.11, and the analysis is organized by general firm and network characteristics, followed by a discussion of corporate linkages among and within firms, export performance, and capital sourcing.

Table 4.7 describes the sample firms by investment source (foreign or local) and by industry. In electrical and electronic products, 18 firms were interviewed, 14 of which were foreign. In textiles and garment manufacturing, 9 firms were interviewed, and 4 of these were foreign. We deliberately distinguished between US and Japanese firms to compare their networking behaviour.

Table 4.8 presents an analysis of corporate linkages by corporate nationality, firm size, and product line. Because International Standard Industrial Classification (ISIC) codes have been twice revised (in 1989 and 1992) in the Government of Hong Kong industrial census, adjustments have been made in the census to ensure consistency in product lines.[1]

Sample firms were selected using three criteria: source of investment (foreign or local, with special attention given to US and Japanese firms), product line, and firm size. Company information

---

[1] Manufacturing of computer products, parts and components (Standard International Trade Classification [SITC] 3838, equivalent to ISIC 382) was included because these products represent a significant share of the manufacture of electrical and electronic consumer products (33.8% in 1993). The analysis of networking will not be meaningful without looking at this product category. We also interviewed five firms in leather manufacturing (ISIC 323) and one firm in plastic products (ISIC 356). The manufacture of plastic products is still a fairly important traditional industry in Hong Kong, especially the manufacture of plastic household utensils and plastic toys. The manufacture of leather products is a traditional industry that still enjoys steady growth.

Table 4.8. Extent of corporate linkages by corporate nationality, firm size, and product line (number of firms).

	Linkage with parent			Linkage among affiliates			Market linkage, including suppliers			Intrafirm trade as percentage of total trade		
	S	M	W	S	M	W	S	M	W	<30%	30–70%	>70%
Source of investment												
Local	—	—	—	10	2	0	0	4	8	4	6	2
Foreign	1	6	14	9	10	2	8	10	3	9	10	2
Japanese	0	3	4	2	5	0	2	3	2	NA	NA	NA
United States	1	3	5	5	3	1	5	4	0	NA	NA	NA
Others	0	0	5	2	2	1	1	3	1	NA	NA	NA
Firm size												
Small (<400 employees)	UA	2	3	2	2	1	1	4	1	4	1	1
Medium (401–1 000 employees)	UA	1	2	9	2	0	1	5	5	2	7	2
Large (1 001–5 000 employees)	1	1	2	4	2	1	2	4	1	2	4	1
Extra large (>5 000 employees)	4	2	3	2	7	0	4	4	1	4	5	0
Product line												
Textiles and garments	UA	1	3	7	1	1	2	4	4	5	3	2
Leather	UA	1	UA	3	1	0	0	1	3	0	4	0
Electrical and electronic products	5	3	6	7	10	1	5	9	4	7	9	2
Plastics	0	1	0	0	1	0	1	0	0	1	0	0

Source: Survey results.

Note: S, strong linkage: the firm's capital investment, machinery, parts, and components are almost entirely sourced from the parent, other affiliates, or outside firms (i.e., 80–100%), and (or) a considerable portion of its outputs is marketed or further processed via the parent, other affiliates, or outside firms; in the market, strong linkages also imply that the firm sources from a fixed group of supplier(s). M, medium linkage: approximately 30–80% of the firm's technology and inputs are sourced from the parent, other affiliates, or outside firms, and (or) a similar percentage of its outputs is marketed or further processed via the parent, other affiliates, or outside firms; in the market, medium linkages also imply that the firm sources from a fixed group of suppliers in some product line. W, weak linkage: less than 30% of the firm's technology and inputs are sourced from the parent, other affiliates, or outside firms, and (or) a similar percentage of its outputs is marketed or further processed via the parent, other affiliates, or outside firms; in the market, weak linkages also imply that the firm has to shift to new supplier(s) from time to time. UA, unquantifiable linkage. Our measurements on the extent of linkages also take into account the prevalence of nonquantifiable linkages, such as technology and training cooperation among firms having subcontracting and (or) outward-processing agreements or forming strategic alliances of a different nature, etc. NA, not available.

was obtained from publications on FDI by the Government of Hong Kong Department of Industry (Government of Hong Kong n.d.c) and the Hong Kong Productivity Council (n.d.). We then confirmed the product line and firm size by phone.

We regard firm size as a major factor affecting business networking in Hong Kong. We deliberately avoided interviewing small firms, for various reasons. Small firms either are unable to network successfully or do not find networking essential for their business success. We purposely concentrated on medium-sized and large firms but interviewed a few smaller ones as well.

Firm size is defined by the number of employees:

❖ Small firms, fewer than 400 employees;

❖ Medium-sized firms, 400–1 000 employees;

❖ Large firms, 1 000–5 000 employees; and

❖ Extra-large firms, more than 5 000 employees.

Because, in most cases, affiliates in Hong Kong do not engage in manufacturing activities at all, firm size is defined in this study as the total number of employees in both Hong Kong and China (that is, the greater China operation) in the same corporate group. This is why we define small firms to be larger than is usually the case. Southern China is the principal manufacturing site for both foreign affiliates and local firms in Hong Kong.

Characteristics of Hong Kong manufacturing

Manufacturing in Hong Kong has three characteristics: the nonmanufacturing nature of manufacturing companies based in Hong Kong; the prevalence of subcontracting in skills or technology acquisition, or both; and close investment and production ties with hinterland China. Interviewees strongly stated that overseas investors no longer viewed Hong Kong as a profitable manufacturing base in the region but as the regional operations centre, that is, as a business and financial centre and base for the RHQs that oversee the greater China group of companies. Only 5 of 33 firms (15%) in our sample indicated that they had some manufacturing activities in Hong Kong. The rest declared no manufacturing in Hong Kong because production had been entirely relocated to southern China.

Unilateral trade-and-investment liberalization introduced by many governments in the Asia–Pacific region has made possible the distribution of value-chain segments over a greater area. Economic reforms in the former socialist economies have improved their locational characteristics, thereby extending the value-added activities possible in the region. In turn, coordination through RHQs in a central location with good infrastructure has become essential. Land and human-resource costs are important but not crucial to determining location. More important are ample supplies of professionals and skilled labour, as well as availability of financial and commercial services. These are factors that explain the choice of Hong Kong as a major centre for RHQs despite the high costs of land and professionals. For a relatively small office (in terms of space and employment) engaged in coordinating a huge volume of businesses in the Asia–Pacific region, Hong Kong provides the ideal location.

Operations in Hong Kong, either foreign or local, perform one or more of the following roles in support of their affiliates undertaking manufacturing in China: the sourcing of capital, technology, and other production factors; distribution; sales and marketing; coordinating the group members; and undertaking product design and R&D. In other words, the Hong Kong affiliate serves as an intermediary between its manufacturing partner in China and all other business associates in and outside the corporate group and acts as a core participant in intrafirm trade. Therefore, a manufacturing firm in Hong Kong is increasingly becoming only a "shell" serving its production partners in China.

As foreign and local firms in Hong Kong merely sell, export, and procure for other affiliates in the group, the objective of this research project — namely, to investigate the sales and procurement behaviour of foreign firms in the Asia–Pacific region — is strictly speaking not applicable to Hong

Kong. Therefore, to make sense of our study, we need to view the greater China group of affiliate firms as a single entity; therefore, data on output and exports in the tables refer to the output and exports of all the affiliates of the greater China group together.

Subcontracting is very common in Hong Kong manufacturing industries: 52% of the sample firms subcontracted, and all of them indicated that they subcontracted more than 25% of their production. On average, 41% of their products were produced by the subcontractors. Foreign affiliates (and also local firms) subcontracted their production to both local firms and other foreign affiliates in Hong Kong and China. In this way, foreign firms in Hong Kong promote trade.

Subcontracting usually refers narrowly to subcontractors doing anything in the range of rendering labour services to processing raw materials provided by the subcontracting firm. In this study, we found subcontracting in Hong Kong actually encompasses a wider range of backward linkages, including the processing of high-end, high-precision intermediate products. When producing precision products, the Hong Kong firm maintains longer-term relationships with a very small number of selected subcontractors.

Subcontracting in developed economies, such as Japan, is becoming a channel for technology acquisition (Bhote 1989; Government of Japan 1989b). After years of evolution, subcontracting in Hong Kong is also becoming increasingly sophisticated: a few of the larger foreign affiliates indicated that they subcontract to gain access to complementary assets and know-how unavailable in house. They found that smaller firms, even local ones, possess specialist knowledge that larger firms lack. For these reasons, subcontracting in Hong Kong is no longer a way to obtain low-cost labour; it can be a loose form of strategic alliance.

It is believed that Hong Kong is poised to extend its economic frontier into its neighbouring region, through more intensive economic interactions, to gradually become the hub of the South China Economic Zone. It will serve as the focal point of economic exchange, distribution of goods and services, dissemination of knowledge and information, and coordination of economic transactions (Wong and Kwong 1994). Our empirical findings lend support to this belief.

About 89% of the firms interviewed had established affiliates in China or Taiwan, or both. Japanese firms in Hong Kong, more so than US firms, were particularly fond of establishing affiliates in China. Almost all local firms have Chinese affiliates. This suggests that foreign investors invest in Hong Kong because they want to invest in China; they locate in Hong Kong, not just to exploit Hong Kong's locational advantages but also to exploit the locational advantages of the entire South China Economic Zone.

Business linkages with the parent

Our survey results show that the behaviour of Japanese firms concerning the export and sourcing linkages with their parents is significantly different from that of US firms. All Japanese firms indicated strong to medium linkages with their parents. In contrast, five out of nine US firms, as well as other foreign firms, indicated weak linkages with their parents.

Table 4.9 analyzes exports by affiliates to their parents. The home market is still important to many Japanese firms (exports to parents averaged around 20%). Significant differences among firms in reasons for exporting were not apparent; most indicated that they wanted to capture the parents' market, with the parents' assistance, and the affiliates considered networking their corporate strategy.

Table 4.10 presents the sourcing of technology by foreign and local firms and reveals a wide technology gap between foreign and local firms in Hong Kong's industry. Of the sample foreign firms (mostly Japanese), 45% stated that they relied considerably on their parents for supply of technology, and 32% of these firms (also mostly Japanese) indicated that they acquired technology via technological cooperations with other firms. On the other hand, most local firms in our sample stated that their technology came mainly from other affiliates in the group and through licencing. Although 27% of the foreign firms acquired their technology through in-house innovation, none of the local firms indicated that in-house innovation was relied on. Table 4.10 also shows that more

Table 4.9. Export performance of foreign and local firms.

	Average percentage of total exports [a]	Reasons for exporting (more common reasons in bold)
To parent [b]		
US firms	Negligible	A **C** D
Japanese firms	20	A **C** D
To other affiliates [c]		
Foreign firms	33	**A B** C D
US firms	34	A C **D**
Japanese firms	25	A D
Other firms	41	**A B** D
Local firms	45	**A B** C D
To outside firms [d]		
Foreign firms		
US firms	55	A D
Japanese firms	35	A B **D** E
Other firms	47	A C D
Local firms	53	A B C **D**

Source: Survey results.

Note: A, further processing; B, re-exporting through the parent firm, other affiliates, or outside firms; C, sales in the parent country's market, promoting sales in the affiliate's country, or diversification of markets; D, sales networking as a corporate strategy or contractual agreements with some buyers in outside firms' countries; E, joint venturing with some companies and supplying parts to them.

[a] Exports to parent, other affiliates, or outside firms as percentage of total exports of the companies in Hong Kong and China within the same corporate group.

[b] Ten foreign firms did not respond.

[c] Four foreign and two local firms did not respond.

[d] Four foreign and seven local firms did not respond.

than 90% of local firms indicated that their technology was standardized, mostly manual, highly labour intensive, and low cost. In contrast, a fairly high percentage of foreign firms indicated higher technology sophistication: 26% adopted fairly specialized technology; 42% were automated; 42% indicated medium labour intensity; and 32% indicated fairly high expenditures on technology.

Japanese and US firms alike sourced almost all their capital from their parents (Table 4.10). Japanese affiliates sourced significantly more from their parents than did US affiliates, especially machinery, equipment, and parts and components (Table 4.11). Foreign companies from other home countries — Singapore, the United Kingdom, and Canada — also relied heavily on their parents for materials and parts. Of seven US firms, four stated that they were reducing sourcing ties with their parents because of a shift in corporate strategy to source more from other affiliates in the group.

The reasons cited by foreign firms for sourcing their machinery, materials, and parts from their parents were similar (Table 4.11). The more common reasons in the order of importance were that only the materials and parts from the parent firm could be used when operating the parent-supplied machinery; parents could provide a more reliable source of supply; and supplies had lower prices and better quality.

Our evidence indicates that parent firms still have an important role to play in the supply of capital, machinery, components, and parts, as well as in home-market sales. This is particularly true of Japanese affiliates in Hong Kong, which still highly value the group-loyalty concept and are relatively conservative in following the global trend of moving from intrafirm to interfirm linkages.

Business linkages with other affiliates in the same group

All sample firms, foreign and local, of all sizes and with all product lines, were found to have close linkages with other affiliates in the group. Their linkages were built particularly on the trading of parts and components, aiming at intragroup vertical integration. Horizontal integration was also

Table 4.10. Sourcing of technology and capital.

	Sources of technology [a] (more important sources in bold)	Characteristics of technology [b]	Supply of initial capital by parent capital by parent (number of firms)		
			100%	50–99%	0–49%
Foreign firms	**A B C D** E F G	3, 5, 8, 11, 12	14	4	2
US firms	**A** C **D** F	3, 5, 6, 7, 8, 11, 12	4	1	1
Japanese firms	**A C D** E	2, 5, 8, 10	6	1	0
Other firms	**A B C D E G**	3, 6, 8, 12	4	2	1
Local firms	**B** C **D** E F G H	3, 6, 7, 12			

Source: Survey results.

[a] A, parent firm; B, other affiliates of parent firm; C, in-house innovations in Hong Kong; D, other firms with which the company has technological cooperation; E, licencing; F, exchange of equipment; G, customer specifications; H, suppliers.

[b] 1 = highly specialized; 2 = fairly specialized; 3 = standardized; 4 = highly automated; 5 = fairly automated; 6 = mostly manual; 7 = high labour intensity; 8 = medium labour intensity; 9 = low labour intensity; 10 = high cost; 11 = fairly high cost; 12 = low cost.

Table 4.11. Sourcing of machinery, materials, and parts.

	Average procurement by type of resources (%) [a]			Reasons for sourcing [b] (common reasons in bold)	Major form of business relationship [c]
From parent					
US firms	R: 10–15	M: NA		**A B C** D	
Japanese firms	P: 40–50	M: 60–80		**A B** C	
Other firms	R: 70–80	P: 60–70	M: 30–70	**A B C**	
From other affiliates					
Foreign firms					
US firms	M: NA				F
Japanese firms	R: 15–30	M: 5–15			E, F, H, I
Local firms	R: 30–50				E, G
From outside firms					
Foreign firms					
US firms	R: 50–90	P: 50–90	M: 50–90		E, F
Japanese firms	R: 5–30	P: 20–40	M: 10–40		E, F, I
Other firms	R: 20–30	P: 45	M: 45		E, F
Local firms	R: 30–70	P: 20–100	M: 30–100		E, F

Source: Survey results.

Note: NA, not available.

[a] R, raw materials; P, parts and components; M, machinery and equipment.

[b] A, low prices and better quality; B, more reliable source of supply; C, only materials and parts from parent can be used when operating machinery, as machinery originates from parent; D, corporate strategy is to establish sourcing network.

[c] E, raw materials trade; F, parts and components trade; G, exchange of managers; H, exchange of technicians and skilled workers; I, technology and labour-training cooperation.

commonly found among sister companies in the same corporate group (*sister companies* refers to group members engaging in different services or producing different products, or both). Among local firms, it was not unusual to find that other affiliates were run by family members.

Table 4.9 shows the findings on exporting to other affiliates. Almost all local and foreign sample firms indicated that they were responsible for exporting to other affiliates in China and elsewhere most of the inputs required for manufacturing. They also exported (or re-exported) semifinished products to these companies for further processing and final assembly. We made no attempt to investigate the value added by further processing in China. In view of the prevalence of the back and forth transportation of inputs, accessories, and intermediate products between Hong Kong and China, the trade between these two places must be overstated.

Table 4.11 shows the sourcing of machinery, materials, and parts from affiliates. Foreign firms did not source inputs from their other affiliates because machinery, materials, and parts used in production are relatively simple and widely available on the market, and therefore the foreign firms had no need to procure them through intrafirm trade. For less sophisticated production, the value chain tends to be shorter. From our interviews, we obtained the clear impression that the sourcing of raw materials and parts and components from other affiliates has become increasingly important, especially for US firms. If external sources of supply can sometimes be unstable, and prices can sometimes be volatile, modern corporations seek greater self-sufficiency. The foreign firms indicated that their business relationships with other affiliates mainly took three forms: trade in raw materials, trade in parts and components, and technological and labour-training cooperation.

Among local firms, all of which had affiliates in China, exporting to their affiliates in China was common, but sourcing materials and parts from them was rare. The reason is that local firms in Hong Kong sourced their supplies significantly more from firms outside their corporate group, either in Hong Kong or overseas, for their affiliates in China. In a few cases, sourcing from China through Chinese affiliates for further processing or manufacturing in Hong Kong occurred.

An interesting observation is that our sample firms, both foreign and local, preferred to set up two separate companies (or two groups of companies) in Hong Kong, performing mutually supportive duties. Company A was responsible for sourcing and engineering, and company B was responsible for trading and marketing, in both cases in support of a common manufacturing base in China. To compete successfully in the complex global market, intrafirm division of labour has become prevalent and sophisticated.

Business linkages with competitors

The findings reported in Table 4.8 clearly show that most of the local firms indicated weak linkages with competitors, whereas most foreign affiliates indicated medium to strong linkages with competitors. The management of three large local firms explained that they deliberately avoided unnecessary contacts with firms outside the group because such deeds were risky and invited copying. Above all, Chinese cultural values favour family businesses and oppose outsiders as intruders. "It is better to rely on someone you know rather than someone you don't," they said. We also found that all the firms claiming to have strong links with competitors were US companies, but the evidence is insufficient to suggest that Japanese affiliates have weak ties with competitors.

Table 4.9 provides information on exports of foreign affiliates to competitors and external buyers. The share of total exports to competitors averaged around 50% in most cases, even for local firms. The two major reasons given for exporting were further processing and cooperative contractual supply agreements with other firms. Indeed, a form of cooperative contractual agreement called the Global Account System was prevalent in the electronics industry. Under this type of agreement, two or more companies serve the same client (or clientele). Usually, this happens when the business involved is too large to be handled by a single company. For example, two chemical companies collaborated to serve the demand of a third company; two major electronics producers collaborated to manufacture mini diskettes for a third firm.

Almost none of the sample foreign firms indicated that they obtained capital from outside the group (Table 4.10). About 40% of foreign affiliates indicated that they sourced technology through technological cooperation with other firms (Table 4.10). Cooperative agreements and partnerships for the sake of the acquisition of technology have become increasingly common in Hong Kong.

Almost all foreign affiliates sourced raw materials from outsiders, rather than sourcing from other affiliates within the group, the percentage being significant in most cases (Table 4.11). (This is understandable because raw materials supplies are difficult to integrate vertically, except in the case in which a local textile firm owns a sheep ranch in northern China, enabling it to ensure a steady supply of woolen yarn for its manufacture of woolen garments.)

Interviews indicated, however, that some foreign affiliates were building strategic alliances as part of a global-investment trend in which strategic alliances were being formed among firms with high technological capabilities to obtain market access (horizontal internationalization) or to relocate production overseas (vertical internationalization). Strategic alliances are no longer confined to developed countries; in recent years, the Asian NIEs have also augmented their technological capability by building strategic alliances (Wong 1994).

Strategic alliance, defined in a strict sense, refers to partnerships entered into by parties usually from different nations for strategic cooperation or acquisition of technology, or both. Defined more broadly, it also refers to interfirm relationships set on an equal footing, involving joint effort of some sort and long-term strategic goals rather than short-term operational gains. Under the broader definition, strategic alliances may not necessarily be technology specific; they may even include long-term supplier–buyer relationships, consortia for R&D, and joint product development and marketing contracts.

Whether an alliance is strategic is thus difficult to determine. Sometimes the strategic partnership is intermingled with other interfirm relationships. For example, the triple alliance among Digital Equipment Company, IBM, and Apple, in 1991, allowed these firms to share advanced technology, but all three continued their competitive manufacturing and marketing activities. By pooling their technological resources, the three computer giants hoped to accomplish something that one company alone cannot do — develop a new array of technology and software in computing. At present, Digital is a member of the triple alliance and is at the same time an original-equipment-manufacturing subcontractor for IBM, manufacturing strategic computer parts for IBM with the IBM label on them.

In the Hong Kong manufacturing sector, one finds three major forms of interfirm cooperation, only one of which is a strategic alliance. The first form is subcontracting, which has relatively low strategic intent and technological content. The second form is the cooperative contractual agreement, such as the Global Account System, in which one firm licences another firm's products, provides services or technology to another company, or franchises the entire business to an independent franchisee. In recent years, franchising businesses has become popular in retailing and the textile industry in Hong Kong. For example, Esprit and Theme sell limited rights to produce and market products to overseas franchisees in return for royalty payments. The Hong Kong firm gains access to overseas markets without making large financial or technical investments. The cooperative contractual agreement should not be considered a form of strategic alliance because cooperative contractual agreements are agreements rather than partnerships, and the parties involved are often not set on equal footing in the value chain; franchising business in retailing is a downstream activity, which is quite a distance from production undertaken by the parent firm. Hence, it is more likely that interfirm cooperation will be established.

The third form of interfirm cooperation emerging in Hong Kong is a loosely structured form of strategic alliance that usually does not involve equity investment. Joint ventures formed between MNEs aiming at market or sector penetration, or both, and long-term supplier–buyer relationships are the most common forms of strategic alliance. Technological alliances are beginning to emerge, usually in the forms of the R&D consortium, in the areas of electronics, biotechnology, and materials science. Joint product development in technology-intensive products requiring high precision is also becoming prevalent.

It is also common for foreign firms to form joint ventures with local firms in the same industry to find local subcontractors or to penetrate the Hong Kong market. Some foreign firms share corporate decisions, orders, markets, technology, and training facilities with their local counterparts. Whereas traditional joint ventures are made between MNEs and local firms for local-market penetration, strategic alliances are made between MNEs to penetrate regional and global markets (Jung 1994). In the case of Hong Kong, conventional joint ventures are often formed to achieve unconventional objectives. Whether these should be classified as strategic alliances is controversial.

Firm size and business linkages

There are *a priori* reasons to believe that large firms with strong financial backup and substantial production and transaction volumes are more able and obliged to network. However, Table 4.8, which shows the extent of corporate linkages by firm size, contradicts this notion. We found that although subcontracting and cooperative contractual agreements, such as licencing and franchising, are prevalent among medium-sized to large firms in Hong Kong, strategic alliances can only be found among extra-large firms, employing more than 5 000 workers. Large foreign companies in Hong Kong seem to have two types of partnership, vertical and horizontal. The vertical partnership is formed on a division-of-labour basis. One firm may concentrate on design while others concentrate on manufacturing and marketing, such as in the case of Digital Equipment Hong Kong Ltd (USA) and its partners and NEC Electronics Hong Kong Ltd (Japan) and its partners. Horizontal cooperation engages in similar activities, such as joint research ventures or joint production schemes. Asea Brown Boveri, for example, is keen to find a partner to share the high cost and high risk of developing a new generation of power plants and power-transmission and -distribution equipment.

Product line and business linkages

Table 4.8 also shows the extent of corporate linkage by product line. Product line does not seem to affect the extent of linkage between an affiliate and its parent. All the garment and electronics firms that indicated weak ties with their parents share a characteristic: either they are RHQs or their products are mainly manufactured, distributed, and marketed in the Hong Kong–Macao–China region. They network with a cluster of other affiliates in the corporate group and are largely self-sufficient within the cluster. By consequence, their ties with parents and firms located outside the region are actually quite weak.

As we pointed out earlier, regardless of product line, linkages are strong with other affiliates that are competitors. These linkages are strong in both electronics and garments. The reason is that many of the large-scale, garment chain retailing outlets in Hong Kong also have their own manufacturing base in Hong Kong or China. For example, Esprit Asia (Distribution) Ltd (USA) undertakes 15–20% of its own apparel manufacturing, and the Fang Group (local) manufactures for its sister, Toppy International.

The product-line factor alone is not sufficient to determine the extent of business links with competitors; we have to put together the three variables — origin of investment, firm size, and product line. We have, for example, found that extra-large US firms manufacturing technology-intensive products are more likely to network with their competitors and buyers–suppliers.

Intra- and interfirm trade and networking in Hong Kong manufacturing

In summary, several generalizations can be made from the firm-level survey. First, foreign affiliates have a strong networking relationship with their parents when sourcing technology, machinery, and equipment but not when sourcing intermediate products. The foreign affiliates also depend on their parents for exports of manufactured products from China. In this case, the foreign affiliates act as re-exporters.

Second, the networking relationship among foreign affiliates in the same group is strong for sourcing of intermediate products but not for sourcing capital goods. This is reversed from the parent–affiliate relationship. However, foreign affiliates also re-export considerably more to other affiliates in the group, again acting as agents for their fellow affiliates that undertake manufacturing in China. It is interesting to note that the behaviour of local firms is similar to that of foreign affiliates in this kind of intrafirm relationship. Local firms in Hong Kong also have a strong networking relationship with other affiliates in the same group with regard to sourcing of intermediate products but a weak relationship with regard to the supply of machinery and equipment. Local firms also export considerably to other affiliates in the same group.

Third, a sharp distinction can be drawn between the behaviour of foreign affiliates and local firms in interfirm networking, that is, networking with competitors in the same or different industries. Foreign affiliates show strong networking relationships when sourcing materials and intermediate products and exporting intermediate and final products. However, foreign affiliates have a weaker relationship with regard to the supply of capital goods. Such an overall strong sourcing relationship with "outsiders" is somewhat surprising and is discussed in the next section.

For local firms, the interfirm relationship is weaker in all respects. This does not mean they do not network with outsiders but that they tend to deal only with a few firms they know really well or with whom they have family ties. This means that for our sample of local firms, at least, the Chinese practice of business networking is still prevalent. It is also worthwhile to point out that these findings hold true for the various industries and product lines included in our survey. The size of a firm also has little influence on the pattern of networking.

Because strong sourcing relationships (whether local or foreign, inter- or intrafirm) were observed, the extent of inter- and intrafirm trade in Hong Kong manufacturing is expected to be significant. Only 40% of the sample firms reported intrafirm trade accounting for less than 30% of total trade (Table 4.8). Although intrafirm trade is undoubtedly important, the accuracy of the figure may be suspect because it was difficult for firms to provide precise figures during interviews. Our survey results, however, indicate that firm size does have some effect on the degree of intrafirm trade. Small firms (in our definition, those employing fewer than 400 workers) seemed to have a lower share of intrafirm trade. Furthermore, product lines and industry types also affected to some extent the degree of intrafirm trade. Our findings indicate that electronics firms engaging in the manufacture of sophisticated products tended to engage more in intrafirm trade. This is, of course, to be expected. High-tech industries have a high degree of division of labour, involving sophisticated parts and components that are normally supplied by many specialized producers in the same group.

Our findings suggest that the conventional form of networking has undergone significant change, from intrafirm relationships only to interaffiliate and interfirm relationships. On the basis of our small sample, it is difficult to determine whether this is an evolutionary process taking place in all developing countries, or whether the observed changes are specific to some industries or to Hong Kong alone. Conventionally, networking takes predominantly the form of the parent–affiliate relationship, or a "hub-and-spoke" relationship. This is particularly true of Chinese business firms. A form of networking that seems to have become increasingly popular is the interaffiliate relationship within the same firm. This is a form of intrafirm networking based on "spoke-and-spoke" relationships. This signifies that affiliates have become increasingly autonomous and are allowed to establish direct relationships with other affiliates in the same group without reference to the parent. This perhaps also signifies the increasing sophistication in the division of labour made necessary by rapid technological change.

In some cases, an affiliate networks with a subparent rather than the parent. A case in point is Motorola Semiconductor (H.K.) Ltd, which has developed business networking with its subparent engaged in semiconductor manufacturing in Arizona, rather than with its parent in the Silicon Valley. In this case, the parent company is still in charge of group management but never participates actively in the day-to-day operations of group members. The Motorola affiliate in Hong Kong receives instructions and the supply of technological and intermediate inputs from the subparent.

However, an interesting difference between US and Japanese firms in developing the "spoke-and-spoke" relationship among affiliates is that the Japanese affiliates in our sample tended to have stronger ties with their parents than did their US counterparts. This is most likely related to the different corporate strategies and cultures of US and Japanese firms (Redding et al. 1987). Typically, a Japanese company provides a strong sense of job security to its staff. Life-long employment is still prevalent in Japan. On the contrary, the management of US firms deliberately creates a sense of job insecurity for its staff, through, for example, intensive job pressure and frequent staff relocation. Whereas the Japanese model aims at promoting productivity and efficiency by creating a sense of loyalty among the staff, the US model aims at promoting productivity and innovativeness by instilling a belief in the survival of the fittest among the staff. Therefore, in the Japanese model, the parent firm is, as a sign of loyalty, expected to have a closer networking relationship with its affiliates. The Japanese parent company is considered by its affiliates a reliable source of supply of technology and capital goods and is expected to provide assistance in an emergency or crisis.

A most interesting phenomenon is certainly the increasing importance of the interfirm-networking relationship between the affiliate of one company and the affiliates of other companies. This does not necessarily occur in the form of a strategic alliance. It could occur in some other form of interfirm relationship related to sourcing, marketing, distribution, and so forth. Such interfirm relationships are more arm's length, less formal, and more uncertain but more flexible. Usually, such interfirm relationships have quite specific objectives. This kind of interfirm relationship seems to run contrary in some ways to the conventional practices of Chinese business firms, which aim to avoid uncertainties by establishing personal relationships. In our study, we found that family ties are unimportant in these interfirm relationships; that is, a foreign affiliate or a local firm cooperates with a wide range of other firms with which it has no family ties. Most often, the relationship is not permanent. This form of networking widens the scope of conventional networking and expands intraregional trade at the macro level. It gives rise to more opportunities for cooperative efforts and a high degree of specialization. It is of course necessary to conduct further research on such interfirm relationships to better understand how they work.

Implications for FDI theories

It is generally accepted that Dunning's (1993) ownership–location–internalization (OLI) framework (ownership-specific advantages, locational factors, and internalization) is most useful in analyzing and explaining FDI. The prevalence of networking in inter- and intrafirm trade demonstrated by the Hong Kong experience does not undermine the OLI framework in any significant way. Indeed, networking is a form of internalizing the cross-border market in intermediate products to minimize transaction costs. Complete internalization occurs in such cases as the parent–affiliate relationship and the interaffiliate relationship in the same group. Interfirm networking is something of greater interest because it represents only partial internalization.

The reason for conventional parent–subsidiary networking is easy to understand. However, it is more difficult to explain the emergence of interaffiliate relationships and even more difficult to explain the increasing importance of interfirm networking. A major reason for the inter- and intrafirm relationships is to be found in technological factors. With rapid technological change and a high degree of specialization in parts and components, the need for networking is greater and the scope for networking is wider. In the context of the value chain, this means that when production becomes more complex and sophisticated, the value chain becomes longer and the possibility of, and need for, establishing inter- and intrafirm networking become greater. The different degrees and patterns of networking found in different types of firms may not reflect their source of investment (local or foreign) but are related to the nature of the different value chains. After economic and technological conditions change, the patterns of networking will be different, reflecting business firms' search for the optimal mix of internal organization and the market. Parent companies have to give up some of their control over their subsidiaries so that the subsidiaries can have a wider choice in procuring the required parts and components. Firms also have to sacrifice certainty for greater exposure to the technological resources available elsewhere among competitors. Traditional Chinese business firms network on the basis of cultural affinity, which helps to reduce transaction costs (particularly legal costs). However, in a technology-dominated environment, the need to pull technological resources together overrides the importance of common cultural values.

In our survey, we found that a significant proportion of business-networking arrangements can be explained on the basis of buyer-induced backward integration. This means that buyers today are very particular about the quality, specifications, and reliability of the product they order. To ensure quality control, firms undertake backward integration or networking with firms they can rely on. We also found that factor markets are increasingly imperfect because of rapid technological change and increasing specialization. Many of the suppliers of intermediate products enjoy oligopolistic power. The buyers of intermediate products (as well as producers of final products) have tried to overcome the market power of the suppliers by buying through agents. Some interfirm relationships in marketing and distribution are established on this basis. Thus, the prevalence of networking of firms has enriched internalization theories in the OLI framework.

Networking also has some impact on the conceptualization of ownership-specific advantages in the conventional OLI framework. Networking is an indication of a longer value chain and disintegration of ownership-specific advantages into many highly specialized advantages. At the same time, networking induces further disintegration of ownership-specific advantages because it is in the interest of a firm to unbundle its ownership advantages in networking relationships, so that cooperation with outsiders, as in strategic alliances, will be confined to a specific area, without involving the entire firm. Today, the major ownership-specific advantage is technological knowledge, which is a form of intangible asset with transaction costs that can be significantly reduced through the internalization of markets. This also helps to explain the increasing importance of firms' networking activities.

An investing firm tends to be attracted, not just by a particular location, but also by the entire subregion. For example, many of the firms investing in Hong Kong are attracted by Hong Kong's being a focal point in the South China Economic Zone. This is one reason why so many manufacturing companies have set up their RHQs in Hong Kong. A case in point is Digital Equipment Company. Its affiliate in Taiwan is responsible for sourcing machinery and equipment and intermediate products; Digital in Hong Kong is the RHQ that oversees corporate management, planning, and coordination; and Digital in China does all the manufacturing. Most firms are taking a subregional strategy when making decisions about FDI in the Asia–Pacific region. This is a form of internalization of the regional economy. Disintegration of ownership-specific advantages has also given rise to the exploitation of different highly specialized advantages in different parts of a subregion. It is commonplace today to find a foreign firm setting up more than one affiliate, even in one locality in the host country.

Also, locational advantages are disintegrating because of the unbundling of ownership advantages and a longer value chain. A location does not have to possess many locational advantages to attract FDI; one or two advantages will do. Production is increasingly distributed among numerous locations that each offer a few specialized locational advantages for a particular activity in the value chain.

In sum, networking of business activities among firms does not fundamentally undermine the OLI paradigm for FDI. However, some modifications should be made to the concepts of ownership-specific advantages and locational factors in the conventional framework. More importantly, studies on the networking activities have thrown important light on the nature of internalization. This has given the conventional OLI paradigm even greater explanatory power in the analyses of FDI.

Policy implications

The foregoing discussion gives a clear indication that networking of business activities means an increased volume of inter- and intrafirm trade. Inasmuch as affiliates are widely spread over all parts of the Asia–Pacific region, such an increase in inter- and intrafirm trade will give rise to rapid growth in intraregional trade. This is confirmed by the macroeconomic statistics presented. To the extent that FDI accompanies intrafirm relationships, networking also offers an explanation for the creation of FDI–trade linkages.

To sustain this process of creating FDI–trade linkages in the Asia–Pacific region, the following policy options are recommended. First, economies in the region should continue their process of economic liberalization in both the foreign-trade and financial sectors. It is of course recognized that the process of liberalization should be gradual; its sequencing is not only an academic but also a practical issue. With the formation of the World Trade Organization, it is expected that trade liberalization and facilitation will become a matter of course. How financial liberalization will proceed both in less- and more-advanced developing countries remains to be seen. Financial liberalization is important to promoting outward and inward FDI. Economic liberalization is important to bringing about a reallocation of resources so that the static and dynamic comparative advantages of a country will not be distorted. It is of paramount importance that economic liberalization in the external sector be accompanied by deregulation in the domestic sector to ensure a level playing field for domestic producers and their competitors.

Second, genuine economic cooperation, free from the influence of political and security considerations, should be promoted at the regional and subregional levels. Block-building approaches can be adopted in this effort. Both functional block-building with respect to sectoral activities, such as telecommunications, financial services, and manufacturing, and geographical block-building on the basis of subregional divisions should be undertaken. Regional and subregional economic cooperation plays an important role in promoting intraregional trade and investment.

Economic cooperation should not, however, be confined to the general macroeconomic level. Efforts should also be made to encourage and promote economic cooperation among different economies at the industry and firm levels. The close linkages between FDI and trade observed recently are largely the result of extensive networking systems based on inter- and intrafirm ties. Many new forms of nonequity FDI have become prevalent. These strategic alliances increasingly involve not only developed but also developing countries. Such new forms of economic cooperation at the microeconomic level provide for more flexible cooperation. Restrictions on such microeconomic ties across national borders should be removed as far as possible in individual countries. In particular, cooperative activities in human-capital formation and technology transfer should be facilitated.

Chapter 5

THAILAND

International Trade, Multinational Firms, and Regional Integration

Eric D. Ramstetter

In the last two decades, especially since 1986, Thailand has experienced a rapid increase in merchandise exports, and this growth has in turn proven to be a major source of overall growth for the Thai economy. The rapid growth of exports in the late 1980s and early 1990s has also been accompanied by rapid growth in private investment, both investment by local firms and foreign direct investment (FDI) by foreign multinational firms. Indeed, the growth of FDI by multinational firms in Thailand and elsewhere was so rapid in the late 1980s that it created the popular perception that multinational firms and their control of internationally integrated production activities are becoming more important in the world economy.[1] Parallel to these events has been the proliferation of agreements facilitating regional economic integration in Europe, North America, and Southeast Asia. Combined with the rapid growth of intraregional trade in these regions, this proliferation has created another popular perception that intraregional integration is also becoming a more important force in the world economy.[2]

Against this background, this chapter attempts to evaluate the effects of intra-Asian integration and foreign multinationals, as well as their interaction in Thailand. To do this, I first review some points that emerge from the theory of the multinational corporation, as well as elements of Thai economic policy. Thailand's trade and the role played by foreign multinationals are then examined, first by focusing on the industry dimension and then by focusing on the direction of trade in machinery

---

[1] See, for example, United Nations (1993). Assertions that multinationals are becoming more important are often based on the observation that FDI flows have grown far faster than GDP in many economies. In contrast, in most Asian economies, the shares of foreign multinational firms in production appear to have been more stable and were often lower in the early 1990s than in the mid-1970s (Lipsey et al. 1995). Evaluating the assertion that internationally integrated production is growing in importance is far more difficult, but intrafirm trade does not appear to have grown in importance for Asian manufacturing affiliates of Japanese and US firms in their trade with the home economy, although there is indication of its increased importance for Japanese-firm trade with Japan in the early 1990s and Japanese-firm trade with other regions. Specifically, for majority-owned US firms in Asia's nonoil manufacturing, the share of intrafirm trade exports to the United States has always been very high, in the 88–100% range in 1982 and in the 82–95% range in 1989, whereas corresponding ratios for imports from the United States fell from 93% to 86% (US Department of Commerce 1985, 1992). For Japanese firms in Asian manufacturing, intrafirm shares of affiliate exports to Japan were 74% in 1983, 77% in 1986, 59% in 1989, and 84% in 1992, whereas corresponding shares on the import side were 66, 67, 63, and 78%, respectively. Intrafirm shares of affiliate trade with other countries were 24% in 1987, 37% in 1989, and 43% in 1992 on the export side and 34, 24, and 43%, respectively, on the import side (Government of Japan 1986, 1989a, 1991, 1994a; note that figures on sales and purchases by direction cover only about half of all sales and purchases, and samples for intrafirm-trade estimates are thought to be even smaller).

[2] Here again, the popular perception clearly tends to exaggerate the trend and may actually be incorrect regarding the Asian region because a large part of the integration observed was due to the relatively high rate of growth in the region (Frankel 1993).

industries. Finally, the interaction of intra-Asian trade and foreign multinationals is examined by analyzing the role of intrafirm trade in a small sample of firms in the nonelectric-, electric-, and transport-machinery industries. The last section summarizes the main conclusions.

Theoretical considerations

As previously explained (Ramstetter 1992a, b, 1994c, d), a very clear theoretical rationale suggests that multinational firms will play a larger role in international trade than in production or other economic activities, and a growing stock of empirical evidence is consistent with this expectation.[3] The theoretical rationale stems from the assertion that multinationals often possess more intangible, knowledge-based assets than do nonmultinationals.[4] The possession of such assets is important because it suggests that multinationals tend to be more efficient than nonmultinationals and hence better able to produce internationally marketable products. If it is further hypothesized that marketing-related assets in multinationals are concentrated in international marketing, it also follows that multinationals will tend to be better able to exploit trading opportunities in foreign markets than nonmultinationals. These two factors suggest that multinationals will be more dependent on exports or imports, or both, than nonmultinationals.

In the Thai case, as in many others, considerable evidence from casual observations indicates that multinationals tend to have relatively high labour productivity and trade propensities, both when parents are compared with nonmultinational firms in home economies and when foreign affiliates are compared with other host-economy firms (Sibunruang and Brimble 1987; Sibunruang et al. 1991; Tambunlertchai and Ramstetter 1991; Ramstetter 1994a, c). Although these theoretical propositions and casual empirical observations are quite common (Ramstetter 1992a, c), data constraints often make it difficult to conduct a formal statistical analysis of the relationship between ownership and trade performance. In the Thai case, some of my previous studies are the only known attempts at formal statistical tests of the relationship between foreign firms and trade performance. Of these studies, the results from a large cross section of nonoil manufacturing firms in 1990 (Ramstetter 1994a, c) are perhaps the most interesting, indicating that after industry-wide variation is accounted for, export propensities tended to be higher in firms that had relatively low total-asset–employee ratios, were promoted by the Board of Investment (BOI), were relatively new, and had foreign-ownership shares of at least 90%.[5] However, it was also found that export propensities were identical in local firms and in foreign firms with foreign ownership shares of 10–89%, whereas import propensities were unrelated to foreign ownership.

The finding of relatively high export propensities in firms with high foreign-ownership shares is also consistent with a time-series finding for Singapore (Ramstetter 1994d) and with the observation that majority-owned affiliates account for a disproportionately large share of exports to the United States by US affiliates operating abroad (Ramstetter 1992b). Thus I have speculated (Ramstetter 1994c, d) that this may reflect the tendency of multinationals to treat their marketing

---

[3] This is relevant here because comparisons of foreign and local firms in Thailand are essentially comparisons of multinationals and nonmultinationals. Foreign firms in Thailand are by definition multinationals, and there are few Thai multinationals. Note that the ratio of outward to inward FDI was only 7% in 1978–93 (Bank of Thailand 1983, 1986–94).

[4] An extensive theoretical debate occurs over whether these so-called ownership-based advantages are necessary conditions for FDI. However, in this context, only the empirical fact that multinationals tend to possess relatively large amounts of production-technology-related intangible assets, as well as marketing-related intangible assets, is important. For reviews of this literature, see Rugman (1980, 1985), Dunning (1981, 1993), Caves (1982), Casson (1987), Buckley and Casson (1991), and Markusen (1991).

[5] Some work has also been done relating the ratio of FDI stock to the total capital stock (Ramstetter 1990, 1993b), indicating a positive and significant relationship for 1972–88; this relationship becomes statistically insignificant for 1972–89, which suggests that the post-1986 structural changes had strong effects. However, the samples are so small that these findings are not very reliable.

networks as proprietary assets and limit the access of affiliates outside their control to those networks.[6] I also showed (Ramstetter 1994a, d) that differences in export propensies are not necessarily accompanied by significant differences in average labour productivity, capital intensity, or wage levels, implying that stronger export performance in multinationals may be due more to their possession of marketing networks than to technological advantages.[7] On the other hand, the failure to find a consistent relationship on the import side was thought to be curious because the same access to marketing networks that facilitates better export performance was expected to facilitate easier importing.

Although a clear rationale can be given for expecting multinationals to depend more on trade than do their nonmultinational counterparts, whether multinationals tend to be more regionally oriented than nonmultinationals has been far less studied, either theoretically or empirically. In a number of cases, as will be clear, it is certainly true that the networks developed by multinationals are regionally oriented, and to the extent that multinationals are better able to exploit international markets, both in the region and beyond, one might expect that such multinationals are more regionally integrated than nonmultinationals. On the other hand, it may also be true that nonmultinationals have far less marketing disadvantage in regional foreign markets than in markets located far away, and I know of no theoretical or conceptual work formalizing such issues. Thus, I am extremely hesitant to advance any hypothesis on whether multinationals depend more on regional markets than do nonmultinationals.

The policy environment in Thailand

Although economic principles often generate powerful explanations of economic patterns, such as the disproportionate role of multinationals in trade, economic policies also have important and independent effects on the patterns observed. In Thailand, at least four aspects of economic policy are extremely important in evaluating relationships between trade and multinational firms.

First, Thai industrial and trade policies have gradually shifted from an emphasis on import substitution in the 1960s and early 1970s to an emphasis on export promotion in the 1980s and 1990s. It is difficult to come up with a precise measure of these shifts, although Warr (1993) reported that the effective rate of protection declined between 1969 or 1974 and 1984 or 1987 for import-competing products (from 54% and 63% to 21% and 39%) and nonimport-competing products (from 187% and 77% to 53% and 55%) and converged to zero for export products (from −35% and −47% to 2% and 4%).[8] Combined with devaluations of the baht, these changes in the structure of protection removed much of the bias against exporting industries that resulted from the pursuit of import substitution in the 1960s and much of the 1970s. Moreover, the trend toward a more balanced structure of protection appears to have continued, with further reductions of import duties on machinery and other products in the early 1990s.

Second, Thailand has a long history of openness to FDI, especially FDI in the industrial sector, although foreign investors are, in principle, limited to minority-ownership shares. The BOI was

---

[6] Some commentators have suggested that the high export propensies in firms with large foreign-ownership shares may indicate that causation runs from export propensies to ownership shares, rather than the other way, and that this is partly a result of a Thai policy that allows firms with high export propensies to have high foreign-ownership shares. On the other hand, the similar findings in countries with no ownership restrictions, such as Singapore, and theoretical findings and logic suggest that Thai policies have simply conformed to multinational-firm practices, rather than actually creating high foreign-ownership shares in firms with high export propensies.

[7] Note that many studies using a wide range of methodologies have found it difficult to identify statistically significant differences in the technology of foreign and local firms in Thailand (Khanthachai et al. 1987; Tambunlertchai and Ramstetter 1991; Brimble 1993; Ramstetter 1993c).

[8] A product is classified as import competing if net imports are positive and imports account for more than 10% of consumption and as export competing if net exports are positive and exports account for more than 10% of production. Remaining products are classified as nonimport competing.

founded in 1959, with the explicit aim of promoting FDI and domestic private investment. The BOI has wide discretionary power to grant incentives to businesses investing in promoted projects and has granted incentives based on a number of criteria. Projects that create a large number jobs and generate technology transfer in key sectors, such as steel and automobiles, have traditionally been favoured. Since the early to mid-1970s, projects with high export propensities have also been given priority, and since the mid-1980s, preference has also been given to projects located outside the Bangkok area. Among the incentives the BOI has offered, the exemption on import duties for raw materials and capital goods has historically been among the more important, although this importance was diminished by general tariff reductions in the early 1990s. Income-tax holidays are another important incentive in some cases, as are exemptions from the legal principle that foreign investors be restricted to minority-ownership shares.

Third, a moderate amount of FDI in Thailand does not go through the BOI, and BOI approval is not a necessary condition for FDI if the investor gets the necessary industrial and commercial licences. An important element in this respect is a clause in a bilateral treaty with the United States granting US firms national treatment, thereby exempting them from ownership restrictions. As a result, a relatively large proportion of US firms appear to invest directly, rather than going through the BOI. Another important element is the large number of industries, mainly in trade and other services, ineligible for BOI promotion but in which FDI is allowed. Note that FDI is prohibited in a few industries, mainly those related to agricultural production.

Fourth, large and important changes occurred in macroeconomic policy from the early 1980s. Devaluations of the baht were traditionally avoided but were implemented in 1981 and 1984 to spur exports and reduce the rate at which foreign debt was accumulating. Fiscal policy was also revamped, with the growth rate of nominal general government expenditures slowing markedly from an average of 17% in 1970–82 to 6% in 1982–88 (Sahasakul 1993). Meanwhile, monetary policy has always been rather conservative, and inflation has generally been very moderate (Nidhiprabha 1993). Partially as a result of steady monetary policies and the gradual structural adjustments in trade, industrial, and fiscal policies in the 1970s and early 1980s, the Thai economy was well positioned to benefit from the favourable external environment that emerged in the late 1980s, and the growth of real gross domestic product (GDP) accelerated from an average of 6.5% in 1980–87 to 10.2% in 1987–93 (Thailand NESDB 1988, 1992, 1993b, 1994).

Coinciding with these changes, there have been extremely rapid increases in FDI, total private investment, and exports. The ratio of FDI to nominal GDP rose from an average of 0.6% in 1970–87 to 2.0% in 1988–93; the ratio of total private fixed investment to GDP rose from 20% to 32%; and the ratio of merchandise exports to GDP rose from 19% to 28%. Much of this change was concentrated in the manufacturing sector, where the FDI–GDP ratio went from 1.0% in 1970–87 to 3.3% in 1988–93, and the merchandise export–GDP ratio rose from 58% in 1970–87 to 83% in 1988–92.[9] These changes have contributed to the popular perception that increases in FDI by foreign multinationals and, in particular, the growth of manufacturing exports from foreign firms have been a key cause of the economic boom in Thailand since the late 1980s. On the other hand, strong reasons can be given for assuming mutual causation in the FDI–growth relationship, and I tend to view the increase in growth as a primary cause of increased FDI, whereas increased FDI seems to be a much more minor cause of growth.[10] Whether as a cause or a result of the changes observed, or both, foreign multinationals have played a role in the recent growth in nonoil manufacturing exports from Thailand.

---

[9] FDI data are from the Bank of Thailand (1983, 1986–94); GDP and private fixed investment data, from Thailand NESDB (1988, 1992, 1993b, 1994); total export data, from IMF (1994b); and manufacturing export data, from an International Standard Industrial Classification (ISIC)-based compilation by ANU (1995).

[10] Indeed, I tend to view the fact that FDI began to increase rapidly in 1988, only after the Thai economy took off in 1987, as evidence that the growth of the local economy was more a cause than a result of increases in FDI, a viewpoint that is also broadly consistent with the results of Granger causality tests at the major industry level for 1972–92 (Ramstetter 1995). On the other hand, Granger causality tests are highly suspect statistically, and the sample is very small, so I would be unwilling to use such evidence to suggest that FDI increases have not increased growth, although I would be willing to use it to suggest that growth is probably a much more important determinant of FDI than vice versa.

Table 5.1. Thailand's export structure and revealed comparative advantage indices by ISIC category.

Industry	Industry shares (%)					RCA indices				
	1973	1980	1986	1989	1992	1973	1980	1986	1989	1992
Total exports (US$ billions)	1.6	6.5	8.9	20.1	32.5	NM	NM	NM	NM	NM
Nonoil manufacturing	44	60	69	80	83	0.6	0.9	0.9	1.0	1.0
Food, beverages, tobacco	21	24	25	23	17	2.2	3.4	3.8	3.7	2.7
Textiles, apparel, etc.	9	10	17	20	20	1.1	1.6	2.2	2.5	2.4
Wood, paper, printing	3	2	2	3	3	0.6	0.4	0.5	0.6	0.6
Chemicals	1	1	2	2	2	0.1	0.1	0.2	0.2	0.3
Synthetic fibres	0	0	1	1	1	0.0	0.1	0.3	0.4	0.4
Rubber and plastics	0	1	2	3	3	0.2	0.9	1.1	1.5	1.5
Nonmetallic mineral products	1	0	1	1	1	0.9	0.4	0.6	0.8	1.0
Metals and metal products	7	14	3	3	2	0.6	1.4	0.4	0.3	0.3
Nonelectric machinery	0	0	2	7	11	0.0	0.0	0.2	0.6	0.8
Office and computing machinery	0	0	1	5	7	0.0	0.0	0.2	1.5	1.9
Electric machinery	0	5	8	9	14	0.0	0.9	1.0	1.0	1.5
Transport machinery	0	0	0	1	2	0.0	0.0	0.0	0.1	0.1
Automobiles, motorcycles	0	0	0	1	1	0.0	0.0	0.0	0.1	0.1
Precision machinery	0	0	1	1	2	0.1	0.2	0.2	0.3	0.7
Miscellaneous manufacturing	2	3	6	7	6	1.3	1.8	3.6	3.6	3.4

Source: IMF (1980–93) and ANU (1995).
Note: ISIC, International Standard Industrial Classification; NM, not meaningful; RCA, revealed comparative advantage.

The structure of trade and the role of foreign firms

The rapid growth of Thai exports is illustrated in Table 5.1, with three identifiable periods, 1973–80, 1980–86 and 1986–92. In the first and last periods, exports grew extremely rapidly (23% and 24% annually in nominal US dollars, respectively), but in the interim period growth was much slower (5%). Perhaps even more conspicuous than the rapid overall growth of exports was the shift in the structure of those exports, with the share of nonoil manufacturing rising from 44% in 1973 to 83% in 1992.[11] Corresponding largely to this structural change, calculated values for the revealed comparative advantage (RCA) index indicates that Thailand has moved from a position of comparative disadvantage in nonoil manufacturing to one of neutrality in the last two decades.[12]

Much of the increase in manufacturing exports was due to two traditional export industries that have always had RCA indices greater than 1: food (including beverages and tobacco) and textiles (including apparel, leather, and footwear; Table 5.1). Food was by far the largest manufacturing export industry in 1973, and despite declining shares of nonoil manufacturing exports after 1986, this industry remained the second largest source of nonoil manufacturing exports in 1992. In contrast, textiles grew relatively rapidly through the middle to late 1980s, with its share of total exports rising to 1989 and flattening out thereafter. In both food and textiles, RCA indices rose through

[11] Note that using the Bank of Thailand's somewhat more narrow definition of manufactured exports, total manufacturing's share rose from 76% in 1991, to 77% in 1992, and to 80% in 1993 (Bank of Thailand 1994). Note also that oil manufacturing exports are unimportant in Thailand, accounting for only 1.2% of total exports in 1973 and 0.4% or less in 1980 and 1986–92.

[12] The RCA index is calculated as $(XT_i/XT)/(XW_i/XW)$, where XT and XW are total merchandise exports for Thailand and the world, respectively, and XT_i and XW_i are exports of industry i for Thailand and the world, respectively. An RCA index less than 1 implies that Thailand exports relatively large amounts from industry i, which is interpreted as an ex post expression of comparative advantage for Thailand in industry i, whereas an RCA index greater than 1 implies a comparative disadvantage for Thailand in industry i.

1989 but then declined somewhat in 1992, indicating that Thailand's comparative advantage strengthened in these industries through the 1980s but may be weakening in the 1990s. A similar pattern was also observed in miscellaneous manufacturing, a smaller but still important export industry.

In recent years, by far the most conspicuous export growth has been in two closely related machinery industries, office and computing machinery (OCM) and electric machinery (Table 5.1).[13] Shares of both industries in total exports started at 0% in 1973, with electric machinery's share rising first to 8% in 1986 and then to 14% in 1992. The share of OCM was still only 1% in 1986 but then exploded to 11% in 1992.[14] Correspondingly, RCA indices also increased rapidly in these two industries, from 0.2 in 1986 to 1.9 in 1992 in OCM and from 0.0 in 1973 to 0.9–1.0 in 1980, 1986, and 1989 and then to 1.5 in 1992 in electric machinery. The more gradual rise in electric machinery reflects in part the more diversified nature of this industry, in which labour-intensive production of parts, an activity in which Thailand has developed a strong comparative advantage, plays a less dominant role. Rubber and plastics is another industry that has experienced rapidly rising shares of total exports and an emergence of RCA since the mid-1980s. However, this industry is much smaller than the machinery industries, and no other industry had consistently high RCA indices or export shares in 1973–92.

On the import side (Table 5.2), Thai trade has historically been much more heavily weighted toward manufacturing, especially chemicals, metals and metal products, and the three large machinery industries, nonelectric, electric, and transport machinery. The former two industries were the largest in terms of imports through the mid-1980s, and they combined to consistently account for about 25–30% of all imports during the period studied. The share of transport machinery has also been rather steady since 1980, fluctuating at around 10%. However, similar to exports, imports of nonelectric-machinery and electric-machinery industries have displayed the most rapid growth. Although the OCM industry plays a smaller role on the import side, its share rose from 0% in 1973 and 1980 to 3–4% in 1986 and thereafter, with shares of electric machinery displaying a similar trend, rising from 6–7% to 11–13% in the same periods. The share of other nonelectric machinery (nonelectric machinery minus OCM) remained rather steady at 7–11%.

Foreign multinationals have played a large and growing role in Thai trade, especially in the export of OCM and electric machinery. Unfortunately, it is difficult to show this unambiguously. On the import side, it is impossible to make industry-wide comparisons between estimates of foreign-firm imports and total Thai imports because no economy-wide compilations of import data exist by importing firm, and one cannot assume that a firm imports products of its industry alone. On the export side, it is more plausible to assume that a firm exports the products of its industry, and comparisons are then possible if one uses an ISIC-based classification of total trade data. However, the existence of multiproduct firms and the imprecise nature of Standard International Trade Classification (SITC)–ISIC conversions of commodity-trade data make such comparisons rough approximations at best. In Thailand, this type of comparison is complicated because it is impossible to compile consistent and comprehensive time series on the activities of foreign multinationals.

The most comprehensive of existing sources are BOI-conducted surveys of BOI-promoted firms, and these surveys are the focus of attention here.[15] However, these surveys are plagued with a

---

[13] These industries are closely related in that labour-intensive production of parts for computers, computer peripherals, and integrated circuits (ICs) is the most important activity involved.

[14] According to the Bank of Thailand (1994), in 1992 computer parts accounted for 6.7% of total exports; finished computer goods, for 2.0%; IC parts, for 1.9%; and finished ICs, for 2.6%. There is obviously a difference in this commodity classification and the ISIC classification used in the text, because the computer-related share appears higher in the commodity classification. However, given the related nature of these industries, neither distinction is very meaningful. More meaningful is that these categories accounted for 13.2% of total exports, or about 65% of the combined exports of OCM and electric machinery.

[15] In addition, surveys of Japanese firms have been completed by the Japanese Chamber of Commerce; of US firms, by the US Department of Commerce (see Table 5.8). Japan Ministry of International Trade and Industry (Government of Japan 1986, 1989a, 1991, 1994a) also conducted surveys of Japanese firms but provided only a limited number of indicators by country for 1988–92.

Table 5.2. Thailand's import structure by ISIC category.

Industry	Industry shares (%)				
	1973	1980	1986	1989	1992
Total imports (US$ billions)	2.0	9.2	9.2	25.8	40.7
Nonoil manufacturing	81	61	74	79	82
Food, beverages, tobacco	3	4	4	3	4
Textiles, apparel, etc.	5	2	4	4	4
Wood, paper, printing	4	3	3	3	3
Chemicals	17	12	16	11	11
Synthetic fibres	5	2	4	3	3
Rubber and plastics	2	1	2	2	2
Nonmetallic mineral products	1	1	1	1	1
Metals and metal products	16	12	13	16	15
Nonelectric machinery	11	8	10	15	15
Office and computing machinery	0	0	3	4	4
Electric machinery	6	7	11	11	13
Transport machinery	14	9	6	9	10
Automobiles, motorcycles	11	6	6	8	7
Precision machinery	1	1	2	2	2
Miscellaneous manufacturing	1	1	2	2	2

Source: IMF (1993) and ANU (1995).
Note: ISIC, International Standard Industrial Classification.

number of problems, the most important being low and variable response rates that make it difficult to discern to what extent observed trends are due to changes in coverage and to what extent they are due to actual changes in economic activity.[16] For example, the data in Table 5.3 indicate that exports of promoted foreign firms (in nominal United States dollars) increased 56–60% annually in 1986–90 (depending on which 1990 sample is used) versus only 16% annually in 1974–86. The contrast in import growth rates, 2% versus 63%, is even more conspicuous. However, it is unclear how much of the difference in growth rates is because the 1990 survey was much more comprehensive than surveys in previous years and how much is because of actual increases in trade flows.[17]

A conspicuous pattern emerging from these data is the large increase in trade by nonelectric-machinery (primarily OCM) and electric-machinery affiliates. The share of electric-machinery affiliates in all promoted foreign firms in nonoil manufacturing grew from 1% in 1974 to 34–35% in 1986 and 1990 for exports and from 5% to 8% and then 31% for imports (Table 5.3). In nonelectric machinery, export shares were 0% in the first 2 years but reached 21–22% in 1990, whereas import

[16] In addition, these surveys omit foreign firms that are not promoted or have had their promoted status expire. In 1990, for example, exports of the 523 promoted firms for which exports could be estimated (in the 1990 BOI survey) amounted to US$6.117 billion (Table 5.3), or 94% of the US$6.504 billion in exports by all 582 foreign firms for which estimates could be made for that year. However, sales of these same 523 firms amounted to US$11.994 billion, or only 58% of the sales of all 894 foreign firms for which sales could be estimated for 1990 (Ramstetter 1994c; IMF 1994b). Note also that the results of these surveys have never been formally compiled or published by the Thai government, and one must therefore rely solely on private compilations of confidential data by individual researchers, who sometimes use different methodologies and definitions in their compilations. In this paper, previous compilations from Sibunruang and Brimble (1987) and Tambunlertchai and Ramstetter (1991) were combined with my recent compilations of 1990 survey data (Ramstetter 1993c, 1994a, c) and some additional original compilations of the 1990 data. See Sibunruang and Brimble (1991) for an alternative compilation of the 1990 data

[17] Changes in sample coverage are also thought to be largely responsible for the large increase in exports observed in 1975–79 (33% annually), followed by the decrease in 1979–84 (–11% annually) and the even more dramatic rise in 1984–86 (63% annually). Note also that Table 5.3 shows two export samples for 1990 to show the most comprehensive export estimates (523 firms) and to facilitate direct comparisons with import numbers, which are available only for a smaller sample (469 firms). The larger sample is the focus of analysis of export patterns that follows.

Table 5.3. Exports and imports by BOI-promoted foreign firms (US$ millions).

Industry	Exports							Imports		
	1974	1975	1979	1984	1986	1990	1990[a]	1974	1986	1990
Nonoil manufacturing	151	192	598	329	938	5623	6117	387	470	3304
Food, beverages, tobacco	27	14	114	104	274	865	884	35	72	206
Textiles, apparel, etc.	92	50	196	121	196	455	524	126	162	269
Wood, paper, printing	2	5	12	2	11	100	101	5	5	20
Chemicals	7	1	19	12	30	159	164	57	35	225
Synthetic fibres	NA	NA	NA	NA	NA	62	62	NA	NA	86
Rubber and plastics	2	0	9	0	39	103	118	19	30	90
Nonmetallic mineral products	8	1	4	13	34	51	60	5	16	14
Metals and metal products	10	118	15	3	10	400	401	69	34	298
Nonelectric machinery	0	0	0	0	1	1243	1275	1	19	807
Office and computing machinery	NA	NA	NA	NA	NA	1121	1152	NA	NA	649
Electric machinery	1	1	219	45	315	1887	2162	18	39	1015
Transport machinery	0	0	1	3	3	47	60	50	35	232
Automobiles, motorcycles	NA	NA	NA	NA	NA	47	60	NA	NA	232
Precision machinery	[b]	[b]	[b]	[b]	[b]	81	117	[b]	[b]	31
Miscellaneous manufacturing	2	1	9	17	25	232	250	4	23	97
Sample size (n)	180	106	158	107	202	469	523	180	202	469

Source: Sibunruang and Brimble (1987), Tambunlertchai and Ramstetter (1991), and author's compilations of BOI-survey data for 1990.
Note: BOI, Board of Investment; NA, not available.
[a] As discussed in footnote 17, the reason for having two export samples for 1990 is to facilitate direct comparisons with import data (n = 469) and to show the most comprehensive export estimates (n = 523).
[b] Precision machinery is included in miscellaneous manufacturing.

shares rose from 0% to 5% to 24% in these years, respectively. Indeed by 1990, affiliates in OCM and electric machinery combined to account for more than 50% of all trade on both the import and export sides by nonoil manufacturing affiliates in Thailand. In 1990, the share of food in promoted-foreign-firm exports was the only other share to reach double digits on either the export or the import sides. However, this share (15%) was lower than corresponding shares in 1986 (29%) and 1974 (18%). In previous years, promoted foreign firms in textiles were relatively large traders, accounting for 60% of all promoted-foreign-firm exports in 1974 and 21% in 1986, as well as 32% and 35% of all imports in each year, respectively. In all years, these four industries dominated exports of promoted foreign firms, their combined share of all exports by nonoil manufacturing firms being 77–84%, and came to dominate imports as well, with a combined share of 58–65% in 1986 and 1990, up from 46% in 1974.

Largely as a result of increasing foreign-firm shares of Thai exports in three industries, electric machinery, nonelectric machinery (primarily OCM), and food, the share of exports by promoted foreign firms in total nonoil manufacturing exports in Thailand rose from 12% in 1974 to 15% in 1986 and 33% in 1990 (Table 5.4). Although the growth of these shares between 1986 and 1990 may be overstated by these data for reasons explained earlier, the rapid growth in promoted foreign firms' shares of nonelectric machinery (mainly OCM) and electric machinery do not appear altogether unrealistic and are the major reason for the rapid rise in the overall ratio. The rapid rise in foreign shares in food is also of some interest because this remains one of Thailand's leading export industries. In contrast, the steep decline in the share of foreign firms in textiles appears to indicate that local firms replaced foreign firms as the leading competitors in this industry.

Another result of rapid export growth in foreign firms and in Thailand as a whole has been an increase in export propensities, measured as ratios of exports to total sales or total income. For Thai nonoil manufacturing as a whole, these ratios rose remarkably from 13% in 1974 to 23% in 1986 and then 30% in 1990 (Table 5.4). Again the most conspicuous increases in this ratio were in electric machinery (from 5% to 52% and 76%) and nonelectric machinery (from 1% to 23% and 58%, as a result primarily of the growth of the OCM industry, which had a ratio of close to 100% in 1986 and 1990). However, notable increases occurred in almost all industries, with nonmetallic mineral

Table 5.4. Export propensities measured as ratios of exports to total sales or total income (%).

Industry	BOI-promoted foreign firms' shares of Thai exports			BOI-promoted foreign firms' export–sales ratios			All firms' export–income ratios		
	1974	1986	1990	1974	1986	1990	1974	1986	1990
Nonoil manufacturing	12	15	33	15	42	51	13	23	30
Food, beverages, tobacco	3	12	21	24	54	63	18	27	31
Textiles, apparel, etc.	62	13	11	26	41	55	8	22	29
Wood, paper, printing	4	5	17	16	21	53	8	11	14
Chemicals	44	22	37	6	19	25	4	14	25
Synthetic fibres	NA	NA	30	NA	NA	33	NA	56	186
Rubber and plastics	20	24	17	3	42	33	2	22	39
Nonmetallic mineral products	23	48	22	21	32	9	15	5	8
Metals and metal products	6	3	64	6	5	49	20	22	21
Nonelectric machinery	0	1	58	0	2	79	1	23	58
Office and computing machinery	NA	NA	74	NA	NA	98	NA	102	96
Electric machinery	11	44	82	3	90	81	5	52	76
Transport machinery	2	8	24	0	2	3	0	3	4
Automobiles, motorcycles	NA	NA	26	NA	NA	3	NA	2	4
Precision machinery	[a]	[a]	39	[a]	[a]	97	[a]	[a]	39
Miscellaneous manufacturing	5	5	15	22	26	98	19	53	54
Sample size (n)	180	202	523	180	202	523	NA	NA	NA

Source: Tambunlertchai and Ramstetter (1991), Thailand NESDB (1993a, b), ANU (1995), and author's compilations of BOI survey data for 1990.
Note: BOI, Board of Investment; NA, not available.
[a] Precision machinery is included in miscellaneous manufacturing.

products and metals and metal products being the only exceptions to this trend. In other words, the increase in export propensities was broad based and included industries in which foreign firms had not been major exporters.

On average, export–sales ratios in foreign firms increased much more rapidly than the Thai average in 1974–86 (2.8-fold versus 1.8-fold), but these increases were of similar magnitude in 1986–90 (1.3-fold each; Table 5.4). This pattern is of some interest because it suggests that differences in the direction of change in marketing strategies of foreign and local firms in nonoil manufacturing were greatly reduced after the economic boom of the late 1980s. Notwithstanding this dynamic convergence, however, export–sales ratios remained much higher in foreign firms than in Thailand as a whole (and by implication, higher than in local firms) in 1990. However, as mentioned earlier, closer examination of the 1990 data indicates these differences between foreign and local firms are statistically significant only when foreign ownership shares are large.

Direction of trade in machinery industries and role of foreign firms

Intraregional exports in manufactures (Table 5.5) have grown slightly faster than total manufacturing trade in recent years. For example, the combined share of the Asia-9 (that is, Japan, Asia's four newly industrializing economies (NIEs) — Hong Kong, Korea, Singapore, and Taiwan — Indonesia, Malaysia, the Philippines, and China) in total nonoil manufacturing exports remained rather steady, dropping slightly from 35% in 1986 to 33% in 1989 and then rebounding to 38% in 1992. The import shares of the Asia-9 countries experienced a more marked increase in 1986–89, from 54% to 58% (Table 5.6), but a decline occurred in 1989–92, to 57% in the latter year. In the Asia-9 region, however, large changes occurred on the export side with Japan's share rising significantly from 10% in 1986 to 15% in 1992, whereas shares of Singapore and Malaysia dropped somewhat. On the import side, intra-Asian-9 changes were less dramatic, and Japan accounted for a much larger portion of intra-Asian trade on the import side than on the export side.

Table 5.5. Thailand's exports of nonoil manufactures by selected ISIC category, year, and partner.

Industry	Year	World totals (US$ millions)	Shares of world totals (%)												
			Asia-9[a]	Japan	Hong Kong	Singapore	Korea	Taiwan	Indonesia	Malaysia	Philippines	China	North America	European Community	Other
All nonoil manufacturing	1986	6 199	35	10	4	11	2	1	1	4	0	2	24	18	23
	1989	15 943	33	13	4	7	1	1	1	3	1	2	26	17	24
	1992	26 982	38	15	5	9	1	2	1	3	1	1	26	18	18
Nonelectric machinery	1986	184	59	31	1	16	3	2	2	3	1	0	29	6	6
	1989	1 498	53	14	3	25	2	5	1	1	1	1	30	14	3
	1992	3 529	59	18	5	27	1	3	1	3	1	0	24	12	5
Office and computing machinery	1986	60	22	6	0	5	8	3	0	0	0	0	69	8	1
	1989	1 067	48	8	2	29	3	5	0	0	1	0	37	14	1
	1992	2 358	54	11	2	34	1	2	0	2	2	0	31	13	2
Electric machinery	1986	717	54	1	1	41	1	0	0	9	1	0	32	9	5
	1989	1 823	33	9	4	14	1	2	0	3	0	0	48	17	2
	1992	4 571	44	13	4	18	1	2	0	5	1	0	36	16	4
Transport machinery	1986	38	46	9	1	13	0	16	1	5	1	0	13	22	19
	1989	200	38	20	1	8	0	1	1	3	1	3	41	9	12
	1992	499	36	18	2	10	1	2	1	1	1	0	19	29	16
Automobiles, motorcycles	1986	21	46	12	1	22	0	0	2	8	1	0	20	9	25
	1989	183	37	22	1	8	0	1	1	3	1	0	43	9	11
	1992	362	38	24	2	4	1	3	1	2	1	0	17	24	21
Precision machinery	1986	53	38	11	22	3	0	1	0	1	0	0	6	13	43
	1989	179	38	11	21	4	0	1	0	1	0	0	20	18	24
	1992	654	48	18	21	5	0	2	0	1	1	0	21	12	19

Source: ANU (1995).
Note: ISIC, International Standard Industrial Classification.
[a] Asia-9, China, Hong Kong, Indonesia, Japan, Korea, Malaysia, the Philippines, Singapore, and Taiwan.

Table 5.6. Thailand's imports of nonoil manufactures by selected ISIC categories, year, and partner.

Industry	Year	World totals (US$ millions)	Shares of world totals (%)												
			Asia-9[a]	Japan	Hong Kong	Singapore	Korea	Taiwan	Indonesia	Malaysia	Philippines	China	North America	European Community	Other
All nonoil manufacturing	1986	6 756	54	34	2	4	3	5	1	1	1	3	16	17	13
	1989	20 540	58	37	1	5	3	6	1	2	0	3	13	15	14
	1992	33 639	57	34	1	5	4	6	1	3	0	3	13	16	14
Nonelectric machinery	1986	947	60	38	2	8	1	6	0	0	4	1	13	20	7
	1989	3 938	63	42	1	12	1	6	0	0	0	1	14	17	6
	1992	6 166	61	39	1	8	2	7	0	3	0	1	14	19	6
Office and computing machinery	1986	263	69	21	5	19	4	6	0	0	14	0	21	4	6
	1989	1 014	67	20	1	41	1	4	0	0	0	0	29	3	1
	1992	1 572	74	26	1	25	3	8	0	10	0	1	21	3	2
Electric machinery	1986	1 017	39	27	1	6	2	2	0	1	0	0	40	13	8
	1989	2 743	60	37	2	8	4	6	0	2	0	1	28	11	1
	1992	5 436	67	35	2	14	4	7	0	4	0	1	18	11	4
Transport machinery	1986	596	75	72	0	1	0	2	0	0	0	0	5	17	3
	1989	2 279	81	77	0	1	1	1	0	0	0	1	4	13	2
	1992	4 258	59	55	0	1	2	1	0	0	0	0	16	22	1
Automobiles, motorcycles	1986	518	82	80	0	0	0	2	0	0	0	0	3	13	2
	1989	2 076	82	81	0	0	0	1	0	0	0	0	3	11	4
	1992	3 019	77	75	0	0	1	1	0	0	0	0	2	17	4
Precision machinery	1986	174	39	31	3	2	1	2	0	0	0	0	20	24	17
	1989	468	51	39	4	2	1	4	0	0	0	1	20	17	12
	1992	759	54	40	5	2	2	4	0	0	0	1	16	15	15

Source: ANU (1995).
Note: ISIC, International Standard Industrial Classification.
[a] Asia-9, China, Hong Kong, Indonesia, Japan, Korea, Malaysia, the Philippines, Singapore, and Taiwan.

Among the rapidly growing machinery industries, intra-Asian exports were important for most years in nonelectric, electric, and precision machinery, but closer to the nonoil manufacturing average in transport machinery (Table 5.5). On the import side, Asia-9 shares tended to be slightly above the nonoil manufacturing average in all nonelectric and electric machinery and markedly above the average in office and computing and especially transport machinery (Table 5.6). Of particular interest in this context is the relatively large share of Singapore in OCM and electric machinery on both the export and import sides and the dominant role of Japan in imports of automobiles and motorcycles. However, it is also notable that country shares often fluctuated in a wide range, with no clear trend.

Using data for the larger sample of 523 BOI-promoted firms in 1990, one can also ascertain the country of owner and for a subset of exports the direction of exports for promoted firms, both local and foreign. Table 5.7 gives these ownership and export-direction breakdowns for all nonoil manufacturing, as well as for all machinery categories.[18] By ownership in all nonoil manufacturing, shares of Japanese firms (32%) and North American firms (24%; the vast majority of these are US firms) were the largest, followed by local firms (22%), whereas shares of European firms (12%) and NIE firms (7%) were smaller. Shares of all foreign firms were larger in exports than in cumulative FDI flows for North American and European firms and smaller for Japanese and NIE firms.[19] Export–sales ratios, on the other hand, were on average highest in North American firms and most groups of NIE firms (Singapore firms being the exception) but much lower in Japanese and European firms.

Although foreign and local firms clearly differed in the industrial structure of exports, as did foreign-promoted and Thai firms as a whole, the direction of exports did not tend to differ much in all nonoil manufacturing for the subset of exports for which direction numbers are available.[20] Thai firms and all promoted firms exported mainly to North America (33% or a little more) and Europe (25% or a little less) (Table 5.7). Both of these shares were much larger than the corresponding shares of North America and the European Community (EC) in total nonoil manufacturing exports in 1989 and 1992 (Table 5.5).[21] Japan's share of promoted-firm exports was also somewhat larger than corresponding shares of total nonoil manufacturing exports (Table 5.7). In contrast, Hong Kong's share was similar among local promoted firms, all promoted firms, and total nonoil manufacturing exports. Singapore's share was also similar for all promoted firms and total nonoil manufacturing exports but much lower for local promoted firms. In contrast, the shares of Other Asia and Other regions (for example, the share of developing economies) were much lower for all promoted firms than for Thailand as a whole; and among promoted firms, the share of Other regions was much larger for local firms than for all firms. In sum, promoted firms in Thailand appeared to depend more on developed-economy markets than did Thai nonoil manufacturing exports as a whole. Moreover, the relative similarity of marketing patterns between foreign and local promoted firms suggests that, with respect to the direction of exports, promoted local firms were more similar to promoted foreign firms than to nonpromoted firms, the vast majority of which were local.

---

[18] Here electric and computing machinery are combined into one category because of the difficulty in classifying multi-product firms in these industries.

[19] Shares of cumulative FDI inflows from 1970 to 1990 in nonoil manufacturing were Japan, 50%; NIEs, 24%; United States, 13%; and Europe, 10%. As noted in the text, the US share accounted for the vast majority of the North American share; Canada's FDI in all sectors amounted to only 0.6 of FDI in nonoil manufacturing in this period. Note also that estimates for Europe are for 12 countries: Austria, Belgium, Denmark, Finland, France, Germany, Italy, the Netherlands, Norway, Sweden, Switzerland, and the United Kingdom (Bank of Thailand 1983, 1986–94). Corresponding shares of foreign-firm exports were Japan, 42%; North America, 30%; Europe, 15%; and NIEs, 9%.

[20] Note that the ratio of the subtotal of exports by direction to total exports is very similar for local firms (67%) and foreign firms (68%). Note also that the difference between the subtotal of exports by direction and total exports results from nonreporting and (or) underreporting of exports by direction compared with total exports.

[21] Note that the EC countries accounted for 85% of all merchandise exports to all Europe and 90% of all merchandise exports to industrial (western) Europe in 1990. Hence, shares of the EC (22%), industrial Europe (24%), and all Europe (25%) in all Thai merchandise exports were similar in this year (IMF 1980–93).

Table 5.7. Exports of BOI-promoted firms by ownership and destination, 1990.

Industry	Nationality of firm owner	Number of firms (n)	Total exports (US$ millions)	Total export–sales ratio (%)	Exports by destination, subtotal (US$ millions)	Export shares by destination (%)						
						Japan	Hong Kong	Singapore	Other Asia	North America	Europe	Other
All nonoil manufacturing	All	806	7833	46	5308	16	5	10	4	35	24	6
	Thailand	283	1716	33	1152	19	4	2	4	32	29	10
	Japan	248	2539	39	1471	35	3	10	4	27	14	7
	Hong Kong	23	173	66	109	3	30	5	21	9	20	12
	Korea	16	63	89	56	3	8	5	9	40	35	0
	Singapore	7	25	21	24	7	0	20	31	21	11	10
	Taiwan	63	258	80	238	2	2	0	10	70	14	2
	Other Asia	26	121	49	88	18	2	4	2	16	43	15
	North America	44	1863	91	1541	1	5	21	1	46	24	2
	Europe	80	946	46	521	15	12	1	8	21	34	9
	Other	16	129	38	108	4	5	1	5	22	50	13
Other nonelectric machinery	All	30	128	22	90	52	1	9	11	7	5	15
	Thailand	7	5	4	5	8	0	9	0	82	0	1
	Japan	19	116	28	78	59	1	10	13	0	6	11
	Taiwan	2	1	44	1	0	0	0	0	100	0	0
	Europe	1	1	41	1	40	0	0	0	0	0	60
	Other	1	5	23	5	0	0	0	0	33	0	67
Electric and computing machinery	All	118	3401	86	2466	8	5	18	2	43	21	3
	Thailand	13	86	88	83	0	1	1	1	44	48	5
	Japan	62	1434	73	772	24	3	16	2	40	11	4
	Hong Kong	3	10	91	5	32	18	43	0	0	2	5
	Korea	1	11	62	11	0	0	0	16	0	84	0
	Singapore	1	11	100	11	5	0	45	18	16	16	0
	Taiwan	17	119	99	116	1	0	1	17	69	11	1
	Other Asia	1	3	100	3	0	0	0	0	100	0	0
	North America	11	1653	100	1392	1	5	23	0	45	25	1
	Europe	8	40	92	39	0	82	0	0	0	4	14
	Other	1	34	100	34	0	0	0	0	5	95	0

(continued)

Table 5.7. concluded.

Industry	Nationality of firm owner	Number of firms (n)	Total exports (US$ millions)	Total export-sales ratio (%)	Exports by destination, subtotal (US$ millions)	Export shares by destination (%)						
						Japan	Hong Kong	Singapore	Other Asia	North America	Europe	Other
Automobiles, parts, and motorcycles	All	40	87	3	60	14	6	7	32	9	27	5
	Thailand	9	28	6	12	4	0	0	36	24	28	8
	Japan	24	35	2	29	25	1	6	42	10	11	5
	Korea	1	8	100	8	12	42	30	16	0	0	0
	Taiwan	1	0	6	0	0	0	0	0	0	0	100
	Other Asia	2	14	43	9	0	0	0	11	0	89	0
	Europe	3	2	85	2	0	0	0	25	4	71	0
Precision machinery	All	22	129	95	125	20	40	2	3	11	15	9
	Thailand	3	12	86	12	8	33	0	4	2	1	52
	Japan	7	56	96	53	45	3	5	3	15	29	0
	Hong Kong	2	27	99	27	0	94	0	0	3	3	0
	Korea	1	0	100	0	0	61	0	0	0	0	39
	North America	1	5	100	4	0	0	0	0	100	0	0
	Europe	8	29	94	29	0	67	0	4	1	11	17

Source: Author's compilations of BOI survey data for 1990.
Note: BOI, Board of Investment; *Europe* refers to all western Europe; *Other Asia* refers to South Asia and unspecified Asian countries.

Among machinery industries, the large electric and computing industry had a relatively small share of exports to Japan, whereas shares of North America and Singapore were much larger. In contrast, Japan's share of exports was relatively large in other nonelectric machinery and precision machinery, as were Hong Kong's share in precision machinery and Other Asia's share in automobiles (including parts and motorcycles). Note that all of these shares differed markedly from corresponding shares in total Thai exports. Because foreign firms accounted for the vast majority of exports in these machinery industries, these differences in part indicate differences in marketing patterns between foreign and local firms in Thailand.

The large shares of developed economies in exports of promoted firms, most of which were foreign, are related to the dominance of promoted-firm exports by firms from developed economies (see earlier), combined with the fact that foreign firms tended to export relatively large amounts to their home economies. For example, in all nonoil manufacturing, the home country or region accounted for 35% of exports by Japanese firms, 46% of those by North American firms, and 34% of those by European firms (Table 5.7). All of these shares were substantially higher than corresponding shares of all promoted-firm exports or total Thai exports. Home-economy shares were also large for the Hong Kong and Singapore firms in the sample, suggesting that the tendency for foreign firms to depend heavily on the home market is a common characteristic among foreign firms in Thailand. This dependence on the home-economy market was also observed in electric- and computing-machinery firms from Hong Kong, Japan, and Singapore. Some important exceptions to this pattern occurred: shares of Singapore were large for North American and Hong Kong firms, and shares of Hong Kong were large for European firms.

In sum, therefore, these data suggest that foreign firms tend to depend heavily on home markets, and because most of the exporting by foreign firms in Thailand is apparently done by developed-economy firms, this is a major factor in creating dependence on developed-economy markets. Thus, in 1990 at least, it appears that foreign firms in Thailand may have actually been less regionally oriented than Thai exporters in general, indicating that foreign firms in Thailand slowed Thailand's shift from North American and European to Asian markets through 1990. If the pattern of heavy dependence on home markets and the high export propensities in firms from the NIEs continue, the recent and dramatic increase in FDI from the NIEs suggests that NIE firms will soon stimulate a more marked shift to Asian markets.[22]

In this respect, data on Japanese and US affiliates are useful because they provide a more reliable picture of how export performance has changed over time in these two important groups (Table 5.8).[23] Because recent Japanese data are available only for 1988 and 1992, it is impossible to make direct comparisons with the BOI data, but both Japanese and US figures for total nonoil manufacturing appear broadly consistent with those from the BOI surveys in suggesting a dramatic increase of exports by Japanese firms from 1983 to 1988 (42% annually in nominal United States dollars) and in both Japanese and US firms from 1988 to 1992 (annual rates of 44% and 30%, respectively). The export and sales estimates in these data sets appear similar for Japanese firms, although BOI-based estimates are somewhat lower for US firms.[24] The Japanese and US data also suggest a

---

[22] Note that the share of the NIEs in cumulative FDI flows from 1970 forward increased from 20% at year-end 1987 to 24% in 1988 and remained at 23–24% in 1989–93 (Bank of Thailand 1983, 1986–94).

[23] The Japanese data are also plagued by coverage problems, however, with notably low reply rates in more recent years; hence, estimates for 1983, 1988, and 1992 are often extrapolations based on small samples (Table 5.8). The US data are perhaps more reliable in this respect because the US survey is legally mandatory and the US Department of Commerce attempts to adjust for changes in response rates before publishing the data. On the other hand, the US data have the drawback of covering only export sales for majority-owned affiliates.

[24] The BOI-based estimate of Japanese exports in 1990 (US$2.5 billion) is between the Japanese estimates for 1988 (US$1.2 billion) and 1992 (US$5.1 billion). The US export figures are not disclosed for 1990, but the BOI-based estimate of total sales by North American firms is somewhat below US estimates for US firms in Thailand in that year. Figures on total exports and total export–sales ratios in Table 5.7 imply that total sales of North American firms amounted to US$2.0 billion, whereas US estimates for US firms alone were US$2.6 billion for majority-owned affiliates and US$3.2 billion for all affiliates (US Department of Commerce 1993).

Table 5.8. Trade indicators for Japanese and US affiliates in Thailand.

Variable, industry [a]	All Japanese affiliates					Majority-owned US affiliates			
	1974	1977	1983	1988	1992	1977	1983	1988	1992
Exports (US$ millions) [b]									
All industries	NA	NA	934	3 268	7 255	104	416	831	2 170
Nonoil manufacturing	38	164	203	1 174	5 087	NA	NA	639	1 844
Nonelectric machinery	NA	NA	NA	55	NA	0	0	NA	NA
Electric machinery	NA	NA	NA	422	NA	NA	249	NA	NA
Transport machinery	0	1	NA	108	NA	0	0	0	0
Shares of Thai exports (%) [b]									
All industries	NA	NA	15	20	22	3	7	5	7
Nonoil manufacturing	3	8	5	10	22	NA	NA	5	8
Nonelectric machinery	NA	NA	NA	6	NA	0	0	NA	NA
Electric machinery	NA	NA	NA	29	NA	NA	83	NA	NA
Transport machinery	11	18	NA	64	NA	0	0	0	0
Exports to home economy (US$ millions) [b]									
All industries	NA	NA	475	1 699	4 114	NA	NA	465	804
Nonoil manufacturing	8	25	40	460	2 426	NA	NA	361	NA
Nonelectric machinery	NA	NA	NA	53	NA	0	0	NA	NA
Electric machinery	NA	NA	NA	173	NA	NA	NA	330	387
Transport machinery	0	0	NA	8	NA	0	0	0	0
Shares of Thai exports to home economy (%) [b]									
All industries	NA	NA	49	67	72	NA	NA	15	11
Nonoil manufacturing	3	NA	9	32	57	NA	NA	13	NA
Nonelectric machinery	NA	NA	NA	45	NA	NA	0	NA	NA
Electric machinery	NA	NA	NA	109	NA	NA	NA	134	37
Transport machinery	0	NA	NA	64	NA	NA	0	0	0
Imports (US$ millions) [c]									
Nonoil manufacturing	238	441	461	1 416	2 286	NA	NA	NA	NA
Nonelectric machinery	NA	NA	NA	26	51	NA	NA	NA	NA
Electric machinery	NA	NA	71	403	830	NA	NA	NA	NA
Transport machinery	80	160	168	444	1 061	NA	NA	NA	NA
Imports from home economy (US$ millions) [c]									
All industries	NA	NA	NA	NA	NA	75	318	398	832
Nonoil manufacturing	185	309	331	929	1 839	49	186	327	558
Nonelectric machinery	NA	NA	NA	26	41	0	0	NA	NA
Electric machinery	NA	NA	55	193	584	NA	NA	290	169
Transport machinery	78	155	136	380	1 005	0	0	0	0

Source: Japanese Chamber of Commerce (1978, 1981, 1984, 1990, 1994), United States Department of Commerce (1981, 1986, 1991, 1994), IMF (1980–93), and ANU (1995).

Note: NA, not available.

[a] For Japanese firms in 1974, 1977, and 1983, transport machinery refers to automobiles only.

[b] For Japanese firms in 1983, 1988, and 1992, estimates are for all Japanese firms, based on a sample of replying firms.

[c] For Japanese firms in 1983, 1988, and 1992, estimates are for a sample of replying firms only, not estimates for all firms.

smoother increase in exports before 1986.[25] Despite differences among data sources, it appears clear that Japanese exports grew much more slowly in 1977–83 than in previous or later periods, which is consistent with the slow export growth in the early 1980s indicated by the BOI data. The BOI data are also consistent with the Japanese and US data in suggesting that, first, Japanese and US firms, especially in electric and computing machinery, have become the two largest groups of exporters in recent years; second, US-firm exports have been much more heavily concentrated in electric and computing machinery than Japanese-firm exports; and, third, export–sales ratios have tended to be higher in US firms, largely as a result of the high concentration of activity in the highly export oriented electric- and computing-machinery industry.[26]

Of most interest here, however, is the fact that the Japanese and US data also reveal a strong focus on home-economy markets, with the home economy taking 51–57% of all Japanese-firm exports in 1983, 1988, and 1992 and 56% of US-firm exports in 1988 and 37% in 1992 (Table 5.8). In nonoil manufacturing, home-country shares were markedly smaller for Japanese firms in 1983, 20%, but these shares increased rapidly to 39% in 1988 and 48% in 1992. For US firms, the home-country share was identical in nonoil manufacturing and all industries in 1988. For Japanese nonoil manufacturing firms in 1988, home-country shares were particularly large in metals and nonelectric machinery and slightly above the nonoil manufacturing average in electric machinery. Thus, these figures are again consistent with the BOI numbers in suggesting a heavy dependence on the home market. Correspondingly, shares of Thai exports to the home economy tended to be markedly larger than shares of total Thai exports.

On the import side, information is more limited, but several trends are of note (Table 5.8). First, for Japanese firms, imports exceeded exports by a very wide margin in the 1970s, but by the early 1990s, exports exceeded imports. The decline in the ratio of imports to exports was even more pronounced in terms of trade with the home economy.[27] Second, for Japanese firms, imports were more diversified than exports across industries, and affiliates in transport machinery were the largest importers for most years. Third, trade with Japan accounted for a far larger portion of imports than of exports, with the large amount of imports by transport-machinery firms being conspicuous. In contrast, US firms' imports from the United States, like exports, are highly concentrated in electric and nonelectric machinery, although the figure for nonelectric machinery is again not disclosed.

Thus, these figures reinforce the observation of high dependence on the home market and further suggest that dependence on the home market for exports has risen markedly for Japanese firms and declined for US firms. Thus, in a dynamic sense, it appears that Japanese firms have contributed to the growth of intraregional exports from Thailand, at least to the extent that they have exported more to the home economy in recent years. The decline in US-firm dependence on the US market is also thought to be related to increased reliance on Asian markets, especially Singapore, a point elaborated later.

---

[25] For example, in 1977–83, exports of Japanese firms in nonoil manufacturing grew 4% annually, whereas exports of US firms in all industries (most of which were from nonoil manufacturing) grew 26% annually (Table 5.8), compared with an estimated −11% annual growth for all BOI-promoted firms in 1979–84 (Table 5.3). The growth rate for promoted foreign firms in 1979–86, 9%, is more in line with the Japanese and US data.

[26] Using data for surveyed Japanese firms only (note that the data for 1983, 1988, and 1992 in Table 5.8 are extrapolations from these figures), one finds that exports of electric-machinery and nonelectric-machinery firms amounted to US$2.0 billion, or 75% of the exports of all surveyed firms in nonoil manufacturing (Japanese Chamber of Commerce 1994). The US export figures in these industries are not disclosed for 1992, but total sales amounted to US$1.7 billion; the assumption of a low export–sales ratio of 95% for these industries implies that they accounted for 93% of all nonoil manufacturing exports (Table 5.8). Note that the category of OCM probably accounts for virtually all nonelectric machinery for US firms and most of this category for Japanese firms.

[27] For example, in nonoil manufacturing, import–export ratios were 6.3 in 1974 (Table 5.8) but declined to 1.7 in 1988 and 0.9 in 1992 if data on surveyed firms only are used (estimates of total imports are not available for later years; see Table 5.8 for sources). Similar ratios for trade with Japan fell even more, from 23.1 in 1974 to 2.8 in 1988 and 1.5 in 1992.

Intrafirm trade in foreign firms in selected machinery industries

In addition to examining the role of foreign firms in trade, this study also examines the extent to which the expansion of intraregional trade may be due to the growth of intrafirm trade. Unfortunately, no known source of data exists for intrafirm trade by firms in Thailand, with the exception of the sparse information in the US surveys on US firms in Thailand, much of which is not disclosed for confidentiality reasons. Hence, in the summer and fall of 1994, a survey of foreign firms in electric and computing machinery and automobiles (including parts and motorcycles) was undertaken with the primary aim of ascertaining the scope of intrafirm trade in the surveyed firms. Questionnaires were sent out to more than 200 firms from Japan, the United States, and the NIEs, and 29 firms provided at least part of the information requested. It was then possible to arrange follow-up interviews with 25 of these firms. Although the original intent was to limit the focus to the industries listed above, an attempt was also made to cover all the affiliates of multiproduct parents in these industries, with the result that a few affiliates in the other nonelectric-machinery category, mainly the manufacture of consumer goods, such as air conditioners, refrigerators, compressors, and related items, also got into the sample. Unfortunately, without the ability to vigorously elicit a larger response, this survey was by no means comprehensive, nor can it be considered representative of foreign firms in these industries, as comparison with the BOI data for 1990 earlier (Tables 5.3, 5.4, and 5.7) quickly reveals. On the other hand, a few of the major firms operating in these industries in Thailand did respond, making the results of some interest.

Table 5.9 summarizes the sales and purchases of sample firms. Reflecting the pattern of investment in these industries, the sample is dominated by Japanese firms, 5 in other nonelectric machinery, 13 in electric and computing machinery, and 6 in transport machinery. Note, however, that Japanese firms dominate this sample to a far greater degree than they did these industries as a whole. Also, four NIE firms and one US firm were in the electric- and computing-machinery sample, US firms are thus underrepresented in the sample. Almost 50% of the firms (14 of 29) were small in terms of sales; a little more than 30% of the firms (9 of 29) were large or very large; and the remainder fell in between. The sample does reflect the nature of Thai industry because the firms surveyed, especially those in electric and computing machinery and other nonelectric machinery, were concentrated in parts assembly and simple consumer products. However, a large variation occurs across firms in the sophistication of operations, with some firms simply assembling imported parts but other firms making most of their parts in house or buying them from related firms in Thailand.

Of the responding firms, 27 provided detailed information on sales; 25, on purchases. Most of the firms provided information for the calendar or fiscal year 1993, but a few of the firms provided 1992 data or estimates for 1994. Comparisons of the export numbers for this sample and the BOI figures for 1990 in Table 5.7 indicate that surveyed firms accounted for a substantial portion of exports by Japanese firms in other nonelectric machinery and electric and computing machinery but a much smaller portion in automobiles. Coverage in value terms was also very poor for NIE firms, but the single US firm in the sample is a giant that single-handedly accounts for most US-firm exports from Thailand.

Among the sampled firms, exports were by far largest in Japanese firms and in the US firm in electric and computing machinery; ratios of total exports to total sales were extremely high for all groups of firms in this industry (Table 5.9). Exports to the home region were rather small in this sample, however, with Japanese and NIE firms sending most, by far, of their exports to North America or other regions (primarily Europe) and with the US firm sending the bulk of its exports to Hong Kong or Singapore. Export–sales ratios were also rather high for Japanese firms in other nonelectric machinery, with most of these exports also going to Hong Kong or Singapore. On the other hand, exports from the automobile firms were very small relative to total sales. On the purchase side, the reliance on foreign markets was also high but not quite as high as on the sales side in all groups except the NIE firms. As observed previously, Japanese firms had a strong tendency to source their imports from the home country. The NIE firms also sourced most of their imports from

Table 5.9. Sales and purchases (US$ millions) by market in sample firms, 1992–94.

Variable, firm distribution	Sample total	Other nonelectric machinery (Japanese firms)	Electric and computing machinery			Automobiles, parts, motorcycles (Japanese firms)
			Japanese firms	US firms	NIE firms	
Total sales	3 875	266	1 802	1 356	46	407
Local sales	672	93	167	0	12	401
Export sales	3 203	173	1 635	1 356	34	6
Sales per firm, avg.	134	53	139	1 356	12	68
Sales per firm, SD	259	43	135	NA	4	96
Firms 2–24	14	2	4	0	4	4
Firms 31–101	6	3	3	0	0	0
Firms 141–378	8	0	6	0	0	2
Firms 1 356	1	0	0	1	0	0
Sample size (*n*)	29	5	13	1	4	6
Total sales	3 597	247	1 541	1 356	46	407
Local sales	665	85	167	0	12	401
Export sales	2 932	162	1 374	1 356	34	6
Japan	345	57	286	0	0	2
Hong Kong, Singapore	1 388	94	259	1 024	12	0
Other Asia	80	6	69	0	0	4
North America	774	0	432	321	20	0
Other regions	345	5	328	11	2	0
Sales, intrafirm	3 383	246	1 330	1 356	44	407
Local sales	524	84	28	0	11	400
Export sales	2 859	162	1 302	1 356	33	7
Japan	339	57	281	0	0	2
Hong Kong, Singapore	1 357	94	228	1 024	12	0
Other Asia	61	6	50	0	0	5
North America	773	0	432	321	20	0
Other regions	329	5	311	11	1	0
Sample size (*n*)	27	4	12	1	4	6
Total purchases	2 464	213	774	1 192	26	260
Local purchases	669	104	210	238	4	114
Import purchases	1 795	109	564	954	22	146
Japan	686	72	430	36	3	146
Hong Kong, Singapore	730	16	113	596	5	0
Other Asia	60	21	13	12	14	0
North America	302	0	4	298	0	0
Other regions	17	0	4	12	0	0
Purchases, intrafirm	2 148	213	498	1 192	14	231
Local purchases	467	104	39	238	1	85
Import purchases	1 681	109	459	954	13	146
Japan	644	72	390	36	1	146
Hong Kong, Singapore	675	16	59	596	4	0
Other Asia	43	21	2	12	8	0
North America	302	0	4	298	0	0
Other regions	17	0	4	12	0	0
Sample size (*n*)	25	4	11	1	4	5
Addendum, total sales	3 324	247	1 271	1 356	46	404

Source: Author's field survey, summer–fall 1994.
Note: avg., average; NA, not available; NIE, newly industrialized economy; SD, standard deviation.

the home region (Hong Kong–Singapore or Other Asia), but the US firm sourced most of its imports from Hong Kong or Singapore and then from the home economy.

Perhaps the most interesting result obtained from this survey is that the vast majority of sales and purchases by sample firms were intrafirm transactions, conducted with parent firms or other ownership-related firms.[28] For example, intrafirm transactions accounted for 98% of all export sales and 94% of all import purchases by the reporting firms. Perhaps more surprising, however, is the fact that reliance on intrafirm transactions was also very great for transactions in the local market: 78% in sales and 70% in purchases. On the one hand, high levels of intrafirm transaction were not

Table 5.10. Intrafirm shares of total sales and total purchases by direction and associated frequency distributions.

Destination mean, sample SD, frequency distribution	Sample total	Other nonelectric machinery (Japanese firms)	Electric and computing machinery			Automobiles, parts, motorcycles (Japanese firms)
			Japanese firms	US firms	NIE firms	
World, mean	88.57	84.08	81.03	100.00	97.40	98.88
World, SD	24.49	31.85	31.03	NA	5.20	2.76
Firms 18.18–36.32	3	1	2	0	0	0
Firms 61.16–95.00	5	0	3	0	1	1
Firms 100.00	19	3	7	1	3	5
Thailand, mean	28.70	38.52	1.56	0.00	24.14	84.29
Thailand, SD	40.64	34.62	2.43	NA	48.28	26.86
Firms 0.00–36.04	20	3	12	1	3	1
Firms 75.69–100.00	7	1	0	0	1	5
Japan, mean	18.20	15.42	30.56	0.02	0.00	10.50
Japan, SD	29.33	22.71	35.20	NA	0.00	25.72
Firms 0.00–33.10	22	3	9	1	4	5
Firms 48.38–63.00	3	1	1	0	0	1
Firms 95.00–100.00	2	0	2	0	0	0
Hong Kong – Singapore, mean	20.83	26.03	21.48	75.51	31.25	0.00
Hong Kong – Singapore, SD	29.25	22.86	26.65	NA	47.32	0.00
Firms 0.00–30.00	21	2	10	0	3	6
Firms 40.69–64.60	3	2	1	0	0	0
Firms 75.50–100.00	3	0	1	1	1	0
Other Asia, mean	2.71	2.71	3.12	0.00	0.09	4.09
Other Asia, SD	4.86	2.75	5.32	NA	0.18	6.82
Firms 0.00–18.00	27	4	12	1	4	6
North America, mean	13.13	0.00	14.17	23.66	40.19	0.00
North America, SD	23.90	0.00	19.35	NA	44.53	0.00
Firms 0.00–23.67	22	4	9	1	2	6
Firms 41.00–49.79	3	0	3	0	0	0
Firms 75.00–82.30	2	0	0	0	2	0
Other regions, mean	5.01	1.40	10.15	0.81	1.74	0.00
Other regions, SD	10.11	1.93	13.58	NA	3.48	0.00
Firms 0.00–28.20	26	4	11	1	4	6
Firms 40.62	1	0	1	0	0	0
Sample size (n)	27	4	12	1	4	6

(continued)

---

[28] In the survey, a distinction was made between sales to parent firms and sales to other related firms. However, because it is difficult and perhaps meaningless to distinguish between parents and related firms when there are multiple owners related to each other, a phenomenon not uncommon in this sample, this distinction is not made in the analysis.

Table 5.10 concluded.

Source mean, sample SD, frequency distribution	Sample total	Other nonelectric machinery (Japanese firms)	Electric and computing machinery			Automobiles, parts, motorcycles (Japanese firms)
			Japanese firms	US firms	NIE firms	
World, mean	73.35	94.51	62.98	100.00	65.58	84.27
World, SD	31.92	10.98	34.55	NA	40.77	22.82
Firms 0.00–42.24	6	0	4	0	2	0
Firms 48.90–88.89	8	1	5	0	0	2
Firms 100.00	13	3	4	1	2	3
Thailand, mean	15.52	38.11	10.04	20.00	6.84	17.71
Thailand, SD	22.64	28.18	22.11	NA	9.18	22.63
Firms 0.00–33.61	23	2	12	1	4	4
Firms 54.25–60.17	3	2	0	0	0	1
Firms 79.80	1	0	1	0	0	0
Japan, mean	41.01	43.37	45.78	3.00	2.31	65.27
Japan, SD	30.79	24.31	30.18	NA	2.98	17.50
Firms 0.00–39.15	14	2	7	1	4	0
Firms 42.24–67.80	6	1	2	0	0	3
Firms 72.15–100.00	7	1	4	0	0	2
Hong Kong – Singapore, mean	7.85	5.91	3.57	50.00	22.97	0.00
Hong Kong – Singapore, SD	15.41	4.78	5.35	NA	28.90	0.00
Firms 0.00–31.90	25	4	13	0	3	5
Firms 50.00–60.0	2	0	0	1	1	0
Other Asia, mean	5.38	7.01	0.19	1.00	28.37	0.07
Other Asian, SD	17.19	9.14	0.58	NA	39.97	0.16
Firms 0.00–19.86	26	4	13	1	3	5
Firms 87.50	1	0	0	0	1	0
North America, mean	2.09	0.05	1.63	25.00	2.50	0.00
North America, SD	6.26	0.10	5.60	NA	5.00	0.00
Firms 0.00–25.00	27	4	13	1	4	5
Other regions, mean	1.50	0.06	1.76	1.00	2.59	1.22
Other regions, SD	4.81	0.07	6.31	NA	5.17	2.72
Firms 0.00–22.75	27	4	13	1	4	5
Sample size (n)	27	4	13	1	4	5

Source: Author's field survey, summer–fall 1994.
Note: NA, not available; NIE, newly industrialized economy; SD, standard deviation.

uncommon in these machinery industries, but on the other hand, it is also clear that these were unusually high ratios, even given the industries involved.[29]

Moreover, the distributions in Table 5.10 make it clear that many of the firms in the sample depend heavily on intrafirm transactions. Indeed, 70% of the firms (19 of 27) relied exclusively on intrafirm transactions on the sales side, and almost 50% of the firms (13 of 27) purchased all of their intermediate inputs through intrafirm networks.[30] At the other extreme, only three firms reported low dependence on intrafirm transactions on the sales side, and six firms reported low reliance on the purchase side. Most firms with low dependence on intrafirm transactions were Japanese firms in electric and computing machinery.

[29] For example, for Asian affiliates of Japanese firms in 1992, intrafirm shares of sales flows in nonelectric machinery were 3% for local sales, 97% for exports to Japan, and 71% for other exports, in electric machinery these shares were 8%, 90%, and 56%, respectively, and in transport machinery they were 7%, 74%, and 60%, respectively (Government of Japan 1994a). See footnote 1 for ratios for all manufacturing.

[30] Note that the sample for purchase ratios is larger than for purchase amounts (Table 5.9) because some firms reported shares of total purchases but not the amount of purchases.

If sales and purchases are further broken down by direction, some additional patterns of inter-est emerge. First, ratios of intrafirm transactions in specific markets to total sales and total purchases were in general much lower than ratios covering all markets. In other words, although reliance on intrafirm transactions is extremely high, the markets were often diversified geographically on both the sales and purchase sides.

Second, the Thai market was the market in which intrafirm transactions were most often reported as accounting for moderate or large shares of total sales (seven firms). As might be expected from the heavy local orientation of the Thai automobile industry, five of these seven firms were Japanese firms. Hong Kong or Singapore, or both, were the markets second most often identified in this way (six firms), followed by Japan and North America (five firms each). Of 22 Japanese firms, 5 reported moderate to high dependence on intrafirm sales in Japan, and 1 of 4 NIE firms reported high dependence on Hong Kong or Singapore, or both. The large US firm reported selling most of its output in Hong Kong or Singapore, not the home market, but the magnitude of such sales was so great that a large portion was undoubtably shipped to other markets from Hong Kong or Singapore, probably including a portion destined for the home market.

Third, on the purchase side, Japan was the only market for which more than four firms reported high or moderate dependence on intrafirm transactions. Moreover, all of the 13 firms reporting mod-erate or high ratios of intrafirm purchases from Japan to total purchases were Japanese firms. Although this sample does not contain enough firms from other countries to make rigorous com-parisons, this pattern is consistent with the observation made earlier that Japanese firms tended to depend heavily on the Japanese market on the import side and further implies that a large portion of these imports came through intrafirm channels.

It is interesting to note that these firms shared many of the characteristics that have previously been shown to be associated with high export propensities in Thailand (see earlier). First, most firms in the sample were labour intensive, with 21 firms having total assets per employee of less than US\$77 442. Corresponding figures in two of the automobile firms were more than US\$32 5962.[31] Second, the vast majority of the surveyed firms (22) were new, having been founded after the FDI boom began in 1988. Third, the vast majority of the firms (26) were BOI promoted. Fourth, most of the firms had high foreign-ownership ratios, with foreign-ownership shares exceeding 90% in 17 firms; automobile firms were an exception, with four of the six firms reporting minority-ownership shares.[32] In contrast, and again consistent with the results of previous research, average labour pro-ductivity and compensation per employee varied widely among sample firms.[33]

In addition to inquiring about intrafirm trade and related firm characteristics, follow-up inter-views with 25 firms also sought to find out which policy issues most concerned the sample firms (Table 5.11). Of the 10 sets of policy issues investigated, the only set of issues identified as a mod-erate or large problem by most of the respondents was import regulations. Because many of the BOI-promoted firms have been granted exemptions from import duties and because import duties have recently declined for a wide range of imports in Thailand, levels of import duties or quotas were not an issue for a number of these firms. Rather, most firms citing this problem were more concerned with the lack of transparency in the way duties were assessed and with BOI regulations on how much

---

[31] Note also that most of the firms in the sample employed substantial portions of skilled or semiskilled workers, with ratios of skilled workers to all workers exceeding 20% in 14 firms and ratios of semiskilled workers to all workers exceeding 44% in 16 firms.

[32] Note also that more than 40% of the firms (12 of 29) had more than one foreign parent, and almost 25% of the firms (7 of 29) were at least partially owned by another foreign-owned Thai firm. About 50% of the firms (14 of 29) also had local joint-venture partners. In the locally oriented automobile industry, this was partially due to restrictions on foreign-ownership shares, but in more export-oriented industries these restrictions were a much smaller factor. Recall that the BOI often exempts firms with high export propensities from ownership restrictions.

[33] Net sales (total sales less total purchases) per employee were less than US\$13 911 in nine firms, between US\$16 586 and US\$21 626 in seven firms, between US\$24 944 and US\$36 669 in seven firms, and more than US\$51 689 in two firms. Compensation per employee was less than US\$3 541 in seven firms, between US\$4 018 and US\$5 065 in seven firms, between US\$5 841 and US\$6 401 in seven firms, and more than US\$7 192 in four firms.

Table 5.11. Policy issues by degree of problem presented for 25 firms.

Policy issue, firm distribution	Sample total	Other nonelectric machinery (Japanese firms)	Electric and computing machinery			Automobiles, parts, motorcycles (Japanese firms)
			Japanese firms	US firms	NIE firms	
Export requirements						
No or small problem	24	4	11	1	4	4
Moderate or large problem	1	1	0	0	0	0
Import regulations						
No or small problem	10	1	2	1	2	4
Moderate or large problem	15	4	9	0	2	0
Local content regulations						
No or small problem	22	4	11	1	4	2
Moderate or large problem	3	1	0	0	0	2
Regulations on corporate finance						
No or small problem	23	5	10	1	3	4
Moderate or large problem	2	0	1	0	1	0
Regulations on corporate ownership						
No or small problem	23	4	10	1	4	4
Moderate or large problem	2	1	1	0	0	0
Regulations on foreign-exchange transactions						
No or small problem	23	5	11	1	4	2
Moderate or large problem	2	0	0	0	0	2
Taxation						
No or small problem	25	5	11	1	4	4
Moderate or large problem	0	0	0	0	0	0
Regulations on local management participation						
No or small problem	24	4	11	1	4	4
Moderate or large problem	1	1	0	0	0	0
Difficulties securing labour supply						
No or small problem	16	3	6	1	4	2
Moderate or large problem	9	2	5	0	0	2
Infrastructure bottlenecks						
No or small problem	19	5	6	1	4	3
Moderate or large problem	6	0	5	0	0	1

Source: Author's field survey, summer–fall 1994.
Note: NIE, newly industrialized economy.

and when duty-exempt items could be imported. On the other hand, a few firms also complained about high duties on intermediate goods, combined with recent declines of tariffs on competing final goods. None of the automobile firms reported moderate or large problems in this area, but 15 of the 21 firms among the more trade-oriented firms in other nonelectric, computing, and electric machinery thought related problems were moderate or large.

The only other two categories cited as a moderate or large problem by more than three firms were infrastructure bottlenecks and difficulties in securing labour supplies. The latter problem was cited by nine firms, but none of these respondents saw this as a large problem, and most commentators reflected a degree of resignation, tending to view the problem as an inescapable result of rapid Thai growth. Because all of the firms interviewed were in the greater Bangkok area, Bangkok's infamous traffic problems were often cited among infrastructure bottlenecks, as were a wide range of other issues concentrated in transport and communications, by the six firms reporting this to be a moderate or large problem. Perhaps most significant, however, is that 16 or more of the 25 firms interviewed felt that aside from import regulations, the remaining nine sets of issues, labour supply and infrastructure concerns included, presented no problem at all.

In previous research (Naya and Ramstetter 1992; Ramstetter 1994c), I suggested that trade restrictions harm multinationals more than nonmultinationals because trade restrictions deprive multinationals of the opportunity to fully use marketing-related intangible assets, which are often a source of their competitiveness. These responses suggest a possible corollary, that trade restrictions hurt trade-oriented multinationals more than they do local-market-oriented multinationals. Although the small sample used in this survey certainly cannot be used to rigorously test the importance of trade restrictions among different groups of firms, this and previous evidence regarding the importance of trade restrictions to multinationals is substantial enough to warrant further efforts to clarify the extent to which different groups of firms are affected by trade restrictions.

Conclusion

This chapter reviewed changes in trade structure and direction, the role of multinationals in Thai trade, especially exports, and finally the results of a small survey of intrafirm trade in the other nonelectric-machinery, electric- and computing-machinery, and automobile industries. Thailand's trade structure was seen to have changed dramatically over the last two decades, with marked increases in the export shares of OCM and electric machinery in recent years being of particular note. On the other hand, changes in the direction of Thai trade have been far less dramatic, with only small increases in intraregional shares of trade having been observed. Multinational firms were seen to have played an increasing role in Thai trade and to have dominated the most rapidly growing export industries, OCM and electric machinery. Multinational firms were also seen to rely heavily on their home markets in many cases, suggesting that to the extent FDI has increasingly come from intraregional sources in Thailand (mainly Japan and the NIEs), multinational firms may be contributing to the increased regionalization of Thailand's trade. The survey results then suggested that the majority of the transactions by firms in the surveyed industries were made through intrafirm channels, even when those transactions were confined to the local market. Patterns of disproportionate dependence on home markets were also observed in this sample, especially for Japanese firms importing from Japan. The characteristics of surveyed firms also suggest that they were in many ways typical of firms that previous research suggested would have high export dependence. Finally, out of 10 sets of policy issues, import regulations were the only set viewed as a moderate or major problem by most of the surveyed firms.

In many ways, these findings raise more questions than they answer. For example, one would ideally want to look in more detail at how the direction of trade in multinationals changes over time. Because the 1990 data represent the first attempt at a census of BOI-promoted firms, a similar effort in 1997, for example, could be extremely enlightening. Second, if one could also include information on intrafirm trade in a future census, it might then be possible to model the determinants of intrafirm trade–sales ratios in a manner similar to that of previous models of the determinants of overall import and export propensities (Ramstetter 1994a, c) and thereby ascertain which firm-level characteristics are correlated with the degree of dependence on intrafirm trade. Third, and perhaps most important, a lot remains to be done in the policy arena. The results of the interviews presented here are suggestive at best, and it would be very helpful to undertake a large-scale survey of firms, both foreign and local, in Thailand to ascertain just what policy issues are of major concern to the corporate world there and how they relate to other firm-level characteristics, including the shares of intrafirm and intraregional trade.

Chapter 6

MALAYSIA

Electronics, Automobiles, and the Trade–Investment Nexus

Sieh Lee Mei Ling and
Yew Siew Yong

In many ways, Malaysia's economic development differs little from that of other developing countries. Although initially Malaysia's economic structure was heavily dependent on commodities exports, it has diversified since independence in 1957. Transformation of the industrial base was driven, first, by a period of import-substitution industrialization, during which imports of consumer goods were reduced and natural-resource processing was increased. Subsequently, in the early 1970s, policy shifted to a growth-with-equity export orientation, which was unique to Malaysia's own socio-economic and political circumstances. Trade policies were promoted with fiscal incentives; export-processing and free-trade zones were created to attract foreign investment in particular.

A combination of commodity price shocks and fiscal imbalances in the mid-1980s required major adjustment and liberalization, in which state intervention in the economy was reduced. High rates of economic growth were restored; indeed, industrialization has since proceeded at such rapid rates that Malaysia now faces labour shortages and infrastructural bottlenecks. In the 1990s, during which Malaysia's economic structure has been transformed, investment attracted from abroad has changed. Malaysia's Vision 2020, of attaining developed-country status by the year 2020, includes a policy set that addresses shortages of factors and other constraints to development.

Foreign direct investment (FDI) has played a particularly important role in Malaysia's transformation. Early attempts to attract FDI were made in the electrical and electronics industries to absorb domestic labour. Major producers initially attracted were Matsushita, Sanyo, Toshiba, and Philips. By the mid-1990s, the industrial distribution of FDI has diversified, and the reasons for investing have also changed. Nearly all the major names in electronics have a presence in Malaysia, and their activities are trade creating, that is, they induce significant quantities of exports and imports. The surge in foreign investment has also led to rapid growth of employment and output in the manufacturing sector. In the same period, the manufacturing sector, which accounted for nearly 32% of the gross domestic product in 1994, registered average annual growth of 14.1% and accounted for 78.2% of total exports.

This study intends to examine the trade ties of investing firms and thus to understand the role that foreign firms play in the region's integration. In the first section, we assess the industrial distributions of Malaysia's overall trade flows and stocks of FDI. In the second, primary data from a firm-level survey are presented to throw light on intrafirm trade in two major industries: the electronics and electrical-machinery and the automotive industries. Personal interviews were conducted with personnel in responsible positions at a number of firms and administered using a prepared questionnaire. In the third section, we examine the implications of the survey findings. In the fourth section, sources of capital and policy concerns are surveyed. Overall conclusions and policy recommendations are reported in the final section.

Studies of foreign firms' behaviour in Malaysia are few. Lim and Pang (1991) studied electronics and automobile firms, noting the desirability of developing local links in both. Salleh (1995) interviewed 11 electrical and electronics firms to evaluate intraindustry linkages between multinational enterprises (MNEs) and local enterprises and how these might be improved. Chen (1995a) interviewed a number of Taiwanese firms; most were small and medium-sized enterprises (SMEs) that source 40% of their inputs from Taiwan and behave like extensions of industrial operations in the home economy.

Policy environment and recent trends in FDI and trade

Before independence, FDI inflows to Malaysia were concentrated in the primary sector. Between independence and the late 1960s, FDI was channeled into import-substitution industries. In the 1970s and early 1980s, Vernon's product cycle (Vernon 1966) appeared to explain the behaviour of FDI in Malaysia because foreign producers used the low-cost Malaysian base to produce standard-technology exports, formerly produced at home, for developed-country markets. After 1986, both the sources of FDI flows and the target industries changed. Ownership advantages extended beyond process technologies used in local production to embrace those of coordination and greater division of labour as firms developed globalization strategies. As this occurred, firms depended more heavily on trade to link the more highly divided and geographically dispersed, albeit well-coordinated, production subprocesses to reap the benefits of international division of labour in performing production tasks.

Malaysia successfully exploited its locational advantages, including those of its domestic market, its factors of production, such key intangibles as preferential trade status under the Generalized System of Preferences (GSP), macroeconomic stability, its liberal trade regime, and the attractiveness of such attributes of its business environment as development of local suppliers and investment in infrastructure. Investment in industrial upgrading is encouraged through fiscal incentives to promote investment in research and development (R&D) facilities and in human capital, such as scientific personnel and engineers. Other policies, such as the Ministry of Trade and Industry's (MITI) subcontract-exchange scheme, established in 1986, attempt to draw local suppliers into the production networks of foreign firms through a computerized clearing house of buyers' requirements and vendors' capabilities.

Recent trends in the industrial distribution of FDI inflows (Table 6.1) and in the sources of FDI (Table 6.2) illustrate how both have diversified since 1986. Two strong trends have emerged. First, Japan is the largest source of investment, followed by Singapore. Other Asian investors, particularly Taiwan, have become significant sources. Asian investors have tended to bring smaller-scale operations to Malaysia. Second, the share of investment in electrical and electronic products grew from almost nothing to 39% of all nonoil investment. By 1994, these industries accounted for about 44% of total manufacturing output and 72% of the sector's export earnings (electronics and electrical products were the single largest foreign-exchange earner), an increase from 26% and 19%, respectively, in 1970.

By 1987, Malaysia had become one of the world's largest exporters of semiconductors, being the third largest producer, after Japan and the United States. Malaysia is also the world's largest exporter of room air conditioners and second largest exporter of videocassette recorders (VCRs). Foreign investors began to venture downstream into the production of intermediate products and component parts and the provision of ancillary services, thus forging linkages between domestic and foreign firms while providing substantial demand for locally produced inputs. Thus, SMEs have also begun to establish themselves.

Table 6.1. Gross FDI inflows by sector, 1986–94 (RM millions).

Sector	1986	1987	1988	1989	1990	1991	1992	1993	1994
Nonoil sector	1457	2123	2324	4067	5438	9857	12660	14651	16859
Manufacturing [a]	1357	2023	2119	3824	5102	8330	10467	11972	14951
Electrical and electronic products	96	761	504	1266	1429	1399	796	3592	6578
Petroleum and coal	704	0	0	99	781	1250	6908	0	314
Chemicals and chemical products	107	423	451	543	622	1058	900	3520	1959
Basic metal products	20	81	267	195	1311	1641	461	1497	613
Textiles and textile products	26	55	104	226	255	200	681	910	1630
Property [a]	—	—	101	119	252	1074	1531	2392	1711
Agriculture [a]	100	100	104	124	84	453	662	287	197
Oil sector	1648	1655	1675	2041	2528	2881	2910	3233	3020
Total	3105	3778	3999	6108	7966	12738	15570	17884	19879

Source: Government of Malaysia (n.d.a).
Note: RM, Malaysia ringgit; FDI, foreign direct investment.
[a] Estimates.

Table 6.2. Stocks of inward FDI (% share) by source country. [a]

Source country	1986	1993
Australia	2.4	1.3
France	0.4	0.2
Hong Kong	6.1	5.0
Indonesia	1.1	0.4
Japan	25.7	32.3
Korea	0.1	1.1
Singapore	17.1	15.0
Taiwan	0.4	7.5
United Kingdom	13.0	6.5
United States	10.3	10.6

Source: MIDA (n.d.).
Note: FDI, foreign direct investment.
[a] Based on fixed-asset stocks in manufacturing.

Malaysia's intraregional trade in manufactures is summarized in Tables 6.3 and 6.4. Since 1985, the share of manufactures in total exports has replaced that of agricultural products as the largest one; since 1989, manufactures have accounted for more than half of total export earnings. During 1986–92, in line with Malaysian government measures to increase exports of higher value-added products, exports of electronics products and electrical machinery (mainly television sets, radios, and air conditioners) have grown more than fourfold, accounting for nearly 40% of total manufactured exports during the period. Nearly 50% of Malaysia's manufactured exports in 1992 were electronic components and office and computing machinery (OCM), which highlights the narrow base of Malaysia's manufactured exports.

The main markets for these exports were Europe, Singapore, and the United States. US customers were the largest buyers of Malaysian manufactured exports, accounting for nearly 50% of total exports of electronics and components in 1986. This share dropped to 30% by 1992, replaced mainly by that of Singapore, a large purchaser of components. Exports to Europe comprised mainly machinery and transport equipment, and the United Kingdom was the largest market. Other newly

Table 6.3. Malaysia's exports of manufactures by selected ISIC category, year, and partner.

Industry	Year	World totals (US$ millions)	Japan	Hong Kong	Singapore	Other NIEs	ASEAN-4	China	United States	European Community	Other
All manufacturing	1986	8 038	8	4	19	3	3	1	26	19	17
	1989	17 401	8	4	21	4	4	2	25	19	13
	1992	32 471	8	4	25	4	5	2	23	17	12
Office and computing equipment	1986	13	2	6	30	1	2	0	35	17	7
	1989	241	9	1	45	2	1	0	35	5	2
	1992	2 374	6	4	34	5	6	0	30	13	2
Electrical machinery	1986	2 988	7	6	14	2	2	0	48	18	3
	1989	6 790	7	6	22	3	2	0	40	17	3
	1992	12 688	8	5	25	3	2	0	33	17	7
Motor vehicles and parts	1986	25	26	1	42	0	4	0	8	5	14
	1989	94	2	3	16	0	2	0	4	63	10
	1992	185	3	1	15	0	3	0	3	66	9
Other industries	1986	5 057	9	2	22	4	3	1	13	20	26
	1989	10 276	9	3	20	4	6	3	14	20	21
	1992	17 224	9	4	23	5	6	3	14	18	18

Shares of world totals (%) applies to columns Japan through Other.

Source: ANU (1995).
Note: NA, not available; ASEAN-4, Indonesia, Malaysia, the Philippines, and Thailand; ISIC, International Standard Industrial Classification; NIE, newly industrialized economy.

Table 6.4. Malaysia's imports of manufactures by selected ISIC category, year, and partner.

Industry	Year	World totals (US$ millions)	Japan	Hong Kong	Singapore	Other NIEs	ASEAN-4	China	United States	European Community	Other
All manufacturing	1986	9 611	23	2	16	6	5	2	20	16	10
	1989	19 984	27	2	14	8	4	2	18	13	12
	1992	36 931	28	2	16	9	4	2	17	13	9
Office and computing equipment	1986	137	24	2	6	6	0	0	39	15	8
	1989	414	17	2	19	14	2	0	33	9	4
	1992	1 194	14	9	16	7	16	0	28	8	2
Electrical machinery	1986	2 719	22	1	16	4	6	0	38	10	3
	1989	5 281	27	2	19	9	4	0	29	8	2
	1992	10 266	29	2	25	9	3	1	20	9	2
Motor vehicles and parts	1986	370	69	0	0	4	0	0	6	4	4
	1989	1 072	72	0	0	1	0	0	5	8	8
	1992	1 410	68	0	0	2	1	0	6	17	6
Other industries	1986	6 385	20	3	17	7	5	3	13	18	14
	1989	13 217	24	3	13	9	5	3	15	15	13
	1992	24 061	26	2	13	10	4	2	15	14	14

Shares of world totals (%)

Source: ANU (1995).
Note: NA, not available; ASEAN-4, Indonesia, Malaysia, the Philippines, and Thailand; ISIC, International Standard Industrial Classification; NIE, newly industrialized economy.

industrialized economies (NIEs) and the Association of Southeast Asian Nations (ASEAN) economies were relatively insignificant markets, as was Japan.

On the import side (Table 6.4), manufactured imports also grew nearly fourfold during 1986–92. This rapid growth was the result of continued expansion of economic activity, with investment goods the fastest growing category. The sources of imports were fairly evenly spread among Europe, Japan, Singapore, and the United States. A significant point to note is that for Japan the balance of trade over the whole period was grossly in its favour. (This imbalance would have been smaller if Japanese purchases through their Singapore affiliates had shown up as Japanese purchases.) Trade volumes with Singapore comprise purchases by some Japanese-affiliated companies as intrafirm purchases by centralized buying operations through Singapore-based regional offices.

The ASEAN economies were only significant sources of imports in 1992, when they began to emerge as suppliers of electronic components. The trade pattern of these products is gradually leading to a more intraregional character, with imports from ASEAN countries leading at the expense of imports from Japan and the United States. One reason for this pattern in electrical and electronics is the integration of production on a vertical or horizontal chain through MNEs, with final assembly at export destinations or in ASEAN economies before export. A regional purchase and distribution network is emerging, with Singapore as an important link.

Trade in motor vehicles and parts is of a much smaller order. Motor-vehicle exports grew from a small base in 1986–92, in large part because direct investment was destined for projects designed to serve the domestic market. The value of motor-vehicle exports remained small. Since 1989, Proton, the national car, has been exported to Bangladesh, Brunei, Ireland, Jamaica, Nauru, New Zealand, Singapore, and the United Kingdom. Japanese imports of transport machinery were significant because of Japan's large market share and because of its participation in the national automobile project. Imported knocked-down units from Japan help to account for the disparity with exports (imports were at about 10 times exports). The other explanation, of course, is that the final products were destined mostly for domestic consumption. Moves are being made through vendor development and local content programs to reduce imported components.

In summary, three patterns are apparent from these tables: first, Malaysia's manufactured exports have a very high imported content; second, the export base is still very narrow, centred around electronic components and OCM; and, third, Malaysia's integration with the region appears to be proceeding very slowly, masked in part by Singapore's significant entrepôt role (which also explains some of the asymmetrical pattern of trade with Japan).

The firm-level survey

Primary data were obtained through a survey of the largest firms, both foreign and Malaysian owned, in the two industries. The survey took place in mid-1994 and covered 21 cities and towns, located in eight different states, including the Federal Territory of Kuala Lumpur, in Peninsular Malaysia. Difficulties expected included problems with disclosing figures, partial answers, unavailable data lodged with overseas parent companies, data sensitivity and business confidentiality, and outright refusal to participate. Eventually, usable primary data were collected from 28 respondents, comprising 18 firms in the electrical and electronics industry and 10 automobile firms. The profile of firms for which primary data were analyzed is summarized in Table 6.5.

Personal interviews were conducted with either the chief executive officer, financial controller, marketing director, or production manager, using a questionnaire that was administered in each country in the larger study. The questions were designed to collect quantitative data on sales, sourcing, and investment. Reasons, views, and other insights on business behaviour, pattern of trade, investment, and government regulations that affected the firms' activities were also probed. A total of 81 firms were contacted, that is, the top 30 from each industry, plus others from lists compiled on the basis of sales, revenue, and employment, using the 1993 Federation of Malaysian Manufacturers

Table 6.5. Profile of Malaysian firms surveyed, by country of parent firm, ownership structure, and representation in the industry.

Country of parent firm	Electrical machinery and electronics[a] (n)	Automobile[b] (n)	Total (n)
Japan	4	4	8
Malaysia	2	4	6
United States	6	0	6
Taiwan	2	0	2
Korea	0	1	1
Singapore	1	0	1
Canada	1	0	1
Germany	1	0	1
United Kingdom	0	1	1
France	1	0	1
Total	18	10	28

Source: Survey data.

[a] These firms (3 joint ventures and 15 wholly owned subsidiaries) constitute 9.6% of electrical and electronics firms, 40.9% of industry sales, and 31.6% of industry employment.

[b] These firms (7 joint ventures and 3 wholly owned subsidiaries) constitute 15.6% of automobile firms, 23.2% of industry sales, and 23.6% of industry employment.

Directory for electrical machinery and electronics and the latest Malaysian Automobile Components and Parts Manufacturers Association directory.[1]

Although the 18 electrical and electronics firms represented only 10% of the total number of firms in the industry, they were much more representative in terms of sales (41%) and employment (32%). The 10 automobile firms represented about 16% of the total number of firms in the industry but less than 25% of sales or employment, largely because of ownership being concentrated in the larger firms.

Generally, observations from the secondary data analyzed in the previous section were corroborated by the survey data. However, new evidence began to emerge when we tried to differentiate relationships with parent firms and other affiliates and arm's-length transactions with unaffiliated firms located both overseas and in Malaysia. Specifically, primary data on sales, procurement of raw materials and components, and physical capital-investment inflows permitted further analysis of the forward and backward linkages of the Malaysian operations, not only by country but also within their respective corporate groups across national boundaries.

In the analysis that follows, the trade behaviour of multinational affiliates is presented in ways that isolate industry effects, corporate nationality, and of course location. The electronics industry is analyzed first according to the variations found in sourcing and sales behaviour. This is followed by an analysis of the automobile industry.

---

[1] It should be noted that surveyed foreign firms in the electrical and electronics industry were mostly wholly owned, whereas those in the auto industry were mainly joint ventures. Given the diversity of ownership proportions, legal arrangements, and equity constraints, it was unrealistic to classify the firm by specific proportions of equity held by shareholders from various countries or nationalities. The responsibility for classifying the country of origin of parent companies rested entirely with respondents. For example, joint-venture firms with minority foreign shareholdings were classified as affiliates of their overseas parents, as reported by their management, despite the fact that they were legally defined as majority Malaysian ownership. This classification reflects the fact that parent firms have considerable control over the strategic directions of their affiliates, regardless of whether the latter are wholly owned or joint ventures with minority equity shares. Foreign involvement in nonequity agreements or sales-and-supply arrangements was not included in the ownership definitions in this study.

The electrical and electronics industry

The results of the electrical and electronics survey are presented in Table 6.6. As indicated, the sales in this industry were largely directed to foreign markets — 96.5% of the total in this sample. Local sales were minimal. This result is not surprising because most of the foreign investors were attracted to Malaysia as exporters rather than as producers for the domestic market and were often sited in free-trade zones as a matter of economic development policy. The United States and Europe were the most important destinations for electronics, mainly for semiconductors, accounting for nearly 65% of all exports of the electronics firms surveyed. This was expected because of the traditional sources of capital and technology from these two areas.

Among East Asian countries, Hong Kong, Taiwan, Singapore, and Japan ranked in descending order of importance as export destinations for computers, telecommunications components and equipment, consumer electronic products, and industrial products such as magnetic heads and semiconductor devices. Despite the major role of Japanese FDI in the electronics industry, Japan's relative unimportance as a market deserves closer attention. Japanese firms reported that as they increased global strategies to maintain competitive advantage in the industry, they forged increasingly complex links within the network of overseas affiliates, rather than with the parent companies in Japan. This relationship shows up strongly in Table 6.6, which analyzes the direction of Japanese firms' sales to third countries through intrafirm channels. In specific cases, new markets emerged for East Asian electronics firms located in Malaysia, such as the Thai market for semiconductors, cathode-ray tubes, logic and memory circuits; the Indonesian market for television tubes, computer-display monitors, and cathode-ray tubes; the market of the Philippines for electronic components and communications products; and that of China for computers, telecommunications equipment, and semiconductors. The changing pattern of electronics export sales was also forged by the rapid economic growth taking place in Southeast Asia.

The more traditional, hierarchical pattern of sales to parent firms was more marked among US and European Community (EC) affiliates. The US and EC affiliates exported 63% and 75% of their output, respectively, to the home country, entirely through intrafirm channels. These exports consisted mainly of semiconductors and contributed to the firms' globally organized value-added chains. The Japanese, by contrast, exported 19% of sales to Japan, of which less than 65% was intrafirm.

The US and European firms also sold much less of their output to third countries than did Japanese affiliates, and more of such sales occurred within their own firms. This finding suggests more vertical integration of US and European firms along commercially protected value-added chains strung across different host countries. This structure is not unlikely, considering the intermediate nature of their products. Japanese firms, in contrast, supplied more final goods.

The US affiliates sold some output to the local market, contrary to European and Japanese firms. All local sales were conducted through intrafirm channels with Malaysian affiliates.

NIE firms sold more than 50% of their output to their home economies, but only 35% of these transactions were intrafirm. Why? Because they were young firms without extensive networks to permit much vertical integration. Similarly, although NIE firms sold nearly 30% of their output to third countries, only 50% of the sales were intrafirm. Again, the evidence points to the early stage of growth of NIE electronics firms, compared with that of US, European, and Japanese multinationals, which had spawned production facilities across many countries during the previous two decades. One Japanese producer had more than 11 local affiliates producing a wide range of products. The high correlation between age and size of firms also explains the weaker NIE intrafirm forward linkages, either in home or third countries. As NIE electronics firms grow, such ties can be expected to grow, other things being equal.

An important attribute of NIE firms was their comparatively strong forward linkages with local buyers, all from outside the firm. Compared with long-established US, European, and Japanese firms, with almost no local sales, as much as 14.4% of NIE sales went to local purchasers. This suggests that NIE or East Asian firms were sited in Malaysia not so much to satisfy their own networking

Table 6.6. Electrical and electronics firms in Malaysia, sales and procurement, 1993.

	Japan		United States		NIEs		Europe		Local		Total	
	Amount (RM millions)	Share (%)	Amount (RM millions)	Share (%)	Amount (RM millions)	Share (%)	Amount (RM millions)	Share (%)	Amount (RM millions)	Share (%)	Amount (RM millions)	Share (%)
Sales												
Local economy (of which intrafirm, %)	0.0 (0.0)	0.0	65.9 (100.0)	1.3	273.9 (0.0)	14.4	0.0 (0.0)	0.0	0.0 (0.0)	0.0	339.8 (19.4)	3.5
Home economy (of which intrafirm, %)	251.0 (64.4)	18.7	3 135.3 (100.0)	62.7	1 061.1 (35.3)	55.8	878.6 (100.0)	75.0	59.0 (0.0)	18.2	5 385.0 (84.5)	55.3
Third country (of which intrafirm, %)	1 092.1 (57.1)	81.3	1 801.7 (64.0)	36.0	566.9 (49.8)	29.8	292.6 (100.0)	25.0	265.5 (0.0)	81.8	4 018.8 (58.5)	41.2
Total (of which intrafirm, %)	1 343.1 (58.5)	100.0	5 002.9 (87.0)	100.0	1 901.9 (34.5)	100.0	1 171.2 (100.0)	100.0	324.5 (0.0)	100.0	9 743.6 (71.5)	100.0
Procurement												
Local economy (of which intrafirm, %)	284.7 (0.0)	30.8	385.6 (12.8)	8.7	225.7 (0.0)	46.0	85.5 (11.7)	10.7	12.0 (0.0)	7.7	993.5 (6.0)	14.5
Home economy (of which intrafirm, %)	409.2 (74.0)	44.2	1 785.9 (100.0)	40.0	56.1 (100.0)	11.5	572.2 (100.0)	71.8	17.1 (0.0)	10.9	2 840.5 (95.7)	41.6
Third country (of which intrafirm, %)	231.5 (27.6)	25.0	2 289.2 (64.0)	51.3	208.0 (30.0)	42.5	139.5 (0.0)	17.5	127.4 (0.0)	81.4	2 995.6 (53.1)	43.9
Total (of which intrafirm, %)	925.4 (39.6)	100.0	4 460.7 (74.0)	100.0	489.8 (24.2)	100.0	797.2 (73.0)	100.0	156.5 (0.0)	100.0	6 829.6 (64.0)	100.0

Source: Compiled from interview data.
Note: RM, Malaysia ringgit; NIE, newly industrialized economy.

needs as to service unrelated firms, including other MNE affiliates in Malaysia. Unlike the case of affiliates from elsewhere, NIE firms were probably vendors and not parts of intrafirm value-added chains or networks.

The NIE firms also produced a wide range of electronic final and intermediate goods. Singapore imported more consumer products, such as radio clocks, portable compact-disk (CD) players, cordless phones, and computers than did Hong Kong and Taiwan, where more intermediate goods, such as semiconductors, computer components and peripherals, cathode-ray tubes, magnetic heads, telecommunications components, and silicon wafers, were landed. Singapore could well be a more downstream distribution point, whereas Hong Kong and Taiwan could be locations more for upstream processing and production.

Local firms were the most dependent on exports through arm's-length transactions. The 18% exports to home countries were in fact foreign partners' sales back to their own country of origin.

On the procurement side, distinct differences in behaviour were observed (Table 6.6). European investors, for example, included manufacturers of consumer-electronics goods, such as cordless phones and CD players, as well as electronic components, such as semiconductors. These manufacturers were the most dependent on inputs from parents, all of which were procured through intrafirm channels. Other inputs were obtained on an arm's-length basis from third countries.

The US electronics affiliates were mainly semiconductor producers of a few computer parts, such as hard disks and communications components. (They relied entirely on intrafirm channels when importing from their parent, but only 40% of their input requirements came from that source.) This finding can be explained by the fact that affiliates in third countries were important suppliers to the Malaysian operations, providing half of total inputs, all of which were procured through intrafirm channels.

Japanese electronics affiliates producing industrial or intermediate electronic goods, such as magnetic heads, computer-display monitors, and television sets, imported 44% of their inputs from Japan, mostly through intrafirm channels. Inputs from third countries appeared less important than was the case for US firms (25% versus 51%) and came substantially from unrelated sources, rather than from within the same firm (28% versus 64%). In contrast to popular belief regarding a tightly knit Japanese supply chain within groups, this study of Malaysian-based electronics affiliates suggests that they were more open to interfirm sourcing from home, third, and host countries than were US firms in the industry (40% versus 74%). The reason US and Japanese affiliates sourced differently was because US affiliates as semiconductor producers were higher up the value-added chain and could use inputs only from their own proprietary sources, whereas Japanese firms turning out intermediate products half way down the value-added chain had more procurement options.

The reluctance of US firms to source from unrelated firms in third countries, thus continuing to buy mainly from affiliates, can also be explained by a combination of intrafirm networking behaviour and value-added-chain considerations. For example, a very large US manufacturer of electronic components actually sourced 75% of its inputs from within the group. This was in line with its no-duplication policy, which divided production activities among affiliates in different locations to avoid duplicating the output of another affiliate. Such a policy would undoubtedly lead to heavy intrafirm trade across national borders to link segments of the value-added chain.

Another reason for US affiliates' preference for intrafirm procurement can be the practice of almost-centralized purchasing by international or regional purchasing offices. Concentration of supply will tend to emerge, because internal sources will have been duly, if not favourably, considered. Such a purchasing practice will contribute to dependence on intrafirm trade in materials and components, both with the home country and with third countries. The survey included a Canadian electronics giant, which relied heavily on its North American purchasing office.

The NIE firms relied heavily on the market. They purchased mainly through arm's-length transactions with either local-, or third-country suppliers. In contrast to firms from developed economies, NIE firms received only 11.5% of their inputs from their home countries (all intrafirm). Significantly, they relied heavily on local vendors: 46% of procurement was from the local economy, and it was entirely from vendors through the market. This pattern of NIE procurement was to be expected because most of the firms from Taiwan (which produced cathode-ray tubes and computer peripherals) and Hong Kong (communications and electronic components) were younger and smaller than their US, European, and Japanese competitors. Their strategy appeared to be more production than market driven; Malaysia offered low-cost opportunities for land and labour. To more established MNEs that needed to import more than half of their inputs, Malaysia provided a suitable location for sections of their international production chain (market-driven strategy).

The local Malaysian electronics firms surveyed engaged mainly in packaging of electronic chips. They sourced primarily from foreign countries and entirely from unrelated firms. This was to be expected because the firms were new and at a technologically dependent stage of their development. (The observed 10.9% of inputs from the home economy, in Table 6.6, is accounted for by a large firm that is a subsidiary of a local investor.) Minority foreign shareholding in joint ventures with the other local firms would be expected to give rise to sourcing from the foreign partner's home country.

Automobiles

One of the startling things about the automobile industry is that US producers are absent from Malaysia (Table 6.7). For the other producers, on the sales side, automobile firms indicated that 57.4% of their output was exported. The large local share of automobile sales may be attributed to a domestic policy designed to create a national car for local needs. Vendors surveyed reported that it was in the interest of their Japanese copartners to cater to Japanese cars in the local market, in line with official policy.

But automobile firms in the survey also produced parts, which accounted for most of their sales to their home countries. Japanese and European firms sold more than 80% of their output, all within the same corporate group, to the home country. Exports to Japan included audio equipment, batteries, car-air-conditioning components and parts, and shock absorbers. Exports to Europe included seat belts, sun visors, and electronic modules for automotive applications. Two interviewees reported that with more than half their sales to Europe through intrafirm channels, they had strong intrafirm links that were intended to yield group synergy.

Local behaviour reflects a growing policy emphasis on strengthening local-content rules for locally manufactured vehicles. The bulk of the local sales, whether intrafirm or otherwise, ultimately ends as inputs to the national car, to local assemblers, who began operating well before the national-car project was piloted, or to the secondary spare-parts market. (Japanese affiliates sold 16.5% of their output locally, of which 50% was intrafirm; European affiliates sold only 10.4% locally, all of it through the market.) These findings suggest that Japanese and European automobile affiliates in Malaysia not only were able to derive gains from ownership (technological), location (low production cost), and market internalization (intrafirm transactions) but also were able to extract further locational and cross-border internalization advantages in the domestic market because of the heavy-industry policy. Clearly, capacity could be expanded to meet local demand. In many cases, this expansion was accompanied by technological upgrading, which in turn permitted intrafirm export of state-of-the-art intermediate products not produced in Malaysia previously.

Japanese and European affiliates clearly focused on local sales. Exports to third countries represented negligible shares of output and were destined for China, Hong Kong, Singapore, and Brunei, which purchased road-transport equipment of all descriptions, except buses, through the market. Singapore also imported automotive electrical and circuitry components. Intermediate products, such as batteries, were sold in Hong Kong through intrafirm channels. Such third-country sales, especially of assembled transport equipment, were probably due to the lack of domestic suppliers in those countries.

Automobile exports to ASEAN countries included shock absorbers for two-wheeler and four-wheeler trucks in Indonesia and the Philippines (mainly to unrelated buyers) and car-air-conditioner components and parts to Indonesia and Thailand (also to unrelated buyers). One reason for sales to

Table 6.7. Automotive firms in Malaysia, sales and procurement, 1993.

	Japan		United States		NIEs		Europe		Local		Total	
	Amount (RM millions)	Share (%)	Amount (RM millions)	Share (%)	Amount (RM millions)	Share (%)	Amount (RM millions)	Share (%)	Amount (RM millions)	Share (%)	Amount (RM millions)	Share (%)
Sales												
Local economy (of which intrafirm, %)	29.6 (49.3)	16.5	0.0 (0.0)	0.0	15.0 (0.0)	100.0	3.7 (0.0)	10.4	95.6 (0.0)	88.7	143.9 (10.1)	42.6
Home economy (of which intrafirm, %)	145.0 (100.0)	80.7	0.0 (0.0)	0.0	0.0 (0.0)	0.0	31.6 (100.0)	89.3	0.0 (0.0)	0.0	176.6 (100.0)	52.3
Third country (of which intrafirm, %)	5.1 (0.0)	2.8	0.0 (0.0)	0.0	0.0 (0.0)	0.0	0.1 (100.0)	0.3	12.2 (73.5)	11.3	17.4 (52.1)	5.1
Total (of which intrafirm, %)	179.7 (88.8)	100.0	0.0 (0.0)	0.0	15.0 (0.0)	100.0	35.4 (89.5)	100.0	107.8 (8.3)	100.0	337.9 (59.2)	100.0
Procurement												
Local economy (of which intrafirm, %)	13.9 (0.0)	13.3	0.0 (0.0)	0.0	5.4 (0.0)	90.0	4.0 (0.0)	17.7	32.0 (5.9)	51.6	55.3 (3.4)	28.4
Home economy (of which intrafirm, %)	79.7 (40.6)	76.6	0.0 (0.0)	0.0	0.6 (100.0)	10.0	10.1 (67.6)	44.7	0.0 (0.0)	0.0	90.4 (44.0)	46.4
Third country (of which intrafirm, %)	10.5 (0.0)	10.1	0.0 (0.0)	0.0	0.0 (0.0)	0.0	8.5 (0.0)	37.6	30.0 (46.6)	48.4	49.0 (28.5)	25.2
Total (of which intrafirm, %)	104.1 (31.1)	100.0	0.0 (0.0)	0.0	6.0 (10.0)	100.0	22.6 (30.2)	100.0	62.0 (25.6)	100.0	194.7 (28.6)	100.0

Source: Compiled from interview data.
Note: RM, Malaysia ringgit; NIE, newly industrialized economy.

new countries was the anticipated saturation in the local market. Because of the Malaysian government's decision to set up a national-car plant in the Philippines, another ASEAN member will be an importer in a few years, thus tying in trade with investment in the region. Although shipments to East Asia and ASEAN countries have been minor, they are indicators of potential trade and investment developments within the region. As the regional automobile industry develops, greater economic linkages will foster regional integration, either through intrafirm business activities or among unrelated firms.

The NIE and local automobile firms surveyed catered mainly to the Malaysian market. They were vendors that supplied the national-car manufacturer and assemblers of franchise holders of other vehicles, as well as the replacement market. Their products included wire harnesses, electronic components, and metal coils for weather strippings. The NIE firms appeared to have located in Malaysia solely to serve the local market. However, local producers exported to third countries through intrafirm channels. Such intrafirm third-country exports can be explained by the interests of foreign partners in the Malaysian joint ventures. Malaysian participation in joint ventures tended to be that of holding or investment companies, often with diverse activities, rather than as manufacturers (Sieh Lee 1992).

On the procurement side, automotive firms sourced 46.4% of their inputs from their home countries; 28.4%, from local sources; and 25.2%, from third countries. Japanese affiliates purchased more than 75% of their inputs from Japan, of which 41% was intrafirm. This finding corroborates the trade balance in automobiles (Tables 6.3 and 6.4), which works very much in Japan's favour. This is not surprising in view of the well-developed vertically integrated operations of Japanese automotive firms. Their Malaysian affiliates produced automobile audio equipment, batteries, air-conditioning components, and shock absorbers. Purchases by Japanese affiliates from third countries were entirely from vendors. Besides conforming to the local-content policy, such interfirm transactions displayed cost advantages because they usually consisted of relatively minor inputs, such as rubber parts, materials for electronic modules, air-conditioning and audio components, and consumable supplies.

The surveyed European automotive firm producing electronic modules for automotive applications and circuitry components was less dependent on home-country supplies than were the Japanese affiliates, although proportionally more of the home-country sourcing was intrafirm. Conversely, inputs procured from third countries and from local sources were more important for the European firm than the Japanese firms. As in the case of Japanese affiliates, all third-country and local purchases by the European firm were transactions with unrelated firms. Such inputs were probably intermediate goods and supplies that were nonproprietary and nonpatented; hence, they need not be obtained from within the group. The large European firm that manufactured automotive electronic modules purchased as much as 40% of its inputs locally.

The Japanese used fewer third-country inputs than the European automobile firms did. Also, the Japanese sourced less from local suppliers than did European firms. However, both Japanese and European firms purchased from unrelated firms when sourcing from outside their home countries. Singapore, Taiwanese, and Thai sources were among the interfirm suppliers from outside the groups. The role of Indonesia will grow from that of a negligible supplier to that of a more significant regional one as its vendors begin to take advantage of the trading arrangements under the ASEAN Free Trade Area (AFTA) agreement. This provides easier access to the Malaysian market because of the accelerated reduction of tariffs. Furthermore, Indonesian automotive parts and components will be counted for joint regional–local content vis-à-vis other trading areas, possibly along different segments of the value-added chain.

The one NIE automotive firm, which was small, sourced almost all inputs locally. Most of these inputs were low-end ancillary inputs. The NIE automotive firm was also new, without a network of subsidiaries built over the years from which to source.

Local firms sourced locally through market channels. The bulk of local materials were channeled to a manufacturer of wire harnesses, which used local rubber-based parts, and to a group of companies that manufactured seat belts and plastic sun visors. The observation that 48.4% of the inputs of Malaysian automotive firms were imported, with 46.6% being intrafirm, was confusing because it is difficult to imagine that Malaysia's automotive industry invested in affiliates outside the country at such an early stage of its development. Closer investigation showed that the two assemblers surveyed were working with completely knocked down parts and components imported from abroad, hence the importance of foreign inputs. Moreover, in the case of one assembler, importing was carried out by a trading affiliate in the group, which was the franchise holder of at least three major foreign passenger-car manufacturers, which explains the intrafirm nature of the transactions. The second assembler manufactured trailers, tankers, and special-purpose vehicles.

Implications of survey results

These survey results suggest a number of observations and generalizations. First, Malaysia is an attractive location for FDI. Foreign investors, facing increased competition in international markets and global business strategies, saw advantages to producing in and exporting from Malaysia. Electronics firms of North American, European, and Japanese origin were able to benefit from the locational advantages of lower wages and land cost in Malaysia's politically stable environment; they were also able to gain more from the technology they developed and owned by dividing production in a network of affiliates in different countries. This division of production into segments of the value-added chain, which are locating in countries most advantageous to the chain, led to internalizing markets across countries. Malaysia continued to be a suitable site for the strategies of the electronics multinationals in the 1990s. On the other hand, automotive firms, primarily from East Asia, saw Malaysia as a low-cost location to which to move expensive home-country production. Others, particularly automotive firms, catered to the rapidly expanding demand of regional markets.

Second, local policies affected industry behaviour. The largest electrical and electronics and automotive firms covered by the survey depended heavily on foreign sources of materials and components. However, the local-content policy for automobiles was in force. Automotive firms sourced nearly 30% of their supplies locally, compared with only 14% sourced by the electrical and electronics firms (despite the latter's longer period of operation in Malaysia). Another effect of policy intervention was the location of many of the wholly owned electronics firms in free-trade zones. Such firms showed strong external linkages, both forward and backward, that were inherent in their initial decisions to locate in Malaysia. Despite the fact that automotive firms were newer in Malaysia, the industry was founded, for different reasons, on firm government initiative and support in every respect. The industry was intended to be instrumental in local development of technology and to be a significant step in the direction of heavy-industry development, thus the high proportion of local inputs.

The backward linkages to unrelated firms in Malaysia found in the survey could be partly explained by the vendor-development program of recent years, particularly after the mid-1980s recession. Buyer firms in government-approved schemes were eligible for tax breaks in return for local procurement. The vendors were often small firms registered with MITI's subcontracting exchange under the *payung* or umbrella concept, designed to build linkages between large MNEs and local SMEs. In the sample, local inputs bought by electronics firms included moulded compounds for plastic casings, silicon-wafer-packaging materials, solder for joints (although its level of purity was not sufficiently high), spare parts and components, supportive tools, industrial chemicals, lubricants, ancillary materials, and final-packing and -shipping materials. Automotive firms also purchased inputs from local vendors, such as rubber-based parts, resins for battery casings, materials for automotive electronic modules and for automobile audio equipment, car-air-conditioner components, paints, and other consumables for transport-vehicle assembly.

The firms surveyed were generally open to domestic sources as more materials and components of high standards became available locally. Some were influenced by GSP requirements, such as those concerning consumer-electronic products, such as radio clocks, portable CD players, cordless phone sets, and certain types of telecommunications equipment exported to the EC. The local-content rules for export-credit-refinancing facilities will also have had some effect on sourcing. Some firms adopted a policy of keeping alternative procurement avenues open as a business practice. Difficulties in increasing local sourcing existed mainly because local suppliers were unable, first, to attain and, then, to maintain sufficiently high technical standards. Developing a network of high-quality local vendors will also take time.

Third, apart from industry differences attributable to policy, other differences can be explained by the time of investment and the vintage and size of firms. The electronics affiliates were generally larger and longer established than those in the automotive industry because most came to Malaysia during the export-orientation phase of industrialization in the late 1960s and early 1970s. By 1993, they had grown to a considerable size and had upgraded their technology; many had shifted from consumer-electrical and electronic-products to industrial-electronic components and semiconductors. The automotive firms were newer and smaller, having been established only after the mid-1980s in the heavy-industry phase of development. Automotive firms are just about to enter their growth stage. With time, experience, and competition in the (small) domestic market, the automotive industry may be expected to increase its exports. Thus, despite the smaller forward export linkages displayed by the automotive firms relative to those found among the electronics firms, external-market ties in East Asia could strengthen in future, particularly in the ASEAN framework.

Fourth, survey results show that East Asian NIEs, such as Korea, Taiwan, and Hong Kong, in that order, are growing electronics suppliers. Korean vendors supplied firms that produced mainly consumer-electronic products and telecommunications equipment. Taiwanese suppliers specialized in electronic components for television and computer manufacturing, which they supplied through intrafirm sources. Hong Kong inputs came from both interfirm vendors and intrafirm exports to Malaysia, which were mainly inputs for semiconductor manufacturers.

The same countries were also playing an increasing role as suppliers for the automotive industry. Unlike procurements in electronics, however, East Asian automotive procurements were met mainly through vendors. They included vendors from Korea, for metal coil for weather strips; Taiwan, for electronic and shock-absorber parts; and Hong Kong, for wire harnesses and electronic components. The ASEAN countries were reported as suppliers for the automotive industry. Singapore provided resins for battery casings and components for electronic modules and shock absorbers. Thai suppliers were also budding sources for some electronic parts. The Philippines and Indonesia had joined in as minor sources for the electronics and automotive industries, respectively. One electronics firm had begun importing small quantities of materials and components for television tubes and computer-display monitors from vendors in China. Other vendors from Australia supplied lead for battery manufacturing, and Indian sources for transport equipment were reported.

The replacement of traditional suppliers with East Asian or ASEAN ones is expected to accelerate as more supporting industries develop in the region. The trend had actually started for some of the firms when they were interviewed. Clearly, if more local and regional vendors with high enough standards and adequate capacity to supply are developed and if they can provide cost advantages without sacrificing quality, further locational advantages will be available to foreign investors. This raises the question whether the shift will be from parent companies to other affiliates in the group or to independent vendors.

Fifth, Japanese investment still dominates the automotive industry in Malaysia. This could be due to the dominant role of Japanese technology and FDI in the early stages of the modern automotive industry in Malaysia. The dominance of the Japanese market was built on strong established business ties. Moreover, at least three of the Japanese affiliates covered by the survey claimed to produce the world's leading brand of their respective products. The business policy of parent firms regarding sale arrangements for market-balancing purposes was also reported. There was also a case of a Japanese parent not itself having the capacity to produce items imported from the Malaysian affiliate, partly because of high labour costs and partly because of the company's policy that all products of the 8-year-old Malaysian affiliate (audio equipment for automobiles) be sold to the parent, which had provided the proprietary technology and which commanded 10% of the global market.

Automotive-industry sales linkages with European markets were partly due to some global business strategy to supply sister companies from a common source. The advantages of exporting from Malaysia to benefit from GSP privileges was another explanation given by a group manufacturing car seat belts and sun visors. Exports of automotive parts to all ASEAN countries were found to be small, except for the Philippines. This exception reflects the emerging development of regional cooperation, which had been discussed at bilateral and formal regional economic meetings. China and Hong Kong were also showing signs of emerging importance, although they were relatively insignificant at the time of the survey.

Finally, the research suggests that US and European electronics affiliates in both industries continue to maintain strong sales ties with their parents. Japanese electronics affiliates definitely showed stronger intrafirm linkages with other affiliates outside Japan than with the home-country parent. Japanese automotive affiliates were beginning to export to neighbouring, especially ASEAN, countries, although such intrafirm sales among affiliates outside Japan were in their early stage of development. The behavioural variations for electronics could be due to different international business strategies between Japanese firms and their Western counterparts, whereas differences between Japanese affiliates in the two industries could be due to the type of products, age, and even size of the investments in Malaysia.

Capital investment and policy concerns

Two other survey topics were designed to probe sources of capital and firms' concerns about host-government policies. The sources of capital available to the surveyed firms are summarized in Table 6.8. Nearly 80%, overall, was from foreign sources. As might be expected from the different industry structures, the automotive industry relied more heavily on local sources than did the electrical and electronics industry. Japan was the major supplier to both industries, accounting for more than 40% overall and channeling more to the automotive than to the electronics industry. Japan was followed by Singapore, the United States, and Taiwan.

The uses of capital included the expansion of the local operation, technology changes, including automation, and the increase of capacity and capability for new product lines and product-line development. The role of investments from Taiwan, Korea, Hong Kong, and Singapore in electronics showed the increasing position of East Asian trading partners as investors because costs in labour-intensive industries had risen at home. Table 6.9 shows that investments from Singapore, Hong Kong, and the ASEAN countries came from affiliates, probably of US and Japanese MNEs in electronics and from Japanese MNEs in the automotive industry. In contrast, US, Taiwanese, and Korean investment originated from the parents. Electronics firms received 63% of their total capital requirements through the market, and parent firms contributed the remainder (Table 6.10).

This pattern may change as internal emphasis in Malaysia shifts toward development of domestic R&D and technological capabilities. For example, one local electronics firm in the survey accounted for considerable capital investment. It was part of a group that manufactured telecommunication products, phones and pagers, facsimile machines, and Private Automated Branch Exchange (PABX) systems, as well as electronic and automotive components.

Evidence of backward investment linkages from Malaysian affiliates to other affiliates in the region is particularly interesting. Such flows are linked to cross-border sales and procurement. The reasons for such links were explored. Were they to serve as technology- or R&D-sharing networks, to secure guaranteed input supplies, to allocate markets, to cement distribution connections, or to provide pieces of the global strategy related to major financial and tax implications? Survey responses tended to confirm that motives related to the protection of ownership advantages. One reason was a

Table 6.8. Capital investment in Malaysia by industry and source.

Source economy	Total sample			Electronics			Automobile		
	Value (RM millions)	Number of firms	Share (%)	Value (RM millions)	Number of firms	Share (%)	Value (RM millions)	Number of firms	Share (%)
Japan	793.38	12	40.8	627.66	8	43.7	14.72	3	54.0
Hong Kong	73.30	3	3.8	73.30	3	5.1	0.00	0	0.0
Korea	108.54	5	5.6	98.94	4	6.9	9.60	1	35.2
Taiwan	264.92	3	13.6	264.48	2	18.4	0.44	1	1.6
Singapore	360.76	10	18.5	28.76	7	2.0	1.01	2	3.7
Indonesia	0.00	0	0.0	0.00	0	0.0	0.00	0	0.0
Philippines	1.38	1	0.1	1.38	1	0.1	0.00	0	0.0
Thailand	1.51	1	0.1	1.51	1	0.1	0.00	0	0.0
China	0.00	0	0.0	0.00	0	0.0	0.00	0	0.0
Canada	2.00	1	0.1	2.00	1	0.1	0.00	0	0.0
United States	274.97	7	14.1	274.97	7	19.2	0.00	0	0.0
European Community	63.40	4	3.2	63.40	4	4.4	0.00	0	0.0
Other countries	1.50	1	0.1	0.00	0	0.0	1.50	1	5.5
Total foreign investment	1945.66	19	100.0	1436.40	13	100.0	27.27	5	100.0
Local investment	522.24	17	21.2	396.34	10	21.6	22.89	6	45.6
Foreign investment	1945.66	19	78.8	1436.40	13	78.4	27.27	5	54.4
Total investment	2467.90	28	100.0	1832.74	18	100.0	50.16	11	100.0

Source: Survey data.
Note: RM, Malaysia ringgit.

Table 6.9. Intrafirm foreign investment from parent and other affiliates: distribution of total FDI (RM millions) by country and industry.

	Parent			Other affiliate			Others	
	Value (RM millions)	Firms (n)	Share (%)	Value (RM millions)	Firms (n)	Share (%)	Value (RM millions)	Share (%)
Total sample								
Japan	16.06	3	3.0	160.84	3	31.2	616.48	68.1
Hong Kong	0.00	0	0.0	1.30	1	0.3	72.00	8.0
Korea	9.60	1	1.8	0.07	1	0.0	98.87	10.9
Taiwan	261.48	1	49.8	0.44	1	0.1	3.00	0.3
Singapore	2.00	1	0.4	342.53	7	66.5	16.23	1.8
Indonesia	0.00	0	0.0	0.00	0	0.0	0.00	0.0
Philippines	0.00	0	0.0	1.38	1	0.3	0.00	0.0
Thailand	0.00	0	0.0	1.51	1	0.3	0.00	0.0
China	0.00	0	0.0	0.00	0	0.0	0.00	0.0
Canada	0.00	0	0.0	0.00	0	0.0	2.00	0.2
United States	220.66	4	42.0	5.09	2	1.0	49.22	5.4
European Community	15.70	1	3.0	0.00	0	0.0	47.70	5.3
Other	0.00	0	0.0	1.50	1	0.3	0.00	0.0
Total	525.50		100.0	514.66		100.0	905.50	100.0
Electronics								
Japan	1.60	1	0.3	9.84	2	33.1	616.22	68.1
Hong Kong	0.00	0	0.0	1.30	1	4.4	72.00	8.0
Korea	0.00	0	0.0	0.07	1	0.2	98.87	10.9
Taiwan	261.48	1	52.1	0.00	0	0.0	3.00	0.3
Singapore	2.00	1	0.4	10.53	5	35.4	16.23	1.8
Indonesia	0.00	0	0.0	0.00	0	0.0	0.00	0.0
Philippines	0.00	0	0.0	1.38	1	4.7	0.00	0.0
Thailand	0.00	0	0.0	1.51	1	5.1	0.00	0.0
China	0.00	0	0.0	0.00	0	0.0	0.00	0.0
Canada	0.00	0	0.0	0.00	0	0.0	2.00	0.2
United States	220.66	4	44.0	5.09	2	17.1	49.22	5.4
European Community	15.70	1	3.2	0.00	0	0.0	47.70	5.3
Other	0.00	0	0.0	0.00	0	0.0	0.00	0.0
Total	501.44		100.0	29.72		100.0	905.24	100.0
Automobile								
Japan	14.46	2	60.1	0.00	0	0.0	0.26	96.3
Hong Kong	0.00	0	0.0	0.00	0	0.0	0.00	0.0
Korea	9.60	1	39.9	0.00	0	0.0	0.00	0.0
Taiwan	0.00	0	0.0	0.44	1	15.0	0.00	0.0
Singapore	0.00	0	0.0	1.00	1	34.0	0.01	3.7
Indonesia	0.00	0	0.0	0.00	0	0.0	0.00	0.0
Philippines	0.00	0	0.0	0.00	0	0.0	0.00	0.0
Thailand	0.00	0	0.0	0.00	0	0.0	0.00	0.0
China	0.00	0	0.0	0.00	0	0.0	0.00	0.0
Canada	0.00	0	0.0	0.00	0	0.0	0.00	0.0
United States	0.00	0	0.0	0.00	0	0.0	0.00	0.0
European Community	0.00	0	0.0	0.00	1	0.0	0.00	0.0
Other	0.00	0	0.0	1.50	1	51.0	0.00	0.0
Total	24.06		100.0	2.94		100.0	0.27	100.0

Source: Survey data.
Note: RM, Mayalsia ringgit; FDI, foreign direct investment.

Table 6.10. Intrafirm foreign investment from parent and other affiliates: distribution of total FDI by firm affiliation.

Industry	Total FDI (RM millions)	Parent (%)	Other affiliate (%)	Other firm (%)
Electronics	1 436.40	34.9	2.1	63.0
Automobiles	27.27	88.2	10.8	1.0
Total sample	1 945.66	27.0	26.5	46.5

Source: Survey data.
Note: RM, Malyasia ringgit; FDI, foreign direct investment.

preference for standardized machinery in the MNE across countries. Equipment interchange among affiliates was reported by a large US semiconductor MNE, for example. Technology transfer within the firm, especially of commercially protected know-how and show-how, was another reason. Quality-standards assurance in a vertically integrated operation, to ensure success along a value-added chain, and other technical considerations were also identified.

Market-related reasons included quality-consistency, price, and delivery concerns. Parent-company policy and strategy were also cited by several firms for such linkages. For example, two Japanese automotive firms clearly explained that their corporate policy was to invest in the countries where they had markets so as to serve and exploit them best. Thus, a car-battery manufacturer with affiliates in 23 countries and a car-air-conditioner MNE with affiliates in 34 countries both had invested in locations close to their major markets.

Another interesting finding in the electronics industry was evidence of capital-investment flows from Japan that were not affiliated with a parent MNE and that corresponded to materials and component inflows apparently from these independent firms. This finding implies that independent, usually small to medium-sized Japanese exporters, possibly vendors, had been relocating to Malaysia. Japanese vendors were engaged in production in Malaysia to meet the needs of the Malaysian or other regional markets, rather than the Japanese market. Similar tendencies were observed for Hong Kong and Korean capital allocated to small and medium-sized East Asian suppliers. Singapore vendors, in contrast, tended to continue to rely on trade, that is, to supply inputs from across the causeway, rather than to invest.

Capital investments in the automotive industry were monopolized by Asian sources, chiefly from Japanese and Korean parent companies. Other intrafirm affiliates' investment in the automotive industry came from Singapore, Taiwan, and elsewhere. Capital from Japan and Singapore also came through the market (Table 6.9).

Policy issues

Several policy concerns emerged from content analysis of the views and opinions of surveyed firms. Electronics firms were concerned with the effects of foreign-exchange fluctuations because most of their output was exported and because inputs of materials and components were imported from parents. Managing exchange risks might render such cross-border strategies too costly to be sustainable in the long term. The outflow of FDI would certainly affect trade negatively if the interactions observed in this study between and among players in the network remained strong.

Firms were also concerned with financial policies, such as disallowing foreign-currency accounts, because of the large volume of foreign transactions in US dollars and yen. Restrictions on interest and currency swaps, even in the international offshore financial centre of Labuan, made hedging of exchange risks difficult, especially when the ringgit appreciated and when interest rates for US currency increased. These were construed as rigidities in the banking system that could be revised if the country valued FDI and the trade it entailed. However, recent decisions on permitting opening of foreign-currency accounts, together with other changes expected under the Interim Accord of the General Agreement on Trade in Services, concluded in July 1995, will bring about significant changes.

Although ownership policies were not a concern, because the electronics firms were either wholly owned affiliates or had already complied with the equity rules, and although much of the past growth had been funded internally, some firms indicated that future expansion might require local borrowing. This would require financial regulations conducive to their obtaining local funds, apart from the question of the availability of funds, especially because the required investment in the electronics industry would be substantial.

Electronics firms whose pioneer status had expired or was about to expire expressed their concern that their reinvestments were not entitled to tax incentives. Some indicated that tax-incentive programs in other countries, particularly in Taiwan, were more extensive. Interviewees faced difficulties with Malaysian tax authorities when finalizing their tax computations like obtaining confirmation of exempt income for the payment of dividends. Such administrative delays were seen to affect their competitiveness, as well as that of the country for FDI.

Other concerns of electronics firms in Malaysia included environmental laws, particularly for discharge of toxic substances, labour shortages and restrictions, the issue of work permits and resident status, and technology transfer for those whose R&D was located with their parent overseas. However, firms with in-house R&D in Malaysia desired tax incentives for such facilities.

Because the automotive firms surveyed needed to borrow for expansion, availability and regulation of financial facilities have important bearings on future investment and trade in the industry. Despite the already high levels of local content achieved, firms were still troubled by the lack of availability of some local materials inputs and the inadequate quality of others. One firm referred to a ban on imported resin as an example. Like electronics firms, automotive firms were concerned about foreign-exchange fluctuations. Shortages of local management were cited as a constraint. Customs and duties were another. Concerns about technology stemmed mainly from firms' dependence on R&D based in Japan. Safety legislation and labour shortages were also regarded as constraints to future investment expansion.

Conclusion

The purpose of this study was to illuminate the trade links of foreign firms in Malaysia's large electronics industry and in its automotive industry. The survey results paint a picture of extensive intrafirm links among the large and more mature investors from industrialized countries, reflecting Malaysia's place in their global strategies. One of the main implications of these patterns is that although these firms are not highly integrated with the local economy, they are contributing to the growth of intraregional ties. In contrast, the newer, smaller international firms from Taiwan and other East Asian economies tended to be more closely integrated with the local economy and to a lesser extent with their parents. The implication is that as they grow they will contribute to more extensive intraregional links.

What are the policy implications? Two areas can be identified. First, policies do influence FDI–trade linkages through their direct effect on FDI inflows and related trade. Second, regional investment and trade cooperation may be desirable to promote regional development.

Policies have encouraged FDI inflows by providing a welcoming investment environment, including incentives and performance requirements. It should be noted that such incentives are unlikely to remain Malaysia's strength in drawing FDI because they can easily be imitated and are indeed subject to competition from neighbouring countries and from newly emerging economies, such as China and Vietnam. Thus, Malaysia should shift to a more broadly based locational strategy to develop a high-quality work force, stable political and economic conditions, better-quality infrastructure, a stable legal and administrative system, and social and cultural acceptability as locational advantages. Malaysia's government has begun investing heavily in human-resource and infrastructural development. In the meantime, pragmatic use of foreign labour and the employment of expatriates should be allowed. Japanese firms in particular tend to employ more expatriates at their production facilities. The main thrust of further pursuit may be to encourage selected industries in a way that suits Malaysia in MNEs' vertical production hierarchies, bearing in mind investors' global strategies. Over the years, the assembly and testing operations of the electronics industry have become more automated. Product complexity and labour-force expertise have increased. At present, most companies have integrated assembly and testing operations in the same facility, and the scope of operations is shifting from one of pure manufacturing to one more integrated with design, reliability, and customer-service functions. In this way, an upward migration has occurred in the production hierarchy. Operations have also diversified into original equipment manufacturing, as has already happened in Hong Kong and Taiwan. As these more advanced economies lose their comparative advantage in manufacturing, as a result of rising costs, Malaysia becomes an alternative location in the telecommunications and computing industries.

Trade linkages of investing firms will be promoted by the availability of local supporting industries. For example, the vendor-development program has been so successful, particularly in the automotive industry, that component suppliers have themselves developed into exporting firms. The vendor program should be extended to more industries, first, by getting firms to support existing FDI firms and, then, by having them establish themselves in the international production network for selected products.

It is not possible to stabilize currency fluctuations to allay fears of exporters and importers of materials inputs and components. The recent practice of hedging foreign currencies by commercial banks, the only legal foreign-exchange dealers in the country, has somewhat lessened the effects of currency fluctuations by allowing firms to predict their cost of inputs and exporters to predict their revenues, without undue effects of currency fluctuations.

Policies that generate regional cooperation are more difficult to implement. Although the division of production among countries to achieve economies of scale could be negotiated, regional cooperation should aim at providing the right conditions for investors to exploit the diversity of locations in the region, rather than having governments dictate the details of cooperative agreements. Accelerated preferential trading agreements among ASEAN members, under AFTA, to reduce tariffs will encourage the sourcing of materials and components from among member countries and will forge trade linkages. Another possibility is the freer flow of production information and integration of information for release to member countries to enhance the chances of partnerships or of production linkages among firms of member countries.

Finally, policies and strategies since Malaysian independence have treated trade and investment separately. Trade policies have shifted to promote exports of higher value-added content, the search for and entrance into nontraditional markets, and the establishment of relations with new trading partners, either bilaterally or multilaterally, that is, with countries sharing areas of common interest; to support greater regional cooperation in trade of goods and services; and to support new changes in the international trading system through active participation in negotiations. On the other hand, investment policies have also evolved, shifting attention from labour-intensive to more skills-intensive industries, from downstream processing of raw materials to technology-based activities, from fiscal incentives to attract investment to political and economic stability and a conducive macroenvironment, from agro-based and manufacturing industries to service-based infrastructural industries, from targeting traditional FDI sources to domestic, though smaller, investors, and from a highly regulated to a more liberal environment. Investment policies have also been guided by the national objectives of ensuring Malaysian, especially Bumiputra, participation in business. As in other developing countries, the negative effects of MNEs are not forgotten.

As Malaysia approaches developed status, the compartmentalized approach to trade and investment policies should be replaced by a more integrated approach because of the increasingly closer relationship between trade and investment in the economy and across countries in East Asia and for several other reasons. First, consistent government treatment will be needed for both traders and investors if their interdependence continues to widen and deepen. Second, synergistic effects may be derived, not only those between host and home economies but also those among other countries in the East Asian region. Such an integrative effect will broaden the role of government in ensuring systematic and fair regulation of investors and traders from different countries.

The main policy implication of growing intrafirm trade with well-knit networks with parents and other affiliates is that a new logic is needed. The tendency has been to look at foreign investors and domestic investors with different mind sets. Similarly, international trade appears to have received more attention than domestic trade. These dividing lines should be de-emphasized because domestic firms will soon be as interconnected with markets and suppliers as foreign firms; and more and more international trade may in fact be transfers between affiliates of the same firm located in different countries.

Malaysia as a host economy requires important economic structural changes for future FDI inflows. It will be of paramount importance to place emphasis on system efficiency, speedy turn-around time, ease of approvals, without administrative delays, and an error- and trouble-free working environment. Another facet of needed structural adjustment will be the readiness of the work force not only to absorb and work effectively with rapidly changing technologies but also to do so with appropriate work ethics, exposure, and responsible attitudes. Reliable telecommunications and transportation services will also be significant. As a host, Malaysia must accommodate the growing phenomenon of key investors who are also major traders. If they are unaccommodated or structural adjustments are not made fast enough, Malaysia may lose to others both as an FDI destination and as a trader.

All these factors point to the need for strategies based on modern infrastructure, speedy information services, adequate transportation and utilities, and skilful professional and business support services. Steps to modernize and develop the service sector should be closely geared to the next industrial master plan. For future economic growth, a holistic approach is needed to make policies in all sectors reinforce each other, particularly as the line between trade and investment is rapidly blurred by factor flows across national boundaries.

Chapter 7

CHINA

A Rapidly Emerging Light-Manufacturing Base in Guangdong Province

*Zhang Zhaoyong and
Chen Kang*

Guangdong experienced an average annual economic-growth rate of 14.1% between 1980 and 1993, which is higher than the 9.5% average for the whole of China during the same period. This impressive economic growth was the result of a swift and profound change in industrial structure that reshaped Guangdong into a large-scale, light-manufacturing base. Guangdong's exports of light manufactures increased more than 26-fold in 11 years, from less than US$800 million in 1982 to more than US$20 billion in 1993. Guangdong also sold a large amount of household electrical products, textiles, apparel, footwear, toys, and other light-manufactured products to the rest of China. According to Guangdong's Governor Zhu Senlin (1993), the rest of China consumed about 33% of Guangdong's manufactured output in 1992, valued at about US$14 billion. Guangdong is ambitiously planning to increase the sale of its output to the rest of China to 40% of Guangdong's gross domestic product (GDP) by 2000.

Lardy (1992) observed that, in the first half of the 1980s, there was little evidence that comparative advantage determined the composition of China's exports. Guangdong has since become a national leader in exploring its comparative advantage. Because of abundant labour supply and low wages, Guangdong shifted its industrial structure to one of labour-intensive production (in the early 1980s), leading to the significant increase in the share of light manufactures in total exports from 34.5% in 1982 to 57.5% in 1986.

This shift in industrial structure was the result of China's open-door policy, introduced in 1979, which allocated to Guangdong various rights and privileges to promote exports and attract foreign direct investment (FDI). Having three of the four special economic zones (SEZs) in Guangdong was the most important privilege that the province received.[1] These SEZs attracted Hong Kong investors. As a trading partner, financier, intermediary, and facilitator, Hong Kong has had a profound and pervasive effect on the development path and the industrial structure of Guangdong (Sung 1991). About 80% of Guangdong's exports go to Hong Kong, and about 80% of its imports now come from there. Hong Kong is overwhelmingly Guangdong's largest source of FDI, accounting for more than 90% of total inflows since the mid-1980s. In effect, an integrated economic area has developed since the late 1980s. The degree of interpenetration is so high that only limited value

---

[1] These three SEZs were Shenzhen, Zhuhai, and Shantou, and the fourth was Fujian. Subsequently, in 1984, Guangzhou and 14 other coastal cities were opened up and, in early 1995, the Pearl River Delta, the Yangtze River Delta, and the Zhangzhou–Quanzhou–Xiamen region in Fujian Province were also opened to FDI. In the late 1980s, China also designated Hainan as an SEZ. In the SEZs and the opened areas, the planning controls are relaxed to promote FDI and the growth of market forces. Foreign investors are given preferential treatment in the form of tax exemptions and other incentives.

can be derived from analyzing the activities of Guangdong and Hong Kong separately (Goodman and Feng 1993). This economic transformation of Guangdong has extended to other parts of China. Thus, Hong Kong has contributed significantly to making China's pattern of trade much more congruent with the country's underlying comparative advantage than it was in the prereform era.

Foreign investors have been attracted to China by its low production costs (especially low labour costs) and by its large domestic market. The restrictions initially set up to prevent foreign businesses from penetrating the domestic market have been gradually relaxed, either in their scope or in their enforcement, especially at provincial and local levels. This is only one example of how China has continuously liberalized its foreign-investment regime to overcome such negative factors as a limited legal structure, nonconvertibility of the currency, and growing corruption. In the 1990s, China has been rapidly becoming one of the most liberal foreign-investment environments in the developing world. China also restricts foreign ownership less than do Japan and South Korea and is more liberal in opening up additional sectors to foreign investment (Lardy 1994).

In this chapter, we study the role of FDI in Guangdong's rapid emergence as a light-manufacturing base. Our focus is on two light-manufacturing industries: household electric and electronic appliances and textiles and apparel. The next section analyzes trade–investment linkages by studying aggregate trade and FDI-flow data at the national and provincial levels. The aggregate analysis is complemented by firm-level surveys, discussed in the third section, using sales and sourcing data to examine the behaviour of foreign firms investing in Guangdong. Finally, we combine the results derived from the aggregate and survey data to draw some conclusions about the relationship between FDI and the rapidly emerging light-manufacturing base in Guangdong.

FDI and trade

National level

China's open-door economic policy did not lead to an early specialization in manufactures. Between 1980 and 1985, the growth rate of manufactured exports matched the 8.5% average annual growth rate of total exports. However, after the implementation of domestic-market reforms in the mid-1980s, such as price reforms and foreign-trade reforms, the open-door policy started to show major results. Manufactured exports grew by 23.9% annually between 1985 and 1993, which exceeded the average annual growth rate of total exports by 7.6% during the same period.

Low production costs, a huge domestic market, favourable investment incentives (such as tax holidays and lower land-use fees), and flexible foreign-investment policies (whereby investors are given latitude regarding investment forms, location, management, and so forth), from 1979, turned China into an attractive location for foreign investors. Between 1979 and 1994, China absorbed an estimated US$57 billion of FDI (UNCTAD 1995). The sectoral distribution of FDI was widespread, including high-technology-oriented industries, raw-materials exploration and extraction, and service-oriented operations. The bulk of foreign investment, however, targeted labour-seeking, resource-extracting, and service-oriented industries.

Because most FDI focused on industries in which China has a comparative advantage, the inflow of FDI was trade promoting (United Nations 1993). Increasingly, the country's export growth became dependent on investments by foreign firms. China's total exports tripled in a 7-year period, from US$30.9 billion in 1986 to US$91.8 billion in 1993, and the share of total exports produced by foreign firms increased from 1.6% to 27.5% — in 1993 foreign firms accounted for 70% of China's total export growth (Lardy 1994).

The dynamic manufacturing sector has been the major driving force behind China's trade expansion. In 1986, manufactured exports were only US$23.7 billion; by 1992, they had risen to US$116.3 billion (Table 7.1), an increase of almost 400%. Exports of manufactures to the United States and the European Community (EC) grew even faster, by 500% and 480%, respectively,

Table 7.1. China's exports of manufactures by selected ISIC category, year, and partner.

Industry	Year	World totals (US$ millions)	Shares of world totals (%)							
			Hong Kong	Japan	Singapore	Other NIEs	ASEAN-4	United States	European Community	Other
All manufacturing	1986	23 718	38.2	11.0	2.5	NA	2.7	18.2	13.2	14.2
	1989	59 318	39.6	11.7	1.8	NA	2.6	19.6	13.7	11.0
	1991	93 087	38.7	10.5	1.7	2.5	2.5	20.4	16.7	7.0
	1992	116 252	37.7	10.6	1.5	2.0	2.0	22.2	15.6	8.4
Textiles	1986	5 208	45.0	13.0	2.0	0.0	2.0	10.0	15.0	13.0
	1989	8 502	49.0	15.0	2.0	0.0	3.0	7.0	14.0	10.0
	1992	10 494	47.0	11.0	2.0	8.0	3.0	9.0	12.0	8.0
Apparel	1986	5 883	36.0	9.0	0.2	0.0	0.0	32.0	11.0	11.8
	1989	13 245	37.0	17.0	0.2	0.0	0.1	24.0	12.0	9.7
	1992	26 419	35.0	18.0	0.3	0.3	0.1	21.0	16.0	9.3
Electrical machinery	1986	1 064	75.0	2.0	0.7	0.0	1.0	9.0	5.0	7.3
	1989	6 904	53.0	4.0	0.7	0.0	0.7	24.0	11.0	6.6
	1992	14 812	49.0	5.0	1.1	0.7	1.3	23.0	14.0	5.9
Other industries	1986	11 562	33.0	12.0	4.0	0.0	5.0	16.0	15.0	15.0
	1989	30 667	35.0	10.0	3.0	0.0	4.0	20.0	15.0	13.0
	1992	64 527	35.0	9.0	2.0	2.0	3.0	25.0	16.0	8.0
All manufacturing (absolute measure of trade intensity) [a]	1986		0.63	0.18	0.04	0.00	0.04	0.30	0.22	0.21
	1989		1.11	0.33	0.05	0.00	0.07	0.55	0.39	0.27
	1991		1.15	0.41	0.07	0.10	0.10	0.79	0.65	0.21
	1992		1.72	0.48	0.07	0.09	0.09	1.01	0.71	0.30
All manufacturing (growth rates)	1986–92	390.1	384.0	374.1	201.0	NA	261.0	497.6	479.3	153.5
	1989–89	150.1	159.1	166.7	85.9	NA	134.7	169.8	159.3	83.4
	1989–91	56.9	53.3	40.8	46.3	NA	51.1	62.6	91.8	–10.0
	1992	24.9	21.8	26.3	10.6	–0.68	1.8	36.2	16.5	53.5

Source: ANU (1995) and UNCTAD (n.d.).

Note: NIE, newly industrialized economy; ASEAN-4, Indonesia, Malaysia, the Philippines, and Thailand; NA, not available; ISIC, International Standard Industrial Classification.

[a] For exports, we define absolute trade intensity as $A = X_{cj} / X$ where c is the country of interest (in our case, China); j is the country's export partners (j in our case, Hong Kong, Japan, Singapore, other NIEs, ASEAN-4, the United States, the European Community, and the rest of the world); X_{cj} is China's exports to one of its export partners; and X is total world exports.

whereas manufactured exports to Hong Kong and Japan grew at roughly the same rate as total exports. Manufactured-export growth to East Asian countries lagged behind but still grew at a respectable 260%.

China's imports of manufactured goods show a similar, though less pronounced, growth pattern (Table 7.2). Total imports increased from US$31.0 billion in 1986 to US$70.6 billion in 1992, or slightly more than double the value of 1986. The growth of manufactured imports from East Asia — particularly from Hong Kong, Singapore, and the ASEAN-4 (Indonesia, Malaysia, the Philippines, and Thailand) — was stronger than the growth of manufactured imports from the rest of world. Thus, China's rapid trade development appears to have had a strong regional component. This implies that the Chinese economy is likely to be integrated more rapidly with the East Asian region — in particular, the Asian newly industrialized economies (NIEs) and ASEAN-4 — than with the rest of the world.

Economists have used different approaches to measure the degree of regional integration. Lawrence (1991) used a measure of extraregional trade to study East Asian integration, whereas Drysdale and Garnaut (1993) applied measures of intraindustry trade.[2] Petri (1993) applied measures of trade intensity similar to our own.[3] We define absolute trade intensity for exports as the ratio of a country's bilateral exports (to each trading partner) to total world exports. Similarly, for imports, the absolute trade intensity is the ratio of a country's bilateral imports (from each trading partner) to total world imports. The relative trade intensities are simply a country's bilateral exports or imports as shares of its total exports or imports. Because this chapter focuses on Guangdong's manufacturing sector, all of our trade-intensity calculations are limited to this sector.

The trade intensities allow us to compare China's share of world trade through time and the changing distribution of its trade with the East Asian economies, on the one hand, and the rest of world, on the other (Tables 7.1 and 7.2). China's share of manufactured world exports increased rapidly between 1986 and 1992. The absolute trade intensities of China's manufactured exports to Hong Kong, Japan, the United States, and the EC nearly tripled in this period, indicating the increased importance of China as a manufacturing base. The sum of the absolute trade intensities of China's imports of all manufactures from the nine East Asian economies is considerably higher than the sum of the indices with the rest of the world for the same time, which reflects the regional component of China's trade development. Most notably, the absolute measures of trade intensity reveal that China's trade in manufactured goods with Hong Kong was considerably larger than that with any other region between 1986 and 1992. Even taking Hong Kong's entrepôt role into account, we found the trade interdependence between China and Hong Kong appeared to be strengthening with time (Chapter 4).

The export and import shares of China's trade in manufactures show that Hong Kong, the United States, the EC, and Japan are China's most important markets. Although the export share to these economies increased modestly from 42% to 48% between 1986 and 1992, the import share declined from 61% in 1986 to 38% in 1992. This seems to contradict the casual observation that China depends heavily on developed market economies for manufacturing imports and on developing economies as a market for its exports, especially when taking into account that about 40% of Hong Kong's re-exports were destined for the developed world. The relative importance of China's exports to the Asian NIEs, especially Hong Kong, remained stable in the 1980s but declined in the early 1990s, whereas imports from this region grew rapidly in the 1980s and leveled off in a dominant position in the early 1990s.

---

[2] See Chapter 1 for a definition of these concepts.

[3] In terms of exports, we define absolute trade intensity (A) to be $A = X_{cj}/X$ where c refers to the country of interest (in our case, China); j refers to the country's export partners (in our case, Hong Kong, Japan, Singapore, other NIEs, ASEAN-4, the United States, EC, and the rest of the world); X_{cj} refers to China's exports to one of its export partners; and X refers to total world exports. Obviously, the definition of the equation for imports is analogous. This definition differs from the one used by Petri (1995) because Petri uses total world trade rather than world exports or imports in the denominator.

Table 7.2. China's imports of manufactures by selected ISIC category, year, and partner.

Industry	Year	World totals (US$ millions)	Shares of world totals (%)							
			Hong Kong	Japan	Singapore	Other NIEs	ASEAN-4	United States	European Community	Other
All manufacturing	1986	30 965	23.3	31.5	1.6	NA	1.2	9.2	19.9	13.3
	1989	43 478	41.8	19.3	2.4	NA	2.3	9.7	14.5	10.0
	1991	52 106	49.7	16.3	1.5	1.9	2.6	10.3	11.7	6.0
	1992	70 638	48.4	16.7	1.5	3.7	2.2	9.5	11.5	6.5
Textiles	1986	2 788	69.0	9.0	0.0	0.0	0.6	2.0	4.0	15.4
	1989	4 798	78.0	8.0	0.0	0.0	0.2	2.0	4.0	7.8
	1992	8 441	77.0	11.0	0.1	4.0	0.4	1.0	1.0	5.5
Apparel	1986	152	90.0	5.0	0.2	0.0	0.1	0.9	3.0	0.8
	1989	375	91.0	5.0	0.2	0.0	0.2	1.3	2.0	0.3
	1992	744	85.0	8.0	0.3	0.3	0.2	0.8	2.0	3.4
Electrical machinery	1986	3 091	31.0	39.0	2.1	0.0	0.1	7.0	13.0	7.8
	1989	5 621	50.0	30.0	2.0	0.0	0.4	4.0	8.0	5.6
	1992	8 622	51.0	25.0	1.1	2.0	0.2	5.0	10.0	5.7
Other industries	1986	24 934	17.0	33.0	2.0	0.0	1.0	10.0	23.0	14.0
	1989	32 684	34.0	19.0	3.0	0.0	3.0	12.0	17.0	12.0
	1992	52 830	43.0	16.0	2.0	4.0	3.0	12.0	14.0	6.0
All manufacturing (absolute measure of trade intensity)[a]	1986		0.51	0.70	0.03	0.00	0.03	0.20	0.44	0.26
	1989		0.86	0.40	0.05	0.00	0.05	0.20	0.30	0.18
	1991		1.03	0.34	0.03	0.04	0.05	0.21	0.24	0.09
	1992		1.26	0.43	0.04	0.10	0.06	0.25	0.30	0.14
All manufacturing (growth rates)	1986–92	128.1	373.8	21.2	211.0	NA	314.2	136.9	32.2	2.6
	1989–89	40.4	151.7	-13.8	110.0	NA	174.2	49.0	2.2	3.2
	1989–91	19.8	42.4	1.3	-25.6	NA	35.2	27.0	-3.2	-38.3
	1992	35.6	32.2	38.9	35.0	164.0	11.7	25.2	33.7	61.1

Source: ANU (1995) and UNCTAD (n.d.).

Note: NIE, newly industrialized economy; ASEAN-4, Indonesia, Malaysia, the Philippines, and Thailand; NA, not available; ISIC, International Standard Industrial Classification.

[a] For imports, we define absolute trade intensity as $A = M_{cj}/M$ where c is the country of interest (in our case, China); j is the country's import partners (in our case, Hong Kong, Japan, Singapore, other NIEs, ASEAN-4, the United States, the European Community, and the rest of the world); M_{cj} is China's imports from one of its import partners; and M is total world imports.

Tables 7.1 and 7.2 also reveal China's trade relationship with the various regions in textiles, apparel, electrical machinery, and other industries. China has an increasing dependence on the East Asian region in textile and apparel products. In 1986, the share of textile exports to East Asia was 62%, and the share of textile imports from the region was about 79%. By 1992, these shares had reached 71% and 93%, respectively. Within the region, Hong Kong and Japan were China's leading trading partners, with Hong Kong accounting for 47% of exports and 77% of imports. The US and EC markets, as well as those of other regions, absorbed together about 30% of China's textile exports, with a declining trend over time; they were not an important source of textile imports.

Hong Kong and the United States were the most important markets for China's apparel exports, accounting for 36% and 32%, respectively, in 1986. These shares declined to 35% and 21%, respectively, by 1992. It is noteworthy that the Japanese and European markets became increasingly important, rising from a common share of 20% in 1986 to 34% in 1992. In 1992, 85% of China's imports of apparel came from Hong Kong and 8% from Japan.

The export and import shares for electrical machinery show that Hong Kong, the United States, and the EC were the most important markets for China's exports and that Hong Kong, Japan, and the EC were important importers. It is worth noting that the export share of electrical machinery to Hong Kong dropped sharply from 75% in 1986 to 49% in 1992. However, Hong Kong's share of China's imports of electrical machinery increased rapidly from 31% to 51% in the same period. The US market became increasingly important for China's electrical-machinery exports, increasing from 9% in 1986 to 23% in 1992 after the rapid development of China's direct trade with other economies in the early 1990s. This development coincided with the onset of foreign firms' exporting their output. It is interesting to note that, by 1992, the United States was no longer an important market for China's imports of electrical machinery, which were mainly sourced from the East Asian economies, especially Hong Kong and Japan. This reflects China's search for cheaper and more adequate technology transfers.

The import and export performance of China's other manufactures displays a pattern similar to that for its trade in electrical machinery. Hong Kong gained rapidly in importance as China's major import market for other manufactures, rising from a share of 17% in 1986 to 43% in 1992. The relative importance of Hong Kong as China's export market was successfully maintained at around 35%. In contrast to the shares of Hong Kong, the shares of Japan in China's two-way trade of other manufactures experienced a significant decline between 1986 and 1992: imports dropped from 33% to 16%, and exports declined from 12% to 9%. Whereas the share of China's imports of other manufactures from the EC declined from 23% in 1986 to 14% in 1992, the relative importance of the EC market for China's exports rose slightly from 15% to 16% in this period. The US market became increasingly important to China's exports of other manufacturing between 1986 and 1992, with export shares rising from 16% to 25%. Nevertheless, China's trade with the East Asian region (including Hong Kong and Japan) accounted for the bulk of trade in other manufactures, with export shares steady at just more than 50% and import shares holding at more than 60% for the 7-year period.

In conclusion, China's manufactured exports to all regions increased in intensity, showing slightly more dependence on the US and EC markets for exports over time, with expanding markets for electrical machinery and other manufactured products in the United States and expanding markets for apparel in the EC. At the same time, China was increasingly dependent on the East Asian economies for manufactured imports.

The growing importance of the interdependence of China's trade with the East Asian economies can most probably be explained by deterministic factors, such as, other things being equal, transportation costs and international-transaction costs, which depend in part on past investments in physical infrastructure, information, and education (Frankel 1993; Petri 1993). Moreover, the rapid growth of foreign-investment inflow from this region promotes China's regional integration with these economies. This will become more evident as we look at the development of the economic integration of Guangdong and Hong Kong, an area referred to as Greater Hong Kong (Goodman and Feng 1993).

Guangdong Province

Guangdong emerged as China's wealthiest province in the early 1990s. Its rapid economic growth and export expansion relied heavily on the influx of foreign investment, which was a result of China's special regional-development strategy, including the establishment of three SEZs in Guangdong. Foreign investment surged, growing at 49% annually between 1986 and 1993, from US$0.6 billion in 1986 to US$7.5 billion in 1993. This is equivalent to about 33% of China's total FDI inflow. Although FDI data by sector are not available at the provincial level, it is evident from the available aggregate data that FDI and exports are strongly correlated.

The most important forms of foreign investment in Guangdong are equity joint ventures, contractual joint ventures, and wholly foreign-owned enterprises. These FDI forms differ in the degree of risk involved and the permanence of cooperation. A contractual joint venture is an arrangement whereby the local and foreign partners loosely cooperate in joint projects or activities, according to terms stipulated in a contract. It involves less of a long-term investment commitment and risk than do equity joint ventures and wholly foreign-owned enterprises. Equity joint ventures grew rapidly in the 1980s, although the growth was to some extent cyclical. Wholly foreign-owned enterprises gained rapidly in importance as a form of capital commitment, rising from 1.6% of total FDI in 1985 to 24% in 1993. Difficulties finding a reliable local partner and cooperating in control management have led foreign investors to prefer wholly owned investments in some cases. The sectoral distribution of FDI shows that a significant proportion was injected into resource-extracting and -processing industries, which are labour-seeking, followed by real-estate development and service-related investment (Table 7.3).

Hong Kong was overwhelmingly Guangdong's largest source of foreign investment. The FDI from Hong Kong increased from US$0.6 billion in 1986 to US$6.8 billion in 1993. For four of these years, FDI from Hong Kong accounted for about 90% of total FDI and was never less than 70% of the total (Table 7.4). The low share in total FDI of the rest of the world has a downward bias, however, because many countries routed their investments in Guangdong through Hong Kong, using its entrepôt role in trade and investment. For instance, much of the Taiwanese investment in China was committed through Hong Kong. Similarly, some US and EC multinational enterprises (MNEs) also routed their investments through their branches or companies incorporated in Hong Kong.

Because of Hong Kong's dominant share of total FDI, Hong Kong is determined to extend its economic frontier into neighbouring regions through more intensive economic integration, thereby gradually becoming the hub of the South China Economic Zone, as portrayed by Chen and Wong (in Chapter 4). To some extent, this rapid economic integration is affected by complementary factors. Hong Kong has severe shortages of labour and land but has expertise in financial and commercial services, as well as an abundance of capital and many industrial entrepreneurs, whereas Guangdong has plenty of land and a large pool of trainable labour but is poorly endowed with factors such as entrepreneurship, soft and hard technology, capital, professional skills, and infrastructure. In 1990, monthly wages in Guangdong's most developed areas were no more than 20% of those in Hong Kong. Rent for land in the SEZs was between 5% and 14% of that in Hong Kong. Such large differences in the cost of production inputs are the driving forces behind increased economic integration, which is also due to the geographical proximity and cultural affinity of the two regions.

Hong Kong also played a dominant role in Guangdong's foreign trade, accounting for about 80% of Guangdong's exports and imports. Guangdong's exports to Hong Kong maintained a higher growth rate than to any other region since the mid-1980s, the share rising from 72% in 1986 to 86% in 1993 (Table 7.4). Hong Kong's import share grew as well, albeit not as rapidly, rising from 73% to 79% of total imports in the same period. Unfortunately, no cross-sectoral data are available for

Table 7.3. Foreign direct investment in Guangdong: forms of ownership and sectoral distribution (%).

Year	Ownership forms			Sectoral distribution						
	Contractual joint venture	Equity joint venture	Wholly foreign-owned enterprises	Resource-extracting and -processing industries	Real estate, public utilities, and services	Construction	Commerce and catering	Agriculture, forestry, and fishery	Communications	Others
1985	65.2	33.2	1.6	39.8	31.7	8.8	6.4	4.9	7.1	1.3
1986	75.1	22.8	2.1	75.7	13.7	0.6	3.3	1.9	2.9	1.9
1987	64.1	33.5	2.4	79.5	9.6	3.5	1.5	2.5	1.4	2.0
1988	47.5	41.0	11.5	80.3	11.2	0.3	1.9	2.4	2.9	1.0
1989	36.8	48.8	14.4	84.1	8.9	0.2	1.5	1.9	2.3	1.1
1990	31.0	44.2	24.8	86.3	6.3	0.1	2.8	0.9	1.3	2.3
1991	29.1	43.1	27.8	86.1	9.3	0.2	1.0	0.9	1.9	0.6
1992	38.8	36.6	24.6	84.2	11.8	0.9	0.5	1.0	0.7	0.9
1993	38.9	37.6	23.5	74.0	17.9	1.1	2.0	0.5	2.8	1.7

Source: Guangdong Statistical Bureau (n.d.).

Table 7.4. Guangdong's exports, imports, and FDI by geographic and sectoral distribution.

	Year	World (US$ millions)	Geographic distribution (%)					Sectoral distribution (US$ millions)			Share of exports by foreign firms in Guangdong's total exports (%)
			Hong Kong	Japan	Singapore	United States	Others	Textiles	Apparel	Electric and electronic products	
Exports	1985	2 953	NA	NA	NA	NA	NA	179.3	99.3	NA	NA
	1986	4 290	72.0	2.4	2.0	6.6	17.0	250.6	192.6	NA	9.1
	1987	5 444	75.4	2.8	2.0	5.9	13.9	353.5	356.1	NA	11.2
	1988	7 484	78.4	3.5	1.3	4.4	12.4	1 230.0	517.8	NA	16.1
	1989	8 168	79.8	3.7	1.4	4.0	11.1	1 315.0	398.7	798.4	27.9
	1990	10 560	82.5	2.7	1.3	3.8	9.7	1 508.0	724.0	1 252.0	35.3
	1991	13 688	84.7	2.8	0.9	3.7	7.9	1 974.0	1 236.0	1 675.0	38.9
	1992	18 440	85.7	2.6	0.8	4.2	6.7	2 562.0	2 197.0	2 113.0	44.2
	1993	27 027	85.8	2.5	0.8	4.1	6.8	3 620.0	3 642.0	3 527.0	38.3
Imports	1985	2 812	NA	NA	NA	NA	NA	NA	NA	291.3	NA
	1986	2 626	72.9	18.5	1.3	1.9	5.4	120.6	31.6	91.1	NA
	1987	3 627	82.9	9.7	0.6	2.0	4.8	417.5	222.8	108.9	NA
	1988	5 110	81.3	8.0	0.7	2.0	8.0	38.6	256.4	213.3	NA
	1989	4 831	73.7	6.4	2.0	3.6	14.3	71.6	65.7	213.9	NA
	1990	5 749	72.2	4.4	1.1	1.8	20.5	71.3	109.9	259.5	NA
	1991	8 510	74.0	4.6	1.3	2.8	17.3	75.7	228.2	366.4	NA
	1992	11 179	75.1	5.0	0.9	2.5	16.5	101.8	374.1	484.8	NA
	1993	19 899	78.8	4.0	1.2	2.2	13.8	90.8	873.1	751.1	NA
FDI	1985	515.3	NA	NA	NA	NA	NA	NA	NA	NA	NA
	1986	643.9	93.7	1.3	0.2	4.7	0.1	NA	NA	NA	NA
	1987	594.0	84.6	1.7	0.8	6.4	6.5	NA	NA	NA	NA
	1988	919.1	91.0	3.6	0.3	1.6	3.5	NA	NA	NA	NA
	1989	1 156.0	82.4	3.3	2.1	4.5	7.7	NA	NA	NA	NA
	1990	1 460.0	69.8	9.1	0.9	9.3	10.9	NA	NA	NA	NA
	1991	1 823.0	79.5	4.3	0.4	5.4	10.4	NA	NA	NA	NA
	1992	3 552.0	89.0	0.5	0.5	2.0	8.0	NA	NA	NA	NA
	1993	7 498.0	90.3	1.4	0.4	1.2	6.7	NA	NA	NA	NA

Source: Guangdong Statistical Bureau (n.d.), China SSB (n.d.), and authors' own compilations.

Note: FDI, foreign direct investment; NA, not available.

analyzing the sectoral distribution of Guangdong's exports and imports to and from different regions in the world.

A sectoral analysis of Guangdong's overall trade performance shows that the shares of textiles and apparel in total exports grew rapidly, increasing from 6% and 3.4%, respectively, in 1985 to more than 13% each in 1993. Exports of electrical and electronics products accounted for about 10% of total exports in 1989, reaching a share of 13% in 1993. On the other hand, imports of textiles experienced a decline between 1986 and 1993, with the share in total imports dropping to 0.5% by 1993. Imports of apparel and electrical and electronics products grew slowly, each only accounting for a share of about 4% of total imports by 1993. This analysis shows that the structural distribution of Guangdong's exports and imports appears to be highly correlated with the sectoral distribution of FDI, the bulk of which was in traditional, labour-intensive industries, as well as in offshore assembly operations and other kinds of vertical cooperation, with Hong Kong being the primary investor and dominant trading partner. This correlation between FDI and export performance confirms the hypothesis that FDI in industries in which a country has a comparative advantage is trade promoting.

FDI not only turned Guangdong into an export production base but also brought about its specialization in light manufacturing. The share of China's textile exports produced in Guangdong increased from 4.8% in 1986 to 24.4% in 1992; the share of apparel exports increased from 3.3% to 8.3% in the same period; and the share of exports of electrical and electronic products increased from 11.6% in 1989 to 14.4% in 1992 (Guangdong Statistical Bureau n.d.; China Resources Trade Consultancy n.d.).

Initially, by transforming Guangdong Province and then by fanning out to other parts of China, Hong Kong has helped to bring China's pattern of trade into line with its comparative advantage. Hong Kong's manufacturing sector, traditionally less important than in other NIEs, joined forces with South China in the last 15 years to form a much more self-sufficient "national" economy (Chen, P. 1994). By 1992, about 3 million people were employed by Hong Kong firms with investments in Guangdong or, more accurately, in the Pearl River Delta. Thus, Greater Hong Kong is a growing area of economic integration that originated in economic interaction of Hong Kong and the Pearl River Delta.

Guangdong's economic integration with Hong Kong has been driven by independent enterprises searching for profitable patterns of trade or, in other words, purely by market forces in the sense described by Dobson (in Chapter 1) and by Drysdale and Garnaut (1993) in their analysis of East Asian integration. The advantages of Guangdong's geographical proximity and cheap supply of production inputs were important reasons explaining why much of Hong Kong's industrial capacity was transferred across the border. Nonetheless, China's open-door economic policy as a stimulus to rapid economic integration cannot be overestimated. With this new policy, international trade was decentralized, prices for traded goods were partly liberalized, and foreign-exchange controls were relaxed. Preferential treatment and tax incentives were granted to foreign firms in the SEZs. A multiple-foreign-exchange-rate system, foreign-exchange control, and rent reduction were also effective measures for subsidizing exports and attracting foreign investors (Chen, P. 1994).

Interprovincial level

Because the economic development of Guangdong has been closely linked to developments in Hong Kong, one tends to overlook the economic relations between Guangdong and other areas of China, which are quite extensive. China's regional-development strategy in the prereform era was to treat each province as a separate economic entity to be developed more or less independently of the others. The central-planning system's overemphasis on vertical leadership resulted in the atomization of various ministries, industries, and localities. Virtually no horizontal economic links existed between different provinces. As a result, the interior of China pursued import substitution in the consumer-goods sector by effectively banning most imports. Similarly, coastal China broadened the scope of its own development to embrace the capital-goods industry, thereby further increasing its dependence on imported raw materials.

According to the World Bank (1990), the lack of horizontal economic links between the provinces could potentially result in either of two opposing scenarios for the country's economic development. In the first scenario, the less-reformed interior would erect protective barriers, selling less of its raw materials to coastal regions and buying fewer consumer goods from these regions. Such barriers would perpetuate the autarkic development strategy for the interior, thus depressing its economic growth. As a result, coastal provinces would have to import more raw materials from abroad, which requires pursuing a manufactured-export-led growth strategy. Under this scenario, the economic disintegration of China could become reality.

In the other scenario, market reforms would spread into the interior. As barriers to trade and factor mobilities were dismantled, the interior would benefit from spill-over effects from the coastal provinces, thereby accelerating its pace of progress. This process would enhance the economic integration of the coast and the interior.

It is not immediately obvious which scenario is prevailing in the reform era because of the lack of data on interregional trade. There are many reports about increasing regional protectionism, which characterizes the first scenario. Some provinces have gone as far as setting up checkpoints along their borders with Guangdong or erecting other trade barriers to curb the outflow of agricultural products and raw materials. One extreme example is the rice war that appeared to have developed between Guangdong and Hunan during 1990 and 1991 where barriers to the movement of rice were erected (Chao 1991). On the other hand, strong evidence indicates an increasing interdependence of Guangdong and the rest of China. According to one estimate, in the 10 years from 1982 to 1991, an average of 20% annual growth in Guangdong's industrial output was the result of demand from other provinces (Zhu 1992). What makes this estimate even more noteworthy is the fact that Guangdong tends to run a trade deficit with other provinces because of its large raw-materials imports. For example, in 1986, Guangdong imported raw materials worth 1.52 billion yuan from the rest of China while only exporting goods worth 0.35 billion yuan (Zhu 1992).

Because only a few statistics on interprovincial trade are publicly available, indirect methods must be used to estimate the magnitude of Guangdong's trade with the rest of China. Guangdong's total net exports are provided by the accounting framework of the Material Product System (MPS). The net overseas exports are subtracted from this figure to obtain Guangdong's net exports to other provinces (Chong 1993). These residual net exports to other provinces are summarized in Table 7.5.

Table 7.5. Guangdong's net exports (billions of yuan).

Year	Net exports		
	Total	Overseas	Other provinces
1985	−1.803	1.484	−3.287
1986	−2.282	5.834	−8.116
1987	−1.416	6.744	−8.160
1988	0.054	8.813	−8.759
1989	2.107	12.533	−10.426
1990	10.769	22.959	−12.190
1991	15.963	27.491	−11.528
1992	3.801	39.940	−36.139
1993	5.020	31.994	−26.974

Source: Guangdong Statistical Bureau (n.d.) and Hainan Statistical Bureau (n.d.).

Note: Total exports are estimated as the difference between national income and national income available according to the Material Product System (MPS) account (World Bank 1990). Because net exports are derived as a residual, they include any statistical discrepancy. Net exports to other provinces are derived as the difference between total net exports and net exports to overseas; hence, they, too, include statistical discrepencies.

The most striking feature of Table 7.5 is the significant increase of Guangdong's net imports from other provinces between 1985 and 1993, which indicates that Guangdong's imports from other provinces grew much faster than its exports to the other provinces. This is consistent with the observation that Guangdong's market share of manufactured goods in the inland area peaked in 1988 but started to decline as Guangdong-made products met strong competition from inland producers after reforms had spread into the inland areas (Yuan 1995).

The actual magnitude of interprovincial trade between Guangdong and other provinces is still unknown. We know that Guangdong became attractive to foreign investors, that its industry was rapidly upgraded, and that its products penetrated the markets of other provinces. Goodman and Feng (1993) estimated that, in recent years, the goods produced in Guangdong were split equally between sales to other provinces, to international markets, and to the market in Guangdong itself. Assuming as a plausible benchmark that one-third of total exports was exported to other provinces, we can estimate the value of exports to other provinces in 1993 at 84.1 billion yuan. This implies that the estimated value of imports from other provinces for the same year is as high as 111.1 billion yuan, or 34.4% of Guangdong's GDP. Therefore, imports from other provinces have been extremely important in sustaining Guangdong's remarkable export expansion overseas. Furthermore, inland provinces benefited greatly from Guangdong's integration with Hong Kong and its specialization in light manufacturing for the international market. (This observation lends support to the hypothesis of Guangdong's increased economic integration within China.) The impact of FDI on Guangdong would be substantially underestimated if its role in boosting interprovincial trade were ignored in favour of its role of promoting external trade.

Guangdong's economic exchange with inland areas takes on other forms as well, such as domestic-linkage (*neilian*) investments and labour services (Yukawa 1992). With the help of investments in other provinces, Guangdong established supply bases for raw materials and energy, as well as sales bases and marketing networks for Guangdong enterprises. Guangdong's economic boom created a huge demand for labour, which was satisfied by large numbers of migrant workers from other provinces, more than three million by the early 1990s.

Inland provinces also benefit from these forms of economic relationship with Guangdong. The inland provinces invested in Guangdong to establish marketing and sales networks and, more importantly, to establish export channels for their enterprises (Zhu 1992). Moreover, labour inflow into Guangdong not only eased the unemployment problem for inland areas, it also generated significant amounts of income when migrant workers gave money to their families. Money sent back by migrant workers to one county in Sichuan was at times more than the total GDP of that county (Fan 1994).

In sum, despite some evidence to the contrary, it appears that interprovincial economic relationships have intensified since China adopted its economic open-door policy. Guangdong, which achieved prosperity through participation in international markets, also strengthened its ties with inland areas through various forms of economic exchange and has thus become the "locomotive" pulling the inland economies.

Firm-level analysis

The firm-level survey,[4] conducted in August 1994, covered 30 foreign firms in Guangdong, of which 15 belonged to the household electric- and electronic-appliances sector and 15 belonged to the textiles and garment sector. These firms were the top 15 recipients of foreign investment in their respective sectors in 1993, the year for which data were obtained.

The 15 firms in the electric- and electronic-appliances sector were concentrated in three cities: Guangzhou, Shenzhen, and Huizhou. The 15 firms in the textiles and garment sector, on the other

[4] Assistance of the Economic Research Centre of the Guangdong Provincial Government is gratefully acknowledged.

hand, were spread among 10 cities and counties: Guangzhou, Shenzhen, Zhuhai, Jiangmen, Fushan, Shunde, Xinhui, Kaiping, Yangjiang, and Chaozhou. Only 3 of the 30 firms were wholly owned; the remaining 27 were joint ventures. Considering the parent's home country or region, we found that 23 firms were based in Hong Kong and Macao; 5, in Japan (all in the electric- and electronic-appliances sector); 1, in the United States; and 1, in Singapore. This distribution is consistent with the overall distribution of foreign equity ownership.

The average annual sales amounted to US$41 million, with the highest being US$282 million and the lowest being only US$2.4 million. The local and international markets were equally important to the sample firms (Tables 7.6–7.9). Although 12 firms, or 40% of the sample, exported more than 67% of their output, another 12 firms sold more than 67% of their output to the domestic market. This means that market penetration and industry relocation were key factors for FDI in Guangdong. Furthermore, Guangdong seemed to be very lax in enforcing the requirement that all output be exported. The existence of such requirements was reported by 28 firms, but only 10 actually met them in 1993.

Most of the firms sold a large share of their output to their parents, although seven firms did not export to the respective parent at all (Tables 7.6 and 7.7). This suggests that firms were largely relying on their parents to market their output in international markets. In other words, networking was considered a corporate strategy through which markets were penetrated and developed. This was

Table 7.6. Surveyed firms in electronics by investing country and destination of sales.

Firm nationality (% sales)	Surveyed firms (*n*)		
	Exported	To parent	To home country
Hong Kong	9	9	9
>90	4	5 [a]	3 [a]
67–90	1	2	1
33–67	0	0	0
<33	3	0	0
0	1	2	2
Unknown	0	0	3
Japan	5	5	5
>90	0	2	2
67–90	0	0	0
33–67	2	0	0
<33	1	0	0
0	2	3	3
Unknown	0	0	0
United States	1	1	1
>90	1	1	1
67–90	0	0	0
33–67	0	0	0
<33	0	0	0
0	0	0	0
Unknown	0	0	0
Total	15	15	15
>90	5	8	6
67–90	1	2	1
33–67	2	0	0
<33	4	0	0
0	3	5	5
Unknown	0	0	3

Source: Interviews and questionnaires.
Note: Numbers of firms with interaffiliate sales are not available.
[a] This inconsistency is due to the fact that some MNEs committed FDI in Guangdong through their subsidiaries or companies incorporated in Hong Kong, which makes the percentage of sales to parent company and to home country different in the table.

Table 7.7. Surveyed firms in textiles and garments by investing country
and destination of sales.

Firm nationality (% sales)	Surveyed firms (n)		
	Exported	To parent	To home country
Hong Kong	12	12	12
>90	2	8 [a]	11 [a]
67–90	4	1	1
33–67	3	3	0
<33	3	0	0
0	0	0	0
Unknown	0	0	0
Macau	2	2	2
>90	0	0	0
67–90	0	0	1
33–67	1	0	0
<33	1	0	0
0	0	1	1
Unknown	0	1	0
Singapore	1	1	1
>90	0	0	0
67–90	0	0	0
33–67	0	0	0
<33	1	0	1
0	0	1	0
Unknown	0	0	0
Total	15	15	15
>90	2	8	11
67–90	4	1	2
33–67	4	3	0
<33	5	0	1
0	0	2	1
Unknown	0	1	0

Source: Interviews and questionnaires.
Note: Numbers of firms with interaffiliate sales are not available.
[a] This inconsistency is due to the fact that some MNEs committed FDI in Guangdong through their subsidiaries or companies incorporated in Hong Kong, which makes the percentage of sales to parent company and to home country different in the table.

Table 7.8. Surveyed firms in electronics: intrafirm sales and procurement by foreign affiliates, 1994.

	Japan	United States	European Community	Hong Kong	Local
Sales					
Total (US$ millions)	65.35	33.30	NA	48.26	NA
Home economy and third country (%)	31.30	99.30	NA	29.30	NA
Local economy (%)	68.70	0.70	NA	70.70	NA
Procurement					
Total (US$ millions)	43.69	28.19	NA	29.67	NA
Home economy and third country (%)	37.00	100.00	NA	47.00	NA
Local economy (%)	63.00	0.00	NA	53.00	NA

Source: Interviews and questionnaires.
Note: NA, not available.

Table 7.9. Surveyed firms in textiles and garments: intrafirm sales and procurement by foreign affiliates, 1994.

	Hong Kong	Macau	Singapore	Local
Sales				
Total (US$ millions)	32.66	19.02	11.49	NA
Home economy (%)	49.50	13.30	2.60	NA
Local economy (%)	50.20	73.20	80.00	NA
Third country (%)	0.30	13.50	17.40	NA
Procurement				
Total (US$ millions)	14.79	14.32	5.00	NA
Home economy (%)	63.80	0.00	0.00	NA
Local economy (%)	29.80	96.20	80.00	NA
Third country (%)	6.40	3.80	20.00	NA

Source: Interviews and questionnaires.
Note: NA, not available.

Table 7.10. Surveyed firms in electronics by investing country and sourcing of materials and components.

	Surveyed firms (n)		
Firm nationality (% sourcing)	Imported	From parent	From home country
Hong Kong	9	9	9
>90	3	7 [a]	6 [a]
67–90	2	0	0
33–67	1	0	0
<33	3	0	0
0	0	2	2
Unknown	0	0	1
Japan	5	5	5
>90	3	1	3
67–90	0	0	0
33–67	1	1	1
<33	1	0	0
0	0	1	1
Unknown	0	2	0
United States	1	1	1
>90	1	1	1
67–90	0	0	0
33–67	0	0	0
<33	0	0	0
0	0	0	0
Unknown	0	0	0
Total	15	15	15
>90	7	9	10
67–90	2	0	0
33–67	2	1	1
<33	4	0	0
0	0	3	3
Unknown	0	2	1

Source: Interviews and questionnaires.
Note: Numbers of firms with interaffiliate sales are not available.
[a] This inconsistency is due to the fact that some MNEs committed FDI in Guangdong through their subsidiaries or companies incorporated in Hong Kong, which makes the percentage of purchases from parent company and from home country different in the table.

Table 7.11. Surveyed firms in textiles and garments by investing country and sourcing of materials and components.

Firm nationality (% sourcing)	Surveyed firms (*n*)		
	Imported	From parent	From home country
Hong Kong	12	12	12
>90	2	10 [a]	5 [a]
67–90	7	1	0
33–67	2	0	2
<33	1	0	1
0	0	0	3
Unknown	0	1	1
Macau	2	2	2
>90	0	0	0
67–90	0	0	0
33–67	0	0	0
<33	2	0	0
0	0	2	2
Unknown	0	0	0
Singapore	1	1	1
>90	0	0	0
67–90	0	0	0
33–67	0	0	0
<33	1	0	0
0	0	1	1
Unknown	0	0	0
Total	15	15	15
>90	2	10	5
67–90	7	1	0
33–67	2	0	2
<33	4	0	1
0	0	3	6
Unknown	0	1	1

Source: Interviews and questionnaires.
Note: Numbers of firms with interaffiliate sales are not available.
[a] This inconsistency is due to the fact that some MNEs committed FDI in Guangdong through their subsidiaries or companies incorporated in Hong Kong, which makes the percentage of purchases from parent company and from home country different in the table.

Table 7.12. Imported capital goods from parent.

Sourcing from parents (%)	Number of firms		
	Electronics	Textiles and garments	Total
100	10	9	19
50–99	2 [a]	—	2
1–49	—	2 [b]	2
0	—	1	1
Unknown	3	3	6
Total	15	15	30

Source: Interviews and questionnaires.
[a] Both firms sourced 70% from the parent.
[b] One firm sourced 5% from the parent, the other, 12%.

especially true of Hong Kong firms, of which 7 of 9 firms in electronics and 9 of 12 firms in the textiles and garment industry shifted back more than 67% of their output to their parents. Such wide marketing–networking tended to be one of the most important firm-specific characteristics of Hong Kong enterprises. From our conversation with firm managers, foreign firms in China were also very keen on developing their own export channels.

Eighteen firms imported more than 67% of input materials and components. Local sourcing was important to eight firms that purchased more than 67% of their inputs from the domestic market (Tables 7.10 and 7.11). Eleven firms reported that they were subject to local content rules, but only seven met these requirements in 1993. Overall, there seemed to be a correlation between sourcing and sales behaviour. In other words, firms producing for the domestic market sourced mainly from local suppliers, whereas highly export-oriented firms imported most of their inputs.

Almost 67%, or 19 firms, procured all imported inputs from their parents (Tables 7.10 and 7.11). Similarly, 19 firms bought all imported capital goods from their parents (Table 7.12). The main reason for sourcing capital goods, materials, and components from parents was that parents supply better-quality and lower-priced goods, besides providing updated technology and know-how. This is consistent with the theory that MNEs tend to internalize firm-specific capital; that is, they take advantage of the firms' ownership relations (Dunning 1993). This implies that intrafirm trade increases internalization.

That Japanese firms behaved differently from other firms in the sample is notable. All five Japanese firms sold a high proportion of their output in China's domestic market while sourcing a large share of inputs from abroad, which suggests that their main interest in Guangdong was to penetrate China's domestic market. The analysis of Japan's investment strategy in China leads to the conclusion that Japanese outward direct investment was motivated by securing vital resources, circumventing trade barriers, and strengthening competitive powers by penetrating local markets. Instead of committing large amounts of direct investment in the early 1980s, Japanese firms believed that exporting was a better approach to penetrating the newly opened, unpredictable Chinese market. As might be expected, when local market shares were threatened by the loss of international comparative advantage, direct investment in China by these Japanese industries surged. In contrast to Japanese firms, most Hong Kong firms established production bases in China with the intention of exporting a large share of the output.

Anecdotal evidence

Personal interviews were conducted with the general managers of two household electric- and electronic-appliances firms and two textiles and garment firms. For the sake of confidentiality, we shall refer to these firms as electric firms A and B and garment firms A and B.

Electric firm A is an air-conditioner manufacturer with an equity investment of US$5 million in 1984, of which the Japanese and the local partners own equal shares. Electric firm B is also a joint venture with a Japanese firm; it produces refrigerators and other appliances. Garment firms A and B are both joint ventures with Hong Kong firms. The shares of foreign and local contributions in garment firm A were 49% and 51%, respectively, of total equity investment; in garment firm B, 51% and 49%, respectively.

The survey findings, which demonstrated that Hong Kong firms tend to export to international markets whereas Japanese firms tend to target local markets, appear to be confirmed by the interviews. Garment firm A produced 8 of the 10 well-known Hong Kong brands of clothing and exported 100% of its output to the North American market through its parent's marketing network. Guangdong's cheap labour and land prices were the major reasons behind setting up this facility. In comparison, the Japanese electric firm A exported 60% and electric firm B exported nothing of their respective outputs to international markets. Most of their products were absorbed domestically. One of the firms' managers mentioned that exporting was the only way to generate the foreign exchange needed to balance foreign-currency requirements.

Export orientation seemed to be negatively correlated with local input procurement. Garment firm A produced 100% for the international market and imported 100% of input materials from Italy. Electric firm A procured all supporting parts from local suppliers and imported only the core component — compressors — from the parent in Japan. Similar behaviour was observed in other firms that procured to a large extent locally and imported only the core components for which local supplies did not meet the quality requirements. Establishing good local linkages and networks was considered very important for foreign firms operating in China.

Foreign firms were likely to follow a "snow-ball" development pattern. The parent company usually established a small joint venture in the beginning and expanded its business later through additional investments, openings of new subsidiaries, or both. Garment firm A's initial equity capital was only HK$2 million. After a few years of operating, it became quite successful; total sales reached HK$100 million in 1993. A new and larger factory was built to meet the additional demand. Electric firm A presented a similar picture. To meet the rapidly expanding business, additional capital of US$3.5 million was invested to enhance its production capacity. At the same time, about 10 sister companies were established across the country in Beijing, Shenyang, Changchuen, Dalian, Fushan, and Shenzhen among others.

Some advantages of FDI are believed to be the transfer of foreign capital and marketing and management skills to the host economy. Our interviews showed that the foreign partner tended to be responsible for technology and production management, but the local partner was in charge of personnel and other administrative management. Garment firm A reported that all technicians were hired from Hong Kong and were responsible for design and quality control. In electric firms A and B, Japanese engineers and technicians were found in the assembly shops training the Chinese workers at the time of the interview. The Japanese firms followed more closely their parents' management styles, such as close, friendly, and cooperative relationships between workers and management. The Japanese firms also had well-managed workshops and employee-welfare programs. A unique characteristic of investing in China is the need to provide staff with food and appropriate accommodation. Hence, the four firms interviewed had to set up their own staff canteens before they could formally open for production.

In sum, the firm-level studies confirm that both international and domestic markets were equally important to foreign firms as sources for inputs and markets for output. Both market penetration and industry relocation seemed to be key reasons for the presence of FDI in Guangdong. Foreign firms relied heavily on their parents to provide them with technological support and management know-how by supplying firm-specific capital and technical and management personnel. FDI has transformed Guangdong into a light-manufacturing base by supplying this important package of foreign capital and marketing and management skills specifically tailored for such production processes.

Conclusion

Before China started its economic reform in 1979, there were large differences between the returns to the production factors of labour, land, and capital on the two sides of the Hong Kong–Guangdong border. At that time, Hong Kong was already very integrated in the world economy; its export-oriented manufacturing sector specialized in the production of light manufactures. However, further development was constrained by high labour costs and escalating land prices. Nearby, on the other side of the border, Guangdong had an abundant supply of labour and land, but the economy was underdeveloped and isolated from the rest of the world, thus lacking profitable opportunities for those factors of production. The severe limitations on factor mobility prevented benefits from these differences in factor prices from being explored.

China's economic reforms and open-door policy enabled foreign investors, especially from Hong Kong, to establish production facilities in Guangdong with very low production costs. Hong Kong manufacturers gradually and cautiously moved their production lines across the border, being forced to do so by Hong Kong's escalating rental and wage costs. Eventually, the pace of relocation picked up as remaining firms faced increasing competition from firms that had already relocated into Guangdong.

Hong Kong investors set up production lines for household electrical and electronic products, textiles and apparel, footwear, toys, and other light-manufactured products, in other words, for the goods in which Hong Kong firms had specialized. These labour-seeking industries are resource extracting and processing. As a result, FDI, especially that from Hong Kong, rapidly transformed Guangdong into a light-manufacturing base.

Initially, foreign firms were export oriented. As economic reforms took hold, income levels of the local population increased, and people's tastes changed. This development rapidly increased the local demand for products made in Guangdong by foreign firms. Although China has been slow in removing restrictions on imports of consumer goods from abroad, it seems to be very lax in enforcing export-orientation requirements for foreign firms. Other restrictions preventing foreign businesses from penetrating the domestic market were also gradually relaxed as China liberalized its foreign investment regime and became one of the most liberal foreign investment environments in the developing world. As a result, foreign firms sold increasingly larger shares of output in China's domestic markets. By the early 1990s, the international and the domestic markets became equally important to many foreign firms. This further stimulated Guangdong's specializing as a large-scale light-manufacturing base.

With the rapid growth of its industrial production, Guangdong had to import increasing amounts of raw materials and intermediate products from abroad and from the rest of China. This development accelerated the integration of the province with the rest of the world and the rest of China. The almost unlimited supply of labour from other provinces enabled Guangdong to contain wage inflation, despite the remarkable speed of growth, thereby ensuring its continued comparative advantage as a low-cost producer.

Foreign firms sourced production materials and components both locally and from abroad. Sourcing from the parents seemed to be unsubstitutable and invaluable to many of the firms. Most of the foreign firms in both the household electric- and electronic-appliances and the textiles and garment sectors sold a large portion of exports to their parents and imported at least the core parts of their products from them, implying a high degree of reliance on the parents' technology and marketing networks. Firm-specific capital and technical and management personnel provided by the parent ensured the supply of necessary technological support and management know-how.

The role FDI played in Guangdong's emergence as a light-manufacturing base is underestimated if one focuses only on its role in promoting external trade while ignoring its role in boosting interprovincial trade. In fact, Guangdong's rapid outward integration has been concurrent with its inward integration with the rest of China. The significant increase of interprovincial trade and investment flows, not to mention the labour inflow into Guangdong, created increasingly dense ties between Guangdong and other provinces. Such interprovincial economic cooperation, or integration, between the coast and the interior is now much stronger than in the prereform era. This development puts to rest some concerns about China's economic disintegration as a result of its unbalanced regional development.

Chapter 8

THE PHILIPPINES

The Underpinnings of East Asian Trade and Investment

Florian A. Alburo and
Maria Socorro Gochoco-Bautista

Philippine policymakers have set the goal of achieving newly industrialized economy (NIE) status for the country by 2000. The country's industrialization policy, as embodied in the Medium-Term Philippine Development Plan, is premised on global competitiveness. Policymakers generally use the term *global competitiveness* to emphasize the idea that a nation's industries must actively participate in the greater international division of labour so that the nation can achieve a high and sustained rate of economic growth. Although the development policy has been criticized as lacking in specifics, certain elements are nevertheless clear: the direction of Philippine economic policy will be toward establishing a more open trade regime, continuing liberalization, and attracting foreign direct investment (FDI) into the country.

The reason for giving this direction to economic policy is the greater appreciation by many in government and in the private sector of the close linkages between trade and FDI and the important role that FDI plays in industrial upgrading. There will be no catching up to advanced industrial countries without industrial upgrading — the process by which new, advanced, higher value-added industries are introduced even as old ones are allowed to die or are exported.

Two specific instruments are being employed to advance industrialization. The first is the further intensification of trade liberalization, which started with the previous administration. The measures include continued reduction in the level and dispersion of tariff rates, the removal of remaining import restrictions, and the specification of the long-term border restrictions.[1] The second is the continued modification of the foreign-investment laws to provide wider entry for FDI into such sectors as retail trade, the review of the need for List C (products that are not open to foreign investments for protective reasons), and the provision of added incentives, such as net-operating-loss carryover. These two instruments provide the structure for encouraging foreign investments, as part of the country's promotion of global competitiveness. This industrialization policy will be supported by institutional changes. In particular, the country's Board of Investments (BOI) is to shift its mandate from regulating and providing incentives to selected industries to promoting and providing generalized incentives across all sectors.

---

[1] The latest executive order, No. 264, lays out the complete tariff rates that will eventually prevail until 2004, at which time a uniform rate of 5% shall be effective.

Conceptual framework

Global competitiveness brings about increasing interdependence in trading and investment activities among economies and greater integration of these economies as a result. Understanding how this is achieved requires several levels of analysis. At the macroeconomic level, economists argue that nations can exploit comparative advantage through trade. Governments can adopt measures to attract FDI so as to create new areas of comparative advantage with the technology transfer and other benefits that FDI brings. It bears emphasizing, however, that these government policies are generally geared to influencing the interindustry configuration. Thus, investment policies, for example, may give incentives to particular types of industries deemed consistent with national goals.

At the firm level, Dunning's (1993) ownership–location–internalization (OLI) paradigm posits that a firm's decision to invest in a particular site depends on ownership, location factors, and type of industry. The internalization theory of FDI posits that a firm has certain specific advantages it can exploit in other markets, using the firm's internal organization and structural hierarchy, rather than incurring high transactions costs, using the market-exchange mechanism in transferring intangible assets. Porter (1986) focused on a firm's competitive strategy. He argued that a firm seeks to create or achieve competitive advantage over rival firms in an industry by managing its value chain, or the different types of its activities, in a certain way. His type of analysis, therefore, focuses on intra-industry competition.

Purpose of the study

The phenomenon of global competitiveness is not well documented or systematically and empirically evident in the Philippines, either at the aggregate or the firm level. This study attempts to document how firm behaviour is integrating the region as firms trade within and with one another across borders. We focus on the electronics industry and the textiles and garment industry. The firms included in the study are those that have some foreign equity or partnership. We were able to obtain interview results for 11 firms in the electronics industry and 12 firms in the textiles and garment industry.

In general, the integration of trading nations' economies has increased. In the past, the Philippines was more integrated with Japan and the United States than with other countries in the region because Japan and the United States are the Philippine's traditional trading partners and sources of FDI. Recent investment from the NIEs is changing this. Certain locational factors in developing countries like the Philippines, such as cheap labour and abundant resources, have allowed these countries to serve as manufacturing bases for the NIEs, which take advantage of lower production costs while selling the manufactured output in developed countries. The data on inward FDI show that FDI from Japan and the NIEs, especially Hong Kong and Korea, is increasing, whereas investments from Canada and the United States are declining.

The survey results indicate that greater economic integration in the region has occurred, despite a wide variety of firm arrangements and ownership patterns. The fact that firms compete with other firms in the same industry, regardless of their home country or ownership pattern, is consistent with the value-chain analysis, according to which a firm will locate segments of its activities in particular locations to suit its strategic objectives. This is also consistent with the intuitively appealing notion of a "global" firm, which emphasizes the ways affiliates and the relationships among their activities are managed or coordinated, rather than ownership of the firm. Thus, newer forms of firm relationship evolve, in which all parties have something to contribute to the production process.

Analysis of specific segments of the value chain in the textiles and garment industry shows that cheap labour in the Philippines and the Multifibre Arrangement (MFA) have encouraged firms to import inputs, process them, and export the resulting products to the home country or to third countries. In the electronics industry, all firms were in consumer electronics at the low end of the value chain.

The increased globalization of production is consistent with a variety of networking relationships, or a relatively nonhierarchical structure among independent firms, affiliates, wholly owned subsidiaries, and so forth. The implication of these findings is that there is no reason to expect that the increased globalization of production will lead to convergence in one mode of production.

In some cases, the survey results seem to be consistent with the operation of a vintage effect. As investment matures to the production stage, more localization takes place in the form of more local inputs being used, increased local sales, or increased local ownership shares, or all three. This is true of some firms in the electronics industry.

The rest of the study is divided into three parts. First, we analyze general trends in trade and investment, which illustrate greater regional integration between the Philippines and other Asian economies. From a generally aggregate picture, we pay attention to the flows in the electronics and the textiles and garment industries. Within them, some comparison is made in the trade structure between 1986 and 1992. Next, we analyze the survey results. A final section concludes the chapter by linking the aggregate analysis with the results from the survey. Some policy implications are also drawn.

Like all survey-based analyses, the data are limited by the amount of information provided by respondent firms. This information is not always comprehensive and is subject to the usual limitations concerning accuracy. However, the approach we adopted is to examine aggregate trade data to suggest some patterns of underlying firm relationships, especially in the two industries studied. Working hypotheses are then tested through the surveys and particular accounts given in open-ended questions in the interviews.

To the extent that both the macro- and the microanalyses are consistent and impart similar perspectives, the underlying interdependence across economies in the region is being driven by intrafirm interactions and intraindustry relationships. We can then define the various policy parameters that may have a bearing in supporting such interdependence and the associated regional cooperation.

Trends in regional integration

The increasing integration of the region can be illustrated in various ways. In this section, we focus on several measures and different levels of analysis, namely, trade and FDI trends at the aggregate level, the importance of trade in both the electronics and the textiles and garment industries with other economies in the region, the amount of intraindustry trade (IIT) in the two industries between the Philippines and the other economies in the region, and finally the correlation of shares of total merchandise trade and FDI.

At the aggregate level, in 1986–92, the United States remained the top destination for Philippine exports; the Asian region came third after the European Community (EC) (Tables 8.1 and 8.2). By 1993, though, the Asian region had replaced Europe as the second largest export destination. The Asian group remained the top source of imports for the Philippines; its share of total imports increased from 25% to 27% between 1986 and 1992. The share of imports from Japan, the second major source, increased from 25% to 26% in the same period but fell to 23% in 1993.

According to the foreign-trade statistics, Asia–Pacific economies account for almost 75% of the Philippines' trade among its top 20 trading partners. From having had a share of more than 70% of trade (export or import) more than a decade ago, Japan and the United States together now account for only 50%. Although this share of total trade remains significant, the decline has been substantial. Part of the reason for the decline lies in the political instability and macroeconomic problems of the Philippines in the 1980s, which likewise affected FDI inflows. Consequently, the shares of the other countries have increased. The trade weights, however, continue to be biased toward Japan and the

Table 8.1. The Philippines' exports of manufactures by selected ISIC category, year, and partner.

Industry	Year	World totals (US$ millions)	Japan	Hong Kong	Singapore	Other NIEs	ASEAN-4	China	United States	European Community	Other
						Shares of world totals (%)					
All manufacturing	1986	2 549	12	5	2	6	3	4	35	24	10
	1989	4 221	14	4	3	3	4	1	37	21	13
	1992	5 421	15	5	3	6	3	2	38	20	9
Textiles	1986	105	4	5	1	3	1	1	44	22	19
	1989	211	5	4	1	3	1	0	42	25	19
	1992	310	4	12	1	3	1	1	33	24	20
Apparel	1986	236	4	5	0	0	0	0	44	28	19
	1989	456	3	1	0	0	0	0	55	24	17
	1992	681	4	3	0	0	0	0	51	22	19
Electrical machinery	1986	342	7	11	10	1	9	0	39	23	1
	1989	783	6	9	8	1	5	0	49	19	4
	1992	1 293	22	9	4	3	1	0	43	16	2
Office and computing machinery	1986	5	0	1	85	0	2	0	11	0	1
	1989	55	3	9	0	53	2	0	7	4	22
	1992	194	4	11	12	28	2	0	14	19	10
Other industries	1986	1 861	14	4	1	7	3	5	33	24	9
	1989	2 716	19	3	2	4	5	1	30	21	13
	1992	2 943	16	4	2	8	4	3	33	22	7

Source: ANU (1995).
Note: NIE, newly industrialized economy; ASEAN-4, Indonesia, Malaysia, the Philippines, and Thailand; ISIC, International Standard Industrial Classification.

Table 8.2. The Philippines' imports of manufactures by selected ISIC category, year, and partner.

Industry	Year	World totals (US$ millions)	Shares of world totals (%)								
			Japan	Hong Kong	Singapore	Other NIEs	ASEAN-4	China	United States	European Community	Other
All manufacturing	1986	2 998	25	5	3	12	3	2	21	16	13
	1989	7 395	25	4	6	4	4	2	17	15	23
	1992	10 188	26	4	5	14	3	1	17	15	15
Textiles	1986	215	14	32	0	39	2	1	3	4	5
	1989	465	6	23	3	8	5	2	4	3	46
	1992	645	7	24	1	51	4	2	5	3	3
Apparel	1986	6	13	27	3	26	3	2	14	10	2
	1989	20	13	22	7	6	8	1	10	13	20
	1992	36	11	19	5	23	6	3	16	14	3
Electrical machinery	1986	341	26	3	3	6	0	0	41	19	2
	1989	768	32	4	6	3	1	0	31	13	10
	1992	1 567	36	5	6	10	2	1	24	14	2
Office and computing machinery	1986	34	25	5	2	4	0	0	43	6	15
	1989	109	30	6	8	2	1	0	27	10	16
	1992	371	28	5	6	7	4	0	13	35	2
Other industries	1986	2 402	26	3	3	11	4	3	20	16	14
	1989	6 033	25	3	6	4	4	2	16	16	24
	1992	7 569	26	3	5	12	3	1	17	16	17

Source: ANU (1995).
Note: NIE, newly industrialized economy; ASEAN-4, Indonesia, Malaysia, the Philippines, and Thailand; ISIC, International Standard Industrial Classification.

United States. The other seven economies studied in this book account for about 15% of all export destinations and 21% of all import sources of the Philippines.

Another element that reinforces the increasing interdependence among these eight Asian economies is the amount of FDI these economies have contributed to the Philippines and how much these economies have been associated with the trade generated. Table 8.3 shows that historically the United States has been the major source of FDI in the Philippines. Most of these investments are found in extractive and natural-resource-based industries. Even as late as 1980, the United States accounted for 55% of the inward direct investment stock. Japan accounted for the next significant share but was quite distant from the United States.

In recent years, especially after 1985, FDI has surged into the East Asian region, especially the Association of Southeast Asia Nations (ASEAN) region, and mostly into manufacturing industries as Japan and the NIEs relocated production sites offshore to adjust to currency appreciation and rising domestic costs. Overall, the Philippines did not appear to have benefited from this surge of FDI. Although FDI did grow by about 9.7% annually (based on the stock values of inward direct investment) between 1980 and 1990 and by 10.6% annually between 1990 and 1992 (Table 8.3), this pales in comparison with the surge into Thailand, for example. FDI grew annually in Thailand by an average of 20% between 1988 and 1991.

Independent of this aggregate analysis, however, is the fact that the country's distribution of investment stock changed, in part because of regional flows. Between 1990 and 1992, substantial changes in the distribution of foreign investment stock took place. The significant drop in the US share was matched by surges in FDI from Korea, Japan, and Singapore, such that their shares increased at annual rates of 79%, 13%, and 23%, respectively (Table 8.3). These were higher than the annual average growth rate for all inward direct investment stock between 1990 and 1992.

Table 8.3 confirms that the Philippines missed out on being a frontline recipient of the FDI flows triggered by the 1985 currency realignments. The surge after 1990 is consistent with a related observation that the country became a second-line destination when bottlenecks started to surface in the other economies that were early beneficiaries. This was especially true of Japanese, Korean, and Singapore FDI. For example, total FDI into Thailand declined by 17.7% between 1990 and 1991 (Vasuprasant 1994).

Next, we examine the importance of trade in electronics and textiles and garments between the Philippines and the other seven economies. In particular, several observations can be made about the distribution of trade in three textile and garment products — textiles; spun, woven, and finished textiles; and wearing apparel (Alburo 1994). First, the shares of the seven economies were larger for

Table 8.3. Sources of inward direct investment stocks, 1980, 1990, and 1992.

Home country	Shares of total (%)		
	1980	1990	1992
Canada	3.9	1.6	1.3
United States	54.6	54.0	47.4
China	NA	NA	NA
Hong Kong	4.3	6.9	6.6
Indonesia	NA	NA	NA
Malyasia	NA	0.3	0.3
Singapore	0.4	0.6	0.9
Taiwan	0.2	0.8	0.9
Thailand	NA	NA	NA
Japan	16.8	16.3	21.0
Korea	0.5	0.5	1.6
Total stock (US$ millions)	1 280.9	3 277.0	4 011.2

Source: Bangko Sentral ng Pilipinas (Central Bank of the Philippines) (n.d.).
Note: NA, not available, not separately available, negligible, or zero.

these products than their shares in overall trade with the Philippines (with the exception of wearing-apparel exports). This dramatizes the importance of these industries in the Philippines trade with the seven economies. Second, there was a wide disparity between the shares of exports and those of imports for the seven economies (Tables 8.1 and 8.2), despite the overall importance noted above. This may simply reflect the magnitude of the trade deficits. Third, raw materials and other input sources (including transshipment trade to avoid MFA quotas) came from the region, especially the NIEs, whereas exports were distributed elsewhere, especially Europe and the United States. Only 3.3% of wearing-apparel exports were accounted for by the seven economies, whereas 48.5% of imports came from these sources. Finally, between 1986 and 1992, there appears to have been a substitution of Korea for Japan as a source of textile imports to the Philippines.

In general, the importance, measured by the shares of manufacturing trade, of the seven economies remained the same between 1986 and 1992, except for a slight decline in the share of manufactured exports from 17.1% in 1986 to 15.9% by 1992 (Alburo 1994). However, the underlying changes in two textiles industries (textiles and spun, woven, and finished textiles) reveal the increased importance of the seven economies as destinations for Philippine exports. For these two industries, the export share of the seven economies grew annually at 11% and 10%, respectively, between 1986 and 1992, with insignificant growth in the import shares. In the wearing-apparel trade, the importance of the seven economies diminished between 1986 and 1992, consistent with the earlier observation.

In contrast, the importance of the seven Asian economies for trade in electronics was about even in 1992. Based on the electrical-machinery trade, 16% of exports and 18% of imports were accounted for by these destinations or sources (Tables 8.1 and 8.2). What is noticeable is the decline in the shares of Hong Kong, Malaysia, and Singapore and the increased importance of Japan and Taiwan. Japan has become the second largest export market for electrical machinery and appliances and is the dominant source of imports of these goods. This latter point seems to be consistent with the view of a globalized consumer-electronics industry in which Japanese and Taiwanese firms are seen as the industry leaders.

Such a view would be supported in the context of analyzing specific electronics products in a more widely dispersed destination for exports, where assemblies take place drawing in major components from such electronics centres as Japan, Singapore, and Taiwan. In fact, in the office- and computing-machinery industry (which is a four-digit International Standard Industrial Category [ISIC] industry), the large shares of imports from Japan, Singapore, and Taiwan are matched by even larger exports to these countries (with the exception of Japan), for which Hong Kong and Korea seem to have taken up the task of further assembly (Tables 8.1 and 8.2). In other words, whereas the network of firms in raw-materials sources includes Japan in the final assembly or further value added, the destination is determined by cost considerations, which reduces Japan's potential as a destination.

The underlying integration is even more prominent in the two industries considered here — textiles and electronics. Both in absolute shares and in the growth of those shares, interactions with the Asian economies have increased, at least in the last 6 years, more in these industries than in overall manufactured goods and in total trade.

This, of course, is only part of the story. Another critical part is some quantitative notion of the amount of IIT taking place between the Philippines and these Asian economies in the two industries. IIT is an important element in possible intrafirm trade taking place within the industry. This will further support the argument that participation in the globalization process occurs through network firms, although this is not necessarily conclusive proof of intrafirm trade among affiliates or between parent and affiliate in cross-border transactions. That will have to come from microanalysis at the firm level.

Various estimates of IIT in the Philippines show an increasing trend over the last two decades. Although the overall degree of IIT varies by industry and the average does not seem to indicate sharp increases in the indices, for some industries it shows that a degree of structural change has taken place. The degree of IIT also varies according to the amount of interdependence among the trading partners. Using the Grubel–Lloyd measure, the index for all commodities for the country's overall trade increased from 0.08 in 1970 to 0.30 by 1980 and 0.39 by 1990 (Drysdale and Garnaut 1993). Notice that whereas the index increased dramatically in the first decade, it seemed to have leveled off in the 1980s. The index of manufactures trade appears to have kept pace with the magnitude of IIT — from 0.07 in 1970 to 0.42 by 1990 for world trade.

In the specific industries of interest here, the magnitude of IIT seems greater in the electronics sector than in textiles, a result that is not surprising. For example, the index with Singapore in 1991 in textiles was 0.64, and the index in electronics was 0.93. With Malaysia, the indices were 0.40 and 0.60, respectively (Alburo 1994). The IIT indices reported here are sensitive to the degree of aggregation used in estimating them. In measuring overall IIT, the industries considered were in the three-digit Standard International Trade Classification (SITC) categories. On the other hand, the two-digit harmonized-system codes were used for estimates of the specific industries' IIT. Given the amount of interdependence and integration taking place in the Asian economies studied, the trend of IIT seems to be self-sustaining. In fact, more detailed IIT estimates for semiconductors and integrated circuits and other electronic equipment showed indices of 0.55 and 0.93 as far back as 1985 (Yokota and Imaoka 1993). It is quite likely that intrafirm transactions have been instrumental in the expansion of IIT.

Finally, to what extent have these recent flows of FDI been associated with concomitant trade flows? To answer this question, flows of total trade, that is, exports and imports, must be estimated. After all, in a globalized setting, FDI flows may be meant for importing raw materials or semi-finished products for forward exporting in further processed form and as final products in final-destination markets. A calculation of the correlation of shares of total merchandise trade and inward and outward FDI stocks shows a value of 0.9722 for 1992. This is higher than the 1990 value of 0.9452. The 1980 correlation was 0.9056 (Government of Canada 1995). The correlations for Hong Kong, Korea, and Taiwan exceed 0.98, for an NIE average of 0.99. It should be noted that the correlations are lower for Australia, New Zealand, and the United States.

To summarize, in this aggregate picture of Philippine trade in specific industries, three main points stand out. First, the seven economies are important to overall manufacturing trade and even more so to textiles and electronics. Second, IIT between the Philippines and the seven Asian economies has increased, particularly in the two industries. IIT in electronics is larger than in textiles. Finally, the shares of total merchandise trade and the stock of FDI are highly correlated. These points seem to indicate a greater degree of integration of the Asian economies.

Survey analysis

To test some of the notions suggested by the aggregate analysis in the previous section, we surveyed firms in the electronics and textiles and garment industries. We obtained a universe of firms in these industries from the BOI, which listed 109 and 118 firms in the electronics and textiles and garment industries, respectively.

To start, we sent questionnaires to all those on the lists, by mail or facsimile (where available). Unfortunately, many firms had changed address, although the BOI lists were current at the time of firm registration. Out of the 227 firms to which we sent questionnaires, 82 were returned because the firms were no longer at the address.

Where contacts were successfully made, sustained follow-ups attempted to establish direct interviews with firm managers because some questions were open ended. Subsequently, we were able to complete interviews with 11 firms in the electronics industry and 11 firms in the textiles and garment industry. The surveyed firms represented about 25% of industry sales in electronics and 10% of industry sales in textiles and garments.

This low interview response can be attributed to several factors. First, most firms were generally reluctant to participate in private surveys that seek detailed information on markets and transactions.

Second, some firms were excluded from the coverage of the study in the sense that they had no East Asian transactions. Third, some firms did not consider themselves to be affiliated or have any linkages with other firms. And, fourth, a substantial number of firms from the BOI list could not be located at their original address. Of the 22 firms that were interviewed, some did not reply to some of the questions; we tolerated this, rather than losing the sample altogether. Thus, in the results, the number of firm responses does not always equal the number of firms interviewed.

Many (45.4%) of the firms in the textiles and garment industry had been in the business for less than 10 years, with another 36.4% operating between 11 and 19 years. For electronics, almost 67% of the firms had been doing business in the country for less than 20 years. For both industries, most of the firms had less than 20 years in operation at the time of the interviews. Two firms from each industry reported more than 30 years in the business. The survey results are shown in Tables 8.4–8.9.

We begin our description of the survey results with some characteristics of the firms sampled, knowing that in many instances the sample size is reduced for certain information. Next we describe the underlying trade relations the firms carry out in the course of their business. Some indication of affiliate relations is then noted. Finally, we summarize the results of the survey.

Firm characteristics

In electronics, 36% of the firms had Japan and Korea as the base for their parents; only one came from the United States. The Netherlands was home for two firms. Four firms were wholly Philippine owned. In contrast, half of the firms in textiles and garments had North America as their parents' base (four in the United States and one in Canada), whereas only one reported an East Asian base (Hong Kong). One garment firm had a parent based in Europe. Four firms were purely Philippine owned and thus Philippine based.

The status of the affiliates is classified according to whether the affiliates are wholly owned by the parent, have some foreign equity, or are 100% Philippine owned. About 75% of the electronics firms were either wholly owned by the parent or engaged in a joint venture with local companies. It might be useful to note that in the electronics industry, one firm used to be a subsidiary of a Japanese corporation but had since become a fully Philippine corporation. In textiles and garments, 78% of firms were either wholly owned by the parent (four out of nine, or 44%) or had some foreign equity (33%).

We attempted to elicit some quantitative characteristics of the sample firms. Unfortunately, the responses to questions were so low that care must be taken in interpreting the results. Only five firms in textiles and garments and two in electronics gave numerical data on sales, raw materials, and assets.

The mean sales of electronics firms in the sample in 1994 was US$0.17 million; the mean asset value, US$0.07 million; the mean capital–output ratio, 0.44. The mean annual sales for a firm in textiles and garments was US$10.2 million; medium sales, US$4.3 million; and high sales, US$20.9 million. In this industry, the firms' asset values ranged from a low of US$0.24 million to a high of US$13.4 million.

The electronics firms' assets amounted to only 17% of the textiles and garment firms' low assets. This is indicative of the fact that the electronics industry in the Philippines consists mostly of the assembly of consumer-electronics products or the manufacture of computer chips, or the low-end segment of the value chain.

The mean capital–output ratio for textiles and garment firms was 0.60. In terms of the low-value category, the electronics firms' ratio of 0.22 was about 55% of the 0.40 ratio for the textiles and garment firms.

Although the number of firms reporting assets and sales in textiles and garments is small, the spread across different sizes suggests that they reflect the characteristics of a wide range of firms. These firms included two that were 100% Philippine owned, a German affiliate, and a US affiliate. Two points regarding the quantitative characteristics of the electronics firms assure some reliability

Table 8.4. Surveyed firms in electronics by investing country and destination of sales.

Firm nationality (% sales)	Surveyed firms (*n*)				
	Exported	Intrafirm	To parent	Interaffiliate	To home country
Japan	3	3	3	3	3
>90	1	0	1	0	1
67–90	0	0	0	0	0
33–67	1	0	0	0	0
<33	1	0	1	0	1
0	0	3	0	3	0
Unknown	0	0	1	0	1
United States	1	1	1	1	1
>90	1	0	1	0	0
67–90	0	0	0	0	0
33–67	0	0	0	0	0
<33	0	0	0	0	0
0	0	0	0	0	0
Unknown	0	1	0	1	1
Europe	2	2	2	2	2
>90	1	0	0	0	0
67–90	0	0	0	0	0
33–67	0	0	0	0	1
<33	0	0	0	1	0
0	1	2	1	1	1
Unknown	0	0	1	0	0
Korea	1	1	1	1	1
>90	0	0	0	0	0
67–90	1	0	0	0	0
33–67	0	0	0	0	0
<33	0	0	0	0	0
0	0	1	1	0	1
Unknown	0	0	0	1	0
The Philippines	4	4	4	4	4
>90	1	0	1	0	0
67–90	0	0	0	0	0
33–67	1	0	0	0	0
<33	1	0	0	0	0
0	1	4	1	2	3
Unknown	0	0	2	2	1
Total	11	11	11	11	11
>90	4	0	3	0	1
67–90	1	0	0	0	0
33–67	2	0	0	0	1
<33	2	0	1	1	1
0	2	10	3	6	5
Unknown	0	1	4	4	3

Source: Firm interviews and questionnaires.

of the data. First, an earlier survey of electronics firms in the Philippines (Kim et al. 1994) reported most had sales in the low range (14 out of 23 sampled), which is consistent with the limited information here. Second, the consistency of the responses is surprising (but not unexpected) in the sense that one firm reported figures in local currency and the other in US dollars, but both turned out to have comparable characteristics. One firm had been in the business for 4 years; the other, for 27; both were Japanese affiliates. This gives some assurance that their characteristics at least reflect an average for small firms.

Table 8.5. Surveyed firms in electronics by investing country and sourcing of materials and components.

Firm nationality (% sales)	Surveyed firms (*n*)				
	Imported	Intrafirm	From parent	Interaffiliate	From home country
Japan	3	3	3	3	3
>90	1	0	0	0	0
67–90	1	0	0	0	0
33–67	0	0	0	0	0
<33	0	0	1	0	1
0	1	3	0	2	1
Unknown	0	0	2	1	1
United States	1	1	1	1	1
>90	0	0	0	0	0
67–90	0	0	0	0	0
33–67	0	0	0	0	0
<33	0	0	0	0	0
0	0	0	0	0	0
Unknown	1	1	1	1	1
Europe	2	2	2	2	2
>90	2	0	1	0	0
67–90	0	0	0	0	0
33–67	0	0	1	0	1
<33	0	0	0	1	0
0	0	2	0	0	0
Unknown	0	0	0	1	1
Korea	1	1	1	1	1
>90	0	0	0	0	0
67–90	0	0	0	0	0
33–67	1	0	1	0	1
<33	0	0	0	0	0
0	0	1	0	0	0
Unknown	0	0	0	1	0
The Philippines	4	4	4	4	4
>90	1	0	1	0	0
67–90	2	0	1	0	1
33–67	1	0	0	0	0
<33	0	0	0	1	0
0	0	4	0	3	1
Unknown	0	0	2	0	2
Total	11	11	11	11	11
>90	4	0	2	0	0
67–90	3	0	1	0	1
33–67	2	0	2	0	2
<33	0	0	1	2	1
0	1	10	0	5	2
Unknown	1	1	5	4	5

Source: Firm interviews and questionnaires.

Trade linkages

We examined the underlying trade relations in the two industries by their outward orientation and associated indicators. Of surveyed electronics firms, 64% exported at least 33% of their sales (Table 8.4). Only four firms indicated that exports constituted less than 33% of output. The average share exported by electronics firms was 50%. For textiles and garments, the mean share of exports to total sales was 98%, which indicates that all firms were export oriented. In fact, no firm reported exports of less than 67% of total sales (Table 8.7).

Table 8.6. Surveyed firms in textiles and garments by investing country and sourcing of materials and components.

Firm nationality (% sales)	Surveyed firms (n)				
	Imported	Intrafirm	From parent	Interaffiliate	From home country
United States	4	4	4	4	4
>90	3	0	0	0	0
67–90	1	0	1	0	1
33–67	0	0	0	0	0
<33	0	0	0	0	2
0	0	4	0	3	0
Unknown	0	0	3	1	1
Canada	1	1	1	1	1
>90	1	0	0	0	0
67–90	0	0	0	0	0
33–67	0	0	0	0	0
<33	0	0	0	0	0
0	0	1	1	1	1
Unknown	0	0	0	0	0
Europe	1	1	1	1	1
>90	1	0	0	0	0
67–90	0	0	0	0	0
33–67	0	0	0	0	0
<33	0	0	0	0	0
0	0	1	1	0	1
Unknown	0	0	0	1	0
Hong Kong	1	1	1	1	1
>90	1	0	0	0	1
67–90	0	0	0	0	0
33–67	0	0	0	0	0
<33	0	0	0	0	0
0	0	1	0	1	0
Unknown	0	0	1	0	0
The Philippines	4	4	4	4	4
>90	2	0	0	0	0
67–90	1	0	0	0	0
33–67	0	0	0	0	0
<33	0	0	0	0	2
0	0	4	1	3	1
Unknown	1	0	3	1	1
Total	11	11	11	11	11
>90	8	0	0	0	1
67–90	2	0	1	0	1
33–67	0	0	0	0	0
<33	0	0	0	0	4
0	0	11	3	8	3
Unknown	1	0	7	3	5

Source: Firm interviews and questionnaires.

Four firms in the textiles and garment industry sold all output to parents, five more sold more than 90%, and another firm sold between 68% and 80% to the parent firm. Only one did not report any sales to parents. The four that sold all output to parent firms were the wholly owned subsidiaries; the degree of foreign ownership (through equity) dictated the magnitude of sales to parent firms.

It is unfortunate that we could not get responses for the electronics industry concerning sales to parent firms. However, we surmise that the four firms that reported exports of more than 90% were wholly owned by the parent. This is not necessarily always the case, but the likelihood of a majority (if not all) of sales to parents will be stronger the larger the equity participation.

Table 8.7. Surveyed firms in textiles and garments by investing country and destination of sales.

Firm nationality (% sales)	Surveyed firms (n)				
	Exported	Intrafirm	To parent	Interaffiliate	To home country
United States	4	4	4	4	4
>90	4	0	4	0	3
67–90	0	0	0	0	1
33–67	0	0	0	0	0
<33	0	0	0	0	0
0	0	4	0	3	0
Unknown	0	0	0	1	0
Canada	1	1	1	1	1
>90	1	0	0	0	0
67–90	0	0	1	0	1
33–67	0	0	0	0	0
<33	0	0	0	0	0
0	0	1	0	0	0
Unknown	0	0	0	1	0
Europe	1	1	1	1	1
>90	1	0	1	0	1
67–90	0	0	0	0	0
33–67	0	0	0	0	0
<33	0	0	0	0	0
0	0	1	0	0	0
Unknown	0	0	0	1	0
Hong Kong	1	1	1	1	1
>90	1	0	1	0	0
67–90	0	0	0	0	0
33–67	0	0	0	0	0
<33	0	0	0	0	0
0	0	1	0	1	1
Unknown	0	0	0	0	0
The Philippines	4	4	4	4	4
>90	3	0	3	0	1
67–90	1	0	0	0	1
33–67	0	0	0	0	0
<33	0	0	0	0	1
0	0	4	1	4	1
Unknown	0	0	0	0	0
Total	11	11	11	11	11
>90	10	0	9	0	5
67–90	1	0	1	0	3
33–67	0	0	0	0	0
<33	0	0	0	0	1
0	0	11	1	8	2
Unknown	0	0	0	3	0

Source: Firm interviews and questionnaires.

We compared the destination of sales and the sources of raw materials for the textiles and garment firms with those for electronics firms. A simple tabulation and counting was made of the various destinations of sales; firms reporting multiple destinations gave multiple responses. No weight was assigned to the magnitude of sales (ranging from less than 10% to more than 50%). For the electronics industry, with the exception of the United States and EC, the destinations of the electronics firms' outputs were also the sources of their inputs. A further exception was Singapore, which five firms reported as their source of raw materials but not as a major destination. For textiles and

Table 8.8. Intrafirm trade: procurement and sales of foreign affiliates in electronics.

	Japan			United States	European Community		Korea	Local			
	Firm A	Firm B	Firm C	Firm D	Firm E	Firm F	Firm G	Firm H	Firm I	Firm J	Firm K
Sales											
Total sales (1994)	US$150 000	P 4 800 million	—	—	—	—	—	—	—	—	—
Sales to home country (%)	100	0.6	<50	—	>50[a]	0	0	—	0	0	100[b]
Sales to local markets (%)	0	94.0	>50	—	0	100	33	90	60–70	100	0
Sales to third countries (%)	0	5.6	—	—	50	0	66[c]	<10	30–40	0	—
Procurement											
Total inputs (1994)	US$4 000	P 2 498 million	—	—	—	—	—	—	—	—	—
Inputs sourced from home country (%)	0	17.0	—	—	50	—	50	—	70	—	—[b]
Inputs sourced from local sources (%)	100	31.0	0	—	0	0	50	30	30[e]	—	—
Inputs sourced from third countries (%)	0	52.4	>50	—	50	>50	—[f]	70	0	>50	—

Note: —, no information was supplied; P, Philippine peso.
[a] To Europe.
[b] To principal.
[c] Includes 10% to Sony Japan.
[d] Principal determines the source.
[e] Includes 10% from Sony.
[f] Unknown.

Table 8.9. Intrafirm trade: procurement and sales of foreign affiliates in textiles and garments.

	United States				Canada	European Community	Hong Kong		Local		
	Firm A	Firm B	Firm C	Firm D	Firm E	Firm F	Firm G	Firm H	Firm I	Firm J	Firm K
Sales											
Total sales (1994)	US$21 million	—	—	US$9 million	US$1.9 million[a]	P 70 million[b]	—	—	US$5 758 million	P 319.4 million	P 15 million
Sales to home country (%)	90	90	80	50	80	90	0	80	100	20.8	100
Sales to local sources–markets (%)	0	0	0	0	0	0	<1	0	0	20.8	0
Sales to third countries (%)	10	10	20	50	20	10	100	20	0	80.0	0
Procurement											
Total inputs (1994)	US$16 million	—	—	US$5 million	—	P 120 million	—	—	—	P 194.3 million[a]	—
Inputs sourced from home country (%)	75	<1	20[c]	—	0	0	95	<5	10	0	—
Inputs sourced from local sources (%)	0	10	2	—	1–2[d]	0	<1	15	0	0	—
Inputs sourced from third countries (%)	25	90	80	95	99	80	5	80	60–80	100	—

Note: —, no information was supplied; P, Philippine peso.
[a] 1993.
[b] Value added.
[c] Includes European Community and Canada.
[d] Also imported.

garments, five firms reported the United States as destination for sales, and six reported local sources of raw materials. It is apparent that for textiles and garment firms, the sources of raw materials were not also the destinations of sales. With the exception of Hong Kong and the local market (which were both sources and destinations for firms from these areas), output destinations and input sources differed.

These results suggest that there is greater IIT, if not intrafirm trade, taking place in the electronics' industry than in textiles and garments.

Affiliate relations

Beyond the nature of trade relations or the degree of arm's-length trade transactions among countries, different kinds of interaction between parent and affiliate contribute to greater integration among firms across countries (Tables 8.8 and 8.9). More than 85% of the firms in the electronics industry had at least 10% foreigners among their senior managers, provided by either the parent or the joint-venture partner. In one firm, more than 50% of management staff were foreigners. In contrast, only 2 of 10 reporting textiles and garment firms had foreigners constituting at least 10% of senior managers. Even more interesting is the fact that most textiles and garment firms did not have foreigners among their senior managers. These magnitudes of foreign (or more accurately, parent or partner) participation in senior management do not appear to be consistent with the affiliate status of the firms surveyed. For example, 44% of textiles and garment firms were wholly owned by parent firms and are thus candidates for foreigners in managerial positions. However, only 20% reported a significant share of foreign managers. In the case of electronics, however, the share of foreign managers was higher than the proportion of firms that were wholly owned or joint ventures.

What all this means is that the nature of the industry — its technical structure and needs, among others — dictates the number of foreign managers essential to firm operations. Affiliate relations facilitate collaborative management but are perhaps unnecessary, especially in the case of standardized products.

The survey results also show a high exchange of technical information in electronics firms, whereas in textiles and garments many firms did not obtain technical information from the parent. This may be because, in the Philippines, the textiles and garment industry does not require much of the technical exchange that affiliate relations can provide. This is not the same as saying that the industry itself is not highly technical in structure. In general, affiliation does open up more avenues for embodied technical transfers and information exchange in production processes. State-of-the-art, frontier technology and best practice are characteristics of firms that are wholly owned or are in joint ventures. In textiles and garments, for example, parent firms provide marketing channels, send designs, consign materials and machines, and source supplies. This kind of advantage is also found in the electronics industry.

In our survey, however, some firms were never affiliates or started as partners or affiliates but became part of the network of firms in the industry. In the electronics industry, one firm was established in 1981 as a wholly Philippine-owned company and went into electronics in 1987 by producing audio equipment for Samsung, paying royalty rights. Although it sold locally (60%), it also had sales to the United States and Europe (40%); 70% of its materials came from Korea. Another firm was a foreign affiliate of a major Japanese consumer-electronics MNE between 1965 and 1986, when it became wholly Philippine owned. It continued to produce the MNE's lines of video and audio products. In the past, this firm had had resident Japanese technicians and high levels of parent–affiliate technical relations, but it began to rely on local managers after the change in ownership, with some spot-checking by the MNE of product and manufacturing processes. It purchased raw materials from local sources, as well as from Singapore and Malaysia. This firm concentrates its sales in the local market. There is evidence, therefore, of a vintage effect in the electronics industry, implying that a greater degree of localization takes place as the investment matures.

In the textiles and garment industry, some firms were not originally established as subsidiaries or affiliates but came to form a network in which these firms act as affiliates with mandated activities over which they may have some autonomy. One was established in 1955 but has been associated with a principal (US) long-term buyer for retail chains (JC Penney and Wal-Mart). Although the firm alluded to some personal relations between the owner and the principal buyer, the firm had the characteristics of an affiliate: the buyer was the principal source of materials and the main customer for the firm's output. Even capital equipment was consigned. The firm in turn subcontracted 90% of the work and did the finishing in its factory. Another firm in the industry was a 100% Philippine-owned contractor exporter that served a single buyer. As with the other firm, there was an implied personal relationship between it and the single buyer. The latter supplied the designs, but the firm was free to modify them according to the firm's technical know-how. The buyer, however, determined the destination of sales. All the managers of this firm were Philippine nationals. Although, at the start, the buyer had provided 20% of the capital equipment, the local firm eventually purchased this from an expanding base of Philippine ownership of the firm.

These case studies of Philippine firms in the context of affiliate relations imply a number of salient points. First, it is clearly possible to graduate from an affiliate status to being an independent firm (in the sense of no foreign equity from a parent) without losing access to product lines, processes, and raw materials sources that originally came with being an affiliate. It is the track record of quality control and standards rather than absolute ownership that keeps a firm within a network. In fact, in the case of one firm, sole dealership was retained for a brand name even after the parent lost its equity.

Second, it is possible to start as a purely local manufacturing firm and become part of a network in marketing arrangements, materials sourcing, and production of components. In other words, it is possible for firms to take on segments of higher value in the value chain, depending on parent firms' strategic objectives and the ability of affiliate firms to meet those objectives. Although personal factors may have contributed to the dynamism of these local firms, it seems clear that networking can be achieved without initial formal affiliation or foreign equity.

Third, the networking among these "independent" firms appears to be as strong as that among firms that are connected as affiliates or wholly owned subsidiaries. Again, the emphasis of value-chain analysis is intrafirm competition, regardless of ownership. We need to understand these cases further to argue that affiliation is neither necessary nor sufficient for networking. Finally, exchanges of technical information or expertise would be a function more of the industry structure than of ownership, affiliation, or equity connections. These points of course do not answer the question regarding the motivation for FDI. Perhaps in a more liberalized trade environment, the evolution of the local firm belonging to a network and producing for the world market would be determined simultaneously by FDI and by the opportunities that trade provides in the world market.

To sum up, this survey of 22 firms in two industries provides the basis for understanding their trade relations with other firms in the Asian region and elsewhere and the kinds of exchange taking place among them. Although the responses were limited for a number of questions, the overall results seem to give some interesting information on the ways in which firms evolve; their relations with parents, affiliates, or other firms; and the trade and investment and greater degree of integration taking place in the region.

Conclusion

Global competitiveness has not been well documented, nor is it empirically evident in the Philippines. *Global competitiveness* refers to the increasing interdependence of trading and investment activities among economies and the greater integration of these economies as a result. This study, by analyzing the electronics and textiles and garment industries, attempted to document the ways in which firm behaviour is integrating the region.

Various theories have attempted to explain why firms produce abroad. Dunning's OLI model proposes that the firm's decision depends on ownership, locational factors, and the ability to internalize transactions. The firm can exploit proprietary assets, such as physical assets, technology, brand name, or managerial skills, in markets by using the firm's internal organization and structural hierarchy, rather than operating through open-market channels. In sourcing inputs, for example, it may be less costly for firms to produce these inputs than to overcome the difficulties in external markets identified by Coase (1937). The latter include the transaction costs involved in finding a correct price, the cost of defining the obligation of parties in a contract, and so forth. For several reasons, Arrow (1974) asserted that intrafirm exchange is also a relatively inexpensive way to exchange information or acquire technology. Porter (1986) concentrated on a firm's strategy, arguing that a firm tries to achieve a competitive advantage over rival firms by managing its value chain.

The study's results show that, at the aggregate level, the integration of trading nations' economies has increased. In particular, recent investment inflows from the NIEs into the Philippines, intended to take advantage of locational factors, such as cheap labour, abundant resources, and MFA quotas, have displaced traditional sources of FDI, such as the United States. Such locational factors have allowed the NIEs to use developing countries as manufacturing bases to lower production costs in manufacturing output that is sold primarily in developed countries.

The survey results indicate that greater economic integration has taken place, despite a diversity of firm arrangements and ownership patterns. In a way that is consistent with value-chain analysis, firms compete with other firms in the same industry by locating certain segments of their activities to suit certain strategic objectives, without regard to home country or ownership pattern. In the electronics industry, most production is for consumer electronics at the low end of the value chain. In the textiles and garment industry, cheap labour, high skills in such aspects as design and finishing, and the MFA have encouraged firms to import inputs for processing and to export final products to other markets. Perhaps the main importance of ownership revealed in the survey is in its determining how much affiliates sell to parent companies, generally an increasing function of ownership.

Whereas ownership is less important in this global-competitiveness paradigm, coordination of networks or nonhierarchical structures among all types of firms — independent, affiliate, and wholly owned subsidiaries — is. There is no one mode of production from which such a network typically emerges, nor is there reason to expect that the increased globalization of production will lead to one. A variety of firm arrangements have emerged, from joint ventures to subsidiaries eventually breaking out as independent firms while carrying some licencing arrangements with the previous parent and remaining part of the network. In the textiles and garment industry, firms that were not originally established as subsidiaries or affiliates belong to the network of firms in the industry.

The survey results indicated the operation of a vintage effect in some cases in electronics. As investment matured to the production stage, more localization took place with increased local inputs, sales, or ownership shares. Most firms sourced inputs and sold most of the output in the same market. There was greater IIT in electronics than in textiles and garments, which seems consistent with greater IIT being built along certain segments of the value chain. Another industry effect uncovered by the survey is that the technical needs of the electronics industry, seen for example in the number of foreign managers essential to firm operations, are greater than in the textiles and garment industry.

Our survey results show the increased importance of Japan and Taiwan in the electronics trade of the Philippines. Japan is both the second largest export market for Philippine's electrical machinery and appliances and the dominant source of imports. This finding seems consistent with a globalized electronics industry, with networking in the region using Japanese and Taiwanese firms as the industry hub.

Internalization helps to reduce costs but also prevents the acquisition by others of firm-specific advantages, which would erode the firm's ability to reap profits from their use. One implication of this is that multinational firms will tend to favour imperfectly competitive industries arising from barriers to entry and externalities that are due to technological innovation. This is because this kind of industrial structure is conducive to the firm's extracting "rents" from firm-specific assets.

In the Philippines, until very recently, with the push toward greater trade liberalization, industries such as home-appliance manufacturing and textiles enjoyed significant barriers to entry. Almost all firms in home-appliance manufacturing were either licencees or joint-venture partners of Japanese or American manufacturers (USAID 1992). An oligopolistic structure characterized the industry, with incentives given to local manufacturers, such as lower sales taxes, tariffs, and import restrictions on parts and components. Similarly, the textiles industry has been described as a differentiated oligopoly that developed as a result of high tariffs, import restrictions, and investment incentives (USAID 1992).

Concerning firm-level linkages between trade and FDI, more recent studies suggest that host-country exports expand when FDI flows into a subsidiary producing downstream products, production complements, or demand substitutes (Petri 1995). In value-chain analysis, this simply means that a larger segment of activities can be produced in places with net FDI inflows.

However, the survey results for the textiles and garment industry seem to give evidence to the contrary. It is true that trade within the region in textiles and garments increased, with the region becoming a dominant source of raw materials and other inputs, at the same time as Hong Kong, Japan, Singapore, and Taiwan increased their investments in the Philippines. But in the trade in apparel, a finished downstream product, the importance of the seven Asian economies diminished between 1986 and 1992. This decline may, however, be due to structural factors in the Philippine economy, rather than to a failure of the theory per se. In particular, an important reason for the poor performance of the country's textiles industry has been the requirement to purchase polyester fibre, an input, from an inefficient domestic monopoly, thereby preventing the textiles industry from feeding into the dynamic garment sector (USAID 1992).

In the final analysis, although greater integration was made possible by trade and investment activities across borders, it is clear that nations will have to do their part and continue to open up their economies so that their industries can participate in the greater international division of labour. There are no shortcuts to achieving a high and sustainable rate of economic growth.

Chapter 9

INDONESIA

Trade and Foreign Investment Linkages

Mari Pangestu

A lot of interest has been shown in the issue of trade and investment linkages, especially their contribution to East Asian economic integration. Growing interest in East Asian economic integration since the mid-1980s has been generated by the relocation of production sites from Japan and other Asian newly industrialized economies (NIEs) to lower-cost locations. The conceptual framework explaining why foreign firms produce abroad is that of Dunning's ownership–location–internalization (OLI) paradigm, or ownership of firm-specific proprietary advantages, location-specific advantages (including government policy), and internalization of firm-specific advantages (Dunning 1981). In other words, the pattern of foreign investment can usually be explained by at least one of these factors, whereas trends in foreign-investment behaviour can be explained by differences in ownership (home country of investor, share of ownership by foreign investor), location (effects of host-country policies), and industry.

Until the mid-1980s, Indonesia followed an import-substitution policy under a highly protective regime, so most firms focused on the domestic market. Because of oil revenues and foreign-exchange earnings from oil exports, foreign investment was seen as a supplementary source of capital. Various restrictions on foreign ownership meant that only joint ventures were permitted and that these had to divest to Indonesian majority within a certain period. Thus, until the mid-1980s, most foreign investment was motivated by import substitution and oriented to the domestic market.

Only in the wake of plummeting oil prices in 1986 did Indonesia undertake bold liberalization and deregulation measures. The need to adjust and restructure by increasing nonoil exports led to deregulation aimed at an outward-oriented trade policy and at improving the investment climate. This occurred at the same time as East Asian investors, especially from Japan, Korea, and Taiwan, were searching for lower-cost locations because of the appreciation of their currencies and other rising costs. Therefore, beginning in the late-1980s, a wave of more export-oriented investments entered Indonesia, much of it coming from East Asia. Local firms and existing joint ventures also took advantage of the greater incentives to export.

The objective of this study is to analyze how firms that are engaged in international production may be integrating the region through intra- and interfirm trade. A firm-level survey provides the foundation for this analysis. Dominant domestic firms were included in the sample to capture non-equity-related foreign linkages, as well as their role in trade and investment linkages. The study does not intend to look for new theories to explain the linkages between trade and investment but to use the OLI framework to understand how foreign investors and internationalized domestic firms contribute to regional integration in East Asia.

Nonetheless, I attempt to go beyond the OLI framework and to gain a better insight into the firms' strategies because firms are the ones undertaking the process of integration. This implies that the focus of this chapter is the firm. I will examine similarities and differences in the behaviour of firms by grouping them according to various characteristics, such as industry, ownership, date of establishment, and whether a firm is part of a larger group. Three industrial sectors, textiles and garments, electronics, and automobiles, were selected based on their importance in regional trade, the dominant role of East Asian investors, and the potential for the division of labour among production sites.

The next section describes the patterns of trade and investment in Indonesia and analyzes intraregional-trade developments at the aggregate level. The third section reports and analyzes the survey results for foreign and dominant local firms' sales and procurement behaviour in the three industries. The fourth section analyzes policy implications.

Patterns of trade and investment

Policy framework: trade and investment deregulation

Indonesia's industrialization can be described as oil dependent, dominated by import substitution until the mid-1980s. The investment climate was not conducive to export-oriented investments in 1974–85 because there was a great deal of government intervention; delays and costs resulting from a complex bureaucratic system, especially the customs; lack of a supporting infrastructure for exports, with poorly managed bonded zones and duty-exemption schemes; high levels and a complex structure of protection, which led to high costs of inputs; and restrictions on foreign investment, most notably not allowing 100% foreign ownership and requiring mandatory divestment to Indonesian majority ownership over a fixed time.

The industrial structure was dominated by large state-owned enterprises in strategic industries, such as cement, fertilizers, and steel, which were funded by oil revenues, and foreign and domestic companies engaging in import-substitution activities in various manufactured products, such as textiles, garments, consumer electronics, chemicals, and automobiles. By the mid-1980s, exports of manufactured products were limited to plywood, which benefited from subsidized loans and regulations banning timber exports, and to textiles and garments, which enjoyed the comparative advantage stemming from low labour costs, as well as export subsidies. These export subsidies comprised subsidized export credits and the implicit subsidy inherent in the duty-exemption scheme operating between 1978 and 1985.[1]

Thus, Indonesia is a latecomer, compared with other economies in the region, in embarking on a manufacturing-based, export-oriented drive. It was only in 1986 that a series of adjustments and reforms were undertaken in response to adverse external developments in the form of plummeting oil prices and appreciation of the yen, which substantially raised the country's debt service. The steps taken included a 50% devaluation; substantial improvements in the duty-exemption scheme for imported inputs used in export production; continued improvements in customs and goods clearance after the 1985 decision to replace import inspection by Indonesian customs with Swiss General Surveyor (SGS); relaxation of restrictions on foreign investment ownership linked to export orientation; and a general program of reduced protection.

To reduce protection, the tariff structure was rationalized, tariffs were reduced, and nontariff barriers were replaced with tariffs. The average level of unweighted tariff declined from 27% in 1986 to 15% by May 1995, and the percentage of tariff lines subjected to nontariff barriers declined from 32% to 12% during the same period. However, tariffs and luxury taxes in the automotive sector remain high, and nontariff barriers persist in the agriculture sector.

---

[1] Duty exemption was calculated on an average basis, rather than on actual dutiable inputs used, so that exporters normally received more than the duty drawback. When Indonesia signed the *Code on Subsidies and Countervailing Duties*, in 1985, these subsidies from the duty-exemption scheme had to be modified to an actual dutiable-input basis and subsidized export credits had to be eliminated by 1991.

Foreign-investment deregulation occurred more gradually, culminating in a substantive deregulation in June 1994. Initially, in 1985–86, foreign-ownership restrictions and divestment requirements were relaxed for export-oriented investments and those located in bonded zones. Then, beginning in 1992, 100% foreign ownership and less stringent divestment requirements were allowed for investments greater than US$50 million and for those located in Eastern Indonesia and in bonded zones. To encourage small and medium-sized foreign investments in components and parts in the electronics industry, 100% foreign ownership along with less stringent divestment requirements was extended to investments with a minimum capital of US$2 million in the supplier industry in 1993. A new form of stand-alone export-processing zone (EPTE, Entrepôt Produksi Tujuan Ekspor) was introduced.[2] Finally, in June 1994, 100% foreign ownership, with few restrictions, was allowed; the divestment requirements were virtually eliminated; and nine public goods sectors, such as power generation and telecommunications, were opened to foreign participation. Since 1994, the regulations covering the management of EPTE have seen major improvements. The result was a dramatic growth in exports, as well as export-oriented foreign investments.

Boom in manufactured exports

Historically, as a result of its endowments, Indonesia's comparative advantage has been in natural-resource- and labour-intensive products. Between 1986 and 1992, however, the share of natural-resource-intensive exports fell from 46% to 25%, whereas those of unskilled-labour- and technology-intensive exports increased from 35% to 45% and from 8% to 14%, respectively. This shift in comparative advantage from natural-resource-intensive to technology-intensive products explains the dramatic increase in manufactured exports, from a small base of US$2.6 billion in 1986 to US$20.1 billion in 1994. This amounts to an average annual growth rate of 30%. As a result, the share of manufactured exports in total exports increased from 18% in 1986 to 52% in 1994.

Natural-resource-based exports were dominated by wood and cork products (mainly plywood). The rise in labour- and technology-intensive exports can be attributed to the rise in exports of textiles, garments, and electronics. The value of textile and garment exports increased 10-fold during 1986–94, with the sector accounting for slightly less than 33% of total manufactured exports, whereas the growth of electronics exports,[3] especially audio and video products, increased from negligible amounts to US$1.5 billion in 1994, with this sector accounting for close to 10% of total manufactured exports. Most of the growth of electronics exports occurred between 1992 and 1994, which was related to the realization of foreign investment during that period, as is discussed later. Automobile and parts exports were still very low in value and accounted for only 1% of total manufactured exports.

The slowdown in annual growth of manufactured exports, to 13% in 1992–94, is noteworthy. The main reason for this slowdown was the decline in growth in two major sectors: textiles and garments and wood and cork manufactures (mainly plywood). The decline in the growth of textile and garment exports can be attributed to increased competition with China and other emerging low-cost-production countries; a slowdown in investments; rising minimum wage; and a larger share of output geared to the domestic market. The reduced growth affected low-end textile and garment producers, whereas the medium- and upper-end producers still experienced robust growth rates. The decline in the growth of plywood exports, on the other hand, was mainly due to a decline in demand, lower prices, and a shortage of raw materials.

---

[2] The advantage of EPTE is that imported inputs come in duty free so that companies do not have to go through the SGS and the duty-exemption scheme. Furthermore, a company can obtain this duty free status without being located in one of the previously existing bonded zones. A company can also sell up to 25% of its products to the domestic market after paying the duty on the inputs and the sales tax on the output.

[3] Defined in the *International Trade Statistics* (United Nations n.d.) as Standard Industrial Trade Classification (SITC) 76: telecommunications, video, and audio products.

Trends in foreign investment

Foreign investment has increased substantially since 1986. Inflows of realized net foreign investment, as reported in the balance of payments, increased from about US$300 million in 1986 to US$2 billion by 1994. The same dramatic increase was revealed by the amount of approved foreign investment, which jumped from US$4 billion in 1986 to US$10 billion in 1992, US$24 billion in 1994, and US$40 billion in 1995 (Government of Indonesia n.d.).

This boom in foreign investment was due to a coincidence of push and pull factors (Pangestu 1995). Rising costs in East Asian economies, as a result of currency appreciation and increasing costs of production, led to a wave of production relocations. This occurred around the same time as Indonesia's investment climate improved because of the deregulation and reform measures described earlier. In 1992–93, foreign investment inflows slowed as a result of the increased attractiveness of China as a production site; the recession in Japan, which led to a substantial slowdown in Japanese outward investment flows; and a deterioration in Indonesia's investment climate resulting from inconsistencies of domestic-policy implementation. Since 1994, however, there have been signs that foreign investment has been increasing as a result of the economic recovery in Japan and the resurgence of pressures there to relocate production sites following the appreciation of the yen in 1994. The most important stimulus to the increase in foreign investment, however, was the substantive deregulation undertaken in June 1994, when most restrictions on foreign investment were lifted.

Table 9.1 provides data on approved and realized foreign direct investment (FDI) on a cumulative basis by source country, based on data from the Board of Investment (BOI), which excludes the oil and financial services sectors. The main investors in Indonesia have been Japan and the East Asian NIEs, including Singapore, with the latter gaining in importance. At the end of 1985, Japan accounted for 33% of approved investments, but by 1995, the share had dropped to 14%. In 1985–95, approved investments from the other East Asian economies surged. The share of approved investments from Hong Kong remained important, at around 10–12%, and the shares of Singapore, South Korea, and Taiwan increased substantially. Meanwhile, the shares of other major investors, such as Europe (except for United Kingdom) and the United States, declined.

Table 9.1. Approved foreign investment by source country.

	1967–85		1986–95[a]		1967–95[a]	
	Total (US$ millions)	Share (%)	Total (US$ millions)	Share (%)	Total (US$ millions)	Share (%)
North America						
United States	1094	7.2	6071	5.3	7164	5.5
Europe						
Switzerland	163	1.1	521	0.5	683	0.5
The Netherlands	861	5.7	2136	1.9	2997	2.3
United Kingdom	511	3.4	11606	10.1	12117	9.3
Germany	533	3.5	2888	2.5	3422	2.6
France	104	0.7	404	0.4	508	0.4
Asia						
Japan	5000	33.1	13032	11.4	18032	13.9
South Korea	206	1.4	6022	5.2	6228	4.8
Hong Kong	1817	12.0	11406	9.9	13222	10.2
Taiwan	120	0.8	7674	6.7	7795	6.0
Singapore	222	1.5	8355	7.3	8578	6.6
Others	1532	10.2	9430	8.1	10962	8.5
Joint countries[b]	2933	19.4	35267	30.7	38199	29.4
Total	15095	100.0	114812	100.0	129907	100.0

Source: Government of Indonesia (n.d.).

[a] Up to September 1995.

[b] *Joint countries* refers to investments from more than one source country or from multilateral bodies.

Table 9.2. Approved foreign investment by sector.

	1967–85		1986–95 [a]		1967–95 [a]	
	Total (US$ millions)	Share (%)	Total (US$ millions)	Share (%)	Total (US$ millions)	Share (%)
Primary sector	2 144	14.2	7 066	6.1	9 209	7.1
Food crops	11	0.1	798	0.7	809	0.6
Plantations	236	1.6	1 669	1.4	1 905	1.5
Livestock	26	0.2	301	0.3	327	0.3
Fishery	104	0.7	452	0.4	556	0.4
Forestry	277	1.8	233	0.2	510	0.4
Mining	1 489	9.9	3 614	3.1	5 102	3.9
Secondary sector	11 531	76.4	79 421	69.2	90 952	70.0
Food	406	2.7	4 142	3.6	4 548	3.5
Textiles	992	6.6	4 827	4.2	5 819	4.5
Wood	263	1.7	896	0.8	1 160	0.9
Paper	490	3.2	14 431	12.6	14 921	11.5
Pharmaceutical	216	1.4	92	0.1	308	0.2
Chemical	2 316	15.3	40 283	35.1	42 600	32.8
Nonmetallic minerals	947	6.3	2 961	2.6	3 908	3.0
Basic metals	3 304	21.9	3 629	3.2	6 933	5.3
Metal goods	2 570	17.0	7 780	6.8	10 350	8.0
Other	27	0.2	380	0.3	407	0.3
Tertiary sector	1 421	9.4	28 325	24.7	29 745	22.9
Utilities	0	0.0	8 074	7.0	8 074	6.2
Construction	392	2.6	635	0.6	1 027	0.8
Trades	14	0.1	1 211	1.1	1 225	0.9
Hotel and restaurant	368	2.4	8 205	7.1	8 573	6.6
Transportation	61	0.4	3 621	3.2	3 683	2.8
Real estate	58	0.4	3 392	3.0	3 450	2.7
Office buildings	424	2.8	1 874	1.6	2 298	1.8
Other services	103	0.7	1 313	1.1	1 416	1.1
Total	15 096	100.0	114 812	100.0	129 906	100.0

Source: Government of Indonesia (n.d.).
[a] Up to September 1995.

Apart from the oil, gas, and financial-service sectors, the main sector attracting foreign investment was the secondary or manufacturing sector (Table 9.2). It accounted for 70% of approved investments between 1967 and 1995 (not counting the oil, gas, and financial sectors). In the manufacturing sector, the highest growth in foreign-investment approvals was experienced by the chemicals (33%), paper (12%), and metal-goods (8%) sectors. It should be noted that there was a decline in the share of approved investments going to the secondary and primary sectors between 1965–85 and 1986–95, whereas the share going to the tertiary sector almost doubled. The main reasons for this substantial increase were the high economic-growth rates experienced by the country in the second period and the opening up of some service sectors to foreign participation.

The role of foreign firms in Indonesia's manufacturing sector can also be evaluated from the Central Bureau of Statistics (CBS), *Survey of Manufacturing Industries: Large and Medium Enterprises* (Government of Indonesia 1992). Based on this data set, foreign firms constituted 24% of value added in the industrial sector in 1992 (excluding oil-related industries). This is a slight increase over the 21% in 1986.[4]

---

[4] Comparing data between 1986 and 1992 requires some care because the number of firms surveyed increased after 1986. The data used here are not the "back-casted" series, which would be more accurate to use because it attempts to take data on the newly surveyed firms back to previous periods. These data have only recently become available.

The pattern of intraregional trade

The trade pattern between Indonesia and its major trading partners, with special emphasis on the East Asian region, is captured in Tables 9.3 and 9.4. These tables show a diverse pattern of intraregional trade between Indonesia and each of its East Asian trading partners, both for manufacturing as a whole and for various manufacturing sectors.

Trade in all manufactures

The growth of manufactured exports to Japan was rapid until 1989 because of the appreciation of the yen but declined between 1989 and 1992 because of the recession in Japan. As a result, the share of manufactured exports to Japan fell from 31% to 17% during that period. The share of manufactured imports from Japan declined by 5% per annum in 1986–92, from 33% to 25%. The decline reflects the loss in Japan's competitiveness as a result of the appreciation of the yen and other rising costs.

In contrast, the growth of manufactured exports to Korea and Taiwan increased dramatically from a small base of US$234 million, with an annual growth of 34% during 1986–92. This is higher than the annual growth rate of manufactured exports of 27% to all countries. As a result, by 1992, Korea and Taiwan accounted for 7% of Indonesia's total manufactured exports. A similar trend is evident in manufactured exports to China. Starting from a small base of US$94 million, annual growth rates exceeded 42% between 1986 and 1992, which implies that the relative importance of China as an export market increased by 12.2% annually. Much of the growth in exports to China was due to the increase in the value of plywood exports, an increase that was partly a result of the high prices in 1991–92.

On the import side, there was a dramatic increase in the growth of imports from Korea and Taiwan; by 1992, 8% and 5% of Indonesia's total manufactured imports were sourced from these NIEs, respectively. Imports from China, on the other hand, increased only on par with total manufactured imports, maintaining a steady share of 2% of total manufactured imports.

Manufactured exports to the United States and Europe increased slightly (although exports to Europe increased in importance, whereas those to the United States declined). A similar trend is evident on the import side. This pattern in Indonesia's manufactured trade seems to point to the following conclusion: to the extent that the wave of foreign investments from Japan and the East Asian NIEs was export oriented, these exports seemed to be geared to third markets, especially the United States and Europe. Furthermore, the pattern of imports indicates that there could be a link between increased Korean and Taiwanese investments and increased sourcing from these countries. On the other hand, rising costs in Japan reduced the amount of sourcing from Japan, although Japanese companies may still have been sourcing from other subsidiaries and affiliated companies not located in Japan.

Textiles and apparels

Overall export and import growth rates for textiles were high, much higher than the growth rates for total manufactures. The rate of textile exports to the East Asian region grew significantly, from 31% in 1986 to 48% in 1992. However, a large part of this growth was due to textile exports destined for Singapore, which in 1992 accounted for almost 67% of the exports destined for Asia-10 (China, Hong Kong, Indonesia, Japan, Malaysia, the Philippines, Singapore, South Korea, Taiwan, and Thailand). This emphasizes Singapore's role as an entrepôt. The value of textile exports to the other East Asian economies remained small, although the growth rates were dramatic, despite declining export shares.

Textile sourcing from Korea and Taiwan increased rapidly. By 1992, 37% and 20% of all textile imports were sourced from these NIEs, respectively, whereas the share of textiles sourced from Japan dropped from 23% in 1986 to reach 10% in 1992. The increased sourcing from Korea and Taiwan

Table 9.3. Indonesia's exports of manufactures by selected ISIC category, year, and partner.

	Year	World totals (US$ millions)	Shares (%)									
			Japan	Hong Kong	Singapore	Other NIEs[a]	ASEAN-4[b]	China	Asia-10[c]	United States	European Community	Other
All manufacturing	1986	4 677.0	27.0	6.0	12.0	5.0	3.0	2.0	55.0	19.0	16.0	10.0
	1989	10 650.0	31.0	4.0	9.0	7.0	5.0	3.0	59.0	14.0	16.0	11.0
	1992	19 670.0	17.0	3.0	13.0	7.0	4.0	4.0	48.0	16.0	21.0	15.0
Annual growth rate (%)	1986–92	27.0	−7.4	−10.9	1.3	5.8	4.9	12.2	−2.2	−2.8	4.6	7.0
Textiles	1986	346.0	6.0	7.0	15.0	3.0	0.0	0.0	31.0	21.0	20.0	28.0
	1989	986.0	9.0	6.0	17.0	3.0	3.0	0.0	38.0	14.0	27.0	21.0
	1992	3 222.0	5.0	5.0	32.0	3.0	3.0	0.0	48.0	6.0	23.0	23.0
Annual growth rate (%)	1986–92	45.0	−3.0	−5.5	13.5	0.0	3.0		7.6	−18.8	2.4	−3.2
Apparel	1986	484.0	1.0	6.0	11.0	2.0	4.0	0.0	24.0	50.0	9.0	17.0
	1989	1 004.0	4.0	2.0	5.0	0.0	0.0	0.0	11.0	49.0	26.0	14.0
	1992	2 863.0	8.0	0.0	9.0	1.0	1.0	0.0	19.0	28.0	31.0	22.0
Annual growth rate (%)	1986–92	34.5	41.4	−100.0	−3.3	−10.9	−20.6		−3.8	−9.2	22.9	4.4
Office and computing machinery	1986	0.5	3.0	22.0	5.0	23.0	12.0	0.0	65.0	0.0	0.0	35.0
	1989	0.3	0.0	25.0	15.0	9.0	16.0	0.0	65.0	2.0	16.0	17.0
	1992	140.0	1.0	1.0	80.0	0.0	0.0	0.0	82.0	5.0	10.0	3.0
Annual growth rate (%)	1986–92	156.6	−16.7	−40.3	58.7	−100.0	−100.0		3.9			−33.6
Electrical machinery	1986	59.0	0.0	34.0	46.0	1.0	1.0	0.0	82.0	1.0	5.0	12.0
	1989	146.0	10.0	6.0	12.0	2.0	7.0	0.0	37.0	22.0	13.0	28.0
	1992	890.0	7.0	3.0	16.0	3.0	2.0	0.0	31.0	35.0	19.0	15.0
Annual growth rate (%)	1986–92	57.2		−33.3	−16.1	20.1	12.2		−15.0	80.9	24.9	3.8
Motor vehicles and parts	1986	1.0	9.0	0.0	28.0	0.0	1.0	0.0	38.0	54.0	6.0	2.0
	1989	13.0	9.0	16.0	41.0	1.0	15.0	0.0	82.0	4.0	2.0	12.0
	1992	75.0	11.0	2.0	14.0	1.0	6.0	0.0	34.0	44.0	11.0	11.0
Annual growth rate (%)	1986–92	105.4	3.4	2.0	−10.9		34.8		−1.8	−3.4	10.6	32.9
Other industries	1986	3 787.0	32.0	5.0	11.0	5.0	2.0	3.0	58.0	15.0	16.0	11.0
	1989	8 501.0	37.0	4.0	9.0	8.0	5.0	3.0	66.0	10.0	14.0	10.0
	1992	12 480.0	23.0	4.0	8.0	10.0	5.0	6.0	56.0	14.0	19.0	11.0
Annual growth rate (%)	1986–92	22.0	−5.4	−3.7	−5.2	12.2	16.5	12.2	−0.6	−1.1	2.9	0.0

Source: ANL (1995).
Note: ISIC, International Standard Industrial Classification; NIE, newly industrialized economy.
[a] Taiwan and Korea.
[b] ASEAN-4, Malaysia, Indonesia, the Philippines, and Thailand.
[c] Asia-10 (Hong Kong, Singapore, South Korea, and Taiwan), ASEAN-4, China, and Japan.

Table 9.4. Indonesia's imports of manufactures by selected ISIC category, year, and partner.

	Year	World totals (US$ millions)	Shares (%)									
			Japan	Hong Kong	Singapore	Other NIEs[a]	ASEAN-4[b]	China	Asia-10[c]	United States	European Community	Other
All manufacturing	1986	9406.0	33.0	1.0	10.0	6.0	1.0	2.0	53.0	14.0	19.0	14.0
	1989	14651.0	26.0	1.0	8.0	10.0	4.0	3.0	52.0	14.0	17.0	17.0
	1992	24501.0	25.0	1.0	7.0	13.0	3.0	2.0	51.0	14.0	22.0	13.0
Annual growth rate (%)	1986–92	17.3	-4.5	0.0	-5.8	13.8	20.1	0.0	-0.6	0.0	2.5	-1.2
Textiles	1986	168.0	23.0	6.0	2.0	18.0	4.0	16.0	72.0	13.0	5.0	10.0
	1989	502.0	11.0	12.0	1.0	36.0	2.0	10.0	72.0	11.0	4.0	13.0
	1992	1073.0	10.0	5.0	1.0	57.0	1.0	5.0	79.0	8.0	4.0	9.0
Annual growth rate (%)	1986–92	36.2	-13.0	-9.3	-10.9	21.2	-20.6	-17.6	1.6	-7.8	-3.7	-1.7
Apparel	1986	8.0	12.0	7.0	14.0	29.0	6.0	2.0	70.0	8.0	17.0	5.0
	1989	18.0	9.0	9.0	10.0	29.0	2.0	4.0	63.0	8.0	22.0	7.0
	1992	43.0	7.0	5.0	8.0	40.0	3.0	5.0	68.0	11.0	14.0	7.0
Annual growth rate (%)	1986–92	32.4	-8.6	-5.5	-8.9	5.5	-10.9	16.5	-0.5	5.5	-3.2	5.8
Office and computing machinery	1986	97.0	28.0	1.0	4.0	7.0	0.0	1.0	41.0	37.0	14.0	8.0
	1989	158.0	30.0	1.0	6.0	10.0	0.0	1.0	48.0	32.0	12.0	8.0
	1992	170.0	15.0	1.0	7.0	10.0	1.0	1.0	35.0	28.0	20.0	17.0
Annual growth rate (%)	1986–92	9.8	-9.9	0.0	9.8	6.1		0.0	-2.6	-4.5	6.1	13.4
Electrical machinery	1986	818.0	31.0	1.0	4.0	7.0	0.0	1.0	44.0	8.0	39.0	9.0
	1989	943.0	22.0	2.0	9.0	11.0	1.0	1.0	46.0	16.0	31.0	7.0
	1992	2785.0	20.0	1.0	5.0	9.0	2.0	1.0	38.0	17.0	38.0	7.0
Annual growth rate (%)	1986–92	22.7	-7.0	0.0	3.3	4.3		0.0	-2.4	13.4	-0.4	-4.1
Motor vehicles and parts	1986	794.0	77.0	0.0	0.0	1.0	0.0	0.0	78.0	6.0	12.0	4.0
	1989	998.0	70.0	0.0	1.0	2.0	0.0	1.0	74.0	9.0	13.0	4.0
	1992	1254.0	59.0	0.0	0.0	3.0	1.0	1.0	64.0	13.0	17.0	6.0
Annual growth rate (%)	1986–92	7.9	-4.3	0.0	0.0	20.1			-3.2	13.8	6.0	7.0
Other industries	1986	7521.0	29.0	1.0	12.0	6.0	1.0	2.0	51.0	15.0	18.0	16.0
	1989	12032.0	23.0	1.0	8.0	10.0	4.0	3.0	49.0	14.0	17.0	20.0
	1992	19176.0	24.0	1.0	8.0	12.0	3.0	2.0	50.0	14.0	21.0	15.0
Annual growth rate (%)	1986–92	16.9	-3.1	0.0	-6.5	12.2	20.1	0.0	-0.3	-1.1	2.6	-1.1

Source: ANU (1995).
Note: ISIC, International Standard Industrial Classification; NIE, newly industrialized economy.
[a] Taiwan and Korea.
[b] ASEAN-4, Malaysia, Indonesia, the Philippines, and Thailand.
[c] Asia-10, 4 NIEs (Hong Kong, Singapore, South Korea, and Taiwan), ASEAN-4, China, and Japan.

can be attributed to the relocation of their export-oriented textile factories to Indonesia, as well as to all firms switching procurement patterns in response to the rising cost of Japanese imports.

Apparel exports continued to be destined for the major markets of the United States and Europe. However, although there was a decline in the share of apparel exports going to the United States, from 50% in 1986 to 28% in 1992, apparel exports destined for Europe increased dramatically from 9% to 31% during the same period. Thus, these two regions accounted for 60% of Indonesia's apparel exports by 1992. To the extent that the growth of apparel exports was limited by quotas, the growth of apparel exports to Europe, where apparel quotas are less stringent than in the United States, was not surprising. It is hypothesized that both the foreign investors relocating to Indonesia and the export-oriented local firms benefited from the increase in apparel exports. However, because of government policies in allocating quotas, new entrants into the market were less likely to export to quota markets. Rather, their strategy was to produce items not subject to quotas or items for which the quotas were not filled and to seek out nonquota markets in the Middle East and Africa.

The dramatic growth of apparel exports to Japan is also noteworthy: from just over US$2 million in 1986 to US$239 million in 1992. Because very few Japanese firms were involved in apparel production, apparel exports to Japan were by local or non-Japanese firms that might have had links with Japanese trading houses or with companies that had relocated to Indonesia, especially from Korea and Taiwan. Furthermore, as in textiles, Singapore continued to be an important entrepôt.

Apparel imports were small in terms of value, amounting to US$43 million in 1992. However, apparel imports underwent growth rates of slightly more than 30% per annum, which reflects the rapid increase of middle-income groups because the imported garments were typically high-end, brand-name items. It is worthwhile to note that increasing volumes of these garments were sourced from Korea and, to a lesser extent, from Singapore and Taiwan. Of course, some of these imports were local Korean, Singaporean, and Taiwanese brand names, including brand names produced in those economies. The other important import sources were the United States and Europe.

Electronics

Exports and imports of office and computing machinery amounted to US$140 million and US$170 million, respectively, in 1992. The growth of exports, starting from a very small base, was dramatic. Most of the exports were accounted for by integrated circuits (ICs) and semiconductors, with the majority shipped through Singapore. The final destination was most likely the United States. As for imports, most came from the United States, Europe, Japan, Taiwan, and other non-East Asian countries. In fact, imports from Japan declined during 1989–92, whereas those from Taiwan and Singapore increased rapidly, especially in 1986–89. Unlike imports from Europe, those from the United States did not undergo much increase.

Similarly, exports of electric machinery, parts, and appliances also increased dramatically from a very small base, reaching US$890 million in 1992. Their main destinations were the US and European markets, accounting for 35% and 19%, respectively, of electrical-machinery exports. Singapore as the regional headquarters (RHQ) and international procurement centre accounted for around 16% of electrical-machinery exports, and other non-East Asian countries accounted for another 15%. It is likely that exports to US and European markets were final assembled products, whereas exports to the other East Asian economies, including Singapore, were probably components. The value of exported electrical machinery to the East Asian economies was small, albeit increasing rapidly.

Imports of electrical machinery, parts, and appliances increased at an average rate of 23% during 1989–92, reaching US$2.8 billion. Of these imports, 75% were sourced from Europe (38%), the United States (17%), and Japan (20%). Assuming the hypothesis holds that investments were relocated to Indonesia from Japan and the other East Asian NIEs, one would expect an increase in imports of electrical and electronic parts from these economies. Although the absolute amounts were small, the growth rates of imports from China, Korea, Malaysia, and Thailand were so high that these economies increased their market share of electrical-machinery imports. Imports from Korea can be linked to Korean investments, whereas imports from China and the other two Association of Southeast Asian Nations (ASEAN) countries can be linked to subsidiaries and affiliated firms sourcing components, as these economies are more-established exporters of electrical products and parts than is Indonesia.

Motor vehicles and parts

Indonesia has yet to become part of the global sourcing of components and parts in the automobile sector. Exports of motor vehicles and parts were low but increased significantly from a very small base in 1986, to reach US$75 million in 1992. The main destinations for exports were the United States, Singapore, Japan, and Europe.

Meanwhile, Indonesia imported more than US$1 billion of parts in 1992. The high value of imports was a reflection of an unusually high demand for motor vehicles in 1991–92 as the economy reached a peak in the business cycle. Imports of completely built-up (CBU) vehicles were only permitted in 1993, with high tariffs remaining (200–300%); thus most of the imports consisted of completely knocked-down (CKD) kits, other parts, and raw materials. Because most of the assemblers of motor vehicles, both four- and two-wheel drives, were licencees of Japanese companies, it is not surprising that a large proportion of imports were sourced from Japan: however, the share sourced from Japan fell from close to 80% in 1986 to 59% in 1992. The increase in imports does not appear to have come from other East Asian economies but from Europe, the United States, and other non-East Asian countries. This increase in inputs is thought to be due to increased imports of raw materials and generic or nonbound parts that were not controlled by the foreign principal.

The high reliance on Japan as a source of imports and the consequently continuing close links with the principal meant that, by 1992, no production network had emerged between the East Asian economies and Indonesia in the supply of automobile components and parts. However, this lack of East Asian networking was likely to have been policy induced because the automobile sector remains the most regulated and protected industry in the region.

Linkages between trade and investment: firm-level survey

The analysis of the trade and investment linkages at the firm level is based on interviews with firms conducted in 1994–95, which were supplemented with information on economy-wide trends from the CBS Industry Survey (Government of Indonesia 1992). In all, 36 firms were interviewed, 9 of which were domestic firms. I attempted to choose a representative sample of domestic, East Asian, and non-East Asian foreign firms in the three manufacturing sectors. In several cases in the textiles and automobile industry, the data collected on sales and sourcing behaviour were product specific, resulting in two observations for each manufacturer interviewed. This increased the total number of observations to 40.

Sectoral developments

The sectors chosen for this study were consumer textiles and garments, electronics and electronic components, and automotive assembly and components. Table 9.5 provides a summary analysis of the relative size of these industries and the ownership distribution of the firms interviewed.

Textiles and garments

The textile industry consists of the upstream, highly capital-intensive, large-scale synthetic-fibre industry; the midstream, capital-intensive, large-scale spinning industry; the midstream, moderately

Table 9.5. Background on sector and sample surveyed (shares of value added, %).

Industry (by ISIC code)	Value added (%)				Number of firms (n)						
	Total		Foreign firms' share[a]		Total	Japan	Taiwan	Korea	Singapore	United States and Europe	Local
	1986	1992	1986	1992							
32111 Spinning	4.2	2.3	37.0	25.0	3	1	1	1	0	0	0
32112 Weaving	5.4	4.3	21.0	28.0	9	2	3	2	0	0	2
32210 Garments	1.7	3.5	0.0	24.0	9	0	2	3	0	0	4
38320 Consumer electronics	1.0	0.8	58.0	71.0	9	4	0	2	0	0	3
38324 Subassembly of electronic components	NA	0.6	NA	68.0	2	0	0	0	2	0	0
38430 Motor-vehicle assembly and manufacturing	2.6	1.5	12.0	24.0	6	2	0	0	0	4	0
38433 Motor-vehicle components	14.8	13.7	NA	23.0	2	2	0	0	0	0	0
Subtotal	29.7	26.7									
Total	100.0	100.0	21.0	34.0	40	11	6	8	2	4	9

Source: Government of Indonesia (1992).
Note: ISIC, International Standard Industrial Classification; NA, not available.
[a] Some changes in ISIC definition were made between the 2 years: 38320 in 1986 included telecommunications but did not in 1992; 38430 in 1986 included all three, motor-vehicle assembly, manufacturing, and components, whereas in 1992, 38320 included motor-vehicle assembly and manufacturing and 38433 included motor-vehicle components.

labour-intensive weaving and fabric-producing industry; and the downstream highly labour-intensive garment industry. The synthetic-fibre and modern weaving industry developed during the import-substitution period of the early 1970s, with the dominant investors at that time being Japanese firms. More recently, since the late 1980s, Korean and Taiwanese firms have made investments. Based on the CBS Industry Survey, in 1992 foreign firms accounted for less than 30% of the share in value added in spinning and weaving. Eleven firms were surveyed in the textile industry, of which three firms produced synthetic fibre, one each from Japan, Korea, and Taiwan; and eight firms were in weaving, of which two were Japanese firms; one, Korean; three, Taiwanese; and two, domestic. For the Korean firm, the data collected were product specific, increasing the number of Korean observations to two.

The garment industry emerged as an import-substitution industry in the early 1970s and only began focusing on export orientation in the early 1980s, as a result of the implicit export subsidy under the export-certificate scheme and the subsidized export credit mechanism described earlier. Until the mid-1980s, the sector was dominated by domestic firms, but the share of foreign firms in value added increased to 24% by 1992. In part, this dramatic increase was due to an increase in the number of surveyed firms, but more importantly the number of foreign firms in the garment sector increased after 1986, as a result of the relocation of East Asian NIE firms, especially from Korea and Taiwan.[5] The main reason for relocating to Indonesia was the combination of low labour costs and the improvements in the investment climate. In total, nine firms were interviewed, ranging from large to medium size as measured by the number of employees and comprising three Korean, two Taiwanese, and four local firms. The high number of domestic firms in the survey was in accordance with the more dominant role of domestic firms in the garment industry.

Electronics

One focus of this book is on consumer electronics and subassembly of electronic components. In 1971–85, investment in the consumer-electronics industry was dominated by import substitution. The banning of CBU consumer electronics in the 1970s led to investments by joint ventures and domestic companies producing under licence. At the time, the dominant investor was Japan. Export orientation began in the mid-1980s by some firms in this sector, but exports accelerated only in the early 1990s, after the relocation of a number of large consumer-electronics firms from Japan and Korea.[6] As a result, the share of foreign consumer-electronics firms in value added increased from 58% in 1986 to 71% in 1992. Because of the structure of the industry, nine firms in the consumer-electronics sector were interviewed, of which four were from Japan, two were from Korea, and three were domestic. Once again, the number of large and medium-sized firms in the sample was representative of the industry.

Unlike in some other ASEAN countries, investments in export-oriented electronic components by multinational enterprises (MNEs) failed to take off in Indonesia because of the lack of a conducive investment climate between 1973 and 1985. In the early 1970s, two large MNEs, Fairchild and National Semiconductor, established subsidiaries in Indonesia with 100% foreign ownership, which produced under a special export-processing status. No other MNE entered Indonesia after that because many restrictions were introduced in 1974, such as not allowing 100% foreign ownership, a particular deterrent for firms in higher-end-technology sectors, such as components assembly. The slump in world markets for semiconductors caused by the recession in the mid-1980s and the lack of support from the Indonesian government for these subsidiaries to undertake automation of their factories led to their closure in 1985–86. Since then, a number of joint ventures, none of

---

[5] The role of foreign firms in the garment industry was probably underestimated in the early years because some firms quoted as domestic were in fact owned by non-Indonesians, especially from Hong Kong, Singapore, and Taiwan.

[6] A number of the larger Taiwanese firms in electronics, especially in computers and computer peripherals, came to Indonesia in the late 1980s. However, they were few, and some have not been successful.

which are part of a big MNE, have been set up in the assembly and packaging of semiconductors and ICs. Based on the CBS Industry Survey, foreign firms dominated the consumer-electronics sector in 1992, accounting for 68% of value added. Two of these were interviewed, both joint ventures with Indonesian majority shareholding and foreign partners from Singapore. It should be noted that the Singaporean partners were not in the semiconductor and IC sector.

Automotive

The automotive sector in Indonesia is still oriented to the domestic market. In the early 1970s, imports of CBU motor vehicles were banned, to encourage import substitution in automotive assembly. A domestic-content policy, known as the deletion program, was introduced in 1977 and set target dates for assemblers to meet certain levels of local content. A policy distinction was made between commercial vehicles and sedans, and the former were to have a higher local-content requirement. Many foreign brands, especially Japanese ones, were produced in Indonesia through either joint ventures or production under licence. In some cases, the firms started off as domestic firms producing under licence, with the foreign principal keeping a tight control over operations. Although the target dates for the deletion program were never fully met, a lot of investment went into components and parts production, including engines. Some of the large-scale assemblers invested in backward integration, often in partnership with the suppliers of their principal, mostly Japanese.

In 1993, the ban on imports of CBU vehicles was replaced by tariffs of 200% for vehicles assembled domestically and 300% for those not assembled domestically. Furthermore, the local-content scheme was altered to be more incentive based, that is, the higher the local content, the lower the duty on CKD kits and parts. In 1995, a schedule of tariff reduction for the following 10 years was introduced, and the World Trade Organization (WTO) was notified of the local-content scheme under the *Trade Related Investment Measures Act*, which essentially meant that the scheme would have to be phased out over the following 5 years.

In 1992, the automotive sector consisted of automotive assembly, manufacture of motor-vehicle bodies, and manufacture of motor-vehicle components. According to the CBS Industry Survey, the shares of value added accounted for by foreign firms were 31%, 24%, and 23%, respectively. Even though foreign firms did not dominate these sectors, the influence of the foreign principal was greater than captured by the statistics because all domestic production in automotive assembly was under licence to the principal, who had a great deal of control over sales and procurement.

Japanese brand names dominated both commercial vehicles and sedans. The manufacture of components and parts, however, which was a result of the domestic-content rules, comprised foreign joint ventures, domestic producers producing under licence for foreign brand names, and many local small and medium-sized enterprises (SMEs). Our sample contained three assembly plants, one large stamping and engine factory, and one large consortium of component producers. The foreign investors in motor-vehicle assembly were German, Japanese, and American. Because the answers to the questionnaire varied considerably by specific product, in the case of the automotive sector the questionnaire was filled in for a specific product — one commercial vehicle and one sedan were chosen for each brand. Thus, one firm could be counted twice. However, the results for the consortium of components producers were reported as a consolidated number because of the high number of different components produced.

Destination of sales

The extent of intrafirm sales and the destination of sales varied by sector, the investor's home country, and the vintage of the firm. As a comparison, some supplementary data from the CBS Industry Survey are also provided. Table 9.6 shows the firms' export orientation by sector and ownership. In general, foreign firms tended to be more export oriented than domestic firms, with an average of 36% of production exported in 1992, compared with 24% by domestic firms.

Table 9.6. Export orientation of firms in sectors surveyed. [a]

Industry (by ISIC code)	Export share in firms' output (%)			
	Foreign firms		Domestic firms	
	1990	1992	1990	1992
32111 Spinning	12	18	13	5
32114 Weaving	29	47	16	18
32210 Garments	58	80	39	44
38320 Consumer electronics	6	76	6	41
38324 Subassembly of electronic components	94	87	26	63
38430 Motor-vehicle assembly and manufacturing	0	1	NA	NA
38433 Motor-vehicle components	NA	NA	NA	3
Total manufacturing	17	36	19	24

Source: Government of Indonesia (1992).
Note: NA, not available.
[a] *Export propensity* refers to the share of output being exported. The survey only began collecting information on exports in 1990.

Textiles and garments

The spinning sector is not export oriented because most of the fibre is consumed domestically by export-oriented weaving factories. Based on the CBS Industry Survey, less than 20% of production was exported by foreign and domestic firms (Table 9.6). This was supported by the survey analysis. None of the three sample firms exported their output. These firms were from Japan, Korea, and Taiwan. Taking indirect exports into account, that is, exports of garments made from the fibre produced by these firms, around 50% of fibre sales were indirectly exported. The three firms sold their fibre to the domestic market through open-market channels (Table 9.7). The three firms each belonged to a larger group in their respective home countries, which is consistent with the large-scale and capital-intensive nature of the sector.

The weaving sector, comprising weaving, knitting, dyeing, and finishing, became increasingly export oriented during 1990–92. The share of exports in total production rose from 29% to 47% for foreign firms and from 16% to 18% for domestic firms (Table 9.6). In our sample, firms were more export oriented than at the national level, with seven of the nine sample firms exporting more than 33% of their output (Table 9.7). Export destinations were the US and European markets, rather than the home and other East Asian markets. Most of the sales were not intrafirm; only two firms reported intrafirm sales exceeding 33% of total output.

The survey highlighted interesting differences between firms based on ownership and vintage. Two of the Taiwanese firms came to Indonesia in 1989, one as part of a medium-sized group and the other as a small firm whose owner relocated to Indonesia (that is, with no parent in Taiwan). The former exported 15% of its sales to Taiwan through the parent company and sold the remainder of its output to the domestic market, all of which ended up as indirect exports. The latter exported 20% to Southeast Asia and a little to Europe and the United States and sold 20% to its subsidiary garments factory in Indonesia. The remainder was sold domestically in the open market. The lower degree of export orientation of these two firms was partly because these firms were only established in 1989 and therefore had no quotas to sell to the US and European markets.

The two Japanese companies were affiliates of large Japanese MNEs and had been in Indonesia since the early 1970s. They became export oriented in the mid-1980s and exported more than 50% of their output, predominantly to nonquota markets. There were some intrafirm sales because one of the partners was a Japanese trading company, but these accounted for less than 50% of total sales.

The Korean firm was only established in 1990 and produced two distinct products, Tetoron/Cotton (T/C) gray and polyester fabric, at two separate factories. The firm was part of a large Korean conglomerate with other subsidiaries in Indonesia, including some in garments and electronics, as well as elsewhere in the region. One of the firm's partners was the trading-company

Table 9.7. Surveyed firms in textiles by investing country and destination of sales.

Firm nationality (% sales)	Surveyed firms (n)					
	Exported	Intrafirm	To parent	Interaffiliate	Home country[a]	Other East Asia
Japan	3	3	3	3	3	3
>90	0	0	0	0	0	0
67–90	1	0	0	0	0	0
33–67	1	0	0	0	0	0
<33	0	2	0	2	0	1
0	1	1	3	1	3	2
Korea	3	3	3	3	3	3
>90	0	0	0	0	0	0
67–90	2	1	0	0	1	1
33–67	0	1	1	1	0	0
<33	0	0	0	1	0	1
0	1	1	2	1	2	1
Taiwan	4	4	4	4	4	4
>90	0	0	0	0	0	0
67–90	0	0	0	0	0	0
33–67	1	0	0	0	0	0
<33	2	2	0	2	2	1
0	1	2	4	2	2	3
Indonesia	2	2	2	2	2	2
>90	0	0	0	0	0	0
67–90	1	0	0	0	0	0
33–67	1	0	0	0	0	0
<33	0	0	0	0	0	0
0	0	2	2	2	2	2
Total[b]	12	12	12	12	12	12
>90	0	0	0	0	0	0
67–90	4	1	0	0	1	1
33–67	3	1	1	1	0	0
<33	2	4	0	5	2	3
0	3	6	11	6	9	8

Source: Firm interviews and questionnaire.
[a] Does not include the domestic market for Indonesian companies.
[b] Three firms belonged to the spinning sector, and nine belonged to the weaving sector.

arm of the conglomerate. The firm was export oriented, with 80% of its sales being exported, all to nonquota markets. The T/C gray was largely exported back to Korea; the remainder, to other East Asian locations. Polyester fabrics were exported to Hong Kong and Singapore, en route to other markets, especially China. Dubai was another important destination because it was the gateway to the eastern and central European markets. A high percentage of the sales was intrafirm through the parent company, its trading-company arm, and its RHQ in Singapore.

In contrast, the two large domestic firms sold more than 50% of their exports to quota markets, such as the United States and Europe. The two firms were leaders in the weaving sector and pioneers in exporting in the late 1970s and early 1980s, thus being allocated a large share of the quotas. Because they were domestic firms, no intrafirm sales were reported. However, both firms had very close links with Japanese trading companies dating back to before the 1970s, when they were importers of textiles. A high percentage of their sales was conducted through the Japanese trading company, which also assisted them with their production plans and quality control and arranged for technical assistance and training of the workers. It was pointed out that even though the companies

Table 9.8. Surveyed firms in garments by investing country and destination of sales.

Firm nationality (% sales)	Surveyed firms (*n*)					
	Exported	Intrafirm	To parent	Interaffiliate	Home country[a]	Other East Asia
Korea	3	3	3	3	3	3
>90	3	3	1	1	0	0
67–90	0	0	0	1	0	0
33–67	0	0	0	0	0	0
<33	0	0	0	1	0	0
0	0	0	2	0	3	3
Taiwan	2	2	2	2	2	2
>90	2	0	0	0	0	0
67–90	0	1	1	0	1	0
33–67	0	0	0	0	0	0
<33	0	0	0	0	0	0
0	0	1	1	2	1	2
Indonesia	4	4	4	4	4	4
>90	3	0	0	0	0	0
67–90	0	0	0	0	0	0
33–67	0	0	0	0	0	0
<33	1	0	0	0	0	3
0	0	4	4	4	4	1
Total	9	9	9	9	9	9
>90	8	3	1	1	0	0
67–90	0	1	1	1	1	0
33–67	0	0	0	0	0	0
<33	1	0	0	1	0	3
0	0	5	7	6	8	6

Source: Firm interviews and questionnaire.
[a] Does not include the domestic market for Indonesian companies.

were able to establish their own direct-marketing contacts, they relied on the trading company for the bulk of their exports because of the high fixed costs of negotiating with customers.

Firms in the garment sector, especially foreign firms, were in general more export oriented than those in the textile sectors. The share of exports in total output of foreign firms increased substantially from 58% in 1990 to 80% in 1992, whereas that of domestic firms increased from 39% to 44% during the same period (Table 9.6). The lower export orientation of domestic firms was due to the high number of small- and medium-scale garment firms that were marginal exporters or purely domestically oriented. The increase in exports by foreign firms was the result of export-oriented investments in garments, especially from Korea and Taiwan, which occurred between 1989 and 1991.[7]

Because predominantly medium- and large-scale firms were interviewed, the sample is biased in favour of export-oriented firms. Thus, only one domestic firm reported exports of less than 33% of total sales (Table 9.8). All other sample firms exported more than 90% of their output. Because the sale of garments is conducted mainly in the open market, just less than 50% of the sample firms sold their output through intrafirm channels. Three of these firms were Korean; the fourth was Taiwanese.

The three Korean firms were entirely export oriented. Two belonged to a large Korean group; one had its own clothing brand name and a production base in Korea. The other firm was given instructions by its parent and affiliated companies in the first few years of operation but was told that

---

[7] Firms from Hong Kong and Singapore were also important in the garment industry, but they are not represented in the sample.

this will be phased out. The third firm was not part of a larger group; rather, the Korean owner started off by setting up a trading company in Indonesia, which focused on garments, and later decided to enter the manufacturing sector.

All three firms were established between 1989 and 1990. Their relocation from Korea was motivated by cost considerations. They produced coats and jackets, which are higher value-added items,[8] in which Korean garment manufacturers are known to have a market niche. The main sales destination was western Europe, where, contrary to the United States, most of these products were not subject to quotas. The two Korean firms, which were parts of a larger conglomerate, conducted all of their sales through the parent company, whereas the third firm sold its output through its affiliated trading company.

The two Taiwanese firms were established between 1988 and 1990. One was part of a medium-sized company in Taiwan. It produced under licence for the export and domestic markets, as well as having its own brands. The parent company continued to produce in Taiwan, specializing in children's wear and toys. It also sourced from Thailand on a subcontracting basis and from China, where it had undertaken other investments. The objectives of investing in Indonesia were to find a low-cost production base to supply the Taiwanese market, which meant that all of the firm's exports went through the parent company, and to penetrate the domestic Indonesian market, where goods were sold under the firm's own brand name.

The other Taiwanese firm was small and had no parent in Taiwan; the Taiwanese owner had relocated to start manufacturing in Indonesia. The firm's comparative advantage was the owner's knowledge of the market and his links with the buyers. He maintained a small representative office in Taiwan, through which buyers were channeled. Because manufacturers and exporters prefer to take orders from trading companies or buying agents and not to deal directly with buyers, the competitive advantage of this small firm, as was the case with the parentless Korean firm, was the owner's knowledge of the industry and its trading network linkages, which he used effectively when he switched to his own production and export base.

The four domestic companies were leading exporters in their product type. Two of them had switched sales to the domestic market, with one exporting only 30% of total output by 1992. Both firms sold their output under licence to various brands, besides having their own retail outlets and selling through other retail outlets like department stores. The reason for the switch to the domestic market was the potential for a higher profit margin. However, both firms continued exporting to keep unit costs low through scale economies and to keep abreast of fashion and trends. The other two domestic companies were largely export oriented. The four companies had started exporting in the early 1980s and thus were large quota holders. Therefore, their main export markets were the major quota markets in the United States and Europe. Three of the four companies also exported 5–20% of their output to Japan, with one of these firms producing under licence for a Japanese brand. Although some of the domestic companies had trading representatives in Hong Kong or Singapore, or both, sales were largely conducted through buyers and large trading companies, mostly Japanese.

Electronics

The aggregate analysis indicates that foreign firms in the consumer-electronics sector were also more export oriented than their domestic counterparts, with the degree of export orientation increasing dramatically during 1990–92. The share of output exported by foreign firms jumped from 6% to 76% and that by domestic firms from 6% to 41% in the 2 years (Table 9.6). Export orientation in this sector appeared to have lagged behind that of the ASEAN neighbours because most of the realization of the new export-oriented investments occurred only after 1991. Several of these investments were located in Batam (part of the southern ASEAN growth triangle); it was estimated that 33% of

---

[8] In garments, one measure of higher value added and of the quality of items relates to the number of pieces that it takes to make the garment.

electronics exports came from Batam-based, export-oriented assembly operations. Most of the consumer-electronics exports were videocassette recorders (VCRs) and audio products; exports of colour television sets (TVs) were relatively small.

The development of an increasingly export-oriented production base resulted in a dualistic electronics sector. On the one hand, there were the more established joint ventures and local firms oriented to the domestic market. On the other, there were the new and majority-foreign-owned joint ventures set up in the early 1990s, which tended to export 100% of their output. This pattern is consistent with the survey results (Table 9.9).

The four Japanese sample firms all belonged to large multinational groups with established brand names. One Japanese joint venture was set up in the early 1970s and sold its consumer-electronics output mainly to the domestic market. Subsequently, the same partners, with the Japanese one having the majority share, set up a separate, new export-oriented plant in 1990. Similarly, the other two Japanese export-oriented firms were set up during 1991–92 with majority Japanese ownership, and the domestic licence holder of the product was the minority partner. All exports were intrafirm, through either the parent companies or the RHQ in Singapore. The destination of exports

Table 9.9. Surveyed firms in electronics by investing country and destination of sales.

Firm nationality (% sales)	Surveyed firms (*n*)					
	Exported	Intrafirm	To parent	Interaffiliate	Home country[a]	Other East Asia
Japan	4	4	4	4	4	4
>90	3	4	0	1	0	0
67–90	0	0	2	0	0	0
33–67	0	0	1	2	0	1
<33	0	0	0	1	1	1
0	1	0	1	0	3	2
Korea	2	2	2	2	2	2
>90	1	1	0	0	0	0
67–90	0	0	1	0	0	0
33–67	0	0	0	1	0	0
<33	0	0	0	0	0	0
0	1	1	1	1	2	2
Singapore [b]	2	2	2	2	2	2
>90	2	0	0	0	0	0
67–90	0	0	0	0	0	0
33–67	0	0	0	0	0	0
<33	0	0	0	0	2	2
0	0	2	2	2	0	0
Indonesia	3	3	3	3	3	3
>90	1	0	0	0	0	0
67–90	1	1	0	1	1	0
33–67	1	1	0	1	1	0
<33	0	0	0	0	1	0
0	0	1	3	1	0	3
Total	11	11	11	11	11	11
>90	7	5	0	1	0	0
67–90	1	1	3	1	1	0
33–67	1	1	1	4	1	1
<33	0	0	0	1	4	3
0	2	4	7	4	5	7

Source: Firm interviews and questionnaire.
[a] Does not include the domestic market for Indonesian companies.
[b] Subassembly of components.

was largely the United States. Some exports were products under the companies' own brand names, and some were undertaken under subcontracting arrangements for other brands. Only one firm exported back to Japan, and two exported to other East Asian countries — namely, Hong Kong and Singapore — although some of these exports were destined for other regions, as a result of the two ports' entrepôt roles.

The two Korean firms were established in 1991–92, each being a part of a large Korean conglomerate. The different firm behaviour appeared to relate to the nature of the product. One firm produced VCRs and radiocassettes, exporting almost all of its output, partly as products under the conglomerate's brand name and partly under subcontracting arrangements for other brands. The main destination of its exports was the United States. All of its sales went through intrafirm channels. The other firm produced colour TVs and sold all of its output in the domestic market: however, the firm had plans to export further down the road.

Two of the three domestic firms in consumer electronics and computer monitors sold their output under subcontracting arrangements. One of them was a leader in the domestic market and exported colour TVs under subcontracting arrangements for other brands but also sold colour TVs of its own design. The other firms that manufactured under subcontracting arrangements obtained the design from the buyer.

Firms in the subassembly of electronic components, especially domestic firms, became increasingly export oriented in the early 1990s. The share of output exported by foreign firms decreased slightly from 94% to 87% between 1990 and 1992, but it increased significantly from 26% to 63% for domestic firms (Table 9.6). The two components firms in our sample assembled and packaged ICs and semiconductors. All of their output was exported, the main market being the United States. Other East Asian economies, especially Singapore, were also important destinations for exports. Production took place under subcontracting arrangements with large MNEs. Sales were not intrafirm but occurred through the subcontracting arrangements.

Automotive

Foreign joint ventures and foreign principals dominated activities in the automotive sector. The principal determined how much of sales were exported and controlled the distribution channel. Sales, whether for domestic or export markets, were channeled through affiliated companies; the distribution was controlled by the joint venture or by affiliates and subsidiaries of the foreign principal.

Because of the high degree of protection in the automotive sector, it is not surprising that production in this sector was, by and large, domestically oriented. The share of exports in total output was very low in the early 1990s for both foreign and domestic firms (Table 9.6). Small increases in exports, especially of components, were recorded in 1992, but the absolute values were still modest.

This trend is consistent with the survey results (Table 9.10). Exports were negligible and mainly conducted through intrafirm channels. In one case, an established joint venture (with majority Indonesian ownership and producing under licence for a major Japanese principal) was given some leeway to export commercial vehicles to markets in the ASEAN region. Exports were channeled through the marketing system of the domestic partner and managers and not through that of the principal. The marketing channels included counter trade, or exchanging assembled vehicles for components. However, the amount exported was very small: only 3% of total output.

Sourcing behaviour

As with sales behaviour, differences in procurement behaviour were related to policy issues, sector-specific factors, the investor's home country, and the vintage of the firm. Procurement behaviour across sectors differed, depending on whether final sales were local or export oriented. The general trend indicated that the more export-oriented foreign firms imported a higher percentage of their inputs. The CBS Industry Survey indicates that foreign firms imported 57% of their inputs in 1992, compared with 23% imported by domestic firms (Table 9.11).

Table 9.10. Surveyed firms in automotive assembly by investing country and destination of sales.

Firm nationality (% sales)	Surveyed firms (n)					
	Exported	Intrafirm	To parent	Interaffiliate	Home country[a]	Other East Asia
Japan (assembly)	2	2	2	2	2	2
>90	0	2	0	2	0	0
67–90	0	0	0	0	0	0
33–67	0	0	0	0	0	0
<33	2	0	2	0	1	2
0	0	0	0	0	1	0
Japan (components)	2	2	2	2	2	2
>90	0	1	0	1	0	0
67–90	0	0	0	0	0	0
33–67	0	1	0	1	0	0
<33	2	0	2	0	0	2
0	0	0	0	0	2	0
United States	2	2	2	2	2	2
>90	0	2	0	2	0	0
67–90	0	0	0	0	0	0
33–67	0	0	0	0	0	0
<33	0	0	0	0	1	0
0	2	0	2	0	1	2
Germany	2	2	2	2	2	2
>90	0	2	0	2	0	0
67–90	0	0	0	0	0	0
33–67	0	0	0	0	0	0
<33	1	0	0	0	0	0
0	1	0	2	0	2	2
Total	8	8	8	8	8	8
>90	0	7	0	7	0	0
67–90	0	0	0	0	0	0
33–67	0	1	0	1	0	0
<33	5	0	4	0	2	4
0	3	0	4	0	6	4

Source: Firm interviews and questionnaire.
[a] Does not include the domestic market for Indonesian companies.

Table 9.11. Import propensity of firms in sectors surveyed. [a]

Industry (by ISIC code)	Imported inputs (%)			
	Foreign firms		Domestic firms	
	1986	1992	1986	1992
32111 Spinning	57	50	51	45
32114 Weaving	46	47	11	9
32210 Garments	NA	86	17	23
38320 Consumer electronics	73	87	87	80
38324 Subassembly of electronic components	NA	94	NA	73
38430 Motor-vehicle assembly and manufacturing	68	94	65	50
38433 Motor-vehicle components	NA	91	NA	68
Total manufacturing	53	57	25	23

Source: Government of Indonesia (1992).
Note: NA, not available.
[a] Import propensity is the share of imported inputs in total inputs.

Textiles and garments

The main raw materials for the production of staple fibre and polyester-filament yarn are purified terephthalic acid and ethylene glycol. Until 1993, most of these raw materials were imported. After that time, some producers started to produce these raw materials, thereby reducing imports. An issue that emerged for these new producers was whether these upstream industries should be protected. The synthetic-fibre producers indicated that this would have adverse effects on their industry because more costly inputs would result in increased prices. Their consequently reduced competitiveness would induce the export-oriented weaving mills to purchase their fibre inputs from abroad because, as export-oriented producers, they could import under duty-exemption schemes.

The two firms producing staple fibre and polyester-filament yarn, one Japanese and one Korean, imported between 67% and 90% of their inputs (Table 9.12). The Japanese firm imported through the affiliated trading company, whereas the Korean firm imported through the parent, which produced the upstream raw materials. The Korean firm also imported some inputs from its affiliated trading company, citing lower costs as the main reason. The Taiwanese firm, which produced cotton- and polyester-spun yarn, procured all of its raw materials domestically, with the exception of cotton, which was procured through the parent company. The main reason for procuring through the parent

Table 9.12. Surveyed firms in textiles by investing country and sourcing of materials and components.

Firm nationality (% sourcing)	Surveyed firms (n)					
	Imported	Intrafirm	From parent	Interaffiliate	Home country [a]	Other East Asia
Japan	3	3	3	3	3	3
>90	0	0	0	0	0	0
67–90	1	0	0	0	0	0
33–67	0	2	0	2	0	1
<33	2	1	0	1	1	0
0	0	0	3	0	2	2
Korea	3	3	3	3	3	3
>90	0	1	0	1	0	0
67–90	1	1	1	0	0	0
33–67	1	0	0	0	1	0
<33	0	1	0	1	0	2
0	1	0	2	1	2	1
Taiwan	4	4	4	4	4	4
>90	1	0	0	0	0	0
67–90	1	1	0	1	2	0
33–67	1	1	1	0	1	0
<33	1	0	0	0	1	0
0	0	2	3	3	0	4
Indonesia	2	2	2	2	2	2
>90	0	0	0	0	0	0
67–90	0	0	0	0	0	0
33–67	0	0	0	0	0	0
<33	2	0	0	0	0	0
0	0	2	2	2	2	2
Total	12	12	12	12	12	12
>90	1	1	0	1	0	0
67–90	3	2	1	1	2	0
33–67	2	3	1	2	2	1
<33	5	2	0	2	2	2
0	1	4	10	6	6	9

Source: Firm interviews and questionnaire.
[a] Does not include the domestic market for Indonesian companies.

company was maintaining quality standards and the parent's better bargaining position and ability to negotiate a lower price.

In the weaving sector, foreign firms displayed a higher propensity to import inputs than did domestic firms. In 1992, foreign firms imported 47% of their inputs compared with 9% of inputs imported by domestic firms (Table 9.11). This higher propensity of foreign firms to import inputs was correlated with their higher degree of export orientation.

The survey analysis indicates that the percentage of imported inputs depended on the final product, the degree of integration with mid- and upstream segments of the industry, and the firm's vintage (Table 9.12). The imported raw materials were mainly cotton and some fine polyester yarn; other inputs were procured locally.

The Korean firm imported less than 33% of its inputs from an affiliated trading company. Raw materials for weaving its T/C gray were procured from the local partner, which had mid- and upstream manufacturing operations. Two of the three Taiwanese firms imported more than 33% of their inputs, mostly from Taiwan through open-market channels. One of the firms had no parent in Taiwan; however, relations with the Taiwanese shareholders facilitated importing. The third Taiwanese firm, whose Taiwanese owner had relocated to Indonesia, imported less than 33% of its input. Because only a representative office existed in Taiwan, imports were not intrafirm. Procurement linkages were based on the owner's past experience in trading fabrics and in taking on contracts for dyeing and printing.

The two domestic firms were both leaders in the weaving sector. They belonged to an integrated textile-manufacturing group with mid- and upstream operations. Raw materials were procured mainly through intrafirm channels from other subsidiaries, with only cotton being imported, which accounted for less than 33% of inputs. Because of the strong links of these two firms with Japanese trading companies, as evident from their sales behaviour, imports were also obtained through these trading companies. It is noteworthy that the trading companies provided them with supplier credits and loans to purchase machinery; helped them in the choice of technology, machinery, and plant equipment; and even assisted them with the plant's construction.

In the garment sector, the share of imported inputs was significantly larger for foreign than for domestic firms (Table 9.11). Foreign firms imported 86% of their inputs in 1992, compared with 23% by domestic firms. Once again, import propensities were strongly correlated with export orientation of foreign firms.

In our sample, the share of imported inputs ranged from nil to more than 90%, with only three firms sourcing through intrafirm channels (Table 9.13). The share of imported inputs depended on the firm's export orientation and the kind of output produced. The degree of intrafirm trade and the origin of sourcing were correlated with the size of the group the firm belonged to.

The three Korean firms imported more than 66% of their inputs. Two of the firms belonged to large- and medium-scale conglomerates in Korea, and they procured through either the parent or an affiliated trading company. The third firm had no a parent in Korea and thus imported from the open market. The owner's trading experience and familiarity with suppliers and procurement channels were considered advantageous. All three firms sourced between 33% and 66% of their inputs from Korea and the rest from other East Asian countries, specifically Japan and Taiwan. This was consistent with the aggregate intraregional trends reported by the CBS Industry Survey.

One of the Taiwanese firms produced high-quality socks and procured all of its yarn inputs locally. The other Taiwanese firm, which produced under licence and also had its own brand name, imported between 33% and 66% of its inputs from its parent in Taiwan.

The three domestic garment firms, which were highly export oriented, imported between 67% and 90% of inputs, whereas the fourth domestic firm, which sold largely in the domestic market, imported less than 66% of its inputs. Most imports came from East Asian countries — China, (through Hong Kong), Japan, Korea, and Taiwan. The large domestically oriented firm also imported from Europe because it produced under licence for some European brands. Imports were not intrafirm but were to a large extent determined by buyers and links with the trading companies

Table 9.13. Surveyed firms in garments by investing country and sourcing of materials and components.

Firm nationality (% sourcing)	Surveyed firms (*n*)					
	Imported	Intrafirm	From parent	Interaffiliate	Home country [a]	Other East Asia
Korea	3	3	3	3	3	3
>90	2	0	0	0	0	0
67–90	1	0	0	0	0	0
33–67	0	1	0	1	3	0
<33	0	1	1	0	0	3
0	0	1	2	2	0	0
Taiwan	2	2	2	2	2	2
>90	0	0	0	0	0	0
67–90	0	0	0	0	0	0
33–67	1	1	1	0	1	0
<33	0	0	0	0	0	1
0	1	1	1	2	1	1
Indonesia	4	4	4	4	4	4
>90	0	0	0	0	0	1
67–90	3	0	0	0	0	2
33–67	1	0	0	0	0	1
<33	0	0	0	0	0	0
0	0	4	4	4	4	0
Total	9	9	9	9	9	9
>90	2	0	0	0	0	1
67–90	4	0	0	0	0	2
33–67	2	2	1	1	4	1
<33	0	1	1	0	0	4
0	1	6	7	8	5	1

Source: Firm interviews and questionnaire.
[a] Does not include the domestic market for Indonesian companies.

Electronics

At the aggregate level, firms in the electronics industry displayed a high degree of import propensity, both for consumer electronics and the subassembly of electronic components. In 1992, foreign firms in consumer electronics imported 87% of inputs, whereas domestic firms imported 80% of inputs. Foreign firms in the assembly of electronic components had an even higher share of imported inputs, namely, 94% (Table 9.11). These figures reflect the lack of a core components and supplier industry in Indonesia (Pangestu 1993).

The survey analysis confirmed this pattern. More than 75% of sample firms imported more than 66% of their inputs (Table 9.14). The import share was similar for export-oriented and domestically oriented firms because of the lack of locally available core components, such as cathode-ray tubes for TVs and computer monitors, printed circuit boards, and video heads.

With the exception of one domestically oriented Japanese joint venture, all Japanese and Korean firms imported more than 66% of their inputs through the intrafirm channels of the large MNE to which they belonged. The main intrafirm sourcing was from affiliates rather than the parent; for at least three of the firms, the role of the purchasing office and RHQ in Singapore was important. A significant amount of sourcing was from the home economy, as well as from other East Asian and ASEAN countries. A number of these firms had subsidiaries in other ASEAN economies or affiliates in Malaysia and Singapore, from which the firms in Indonesia imported. This procurement policy was in part the result of local- or ASEAN-content requirements imposed by the preferential-tariff system in Europe and the United States under the Generalized System of Preferences (GSP).

Table 9.14. Surveyed firms in electronics by investing country and sourcing of materials and components.

Firm nationality (% sourcing)	Surveyed firms (n)					
	Imported	Intrafirm	From parent	Interaffiliate	Home country[a]	Other East Asia
Japan	4	4	4	4	4	4
>90	1	1	1	1	0	0
67–90	2	2	0	2	0	1
33–67	1	0	0	0	1	3
<33	0	1	0	1	3	0
0	0	0	3	0	0	0
Korea	2	2	2	2	2	2
>90	1	1	1	0	0	0
67–90	1	1	0	1	1	1
33–67	0	0	0	0	1	1
<33	0	0	0	0	0	0
0	0	0	1	1	0	0
Singapore[b]	2	2	2	2	2	2
>90	2	1	0	1	0	0
67–90	0	0	0	0	0	1
33–67	0	0	0	0	1	0
<33	0	0	0	0	1	1
0	0	1	2	1	0	0
Indonesia	3	3	3	3	3	3
>90	1	0	0	0	0	0
67–90	1	0	0	0	0	3
33–67	1	0	0	0	0	0
<33	0	0	0	0	0	0
0	0	3	3	3	3	0
Total	11	11	11	11	11	11
>90	5	3	2	2	0	0
67–90	4	3	0	3	1	6
33–67	2	0	0	0	3	4
<33	0	1	0	1	4	1
0	0	4	9	5	3	0

Source: Firm interviews and questionnaire.
[a] Does not include the domestic market for Indonesian companies.
[b] Subassembly of components.

The amount of inputs, none of which were intrafirm, sourced from abroad varied widely for the three domestic firms. All of them obtained at least 67% of their imports from East Asia, especially Taiwan, and other ASEAN economies, such as Singapore and to a lesser extent Malaysia. One of these firms, a subcontractor, had its procurement behaviour determined by the European brand-name company, which had its RHQ in Singapore and other manufacturing facilities in Singapore and Malaysia.

The two majority-domestic-owned firms assembling and packaging ICs under subcontracting arrangement to big MNEs sourced most of their inputs from Japan, Korea, and Singapore. One of the firms, which is part of a large Indonesian conglomerate, purchased its inputs through the group's international purchasing office in Singapore. The other was located on Batam and thus had close access to procurement centres based in Singapore.

Automotive

Despite the domestic-content rules, import shares in the automotive sector remained high, especially in the case of foreign firms. In 1992, foreign firms in assembly and manufacturing of automobiles imported 94% of their inputs, whereas domestic firms sourced 50% of their inputs from abroad

Table 9.15. Surveyed firms in automotive assembly by investing country and sourcing of materials and components.

Firm nationality (% sourcing)	Surveyed firms (*n*)					
	Imported	Intrafirm	From parent	Interaffiliate	Home country[a]	Other East Asia
Japan (assembly)	2	2	2	2	2	2
>90	0	0	0	0	0	0
67–90	1	1	1	0	1	0
33–67	1	1	1	1	1	0
<33	0	0	0	1	0	2
0	0	0	0	0	0	0
Japan (components)	2	2	2	2	2	2
>90	2	2	1	0	1	0
67–90	0	0	1	0	1	0
33–67	0	0	0	0	0	0
<33	0	0	0	2	0	2
0	0	0	0	0	0	0
United States	2	2	2	2	2	2
>90	0	0	0	0	0	0
67–90	1	2	0	2	0	1
33–67	1	0	0	0	0	1
<33	0	0	0	0	0	0
0	0	0	2	0	2	0
Germany	2	2	2	2	2	2
>90	0	0	0	0	0	0
67–90	2	2	1	1	1	0
33–67	0	0	0	0	0	0
<33	0	0	0	0	0	0
0	0	0	1	1	1	2
Total	8	8	8	8	8	8
>90	2	2	1	0	1	0
67–90	4	5	3	3	3	1
33–67	2	1	1	1	1	1
<33	0	0	0	3	0	4
0	0	0	3	1	3	2

Source: Firm interviews and questionnaire.
[a] Does not include the domestic market for Indonesian companies.

(Table 9.11). Part of the reason for this discrepancy was that domestic firms producing under licence had to respond to the domestic-content policy by investing in backward integration. The more recently established foreign firms, on the other hand, had not yet invested in backward integration. The manufacture of motor-vehicle components also displayed high import shares in 1992, with foreign firms importing 91% of inputs, compared with 68% for domestic firms.

The survey analysis showed that sourcing patterns depended on product type and policy rules (Table 9.15). The domestic-content policy adopted in the automotive sector required that some amount of the final product, as well as certain parts and components, be produced locally within a specific time after entering the market. As noted earlier, the local-content requirement was higher for commercial vehicles than for sedans. Because the sedan is of a higher quality and value, imports of components for the assembly of sedans relied more heavily on the parent, whereas multisourcing from other affiliates and unrelated companies was more common in the assembly of commercial vehicles. Components procured locally were obtained from both subcontractors and unrelated companies, as well as from the firm's own subsidiaries and affiliated companies.

Two sample firms that assembled light commercial vehicles imported less than 67% of all inputs. This comparatively low percentage revealed the stricter domestic-content requirements for these automobiles. The German assembler of trucks and buses, that is, of commercial vehicles rather than of light commercial vehicles, displayed a higher propensity to import. All sedan assemblers imported between 67% and 90% of their inputs. The strong control of the principal ensured that a large share of sourcing was intrafirm, through the parent and affiliates. There were, however, differences in sourcing behaviour depending on the principal's nationality. The Japanese assemblers imported mainly from Japan; the US assemblers sourced predominantly from affiliates based in Japan; and the German assemblers imported largely from Germany and other non-East Asian affiliates.

The two Japanese firms producing a variety of components imported 90% of inputs, thus displaying the highest propensity to import. All inputs were sourced through intrafirm channels, mostly from the parent company. Only a small amount was sourced from affiliated companies. Furthermore, most inputs originated in Japan, with the remainder coming from other East Asian and ASEAN countries.

So far, despite the appreciation of the yen, there has been little evidence of a shift away from Japan as the major input supplier for both assemblers and components manufacturers. This has been due to the tight control of the principal, who can transfer pricing practices, given the high protection in the domestic markets. With increased competition, a continued risk of appreciation of the yen, and the potential opening of some of the regional automobile markets, changes in sourcing patterns may be expected. Some of the major principals were already planning a regional production strategy, with production sites in different locations in the region complementing each other.

Policy implications

The interviews and questionnaires revealed several policy issues affecting firms' behaviour. In the three sectors analyzed, export orientation started in the textiles and garment industry. Exporting since the late 1970s and early 1980s, firms in this sector took advantage of subsidies inherent in the export-certificate scheme and the subsidized-credit program. Early entrants also benefited from the allocation of large quotas. The late 1980s saw a new wave of investments in this sector, mainly from Korea and Taiwan, searching for lower-cost locations. Although some of the output was directed to servicing the home markets, other exports, geared to the US and European markets, encountered problems obtaining the necessary quotas. Therefore, these firms exported mainly to nonquota markets or exported nonquota items. Some of the problems with the government's administration of the quota-allocation system referred to in the interviews were the lack of transparency and delays in allocating unused quotas, which frequently meant that the orders for the season had passed by the time firms were certain about their quotas.

Other policy issues affecting firms' export and sales decisions related to ensuring a competitive environment. Both domestic and foreign firms identified lower labour costs as a comparative advantage of Indonesia. That is, the proportion of labour costs in production costs was low, ranging from 5% for some electronics companies to around 10–15% for labour-intensive garment firms. However, it is important that this comparative advantage not be outweighed by impediments of doing business in Indonesia. Major impediments, identified by all firms, were the high costs of doing business transactions, the high costs of financing investments,[9] the limited supporting physical and institutional infrastructure, and the lack of a viable supplier industry (given that raw materials and inputs represent the bulk of production costs).

Most of the respondents commented on the red tape and bureaucracy, ranging from investment approvals to ensuring the smooth flow of goods, as major problems in Indonesia compared with other countries in the region. For instance, the processing of documents to obtain duty exemption

---

[9] Indonesian interest rates were higher than those of other countries in the region. The high interest rates were a result of a tight monetary policy combating inflation and to some extent the banking sector's inefficiencies.

for inputs used in the production of exports was considered unduly onerous, starting with the time it took to be inspected by SGS at the port of origin and continuing on to the clearance of the documents needed for exemption. Another related problem was the 10% value-added tax that had to be paid on inputs purchased domestically: this was supposed to be refunded for inputs used in exported goods. In practice, however, it took a long time to get the refund, and usually some of the amount was withheld. This added to the overhead of companies, and in the case of some garment firms it dissuaded them from sourcing domestically. The government has since reduced some of the documentation procedures required for duty exemption, and in January 1996 it ceased withholding the value-added tax.

At the time of the interviews, the export-processing zones — EPTEs — were just being introduced. The main advantage of the EPTE is that goods come in duty free, so a company avoids having to go through SGS inspection and duty-exemption documentations. However, initially, there were some delays in approvals, as well as difficulties related to administrative procedures in transferring goods in and out of and among EPTEs. This made it difficult to subcontract production out of the EPTEs and procure goods and lease equipment from outside an EPTE. Some of these problems were addressed in the January 1996 deregulation, especially those regarding economic interactions among EPTEs.

Our survey confirmed findings of other studies regarding the high import content of Indonesia's exports. Several policy factors pointed out by the surveyed firms kept them from sourcing as much as they might have domestically. Besides the problems relating to refunds of value-added tax on domestically procured goods and the difficulty of moving goods in and out of EPTEs, the procedure for obtaining duty exemption for indirect exports, that is, for domestically produced raw materials, parts, and components used in export production, was considered a problem because it was too complex. These factors contributed to the difficulty in developing an internationally competitive supplier industry; it was simply cheaper and faster for export-oriented firms to import inputs.

Of course, in the case of electronics and automobiles, the lack of an internationally competitive supplier industry was also related to lack of demand. The development of the components and supplier industry in the automotive sector occurred because of the local-content rules, but this sector was not export oriented, with the exception of a few goods, such as car batteries and tires. The recent deregulation in January 1996, which addressed some of the issues referred to as problematic by the survey firms, will go some way to improving the incentives to develop a viable supplier industry. However, the development of a sustainable supplier industry will depend to a large extent on the inflow of foreign investment into these sectors and the upgrading of domestic technological capability and human resources. Some of the electronics firms in the survey that belonged to large MNEs with operations across the region induced some of their suppliers to relocate as well. However, as a result of the lack of a policy environment conducive to the supplier industry, many of the major suppliers have been adopting a wait-and-see attitude. It remains to be seen whether the recent improvements in the policy environment will be sufficient to attract a wave of relocations by supplier industries.

In addition to citing low labour costs, the foreign firms pointed out the potential of the domestic market and the improvements in the investment climate since 1986 as locational factors. All these firms had a domestic partner because, before June 1994, it was impossible for firms to operate with 100% foreign ownership. Typically, the partner they chose was also their domestic partner in previous joint ventures, their licence holder, their distributor, or their previous customer (that is, trader). In the majority-owned, export-oriented joint ventures set up in the early 1990s, the domestic partner played a peripheral role. Only in a few instances did the domestic partner play a greater role or contribute in some way to running the firm by, for example, procuring inputs.

The firms interviewed also pointed out that the availability and trainability of unskilled labour in Indonesia were commendable, especially in comparison with China. However, the firms all faced problems finding capable technical personnel, engineers, and managers. As a result, many resorted to hiring expatriates or recruiting and training new graduates.

Conclusion

Since the mid-1980s Indonesia's trade and investment policy framework has been liberalized and deregulated. With policy changes to promote export manufacturing and allow 100% foreign equity ownership, FDI inflows surged, particularly from the Asian NIEs (which offset the slower growth of FDI from Japan). Manufacturing exports surged as well, with East Asia, particularly through Singapore, being an increasingly important destination for textiles and other products. However, the United States and Europe continued to dominate markets for electrical machinery and textile exports.

The firm-level survey showed that the incidence of intrafirm trade varied by industry, corporate nationality, and vintage. Half of the interviewed textile firms reported intrafirm sales, such sales being more important for Korean than for Japanese or Taiwanese firms. Less than half of the garment firms reported intrafirm sales; again, such sales were more important for Korean firms. Most firms in electronics and nearly all firms in the automobile sector relied heavily on intrafirm channels for sales.

On the procurement side, the use of intrafirm channels varied widely by industry. Garment firms used the market, but automotive-component firms relied on intrafirm sourcing. Sourcing from the parent appeared unimportant for textiles and garment firms and more important for electronics and automobile firms. By corporate nationality, there was no distinctive sourcing behaviour among firms in textiles and electronics, although Korean firms in garments and Japanese firms in automotive assembly appeared to depend more on import sourcing.

Sourcing behaviour was related to market orientation, industry, and policy framework. In general, foreign firms were more import dependent than domestic firms, which to some degree reflected the greater export orientation of foreign firms. The greatest contrast was in the weaving sector, where foreign firms imported 47% of inputs, compared with 9% for domestic firms. The import intensities also varied with industry, which partly reflected the degree of upstream integration. Import dependence was higher for garment, electronics, and automobile firms than for textile firms. No clear evidence of import dependence by corporate nationality was found: in textiles, Taiwanese firms were more import dependent than Japanese and domestic firms; in electronics, most foreign and local firms were highly import dependent; and, in automobiles, Japanese firms were more import dependent than others. The local-content program affected sourcing behaviour in the automotive sector because more-established firms had progressed further in the localization process than those that were newly established.

Indonesia has come a long way in trade and investment-policy liberalization and deregulation, but further efforts are needed if its increasingly outward-looking strategy is to be reflected in larger inflows of FDI and rising international competitiveness. Foreign investors expect transparency and nondiscriminatory treatment, as well as ready and cheaper access to intermediate inputs, both imported and from local suppliers. These efforts may be expected to bear fruit in the form of larger FDI inflows from Japan and the Asian NIEs, which will be attracted by the size of the Indonesian market. Because of the FDI–trade linkages, Indonesia will become increasingly integrated into the East Asian economic region.

Part III

CROSSING BORDERS

Chapter 10

CROSSING BORDERS

Multinationals in East Asia

Wendy Dobson

To this point, our analytical focus has been on firms' activities in individual host economies. In this chapter, the firm becomes the unit of analysis as we examine more closely how firms carry out cross-border operations. What are their strategies? Does location influence these strategies? We expect firms to have made the basic choice among low-cost, differentiation, or focus strategies and to allocate (and reallocate) responsibilities to affiliates so that the advantages of location — such as economies of scale, incentives, and factor supplies — and local specialization outweigh the costs of transferring technology and learning and coordinating these dispersed activities to promote the firm's global competitive advantage in the industry.

The hypothesized synergy between a location and a firm's value-added activities refers to a positive relationship: investment- and innovation-driven economies (such as Malaysia, Singapore, and Taiwan) should be locations for, even agglomerations of, higher value-added industry activities. We expect to see firms, through intrafirm or intranetwork shipments of inputs or sales and technology transfers, contribute to regional integration. The available evidence on corporate nationality suggests that we should not expect to see much evidence of differential behaviour. We might, however, see differentials by vintage and size (that is, small, new internationalizing firms behaving differently than the more mature multinational enterprises [MNEs]). We may also expect evidence that firms change the ways they organize themselves as they internationalize, and if this occurs, ask how it does occur.

The firms studied (their characteristics are summarized in Table 10.1) were Acer, whose home base is Taiwan; AT&T (American Telephone & Telegraph Co.), Motorola, and Texas Instruments (TI), based in the United States; and Matsushita Electric Industrial Co. Ltd (MEI) and Sony from Japan. This analysis is based on two types of data. The first is publicly available data, which I use to map the activities of firms in Tables 10.2–10.7 to study their activities in the region. These firms were chosen over others because their affiliates appeared a number of times in our surveys. The second type of data, presented in Table 10.8, come from our surveys reported in previous chapters. In this analysis, the identities of firms are kept confidential.

The electrical and electronics industry is one of the most rapidly growing and rapidly evolving in the world; thus, classification of the product focus and industry segments of electrical and electronics firms is also evolving. The value chain in the industry includes a wide range of products and services, from low-tech components and assembly to technology- and capital-intensive sophisticated services, like telecommunications.

Table 10.1. Summary of characteristics of six firms, 1994 or latest.

Firm	Revenues, 1994 (US$ millions)	Production abroad[a] (% total)	Affiliates in East Asia (% total)	Location of Asian headquarters	Ranking by foreign assets[b]	Asian R&D facilities
Acer	≥5.0	NA	(n = 3)	Taipei (WHQ)	NA	Taipei
AT&T	75.1	8	NA	Beijing (1) Hong Kong (1)	65	Bell Labs (Singapore, Beijing)
Matsushita	69.9	38	34	Singapore	14	Taipei, Singapore
Motorola	22.2	56 [c]	(n = 24)	Singapore (1993)	95	IC design centres (Hong Kong, Taipei, Singapore), technical support centre (Singapore)
Sony	40.1	36	17 [d]	Singapore	9	Singapore
Texas Instruments	10.3	NA	31	Taipei	NA	Tsukuba (Japan)

Source: Fortune (1995).

Note: AT&T, American Telephone & Telegraph Co.; IC, integrated circuit; NA, not available; R&D, research and development; WHQ, world headquarters.

[a] Foreign production is measured by the value of production abroad divided by total sales.

[b] UNCTAD (1995). Rankings by foreign assets are calculated from Fortune Global 500 or, if not available, estimated from foreign employment, sales, etc.

[c] Fifty-six percent of total sales were outside the United States in 1994; 26% were in Asia.

[d] Sony annual reports (Sony Corporation n.d.). Sony aims for 50% by 1996.

Case studies

To understand a firm's regional strategy, one must also understand its global objectives. Two firms specialize in computers and semiconductors. Acer, with nearly US$5 billion in sales in 1995, is the world's 10th largest producer of personal computers (PCs) and produces components, as well as its own brand-name computers. TI is one of the world's leading semiconductor producers. Its operations are largely upstream, although it also produces its own brand of computers and office equipment. TI has sunk deep roots in the region, as part of its strategy to get closer to its fastest-growing customers. One of the world's largest companies, AT&T has a broader focus that includes its original mandate as a telephone company but has expanded to include telecommunications and information-management services. Motorola began life as a consumer-electronics firm, a business it left in the 1970s. It is now one of the world's largest producers of cellular phones, pagers, and mobile radios (wireless communications and electronic equipment) and is the world's fourth largest semiconductor manufacturer, as well as being a producer of data-communications and information-processing services and equipment. Motorola's operations range from upstream research and production of semiconductors and integrated circuits (ICs) used in its products to consumer products. The other two firms specialize in consumer-electronics. MEI, another of the world's largest companies, occupies the entire value chain producing consumer electronics end products, such as televisions (TVs) and radios; household appliances; and chips, floppy disks, motors, and compressors for its end products. Sony is one of its largest competitors.

Acer is distinctive in this group. It is a relative newcomer, as one of the first Taiwanese multinationals, and has developed from an original equipment manufacturer (OEM) supplier to a brand-name PC supplier that aims to become one of the world's top computer makers by the end of the decade. MEI, on the other hand, first entered Asian markets in 1961, in Thailand. As recently as 1988, only 11% of its production was located overseas, although by 1993, 49% of total sales were foreign. Motorola arrived in Korea in 1967, followed closely by TI, which entered Japan in 1968. AT&T is a latecomer. It grew to its huge size through its US operations (to which it was confined until recent industry deregulation). Only 8% of its revenues in 1993 came from operations abroad. Sony, with its distinctly successful global strategy, which include sales and marketing outlets in the region since the early 1970s, began production in the region only in the wake of the appreciation in the yen in 1986. Sony and MEI control 70–80% of the world market for many kinds of consumer-electronics products. The two giants employ a total of 360 000 workers worldwide and generate total sales, including consumer-electronics goods, equivalent to 2% of Japan's gross national product (de Rosario 1992).

The East Asian region, although it is only half the size of the US market, is important in the global plans of the world's largest electronics firms because of the region's dynamic growth as an end-user market. Large production clusters have developed around certain products, such as disk drives in Singapore, semiconductors and appliances in Malaysia, and PCs and peripherals in Taiwan. In recent years, while markets in the United States, Europe, Japan, and South Korea were in recession, the rest of East Asia remained buoyant; production grew more than 6% annually in 1992–94.

Many East Asian governments, particularly those in Korea and Taiwan, have targeted semiconductors as a major export product. Most exports are to the United States, the European Community (EC), and Japan, but an increasing number of chips are purchased in the Asia–Pacific region as well. Semiconductors are Taiwan's biggest import after oil. Its largest chip consumers are makers of notebook computers, which hold around a 22% share of the world market. In 1992, Taiwan also produced 66% of the world's computer motherboards and held strong positions in digital pocket diaries, computer mice, and other computer peripherals. Korean companies, including Samsung Electronics, Hyundai Electronics, and Goldstar Electron, account for 75% of the Asia–Pacific region's production of high-volume chips used in PCs. Although 90% of Korean memory chips are exported, Korea imports as many chips again, usually custom designed, as components in other products (Clifford 1992a). Singapore has also targeted export markets, using a different approach: by constantly upgrading the skills of its work force, it can staff highly automated factories producing components and end products for such companies as Motorola and Sony.

Acer: an evolving global strategy

Acer is a home-grown Asian firm whose Taiwanese founder, Stan Shih, aims to demonstrate that a Chinese firm that began its life as an OEM can also become a professionally managed global firm marketing a brand-name product.[1] Acer is an example of a firm that began with a low-cost strategy and a broad focus and took the risks of switching to a differentiated strategy to become a global low-cost producer. As this case study shows, the costs of the switch were high: success was contingent on moving production close to sophisticated customers in countries of the Organisation for Economic Co-operation and Development (OECD) and the technology available in OECD markets while pursuing its low-cost differentiation. Acer makes most of the components of its brand itself, ensuring quality while underselling its major competitors, such as Compaq, but also allowing it to continue its OEM business.

Acer's founder set an ambitious goal to achieve in one decade: to become one of the world's top five PC makers by 2000, with worldwide sales of US$10 billion (TI's net revenues in 1993 were US$8.5 billion, by comparison) through a network of 21 companies listed on stock exchanges around the world. By late 1995, Acer was ranked as number seven (Kraar 1995).

At the outset, Acer, as an OEM, took advantage of Taiwan's relatively low labour costs and sold 45% of its output to other manufacturers. By 1991, 70% of Acer's sales were destined for places outside Taiwan. To overcome Taiwan's reputation for low-cost computer components, which leads customers to demand large price flexibility, Acer moved in 1991 to promote the Acer brand globally and to become a full-line PC supplier with a strong brand identity. Even so, in 1995, 29% of sales came from its OEM business: Acer still makes OEM notebooks for Hitachi and Siemens (Kraar 1995).

---

[1] Acer's Chinese name is Hong Chi, which means "grand game of go." Acer was founded in 1987, when its name was changed from Multitech, a company founded in 1976 to distribute electronic imports and produce video games.

The stakes were high. Production was pushed into high-end workstations, more sophisticated laptops, and high-resolution colour monitors. With product cycles becoming ever shorter and prices becoming more volatile, practice time also disappeared, but upgrading key components was essential (Asian Business 1994). In 1989, Acer teamed up with TI to build a US$250 million plant to produce 4-Mb dynamic random-access memory (DRAM) semiconductors at Hsinchu Science Park in Taiwan. Acer owns 58%; TI, 26%; and the Taiwan government, 16%. This facility has since undergone significant expansion.

Because technological capabilities were seen as necessary core competence and proximity to sophisticated customers was important to building these capabilities, Acer invested abroad to be near these customers. Initially, Acer penetrated OECD markets in Europe and North America. By 1993, Acer had moved from assembling PCs in Taiwan and Malaysia and shipping to European and US customers to assembling abroad with strict quality standards.

Acer pursued its investment strategy through a combination of joint ventures and acquisitions of local companies (with mixed results). In 1987, seeking technology, Acer acquired Counterpoint Computers, a small Silicon Valley maker of multiuser systems, which was subsequently folded into Acer's US division. Acer entered into another joint venture, with Smith Corona (which declared bankruptcy in 1995), to produce PCs. In 1990, Acer bought Altos, a small California maker of desktop workstations, to acquire technology and distribution channels. This strategy for entry into the minicomputer business encountered significant problems, causing major losses in 1991; extraordinary gains from land sales were required to put Acer back into the black (Goldstein 1992a).

Acer also entered into agreements with European companies, including International Computers Limited (ICL), in the UK, to build minicomputers in Taiwan; a joint venture with Messerschmitt, in Germany, to manufacture high-density semiconductor packaging; and a technical partnership with National Semiconductor to develop a specialized type of integrated circuit. In 1990, it purchased Kangaroo Computer, a Dutch PC maker, to establish a European manufacturing base and expanded this plant in 1992 (Goldstein 1990)

Because of the time it takes for investments in an international strategy to pay off, the initial financial effect was negative. Between 1985 and 1988, net-income margins averaged a healthy 4.3%. Margins became negative in the early 1990s, as a result of heavy spending and unanticipated declines in revenues as the home currency appreciated, the US market weakened, and a global shakeout occurred in the overcrowded PC industry. Heavy spending on distribution companies in the United States and Europe, improving the overseas sales and marketing staff, and raising the percentage of turnover devoted to research and development (R&D) contributed to expenses. Keeping costs down and inventories under strict control thus became essential to restoring competitiveness.

Acer's management structure evolved, in the wake of these acquisitions, into a decentralized and highly flexible structure, described as being like a client-server computer, with independent units linked into a flexible network. Six groups emerged as accountability centres to cooperate and compete simultaneously. Once the parent has decided major development policies, it leaves implementation to the groups. This structure allows for faster growth than more traditional structures because final products are marketed through joint ventures with local sales firms (Dubashi 1991).

Acer also became dependent on external sources of funding. Financing for the joint venture with TI came from foreign sources, including Barclays Bank, Bank of America, and one of Taiwan's policy banks, the Bank of Communications. Shih also financed his global strategy by finding global partners to buy small stakes in Acer, as well as strategic alliance with a global company.

Not until the OECD-entry thrust had been accomplished did Acer shift its sights to its own backyard. In 1976, attracted by externalities of previous investments made by US and Japanese electronics companies, Acer financed construction of a monitor plant in Penang, Malaysia, where infrastructure was attractive relative to Taiwan. In 1993, these production facilities were doubled. In that year, too, Acer located its Asian sales headquarters in Singapore, taking advantage of its growing reputation as a business centre. Because the Singapore and Taiwanese governments encourage more trade and investment, Taiwanese producers are attracted to Singapore's proximity to key Southeast

Asian markets, its political stability, and its good infrastructure. Two-way trade is growing among computer companies as they tap each other's expertise in certain products. Taiwan buys hard disks from Singapore and in turn sells it large numbers of monitors (Flannery 1993). In 1995, Acer located a new affiliate at Subic Bay, in the Philippines, to produce computer motherboards for export.

In 1992, Acer began exploring possibilities for investing in the People's Republic of China. The strategic rationale was to enter China's service industries, set up PC-sales networks, and gain permission to manufacture components locally (because imported PCs face a 38% import tax), concentrating on low-end assembly operations that were facing intense price competition at home. Cheaper engineering talent could be used.[2]

At this point, Acer encountered government opposition to its strategy. Because the Taiwanese government sees computers as a strategic industry, it fears that production shifts to China will damage Taiwan's high-tech future. Even the manufacture of components in China was prohibited at the time, with the exception of keyboards, despite the fact that Taiwan's industry was under severe cost pressures. The conflict over establishing a presence in China highlights key features of Acer's strategy. Its pursuit of a differentiated strategy has been encouraged by the Taiwanese government through a state-backed group called Brand International Promotion Association: the chief executive officers of Acer, Mitac, Copam, Giant (bicycles), and Kennex (tennis rackets) are members of this group. However, as the industry has expanded successfully abroad, the government has only slowly modified its interventionist approach (in both ownership and participation in firms' direction).

By 1995, Acer, with a market value of US$2 billion, began to split itself into 21 public companies, listed on stock exchanges around the world, to open the company to foreign investment. Acer Computer International, the Asian regional distribution arm, was the first public offering, on the Singapore Stock Exchange. Public offerings in Taiwan were still obstructed by barriers to outside investors in Taiwan's financial markets (no foreign institution is allowed ownership of more than 7.5% of a company in Taiwan) (Kraar 1995).

In summary, Acer's business presence in East Asian markets is still at an early stage because its goal has been to develop a high-quality brand-name PC. It has penetrated OECD markets to supplement its export strategy. Given its background as an OEM, this is a sensible approach to accomplishing its goal. Evidence in 1995 indicates that Acer was branching out into the region to support its low-cost differentiation. Unlike other informatics firms, Acer starts from final products and moves upstream into components. In this way, Acer controls both the quality and costs of its inputs and allows for economies of scope that facilitate successful price competition. As incomes grow and regional markets expand and Acer's own technological and marketing clout continues to increase, its sights can be expected to shift more to its neighbours. At that point, as a more mature international business, Acer could be expected to contribute in a significant way to regional integration through its investments in neighbouring economies and through the trade that will follow. Developments in the global PC market will, however, strongly influence Acer's future. Among the top 10 PC vendors, Acer is one of the few that increased market share in 1995 (Kehoe and Taylor 1996) as the industry was becoming increasingly "commoditized" and competition was becoming strongly price sensitive at comparable levels of quality.

AT&T: latecomer to the region

Until its breakup in 1995, AT&T was one of the world's largest corporations. In the Asia–Pacific region, however, it was a late starter relative to its main competitors. It has followed a broadly based strategy in which it has moved rapidly to build up a wide range of manufacturing and service activities since the early 1990s; many of these activities were divested in the mid-1990s as it switched to

---

[2] Acer's sales in China are handled by Yu Chi Electronics, a Hong Kong-based, mainland-owned company (Goldstein 1992b).

a more focused strategy. Because it is a latecomer, its behaviour as a foreign investor has been that of follow-the-leader; in some cases, the late arrival has made market entry costly.

AT&T grew to its current size and complexity within the US market. Its activities — which extended across computers, telephone products, and services — were manageable as long as it remained within this familiar environment, despite growing competition from new entrants. However, the US market is also a maturing one. To sustain growth, internationalization became an important option. Internationalization of segments with very different industrial structures and competitive conditions created conflicts, raised costs, and increased uncertainty. Although service activities have the highest value added, they are also highly protected in many countries, in contrast to the US business environment. Thus, market entry required that AT&T strike deals with host governments to provide services within domestic competitive constraints. AT&T's open product areas, which include computers, automated teller machines, switches, cables, and transmission systems, face globalized markets with no entry barriers and fierce rivalry. As a late entrant to international markets, AT&T faced the dilemma of seeking highly focused supplier status in established high-income markets (in competition with domestic suppliers) or competing fiercely for some of the world's newer fast-growing markets — many of which are located in Asia — that still lack established suppliers. Breaking up the company into its major business segments is one way to manage the conflicts created by differing industrial and market conditions.

Revenues from operations abroad in 1993 accounted for a mere 8% share of the total; 75% was still derived from US operations. In that year, AT&T invested US$1 billion and had 309 000 employees, of whom 53 000 were working in 100 countries outside the United States. AT&T saw itself as the world's networking leader. It adds value to its networks by combining communications, computing, and network products and systems. It aims to derive 50% of its revenues from international activities by the beginning of next century. In 1993, 60% of these revenues came from telecommunications services; 27%, from products and systems; and 10%, from rentals and services. In developing its global network, AT&T joined in 1993 with Japan's telephone and telegraph corporation, Kokusai Denshin Denwa, and Singapore's Telecom to form WorldPartners Association to provide global companies with services, such as one-stop shopping for service orders, maintenance, and billing. (Other big-company networks are Alliance of France and Deutsche Telecom and Sprint. Each is biased toward EC and US markets.) Services have always been a large part of AT&T's business, but like many of its large competitors producing computers and telecommunications equipment, it has a service business that is evolving rapidly as firms and consumers take advantage of technological changes that are revolutionizing information management and movement.

Because AT&T is a latecomer, its Asian strategy has been to increase market share by locating manufacturing, R&D, and networking nodes in the region. To do this, AT&T has been investing in a wide range of value-chain activities throughout the region (Table 10.2). The communications-equipment market in the region was estimated to total US$70–75 billion in 1991, growing at 10% annually; by comparison, the OECD market averaged around US$64 billion per year.

As we might expect, the focus of AT&T's activities is in Japan, Singapore, and China. Japan-based activities are mainly services and technology development or licencing technologies in joint ventures. High-end manufacturing ventures with Japanese firms give access to Japanese technologies and respond to US pressures for more foreign procurement. One feature of AT&T's strategy has been to capitalize on the Japanese boom that followed deregulation. Nippon Telephone & Telegraph Co. has targeted more than 10% of its annual procurement from foreign suppliers; the rest will be filled by Nippon Electric Company Ltd (NEC) and Fujitsu. Mitsubishi and AT&T cooperate in producing gallium arsenide chips under the Mitsubishi brand name, using Japanese technology. AT&T and Mitsubishi also work together, the latter to buy more foreign-made chips and ease international frictions and the former to expand its distribution channels (Business Times 1993d). In 1991, AT&T and NEC agreed to develop processing technology for future generations of computer chips, leveraging off its NCR Corporation position (which AT&T had acquired) in financial and retail markets (Business Times 1991b).

In Singapore, AT&T's other regional focal point, AT&T operations began with manufacturing (50% of output is destined for the US market; 30%, for Asia) and have since expanded to more sophisticated services, marketing, and R&D with a Bell Laboratories facility located there (Business Times 1991b). Increasingly, manufacturing in Singapore is linked to other Southeast Asian economies. For example, AT&T Microelectronics has 13 manufacturing operations around the world, with two in Asia — in Singapore (begun in 1985) and Bangkok. This affiliate produces advanced integrated circuits and develops integrated-circuits packaging. The factory in Singapore transfers mature products and technologies to Bangkok and supports them technically from Singapore. The Singapore facility also positions the company to move into new markets, including cellular-based personal communicators, interactive video, and high-speed digital-signal processing (Straits Times 1993b).

Hub activities are also located in Singapore, although the Asia–Pacific business centre has been located in Taiwan in a joint venture with the public sector to set up a regional telecom network (Business Times 1993a). AT&T Global Business Communications Systems has its Singapore-based Regional Support Centre as part of a plan to decentralize R&D activities to meet local networking needs, such as particular languages and accents in voice mail (Straits Times 1993a). An international network centre was also set up (linked to four others around the world) to assist multinational clients to manage global information with a 24-hour network.

Singapore is a hub in another sense. AT&T has made it the support base for low-end manufacturing in Indonesia and Thailand. Taking advantage of Batam's proximity to Singapore, low value-added production activities, such as those for cordless phones, were moved there. Indonesian operations are also supplying Indonesian requirements for digital-switching equipment, half of which is made locally by two private companies appointed as local partners (Westlake 1991). In Thailand, AT&T supplies the digital equipment for single-mode fibre cables in cooperation with a Thai partner that provides project services and installation. A factory producing telephones was also set up, but in a 1994 cost-reduction drive this unit was sold to local investors.

China is AT&T's third East Asian focus. After refusing a request in 1979 to enter a joint venture to produce telephone switches, AT&T fell behind its competitors in what is seen as potentially the world's largest telecommunications market. It was not until 1985 that AT&T established fibre-optic joint ventures. In 1993, it scrambled to move ahead of its competitors by agreeing to locate R&D facilities in a Chinese branch of Bell Laboratories. AT&T aims to be one of China's largest telecom suppliers, competing with Nortel, Alcatel, and Ericsson. It plans to engage in production of digital switches, microelectronics, optical-transmission products, and cellular systems as well as network management, training, systems integration, and R&D (FEER 1993), and will build China's largest fibre-optics plant, in Shanghai. Other agreements are being made at the provincial levels; for example, AT&T will supply switching equipment for an advanced communications system in Guangdong Province, including the establishment of a technical-support and training centre in Guangzhou.

AT&T's activities in Hong Kong, South Korea, and Taiwan take advantage of local manufacturing capabilities for the local and export markets for such consumer items as telephone handsets and modem cards for fax machines. Switching gear, which is a high-end product, must be imported. AT&T is active in Taiwan with a manufacturing joint venture, producing half of its output for the local market and half for export. In Korea, Goldstar has teamed up with AT&T to produce fibre optics. The Hong Kong operation exports handsets, cellular phones, and other low-level equipment to the United States (Westlake 1991).

In summary, AT&T is a latecomer to the global and regional marketplace. Because of the conflicting market conditions across its business segments, it has moved to facilitate greater focus in each by breaking up the company. Asian operations are spread across these many segments, and these activities are being adjusted to fit with evolving locational characteristics. In Japan, AT&T's objectives are to obtain technology and a market presence as deregulation of the telecommunications industry proceeds; in Singapore, to do market development, research, and customer support and to

Table 10.2. AT&I: mapping the Asian network.

Economy	Products	Value-added activities				
		R&D	Raw materials–components production	Assembly/manufacturing	Marketing and sales	Services
Japan	Semiconductors, video conference technology, PCs, network systems management, international calling service, WorldPartners	1995, video conference technology licence; 1993, JV with NEC to develop chip-processing technology	1993, Mitsubishi JV to produce chips	1994, AT&T GIS Japan halts production of point-of-sales systems for export; 1984, affiliate opened	1995, sells new family of PCs; 1995, sells voice response system; 1995, sells integrated network system management; 1994, sells ATM device; 1994, sells solid-state relays; 1994, sells wireless LAN system	1995, frame relays division divested; 1995, new ISDN service with KDD; 1994, dial service; 1994, Internet service with NEC; 1993, KDD in WorldPartners
Korea	Large computers, WorldPartners, semiconductors	1995, partnership to develop technology for large-capacity computers	1994, semiconductor division sold to Hyundai		1995, computer systems	1994, Korea Telecom joins WorldPartners
Taiwan	Telecom service, PCs			Telecommunication JV with 4 local partners; 1994, PC plant (Hsinchu)		1995, technical services centre for Asia (excluding Japan); 1947, long-distance service
Singapore[a]	Bell Labs, cordless phones, consumer electronics, WorldPartners, information-management service	1995, business communications research centre; 1993, Centre for Advanced Technology; 1991, Bell Labs Overseas		1995, Batam and Singapore consumer telephone-manufacturing operations sold to Sinoca Enterprises (of Taiwan)	1993, base for new marketing development	1993, Singapore Telecom joins WorldPartners; 1993, doubled regional support centre; 1993, accumaster management service node
Malaysia	Wireless telephones, network service			1995, wireless digital system with Mesiniaga; 1994, restructuring and upgrading of facility; 1993, expansion and upgrade of manufacturing facility; 1991, production facility transferred to Batam; 1986, cordless-phone and consumer-electronics affiliate	1994, O'Connor Engineering and Trading Malaysia becomes distributor; 1993, cordless phones and network operations and sales; 1992, sales office	
Hong Kong	Leasing service, regional office for GIS operations					1994, leasing company acquired

Country	Products/services					
Thailand	Semiconductors, PCs, phone manufacturing	1995, expansion of NECTEC semiconductors 1993, IC expansion 1985, IC facility	1994, sold manufacturing subsidiary to Alphatel Communications 1993, Singapore manufacturing operations transferred		1993, JV to supply optical fibre transmission	1995, subsidiary introduced Accunet Digital Service
Indonesia	Phones, switching and transmission		1991, part of Batam operations from Singapore		1994, switching and transmission equipment 1991, JV to install lines	
Philippines	Optic network, phone operations, phone equipment			1995, constructing national fibre-optic network 1994, JV with Philippine Long Distance Co. to operate international and local phone network	1995, supplying telephone equipment	1995, Aditya Birla (India) Group–Philippine Long Distance Co. JV to bid for licences 1995, telephone service with Islacom JV (Philippine–Thai)
China RHQ	R&D facility, switches, computers, telecommunication systems, direct-call service	1995, technology-transfer contract with Ministry of Electronics Industry for processing and design of semiconductor IC 1993, R&D facility	1995, JV to upgrade switch-manufacturing operations 1993, opened switch JV 1982, refused switch JV 1979, refused switch JV	1995, 9 JVs in marketing wireless systems, long-distance service, computer products, and networks 1994, JV with government and Megga Telecom for manufacture and distribution of telecom products 1992, AT&T fibre-optic cable JV 1989, AT&T of Shanghai JV (digital transmission equipment) 1985, fibre-optics JV	1995, network-infrastructure equipment (Guangdong) 1994, JV to manufacture and sell consumer products 1994, digital-transmission system (Shenzhen) 1994, high-speed telecommunications-transmission equipment 1994, transmission- and network-management equipment (Beijing) 1993, telecommunications supplier	1994, US direct-call service
India	Phones, phone network			3 manufacturing JVs		1995, JV Philippine Long Distance Co.–Aditya Birla

Note: ATM, automated teller machine; AT&T, American Telephone & Telegraph Co.; GIS, geographic information system; IC, integrated circuit; ISDN, integrated services digital network; JV, joint venture; KDD, Kokusai Denshin Denwa (telephone company); LAN, local-area network; NEC, Nippon Electric Company Ltd; PC, personal computer; R&D, research and development; RHQ, regional headquarters.
[a] Singapore is the location of AT&T's procurement office.

provide a manufacturing support centre; and in China, to access the local market. The broad range of AT&T's activities in China is somewhat unexpected in that these activities seem to span the entire value chain. This range is explained in part by the potential size of the local market and by AT&T's late appearance relative to its major competitors, which gave the Chinese government a bargaining advantage and enabled it to push far up the value chain into R&D activities. Government policies have also influenced the restructuring of AT&T's manufacturing activities, such as in taking advantage of the SIJORI growth triangle (**Si**ngapore; **Jo**hore, Malaysia; and **Ri**au, Indonesia).

Matsushita Electric Industrial Co. Ltd: first mover

MEI, like AT&T, is one of the world's largest companies. Unlike AT&T, it has international and regional activities that are quite mature and deeply rooted, beginning with a simple product-cycle approach in the 1960s when low-end appliance production was transferred offshore to Thailand and Taiwan. In the mid-1990s, MEI has 150 plants in 38 countries, which are known as affiliates of Panasonic and MEI and by a variety of local names. Foreign sales make up 49% of its total sales. However, as recently as 1988, only 11% of its production took place abroad.

As one of the world's main consumer-electronics firms, MEI has been forced by currency appreciation, a protracted recession, and decline of Japanese sales, like other Japanese electronics manufacturers, to place most of its labour-intensive, standard-technology production outside Japan and to restructure its Japanese operations into higher value-added activities. The spectacular failure of its expensive acquisition of the Hollywood entertainment firm, MCA, Inc., as part of a multimedia strategy was undoubtedly also a factor.

Restructuring is not new to a Japanese firm. MEI began to exploit the product cycle as early as 1961, with its investment in Thailand. Building factories abroad gave older production systems from Japan a second life. Lately, MEI has been adding full-fledged R&D labs overseas, giving to them authority to redesign products.

Nor is the East Asian market new to MEI. Between 1961 and 1985, it established 19 operations in Southeast Asia, all transplants that assembled products with parts from Japan for sale in the United States. Since 1985, the number of plants has doubled (employing 40 000 workers, 500 of whom are Japanese), and these produce the entire line of MEI consumer electronics and parts. Exports to Japan are expected to account for much of the future growth. These operations and their evolution are mapped in Tables 10.3 and 10.4.

Table 10.4 summarizes MEI's activities in Singapore from 1986 to the present. Since 1990, MEI has located its regional headquarters (RHQ) in Singapore to help manage regional manufacturing and technical and engineering operations. Nine affiliates produce electrical appliances and components, electric motors, electronics, fax machines (MEI has a 25% share of the world market), and refrigerators (the Singapore plant makes 20% of world output of rotary compressors). A technical centre is also located there. Before 1986, Singapore operations consisted of consumer-electronics goods (record and compact-disk [CD] players) and components (semiconductors) for export (50% to the US market; 3% to Japan). After 1987, facilities were upgraded; production was extended to include small motors, fax machines, key components (formerly imported from Japan), and industrial control systems (through a joint venture with a local firm to supply the regional market); and investment was made in higher value-added activities. Regional procurement activities were also added. As part of its localization strategy, MEI began to open up its supply chain; it agreed to join the Local Industry Upgrading Programme (LIUP) to source more inputs from local suppliers. MEI has also taken advantage of the externalities associated with Singapore's cluster of disk-drive manufacturers. MEI's plant will make some components and carry out subassembly. This decision was influenced by the presence of Singapore's skilled human resources, excellent infrastructure, and supportive industrial base.

The evolution of MEI's Singapore operations also illustrates how a company as large as MEI is rationalizing its regional operations (Table 10.4). Former Japanese audio design and production

Table 10.3. Matsushita Electric Industrial Co. Ltd: mapping the Asian network

Economy (affiliates)	Products	R&D	Procurement	Value-added activities		Marketing and sales	Services
				Raw materials–components production	Assembly–manufacturing		
Taiwan (2)	Electrical appliances				1 affiliate	1 affiliate	
Singapore (9) 1990, OHQ	Refrigerator compressors, motors, tuners, CD players, chips	1994, design centre 1993, software JV	1992, IPO 1987, member of LIUP	1994, disk-drive production 1992, key components production	1994, high-end audio production upgrade 1989, upgrade 1987, audio-production expansion 1987, fax machines, small motors expanded	1 affiliate	1988, affiliate invests in US refrigerator plant 1987, technical support centre
Hong Kong (2)	Seiko watches					1 affiliate	1 affiliate
Malaysia (12)	Electric motors, refrigerators, TVs			1993, electrolytical capacitors production 1987, production of ceramic electronic devices	1991, air-conditioners expansion to be the largest plant in the world 1991, audio and video products shifted from Singapore 1988, colour TV production shifted from Japan	1 affiliate	1 affiliate
Thailand (1)	Audio, refrigerators, home appliances					1 affiliate	
Indonesia (4)	Batteries, appliances					1 affiliate	
Philippines (3)	Floppy disks					1 affiliate	
China	Electrical appliances, lighting			CRT plant from Japan 1994, low-end audio production from Malaysia 1992, JV in lighting, home appliances, wiring 1991, components production		1 affiliate	

Note: CD, compact disk; CRT, cathode-ray tube; IPO, international procurement office; JV, joint venture; LIUP, Local Industry Upgrading Programme; OHQ, operational headquarters; R&D, research and development; TV, television.

Table 10.4. The dynamics of upgrading: Matsushita Electric Industrial Co. Ltd in Singapore, 1986 to present.

Year	Activity
Pre-1986	Started production of record players, CD players, chips
1987	Set up technical-support centre Joined LIUP Expanded audio production Invested in facsimile plant; plant for small motors for audio and video products
1988	Refrigerator affiliate, based in Singapore, invested in new plant in the United States making the same products for US market
1989	Upgraded production facilities
1990	Received OHQ status
1992	Received EDB award for pioneer work Opened IPO Invested in key component facilities for CD and high-end audio
1993	Tied up with Eutech (local software company) to produce industrial control systems
1994	Invested in disk-drive plant Upgraded audio to high-end audio production Shifted low-end audio production to Malaysian plant (Malaysian production shifted to China) Opened first design base outside Japan

Source: Author's sources; public information from annual reports and newspaper reports.
Note: CD, compact disk; EDB, Economic Development Board (Singapore); IPO, international procurement office; LIUP, Local Industry Upgrading Programme; OHQ, operational headquarters.

activities have been shifted to Singapore, where facilities have been upgraded. At the same time, low-end activities in Singapore were shifted to Malaysia, and Malaysian low-end production shifted to the plant in Xiamen, China. This move is logical because Southeast Asia now produces 60% of MEI's overseas output.

Table 10.3 maps the location of MEI's value-added activities in the Association of Southeast Asian Nations (ASEAN) and the Chinese economic area. Malaysia hosts an ever-larger cluster of affiliates (15 in 1995), which produce air conditioners and TV sets. When production began in 1965, the local affiliate was a multidomestic firm. Investment increased sharply after 1986 to shift production out of Japan and subsequently to supply the rapidly growing consumer market in the region. These facilities now produce most of MEI's air conditioners, of which 90% is exported elsewhere in Southeast Asia, Japan, and the Middle East. Only high value-added air conditioners continue to be made in Japan. Other MEI facilities in Malaysia produce one million colour TV sets per year for the Japanese market.

China is another major market. There, since MEI's arrival in 1978, a cluster of activities has been created to produce lighting fixtures, home appliances, relays, wiring devices, and laminates in many joint ventures. Production of colour cathode-ray tubes began in Beijing in 1989 using a recycled assembly plant shipped from Japan. Learning from the Malaysian experience, MEI's Chinese production is organized into at least 16 joint ventures, each of which makes specific items in large volumes. Highly automated key components for other Chinese ventures are produced in Dalian (Eisenstodt 1994). The MEI has representative offices in Shanghai and Guangzhou.

Activities in other ASEAN and Chinese-economic-area economies are more modest but appear to be gradually fitting into a region-wide value chain. The Thai affiliate has been assigned audio-product, refrigerator, and appliance production, sales, and service. Siam Matsushita Steel Co. and MEI increased production lines for appliances in 1992 and initiated the manufacture of wiring devices. Hong Kong, Indonesia, and the Philippines are other modest locations. Local economic factors have played a role in limiting the MEI presence in the Philippines; its Indonesian presence is similarly modest, but the Hong Kong affiliates make watches for Southeast Asian markets and provide sales and service support. Activities in Taiwan include sales and service, electrical-appliance production, and engineering activities at the MEI Institute of Technical Engineering in Taiwan, established with Matsushita Denko (note: the MEI affiliate is Taiwan's largest foreign firm). Finally, the company's presence in India is being levered on other activities in Southeast Asia. A joint venture to make air conditioners is planned with a Malaysian affiliate.

In summary, this mapping of MEI's regional activities illustrates that they span many segments. Production is sufficiently mature to obtain substantial economies of both scale and scope. MEI can take advantage of economies' shifting dynamic comparative advantage to advance its global competitiveness. It has also decentralized to some extent through the use of several highly focused affiliates. MEI's Singapore operations also illustrate how it has begun to open up its supplier network as it internationalizes its operations.

Motorola

Motorola is one of the world's largest producers of wireless communications — consumer goods, such as cellular phones, pagers, and mobile radios — semiconductors, and advanced electronics systems and services. In 1995, sales totaled US$27 billion (Motorola 1996), of which 65% were foreign. In 1994, 26% of its sales were in Asia, including 7% in Japan and 8% in China and Hong Kong. Asian demand alone grew more than 20% that year. One of the reasons for this rapid growth is that Motorola derives more than half its revenues from semiconductors and its wireless-communication devices, markets in which Asian growth exceeds that of Europe or North America. Nevertheless, the emergence of competitive pressures in the consumer market in the mid-1990s are forcing Motorola to reconsider the broad base of its overall strategy and to consider returning to its roots in the consumer-electronics industry, in which the brand name counts for so much (The Economist 1996).

Motorola's major businesses include general systems (cellular phones), semiconductors, land-mobile products (two-way radios), messaging, information and media (pagers), government and space technology (including the Iridium satellite-based communication system),[3] and electronic components for auto, energy, and other control systems.

Motorola entered the Asian market in 1967, in Korea; sales agencies were subsequently located in Hong Kong and Japan. By the mid-1990s, decisions about products and marketing in businesses in Motorola's three biggest markets — China, India, and Japan — were decentralized to local organizations. In other parts of Asia, affiliates report to the North American headquarters (The Economist 1992). Asian operations include 3 marketing headquarters; 3 country headquarters; 13 manufacturing facilities; and 11 sales offices in 10 countries, including Australia and New Zealand.

Motorola's marketing and sales activities in the region are extensive (Table 10.5). However, its manufacturing activities are concentrated in Japan, Korea, and Singapore, with some also located in Taiwan. An extensive range of activities have also been located in China, reflecting potential market size. The R&D activities are similarly located in these economies, with Hong Kong playing an important role in design. Motorola's strategy is a differentiated one, built around the high technological barriers to entry of manufacturing semiconductors and associated communications devices and the tight linkages between these products and the Iridium telecommunications network.

Motorola became a serious competitor in the Japanese market in 1982, reasoning that it was necessary to match skills and technologies by being present in a market of that size (accounting for 30% of world's semiconductor demand at the time). Motorola encountered barriers to entry for cellular phones, which required high-level political intervention to overcome in 1994. A technological alliance with Toshiba in chip making in 1987 was an important turning point because Toshiba then

---

[3] Iridium is a major private-sector aerospace project consisting of a satellite-based global mobile-telecommunications network. Although five other consortia have planned similar schemes, Motorola enjoys first-mover advantages. It hopes to attract 1.5 million customers (1.5–2% of cellular phone users) by the end of the century. The network will provide telephone-call, fax, paging, components-data, and radio-determination satellite services. Rockets will be launched in the United States by McDonnell Douglas and in Russia and China (Business Times 1993c).

Table 10.5. Motorola: mapping the Asian network.

Economy (affiliates)	Products	R&D	Value-added activities			
			Raw materials–components production	Assembly–manufacturing	Marketing and sales	Services
Japan	Semiconductors, DRAMs, cellular phones, PCs, network systems	1994, semiconductor technology transfer with Matsushita Electronics Co.	1995, Toshiba JV to produce DRAMs; 1994, new semiconductor plant with Toshiba; 1987, Toshiba JV to develop DRAMs	1993, Shinko Electric Industries Co. JV to produce and market ball-grid array	1995, cable TV equipment; 1994, cellular phones; 1994, Motorola workstations with Komatsu; 1994, cellular phones with Marui Co.; 1994, partnership to supply equipment for cellular franchise; 1989, network infrastructure built; 1960, sales agency	1994, expansion of telephone network and production with IDO
Korea	Pagers, semiconductors, cellular phones, computer hardware, Iridium		1967, semiconductor facility	1995, expansion of cellular manufacturing infrastructure; 1984, opened facility; Late 1980s, pager production	1994, price war; 1992, pagers	1994, Korea Mobile Telecom joins Iridium; 1984, launched operations
Taiwan	PCs, semiconductors, mobile phones, Iridium	1994, JVs to obtain technology or markets	Semiconductors and crystal filters	1994, JV to build mobile-phone communications firm		1994, PEWC joins Iridium
Singapore 1993, OHQ	ICs, software, data terminals, pagers, PCBs	1995, IC centre expanded; 1994, IC design centre; 1993, materials development centre	1983, PCB production	As of 1995, 3 manufacturing facilities; 1992, expansion of paging and mobile data products plants	1994, microcellular loop systems; 1994, production base for China	
Malaysia	Semiconductors, 2-way radios, pagers, cellular phones, Iridium	1976, R&D in Penang	1994, expansion of semiconductor production plant; 1994, Philips JV to establish manufacturing plant; Since 1989, upgrade of chip factory; 1974, Penang plant; Since 1972, 4 manufacturing facilities: semiconductors, integrated electronic systems products		1994, sells new cellular-phone products Sales office	1995, digital cellular network; 1995, Telekom Malaysia joins Iridium

Country	Products					
Hong Kong	ICs, Iridium	1990, developing pocket organizer 1986, IC design centre			1960, sales agency	1995, wireless data service 1993, acquired Hutchison Whampoa mobile data network
Thailand	Pagers, Iridium				1995, pagers with Samart Paging 1994, MPRouter and new cellular phones 1994, digital cellular network	1983, Thai Satellite joins Iridium project
Philippines	Cellular phones, network systems				1994, expansion of Mobiline system 1994, 2-way wireless data network with Easicall Communication	
China	Cellular phones, semiconductors, pagers, consumer electronics products	1995, JV to develop intelligent machine maintenance tools 1994, Beijing Catch JV to design mobile telecommunication network	1993, low-end pager	1995, expansion of cellular phone and chip assembly facility 1995, Panda JV to produce pagers, computers, and other telecommunications equipment	1995, analogue cellular equipment 1994, opened mobile-telephone production line 1994, large-capacity phone system in Shanghai	1994, headquarters in Beijing to handle sales, marketing, and engineering
India	Pagers, Iridium				Martin Telekom JV to supply radio paging infrastructure	1994, Indian consortium joins Iridium project
Australia	Research	1995, opened software research centre				
Vietnam	Paging services				1994, paging services	

Note. CRT, cathode-ray tube; DRAM, dynamic random-access memory; IC, integrated circuit; JV, joint venture; OHQ, operational headquarters; PC, personal computer; PCB, printed circuit boards; R&D, research and development; ; TV, televison.

alliance with Toshiba in chip making in 1987 was an important turning point because Toshiba then provided marketing assistance.

Because of the growing capital intensity of semiconductor production and customer preferences for a full range of chips from any supplier, Motorola has sought alliances with other partners, beginning with Toshiba in Japan. Personal connections are also important in marketing to public-sector customers (Motorola's major Chinese customer, for example, is the Ministry of Post and Telecommunications). Thus, Asian operations have been grown carefully and staffed with locals from the beginning to demonstrate commitment to the local market and access to the right skills. Even so, local materials procurement in these sophisticated businesses has lagged. Local procurement in China, for example, is limited to that of packaging materials.

Hong Kong has until recently been the centrepiece of Motorola's strategy in China. The large chip-making and design centre, opened in 1990, was upgraded to a design facility in 1991, with engineers doing work on pocket organizers that equal in complexity those at any other Motorola integrated-circuit lab.

Motorola's largest investment outside the United States is a US$720 million investment in integrated production facilities in Tianjin, China, with semiconductor, pager, and cellular-phone production. As much as 70% of pager production was planned for export, but domestic demand has risen rapidly. Thus, production has expanded rapidly since the plant was opened, with workers reportedly attaining quality standards achieved in Singapore. Motorola is also under government pressure to transfer technology directly and through training local managers to levels set for US managers (The Economist 1996).

The Taiwanese affiliate focuses on manufacturing and development of new technology through a US$3 billion joint venture with Pacific Electric Wire and Cable and others in wireless communications. Motorola also plans to hook up with TI and nine local firms to develop hardware and applications for the mobile computers of the future ("personal digital assistants"). Motorola, Apple, International Business Machines Corp. (IBM), and seven local firms have also created a strategic alliance to offer Power PCs.

Singapore operations began in 1983 with a single wholly owned affiliate producing printed circuit boards (PCBs). Manufacturing has been expanded and upgraded to include four core products (Table 10.5): semiconductors, high-end PCBs, pagers, and data terminals. Head-office functions, integrated-circuit design and innovation to support Singapore's hard-disk-drive industry, and software development are also located there. One plant (Tuas) is Motorola's sole producer of PCBs and supplies 10% of the company's total requirements; it also provides process development and technology. Singapore operations play a significant role in time-based competition, with which the company brings user-friendly, high-quality products to market.

Although Motorola's East Asian operations are organized around its major markets, Singapore has also played a special role since 1993 as an operational headquarters (OHQ) to coordinate and support 19 affiliates in Southeast Asia, India, and Australia. Local government incentives (including a 10% corporate tax rate for 10 years) were an important factor in this decision. Singapore also provides manufacturing support to facilities in China and India.

In summary, Motorola's Asian operations illustrate a differentiation strategy based on high barriers to entry and rapid technological innovation. Location in Japan was essential to access new technology and potentially large product and services markets. China is seen as a major local-market opportunity, as increasingly is India. Singapore's locational advantages played an important role in its being selected as regional manufacturing support base and software-production site. Increasing competitive pressures in the mid-1990s in its semiconductor and wireless-communications consumer businesses may lead to the strategic conclusion that the range of businesses across both industrial and consumer electronics may be too broad a reach, but the evidence at the time of writing is insufficient to draw such a conclusion.

Sony

Sony is widely regarded as being the most innovative of the Japanese consumer-electronics firms. Engaged in intense competition with MEI, Sony's original strategy was low cost: to make radios that were competitively priced and of better quality than those of competitors. Subsequently, it switched to a differentiated strategy by developing its own brands and products, such as the portable tape and CD players, which attained popularity with consumers worldwide. By 1994, Sony's main product groups included electronics and entertainment, of which video equipment accounted for 18% of sales; audio equipment, for 22%; TVs, for 17%; entertainment, for 21%; and other products, for 22%. Sony restructured its operation in late 1994 into eight independent companies. In that year, the entertainment business wrote off nearly US$3 billion in losses at Sony pictures, its US business.

Situated outside the *keiretsu* structure, Sony traditionally has targeted external markets: 73% of its sales in 1994 were foreign (Sony Corporation n.d.). According to the ranking by the United Nations Commission on Trade and Development (Table 10.1), in 1994 Sony had more foreign assets than MEI.

Because the value of the yen rose in 1986, Sony reevaluated its international strategy and concluded that production had to be moved to lower-cost sites and product design moved closer to customers. By 1994, 36% of total production was foreign. Face-to-face meetings in Tokyo for management decisions began to be abandoned, and decision-making was explicitly decentralized. In that year, its principal research laboratories in Japan were consolidated and directed to collaborate closely with businesses. The next step will be to take advantage of local technological strengths and proximity to customers by expanding international R&D activities.

In the past decade, Sony has built 10 manufacturing plants in the other East Asian economies to supply export and local markets. In 1991, the East Asian plants sold 20% of their output in the region, and this share is expected to rise to 50% by 1995 (Worth 1991). The largest concentrations of affiliates in the region are located in Malaysia, Singapore, and Thailand (Table 10.6). Affiliates in Singapore have expanded into most segments of the value chain. Two of the four manufacturing affiliates produce precision components, including industrial robots. The OHQ carries on most head-office functions, including business planning, marketing, distribution, procurement, international logistical planning, after-sales service, and finance operations.

Indonesia, Malaysia, and Thailand have nine manufacturing affiliates, producing similar consumer products and semiconductors. Sales and service affiliates are also located in Malaysia and Thailand. Sony's most recent manufacturing investment, in Indonesia, provides a glimpse of future strategy. Because output is destined for export, the factory is not a low-tech assembly operation relying on cheap labour. Instead, to meet quality standards, it is almost as automated as its Japanese counterparts. Because just-in-time inventory management is not yet available locally, space is devoted to imported-materials storage (80%, or three times as much space as in a Japan-based factory). Japanese suppliers are encouraged to move from Japan and Malaysia to meet local demand. Sony intends eventually to switch production from exports to the local market. However, with consumer incomes averaging around US$600 in Indonesia, sales are slow; lack of electricity prevents broad-based markets from being developed (Clifford 1992a).

Sony's presence in other East Asian markets is more modest: a sales and service affiliate in Hong Kong and production of components and assembly in Korea and Taiwan (in the late 1960s and 1970s). Plans to penetrate other major Asian markets include entering the Chinese market with video-camera production in Shanghai; consumer-electronics production in Vietnam; and TVs and other consumer products in India.

Sony's Asian operations are more modest than MEI's, reflecting Sony's smaller size and setbacks in its global strategy to remain at the forefront of the consumer-electronics industry. Home sales are depressed; operating margins are much thinner than in the 1980s; the cost of capital has risen; hoped-for demand from Eastern Europe failed to materialize; and, in the US export market, consumers have been more keen to cut debt than to buy new electrical goods.

Table 10.6. Sony: mapping the Asian network.

| Economy (affiliates) | Products | Value-added activities | | | | |
		R&D	Procurement	Raw materials– components production	Assembly–manufacturing	Marketing, sales, and service
Korea (1)	Audio equipment, TV tuners			1993, audio plant 1993, tuners plant		
Taiwan (2)	VCRs, audio products	1991, R&D centre		1984, VTR plant 1967, audio equipment	Radios and cassettes plant	
Singapore (7) 1987, OHQ	Optical pick-up devices for CD players, CRT, Industrial robots (precision components)	Research venture with NUS Factory automation centre Software development	IPO	1994, CRT plant 1993, robots 1992, optical devices plant		1991, distribution centre Sales and service agency
Hong Kong (1)						Sales and service agency
Malaysia (6)	TV components, audio equipment, video cassettes, disk drives			1990, disk drives 1988, camcorders 1988 and 1984, tape recorders	TVs, radios, stereo heads	Sales and service agency
Thailand (4)	Colour TVs, video cassettes, semiconductors			1990, semiconductors 1988, colour TVs 1988, video cassettes	TVs, audio products	Sales and service agency
Indonesia (1)	Audio equipment, audio cassettes			1992, audio cassettes 1992, audio equipment		

Note: CD, compact disk; CRT, cathode-ray tube; IPO, international procurement office; NUS, National University of Singapore; OHQ, operational headquarters; R&D, research and development; TV, television; VCR, videocassette recorder; VTR, videotape recorder.

In summary, Sony has followed a differentiation strategy in East Asia, concentrating its regional activities outside Japan around a Singapore management and innovation hub. Sony's Singapore operations are organized differently than MEI's, with more centralized procurement, for example, and an engineering and manufacturing group that exports worldwide. Its OHQ also has considerable discretion in management functions. Unlike many other Japanese corporations, Sony is not part of *keiretsu* and has more flexibility in going abroad. It, too, has opened up its supply chain to local vendors in Singapore, but its Indonesian operations illustrate continued import dependence in the absence of reliable local suppliers. For the foreseeable future, these are expected to be other Japanese firms.

Texas Instruments

TI is a global supplier of semiconductors to producers of end products. It has one of the most focused strategies of the firms in this sample, producing semiconductors and computers and relying on the barriers to entry posed by the sophistication of its technology and the quality premium commanded by its brand name. Its chips are a brand unto themselves. Many semiconductors produced in East Asia are components for exported products, such as Taiwanese PCs, Singapore disk drives, Japanese video players exported from Thailand and Malaysia, and microwaves from Korea. TI has had a heavy defence-industry focus for many years. It is also a laptop brand name in computers. Historically, TI has been seen as a technology leader (with Kilby's 1958 patent of the integrated circuit) but has been slow to seize market opportunities. Indeed, a group of its executives left the company to start Compaq. Even so, TI has earned sustained market leadership in chosen segments, with long-term sole-source relationships with many customers. Because of the high costs and risks entailed in creating increasingly powerful semiconductors, TI has entered into a number of joint ventures and alliances with regional players, including governments and other firms.

The core of TI's focused strategy is customer support. This means setting up more electronic-circuit design centres and regional technology centres and hiring more technical experts. Customers will then be linked into technical support systems anywhere in the world via the TI satellite network. By forging alliances, the company aims to obtain Asian partners to supply most of the capital for its new factories. TI is also developing a global research strategy that uses university contacts to provide "stocks" of innovations, which are then matched to market opportunities. TI has set up a technology council in the Asia–Pacific region, charged with looking for universities with which to work on information-delivery problems. Its program at the National University of Singapore, for example, sponsors research on integrated circuits, and "failure analysis" needed to reduce cycle time in memory products is being carried out at TI's Singapore semiconductor-wafer fabrication plant.

TI has sunk deep roots in the region to create sufficient semiconductor manufacturing capacity to gain market share. It has interests in a dozen chip factories in East Asia, including five in Japan (Table 10.7) (Clifford 1993a). Its East Asian affiliates (in 1992, Asia accounted for 30% of the company's nonmilitary turnover, with 15 000 workers on payroll) include 13 manufacturing facilities, of which 3 are joint ventures: Kobe–TI in Japan; TI–Acer in Taiwan; and TECH in Singapore. Half of TI's worldwide facilities for the manufacture of submicron complementary metal-oxide semiconductors (CMOSs) are in East Asia. It is difficult, however, to estimate the share of TI production located in the region because of the portability of semiconductors, which are produced at 43 manufacturing operations in 18 countries and are shipped to different locations for packaging and testing before being shipped to the final customer.

TI's first semiconductor plant was located in Japan in 1968. During the next two decades, it built the operations of this subsidiary into three chip factories. Kobe Steel, wishing to diversify its Japanese operations, paid for most of a factory to make 16-Mb DRAM chips. These chips are currently the industry's main technology driver — the grounds providing for new design and manufacturing technologies that will diffuse to other integrated-circuit markets, such as microprocessors. TI also tied up with Hitachi in 1989 to produce chips, to hedge its bets and spread risk; it also joined Motorola,

Table 10.7. Texas Instruments mapping the Asian network.

Economy (affiliates)	Products	Value-added activities			
		R&D	Raw materials—components production	Assembly—manufacturing	Marketing, sales, and service
Japan	Semiconductors, DRAMs	1 facility 1995, Hitachi JV to develop DRAMs 1994, Kobe Steel JV 1989, Toshiba JV	4 semiconductor facilities 1995, expansion of semiconductor plant 1968, opened wholly owned semiconductor plant		
Korea				1 facility	1 facility
Taiwan 1994, RHQ moved from Hong Kong	Logic systems, DRAMs, wafer packaging	1994, cooperation with government 1994, linear logic products and systems products	1995, start-up of TI–Acer 2nd dynamic-memory-chip production line 1994 TI–Acer JV to finance silicon-wafer plant		1994, sales contract with First International Computer Inc. 1994, alliance with government
Singapore	Semiconductors, wafer packaging	1994, government grant (semiconductor packaging) 1990, development of knowledge-based transportation systems	1995 technology consortium (TI, Canon, HP) expanding semiconductor fabrication capacity	1994, Alphatec JV to assemble and test EPROM (2 facilities)	1 facility
Malaysia	Semiconductors, software		1972, opened semiconductor plant		1994, appointed AutoComp as distributor for software products 1994, alliance with Mesiniaga to open sales and support office
Hong Kong TI Asia					1967, headquarters for sales and marketing of semiconductor products
Thailand	Semiconductors		1994, low-end chips facility		
Philippines	Semiconductors		Semiconductors		1 facility
China				1 facility	1 office
India			200 engineers providing semiconductor design support	1 facility	

Note: DRAM, dynamic random-access memory; EPROM, electronically programable read-only memory; HP, Hewlett-Packard; JV, joint venture; R&D, research and development; RHQ, regional headquarters; TI, Texas Instruments.

DuPont, and 40 Japanese companies in a project in atom technology financed by the Ministry of Trade and Industry. TI has a wholly owned R&D centre in Tsukuba.

In Taiwan, TI's joint venture with Acer to produce 4-Mb DRAM chips, initiated in 1989, has been successful and has led to other activities, including major expansions of production,[4] a strategic alliance with the local government to penetrate Asian markets, and cooperation in R&D, marketing, manufacturing, service, and technical training. It has also shifted its RHQ to Taipei. These alliances will help upgrade Taiwan's industrial-technology and manufacturing capabilities and assist in Taiwan's drive to become a regional financial, transportation, and high-tech manufacturing centre.

TI's Singapore operations are even more high tech and also government assisted. It has begun a 5-year US$7.4 million R&D program to develop packaging for 64-Mb and 256-Mb DRAM chips. Critical skill sets and know-how are needed to support its future generation of processes and products, such as large-die–ultra-thin packages, three-dimensional memory-cube packages, multichip modules, and advanced interconnect technology (Business Times 1994). A US$330 million wafer plant is being bankrolled by customers, including Hewlett-Packard and Canon (two customers, each with 24% shares) and the Singapore government.[5] Local partners add to risk of investment but ensure that local players share profits as well as provide access to foreign technologies and managerial expertise. This venture uses TI's CMOS DRAM 0.5 μm technology to produce 16-Mb DRAMs. Each partner is entitled to buy chips at a discount from world prices.

TI's other Southeast Asian operations are few; they include a chip factory in Malaysia and a subcontracting relationship for low-end chips with a Thailand-based producer.

To summarize this sixth and final case, TI is the most focused firm of the study sample. The map of its activities in East Asia (Table 10.7) illustrates the key success factor in its strategy: heavy technology and research orientations. As might be expected, TI's activities are, therefore, located in the more advanced economies: TI is largely absent from China, except for sales and service. Chip-manufacturing facilities are located near research facilities, with location decisions strongly influenced by the availability of joint-venture partners (usually large customers) and government financing. This case illustrates the more general point that governments may have more bargaining power with highly focused firms such as TI if they are willing to share the high costs and risks of technology development.

Cross-border patterns of sales and procurement: survey evidence

The second source of empirical information for this study is survey data gathered by the eight-person research team from affiliates of these six firms, located in seven of the eight economies studied (Guangdong is excluded). Reports of 17 affiliate interviews are available from six host economies. These affiliates produce a wide cross section of products, including colour TVs, heat exchangers, welding machines, hard-disk drives, audio and video cassettes, and other consumer-electronics components, computer peripherals, semiconductors, and communications equipment and services.

Patterns of intraregional (and intrafirm) trade are summarized in Table 10.8. Corporate nationality is controlled for by reporting Japanese and US firms separately. Data for each affiliate, whose identity must remain confidential, are reported separately.

The results in Table 10.8 provide four dimensions of comparison. First, although the behaviour of US affiliates on available measures is reasonably uniform, behaviour within Japanese firms — that is, among affiliates — shows considerable variation. Some affiliates are localized: others sell to Japan;

---

[4] The joint venture's second plant began production in 1995; the third plant is slated to open in 1997.

[5] The Singapore Economic Development Board (SEDB) has a 26% equity share, with an option for TI to buy it out in 5 years, as has TI. SEDB's investment is part of its drive to encourage the development of higher value-added industries in Singapore's increasingly labour-scarce economy and to bring chip manufacture to Singapore to ensure adequate supplies of inputs for customers located there.

Table 10.8. Intraregional and intrafirm cross-border transactions of Japanese and US affiliates, 1994.

Sales (by company)[a]	Destination (%) (% intrafirm trade)						
	Local		Regional		Home country		Third country (non-Asian)
US firms							
Sales							
A1	0		13	(100)	72	(100)	12
A2	21	(80)	6	(100)	73	(100)	0
A3	40		0		27	(100)	32 (NA)
B1	0		0		0		100
B2	0		47	(100)	0		53 (100)
C1	NA		0		0		100 (100)
D1	0		75	(100)	24	(100)	1 (0)
Procurement							
A1	0		36	(100)	43	(100)	8 (100)
A2	0		NA		73	(100)	24 (100)
A3	20	(100)	0		80	(100)	0
B1	NA		NA		NA		NA
B2	0		24	(100)	49	(100)	21
C1	NA		NA		NA		NA
D1	20		53		24		1
Japanese firms							
Sales							
E1	94	(0)	5	(100)	1	(0)	0
E2	0		10	(NA)	16	(NA)	46 (NA)
E3	0		42	(NA)	20	(100)	48 (100)
E4	40	(NA)	0		0		60 (NA)
E5	95	(70)	0		0		3 (0)
E6	73	(0)	0		12	(100)	15 (0)
E7	0		0		0		100 (NA)
F1	90	(NA)	0		0		10 (NA)
F2	1	(0)	65	(0)	20	(0)	15 (0)
F3	0		12		1		82
Procurement							
E1	31	(NA)	52	(NA)	17	(100)	0
E2	52	(NA)	27	(NA)	10	(NA)	11 (NA)
E3	37	(0)	46	(100)	18	(100)	0
E4	NA		NA		NA		0
E5	15	(NA)	8	(NA)	78	(94)	0
E6	50	(0)	0		40	(100)	10 (0)
E7	0		50	(NA)	50	(NA)	0
F1	30	(0)	70	(NA)	0		0
F2	8	(0)	8	(0)	83	(0)	1 (0)
F3	35	(0)	55	(50)	12	(100)	0

Note: NA, not available.
[a] Parent firms are identified by letter; affiliates, by accompanying digit.

but there is not a strong "triangular" trade pattern, in which procurement is from Japan and sales are destined for third countries, particularly the United States and Europe.

Second, in their sales activities, Japanese affiliates are much more local in their orientation. They are more likely to rely on the local and regional markets for sales channels than are US firms. The US firms relied heavily on the home market or on Singapore for sales, whereas 66% of the Japanese firms sold locally or to Singapore; only one firm exported more than 50% of its output outside the region. One of the obvious reasons for this behaviour is that Japanese firms in the surveys are consumer-electronics producers and therefore more likely to supply local markets, whereas US firms are industrial-electronics producers, exporting to the world's most sophisticated markets.

Third, on the procurement side, US firms again relied heavily on the home market or on Singapore; only one firm reported local procurement (20%). Half of the Japanese firms, on the other hand, obtained up to 50% of their inputs locally; 25% obtained 50–70% within the region; and 25% relied heavily on the home market for inputs.

Finally, distinctions were also noticeable in the ratio of intrafirm transactions. For sales, Japanese firms relied less on intrafirm transactions than did US firms. Japanese firms tended to use the market. For procurement, both groups tended to rely heavily on intrafirm channels.

Interviews turned up some of the reasons for these patterns. In Malaysia, for example, many firms operate in the free-trade zones that require that output be exported. These zones also isolate foreigners from local suppliers, however, and reinforce reliance on intrafirm and therefore foreign procurement. More detail on the actual local sources of Japanese firms would be useful; it was not possible to determine, for example, whether local suppliers were other Japanese firms and part of a *keiretsu* grouping. Another explanation for the dissimilarities is in the differences in industrial orientation: consumer-electronics products are in many cases aimed at local markets, whereas industrial-electronics components produced in the region still take advantage of low-cost skilled labour doing subcontracted semiconductor assembly, such as in the Philippines, for products that are assembled elsewhere for export.

This analysis has also illustrated Singapore's major role in the operations of Southeast Asian electronics affiliates. Japanese firms tended more than US firms to use it as a sales channel, but US firms used Singapore heavily for procurement.

Concerning the contribution of firms to regional integration, this analysis suggests that Japanese affiliates contribute more than US affiliates to the growth of intraregional trade because of their heavier reliance on local and regional transactions. The US firms, on the other hand, tie the region into the rest of the world because of their heavy reliance on trade with their parents.

Conclusion

The goal of this chapter was to clarify the role firms play in East Asian integration. Primary data and detailed public information on specific firms were analyzed. The case studies suggest some generalizations about the determinants of corporate behaviour: location, corporate nationality, and vintage.

Location

Locational factors in the form of factor endowments and government policies are important determinants of regional activities. The hypothesized linkages between firms and governments were made quite evident in this chapter. The more advanced economies of Hong Kong, Singapore, and Taiwan are able to attract sophisticated R&D and headquarters activities, including finance, design, and regional procurement. Singapore is a favoured location for advanced manufacturing and service activities because of its sophisticated communications and technical infrastructure, skilled labour, and supportive policy environment. The TI and MEI cases illustrate the clustering of R&D activity in the more advanced economies (where, incidentally, government subsidies are also available for such activities) and location of low-end chip production in the less advanced economies. The MEI case (in Table 10.4) illustrates most graphically the dynamics behind this picture: low-end manufacturing is being skilfully transferred in the region to take advantage of evolving locational advantages.

The diverse roles of governments in influencing particular value-added activities is also evident. The Acer case illustrates government's role in the evolution of an Asian multinational. Financing, guidance in the Brand International Promotion Association, direct subsidies of home-base operations, links with Singapore, and, conversely, opposition to mainland operations have influenced Acer's evolution and its pattern of operations.

Host governments' industrial-upgrading objectives are critical to firms' decisions to allocate value-added activities to particular economies. Governments' contributions take several forms; for example, subsidies for high-risk, technology- and capital-intensive activities are noticeable factors in firms' reported decisions about location. However, governments may also bargain in a sophisticated fashion at the time of firm entry (as in the case of AT&T in China), and some have acted to create locational factors that emphasize upgraded skills and infrastructure (Singapore being an obvious case). Future implications of these kinds of interventions (such as the disappearance of subsidies as a result of World Trade Organization requirements) are examined in the concluding chapter.

Corporate nationality

Few ownership distinctions stand out as possible determinants of variations in cross-border operations of Japanese and US firms. One that does is the greater tendency of US electronics firms to locate R&D facilities in the region. However, industry factors, such as differences in firm strategies in consumer and industrial electronics, for example, and factors such as vintage and capability to manage diverse locational characteristics appear to be more important. Although the structure of ownership in joint ventures or alliances was not a focus of this study, it does help to explain why US firms are present in some economies and absent from others. The US companies are obsessed, relative to the Japanese and other Asians, with majority ownership. They even opt out of markets rather than give up majority control (in large part because it is then easier for the parent to consolidate revenues on financial statements). The *Foreign Corrupt Practices Act* is another reason: when firms have majority ownership, they can control both the venture and the partner's behaviour more easily.

Perhaps of more importance to future studies is the observation that firms are adapting to locational variations by changing the ways they are organized. Japanese firms, both from *keiretsu* and outside *keiretsu*, are opening up their supply chains to local vendors. This is particularly evident in Malaysia, Singapore, and Taiwan, where policy provides inducements for doing so and penalties for not doing so.

Vintage

The Acer case illustrates how vintage matters. As the newest entrant into the group, Acer has relatively few operations in the region, having focused instead on penetrating Western markets. Its few regional operations are divided among Malaysia, where a lower-cost cluster location for computer peripherals has been used to advantage; Singapore, where government inducements have led to a regional sales office; and China, whose huge market offers diverse long-term opportunities. At the other end of the scale, MEI, as one of the longest established MNEs in the region, has developed extensive production facilities tailored to variations in locational characteristics.

Other observations

Several other observations are germane. First, MNEs in the region are not pursuing simple, low-cost strategies. Most are differentiated (as would be expected in an oligopolistic industry with entry barriers), and one is highly focused; in other words, the activities of these firms are highly variable and sometimes very sophisticated. Few systematic differences in strategy could be associated with differences in corporate nationality.

Second, two dimensions of the ways MNEs influence regional integration are suggested by these case studies. First, because affiliates tend to trade with their parents, investments by US and European firms have encouraged extraregional trade with those areas. Further, because many Japanese investments in the late 1980s were aimed at maintaining market share in the United States and Europe, these investments accentuated this interregional trade pattern. Because local incomes have risen in East Asia, however, and because other East Asian investment has appeared, intraregional trade has followed. Second, the ability of firms in oligopolistic industries with differentiated products to locate operations across borders suggests that competition for foreign direct investment (FDI) from newcomers, such as China and Vietnam, should not be viewed as a zero-sum game (in which some economies win and others lose). Instead, the capabilities of these firms to take advantage of variations in locational characteristics means that the newcomers, whose advantage is low-cost labour, will attract investments in low-end production. More sophisticated products and key-component production are moved from home-country plants to the more sophisticated offshore locations, such as Hong Kong, Singapore, and Taiwan. Production is then dispersed within the region. The low-end producers increasingly ship output to other locations in the region and, in this way, increase the intensity of intraregional-trade ties.

Because the appearance of new competitors does not lead to competition for FDI, governments should feel less pressure to use incentives to lure investment to one location rather than another because it is already headed for the region. This focus on complementarity implies that intrafirm and intraindustry trade will also pave the way for a positive-sum game in which all players gain from trade in differentiated products.

Finally, FDI is a means for both home and host economies to adjust to structural changes in the world economy. The movement of manufacturing activities offshore assists home economies to adjust to changing economic and competitive conditions by allowing for greater focus at home on even higher value-added activities that are consistent with highly skilled labour forces and are necessary to sustain rising living standards.

Chapter 11

HARNESSING DIVERSITY

Chia Siow Yue and
Wendy Dobson

How do the links between FDI and trade of firms influence regional integration? Do Asian investors, through their intraregional foreign direct investment (FDI) and trade, exert any special influence on the emerging trends? We addressed these questions by examining trends in FDI and those in trade at national and industry levels. We also surveyed US, Japanese, and non-Japanese Asian firms and affiliates in key industries that account for much of East Asia's trade and for much of the inflows of FDI in manufacturing, including the electronics, textiles and garments, automobile assembly and components, and chemical industries.

Questions posed at the firm level probed intrafirm and intraindustry trade patterns by corporate nationality, location, industry, age and size of the enterprise. Authors investigated what these patterns imply for national trade policies and for intraregional intensity of trade and investment ties relative to those with the rest of the world. Sufficient variation in the responses allowed for useful comparisons of government policies, industrial structures, and corporate behaviour. As often happens in studies of this kind, however, firm-level data in this study are not uniform: some are discrete observations, and others are interval data. These variations precluded econometric testing.

This concluding chapter is organized as follows. In the next two sections, we summarize the implications of our findings on the impact of interactions between multinational-enterprise (MNE) behaviour and locational determinants, particularly government policies, on regional integration. The third section summarizes our finding on corporate strategies. The fourth section contains our findings on firm-level trade and production patterns by corporate nationality. Findings on newly industrialized economies' (NIEs') firms and on the implications of internationalization for the organization of MNEs are also presented. In the fifth section, we draw conclusions on the impact on regional integration of growing intrafirm, intraindustry, and intraregional trade and FDI. In the sixth and final section, we draw the policy implications from the country surveys and from our findings in this chapter.

Our main conclusions were listed in Chapter 1 and are set out at the beginning of each relevant section in this chapter.

This study provides new quantitative estimates of the entrepôt roles of Hong Kong and Singapore, respectively, for Southeast Asia and China. The entrepôt trade of Hong Kong and Singapore inflates the figures on intraregional trade in East Asia, and the sharp growth in Hong Kong–China trade following China's open-door policy of 1979 has a similar exaggerating effect. Chen and Wong made adjustments to the Hong Kong trade data and found that trade intensities with the United States and the rest of Asia were stronger and that with China was smaller than originally thought. Singapore's entrepôt trade in the 1986–93 period accounted for 40% of Singapore's total manufactured exports. Overreporting of Singapore's intraregional trade is less serious than in Hong Kong, as Singapore's official trade statistics exclude all trade with Indonesia, widely acknowledged as a leading trading partner.

Regional integration and global adjustment

Regional integration is influenced by international firms in two ways. First, it is enhanced by NIE producers based in the region who invest defensively in other regional locations and by multinational firms' (or their local affiliates') investments in components, intermediate products, and services that are shipped around the region, both to add value and to reach final customers. Second, regional integration can be reduced by firms from outside the region whose trade is outside the region. Although the relative magnitudes of these offsetting trends are difficult to estimate, the positive influence of investments from within the region is growing.

The trade–FDI linkages driving regional integration are created by changes in comparative advantage and industrial upgrading in East Asian investing countries. Outflows of FDI from Japan and the Asian NIEs (Hong Kong, Singapore, South Korea, and Taiwan) have been growing rapidly since the late 1970s and surged following the post-1985 currency realignments. Investors from these countries were motivated to venture abroad to reduce costs and pursue globalization and regionalization strategies to maintain competitiveness.

Sustained high economic growth in much of the region over the past 30 years has led to labour and land shortages and rising wages and land costs. Export-led growth contributed to improved balance of payments and currency appreciation. As foreign-exchange controls were eased, Japan invested in the United States and western Europe to reduce political pressures arising from the large current-account surpluses and to exploit the market opportunities offered by the large high-income markets. Among Asian NIEs, relaxation of foreign-exchange controls in the late 1980s was key to outflows from South Korea and Taiwan headed for the same markets.

They and the Japanese also became significant investors in the East Asian region. Investments in Asian developing economies were intended to jump trade barriers and to take advantage of host-country Generalized System of Preferences (GSP) privileges and underused Multifibre Arrangement (MFA) textile quotas. Since the early 1990s the Singapore government also actively promoted outward investment in the region to take advantage of regional economic opportunities and to aid its own domestic industrial restructuring program. For both Japan and the Asian NIEs, rapid economic growth and economic liberalization and deregulation in several potential host countries have made these markets increasingly attractive.

The evidence in this study of the impact of these FDI flows on regional integration is reasonably clear. FDI originating outside the region is associated with trade outside the region. FDI inflows into East Asian economies from the United States, Japan, and Europe contributed to trade outside the region because of complementarity between trade and FDI because of the cross-border shipments within production networks. Growing stocks of FDI from Japan and the Asian NIEs in the past decade (see Table 1.2) contributed to increasing regional integration. Tables 1.5–1.8 illustrate trade intensities by industry. Highest intraregional intensities appear, in declining significance, in office and computing machinery (OCM), chemicals, and textiles and garments (T/G). In electronics, trade intensities are highest with the European Union and Japan; in T/G in those economies where FDI inflows from outside the region have been large, trade intensities are high with the United States.

Table 1.1 illustrates the triangular trade pattern whereby East Asian economies import larger shares of manufactures from Japan than they export and they export larger shares to the US–European markets than they import. Although Japan's triangular trade is unidirectional, with large net exports to host countries in East Asia, this pattern may be changing. The chapter on Thailand showed that by 1990, as investments matured, exports to Japan caught up with imports from Japan.

The existence — and possible reversal — of this triangular trade pattern provides insights into the global adjustment process as it contributes to regional integration. As a net saver and capital exporter, Japan augments domestic savings and transfers technology to the host economies in which it invests, thereby accelerating their growth and access to international markets. By relocating uncompetitive low-end production abroad and continuing to invest in high-end production at home, Japan's economy becomes more efficient. As it deregulates and accepts more foreign imports, Japanese consumers also become better off, with wider choice and increased purchasing power derived from the availability of cheaper imports. The host economy also benefits from FDI, first, in terms of access to foreign savings and technology and, subsequently, in terms of increased access to the Japanese market.

Similar patterns with respect to Taiwan were demonstrated in Chapters 1 and 3. Taiwan, in contrast to Hong Kong, until recently was interventionist in its policy stance toward inward FDI and controlled its capital markets. Relaxation of FDI controls stimulated inflows and, with them, more imports. As exchange controls were lifted and the exchange rate appreciated, domestic costs increased and direct investment flowed out to other locations in the region. Dobson's trade analysis showed how intraregional trade within both the electronics and the industrial chemicals industries has grown as Taiwan has become an increasingly significant processor.

Thailand has seen a large increase in exports by affiliates of foreign multinationals, particularly by US multinationals, who dominate electronics and OCM, and by Japanese producers, who dominate autos and bicycles. In part because of these patterns, intraregional electronics exports are growing more slowly than total trade in manufacturing (that is, because of continued dependence on US and European markets). One of the conclusions from this analysis is that intraregional FDI flows will lead to greater intensity of intraregional trade.

Analysis of FDI in Guangdong and Indonesia illustrates cases of subregional integration. By specializing in light manufacturing in low-end electronics and T/G, Guangdong has become closely integrated with Hong Kong, its main source of capital and technology, and with the rest of China, which has provided a continuous supply of low wage labour. In different ways, Japanese and Hong Kong investors have strengthened this regional differentiation within China by the interest of the former in penetrating the domestic market and of the latter in using Guangdong as an export platform. Taiwanese investors in Indonesia have contributed to less significant integration, in part because the investors have tended to be small and medium sized, making small investments. But they, too, have sought to exploit their ownership advantages by penetrating local markets, in many cases, and to maintain exports to their traditional customers, in other cases.

Synergies: governments, industrial upgrading, and MNEs

The region's diversity is "harnessed" by governments intent on industrial upgrading and by MNEs whose objectives are served by exploiting locational differences. Governments, MNEs, and East Asian firms act strategically.

Host-government policies as locational factors

Governments' economic policies, as outlined in parts I and II, have had important impacts on trade and investment patterns. Macroeconomic policies have changed since the early 1980s: currencies have been devalued (except in Singapore), fiscal policy has generally avoided accumulation of large debts (except in the Philippines), monetary policy has been conservative, and inflation has been moderate. Firms benefited from low rates of interest and inflation and high savings. Macroeconomic stability provided firms with a conducive environment for long-term planning and investment.

Tu and Chia each emphasized how, in Taiwan and Singapore, macroeconomic policies have played roles in — even encouraged — the evolution of locational characteristics as these economies respond to higher costs by upgrading to higher value-added activities. They also stressed the more recent role of strategic policies in transforming the industrial structures of Singapore and Taiwan in the direction of more advanced manufacturing and service activities, such as finance and research and development (R&D), and the related rise in outward investment into other economies in the region in order to continue lower value-added manufacturing (we return to the characteristics of the East Asian firm later). Singapore has become a regional hub in which key economic activities, such as finance, shipping, transportation, communications, and information functions, are concentrated to serve a hinterland. Taiwan is leveraging off the political uncertainty surrounding Hong Kong's future. Hong Kong's industrial structure and upgrading are closely linked with China; its manufacturing operations are increasingly relocated to neighbouring south China, and its regional hub activities increasingly focus on the China hinterland.

The regional hubs overlap and compete with each other to some degree but are also developing some distinctive characteristics. Singapore has a strong role in supplying and distributing regional production in the electronics industry and, because of its Southeast Asian location, is a management hub for a wider range of industries as well. Hong Kong has become more and more a managerial hub for activities in China, while production has moved to Taiwan and the mainland. Taiwan is leveraging off the political uncertainty surrounding Hong Kong's future to attract advanced component production and related R&D activities; it also aims to acquire a wider range of managerial activities similar to those in Singapore.

Table 11.1 illustrates how governments' objectives of industrial upgrading are positively related to MNEs' location of higher value-added segments. In this table, the economies in this study are located according to the rankings illustrated in Figure 1.1 (on the vertical axes in Table 11.1) and the value-added business segments in the electronics industry we found in those economies (on the horizontal axis).

At the bottom of the table are the factor-driven economies of Guangdong, Indonesia, and the Philippines. These economies have sales and service affiliates and labour-intensive assembly operations. Each is also increasingly the site of low value-added components production, as is Thailand. Malaysia is moving toward more capital accumulation and related sophistication of production as affiliates located there upgrade components-production facilities. Singapore, Taiwan, and Hong Kong are moving toward the innovation-driven stage; Singapore has benefited from highly focused government policies aimed at attracting managerial, design, and research segments of the value chain, in addition to its high value-added components production. Taiwan is the site of design, R&D, and production of high value-added products and components. Hong Kong, however, is currently affected by its uncertain political future.

Table 11.1. Harnessing diversity: host economies and the allocation of business segments in East Asian manufacturing.

Host economy's comparative advantage	Firm's value-added activity		
	Low	Medium	High
Innovation driven			Hong Kong
			Taiwan
Investment driven		Malaysia	Singapore
Factor driven	Guangdong	Thailand	
	Indonesia		
	Philippines		

Source: Host economies are ranked according to total-factor-productivity estimates reported in Table 1.3; value-added activities are based on the survey results (Chapters 2–9) and the cross-border study (Chapter 10).

Corporate strategies

Firms exploit the region's diversity by slicing up the value chain and allocating and reallocating value-added activities — rather than entire industries — according to a location's comparative advantage.

Similar industries are locating in the region through FDI, but different locations attract different value-added segments, creating the potential for a positive-sum game in which everybody gains.

Firms — particularly MNEs pursuing a variety of strategies as illustrated in the different chapters — are increasingly adept at allocating value-added activities according to two factors: first, as they accumulate experience, as Tu demonstrated empirically for Taiwan; and second, according to the sophistication of the host economy. Thailand and Malaysia are sites, in the electronics and auto industries, for assembly and the production of low value-added components. In contrast, Taiwan has many fewer final-assembly activities in electronics. In keeping with international division of labour within production networks, affiliates are assigned the components they will produce. Whereas components in Malaysia and Thailand include low-end semiconductors and components for consumer products, in Taiwan they are increasingly high-end semiconductors and higher value-added components like liquid-crystal displays, telecom oscillators, and filters. Almost no production in the electronics industry takes place in Hong Kong any more, as Chen and Wong confirmed. Singapore continues to be a production site, but for higher value-added components, such as disk drives, and for costly, high-risk semiconductor production, such as wafer fabrication, in which the government participates as an initial co-investor to mitigate front-end risk.

Dobson's maps of MNE value-added activities in the electronics industry (in Chapter 10) confirm a positive and dynamic relationship between location and business segments allocated by MNEs. Those economies with favourable factor endowments and policies to create new endowments, such as skilled labour, communications facilities, and risk sharing (through capital to invest), attract the costlier, riskier, higher value-added activities. Indeed, the case of Matsushita Electric Industrial Co. (described in Chapter 10) demonstrates the dynamic behaviour of larger firms. As the economies of China and Vietnam open up, low-end production is transferred to these sites from other locations within the region. The other locations do not lose their investments, however. They receive higher value-added mandates. In this way, everyone gains. FDI is a positive-sum game.

Another of our conclusions is that because firms allocate by value-added segment, it is unlikely for the foreseeable future that FDI in East Asia will be a zero-sum game in which one economy gains an entire industry at the expense of its neighbours. Nevertheless, this perception seems to exist as host governments compete, sometimes intensely, for FDI inflows. To promote a positive-sum game, it is essential that economies facilitate movement up the value-added chain by ensuring domestic investment also occurs so that those that restructure are not confronted with a "hollowing out" problem.

Corporate nationality and trade and production patterns

Differences in corporate nationality influence production, but location and industry effects dominate corporate nationality as determinants of trade patterns.

The focus in this section shifts from regional patterns to determinants of firm behaviour. Analysis focuses first on the trade patterns of Japanese and US firms and then on NIE firms. The significance of these results is then interpreted in terms of the production networks within and among firms in these assembly-based industries. We then examine how the organizational characteristics of firms change as they internationalize.

Data sources are as follows. For Indonesia, Singapore, and Thailand, the Indonesian Central Bureau of Statistics Industry Survey (Government of Indonesia 1992), the Singapore Economic Development Board Census of Industrial Production (EDB 1994a), and the Thailand Board of Investment provided data on sales and procurement behaviour of firms for the industries under study; data were also derived from researchers' fieldwork. For the other countries, data were derived primarily from researchers' fieldwork. The data are more complete for the electronics industry than for the T/G, auto, and chemical industries. US firms, for example, are mostly absent from the auto industry and appear in few of the surveys of T/G. The electronics industry is increasingly important. It is covered in all eight economies under study and more clearly demonstrates the importance of FDI, trade–investment linkages, and the regional division of labour.

Corporate trade behaviour by industry and nationality

Tables 11.2 and 11.3 summarize and compare trade and production patterns presented in earlier chapters for the electronics industry. Table 11.4 and 11.5 cover autos and T/G. Table 11.2 covers electronics in Malaysia, Taiwan, and Thailand, where the survey data provide values on firms' sales and procurement activities. The distributions of sales and procurement transactions among local, home, and third countries are compared, as are the intrafirm shares of these transactions. Table 11.3 covers Guangdong Province (China), Indonesia, Singapore, and the Philippines, where interval data were obtained. Entries in that table record the number of firms reporting traded sales and procurement, by interval. The first cell in the table, for example, shows that all five Japanese firms surveyed in Guangdong exported less than two-thirds of their sales. Information on intrafirm transactions was not available. In the cell below, three of the four Japanese firms surveyed in Indonesia exported more than two-thirds of their sales; all of these exports were through intrafirm channels.

Several observations are in order. First, evidence from the electronics industry in three economies at different stages of development is presented in Table 11.2. It should also be noted that

Table 11.2. Traded sales and procurement in the electronics industry, by corporate nationality: Thailand, Malaysia, and Taiwan, 1993–94.

| | Shares (%) (% Intrafirm trade) | | | | | |
| | Japanese firms | | | US firms | | |
	Thailand	Malaysia	Taiwan	Thailand	Malaysia	Taiwan
Sales						
Local economy	10.8 (16.8)	0.0 (0.0)	40.0 (2.0)	0.0 (0.0)	1.3 (100.0)	36.0 (0.0)
Home country	18.6 (98.3)	18.7 (64.4)	20.0 (91.0)	23.7 (100.0)	62.7 (100.0)	48.0 (94.0)
Third country	70.6 (93.8)	81.3 (57.1)	40.0 (49.0)	76.3 (100.0)	36.0 (64.0)	16.0 (76.0)
Total	100.0 (86.3)	100.0 (58.5)	100.0 (39.0)	100.0 (100.0)	100.0 (87.0)	100.0 (57.0)
Procurement						
Local economy	27.2 (18.6)	29.2 (0.0)	46.0 (0.0)	20.0 (100.0)	8.7 (12.8)	19.0 (0.0)
Home country	55.6 (90.7)	45.2 (74.0)	44.0 (63.0)	25.0 (100.0)	39.7 (100.0)	65.0 (84.0)
Third country	17.2 (51.5)	25.6 (27.6)	10.0 (17.0)	55.0 (100.0)	51.6 (64.0)	16.0 (49.0)
Total	100.0 (64.4)	100.0 (40.5)	100.0 (29.0)	100.0 (100.0)	100.0 (74.3)	100.0 (63.0)

Source: Survey data as presented in Tables 3.6, 5.9, and 6.6.

the firms surveyed accounted for 41% of industry sales in Malaysia, 36% in Taiwan and 76% in Thailand (see Table 1.4). Few differences by corporate nationality are apparent in trade behaviour. The main difference is that US industrial electronics firms engage in more intrafirm trade than do Japanese consumer-electronics firms (see bottom lines of sales and procurement panels) and export more of their sales to the home market. What might be the reasons for these differences? One of the most plausible explanations is that US firms, which specialize in the industrial-electronics industry segment, export more of the components produced in these economies back home and procure more from home — mostly through intrafirm channels — to protect proprietary advantages and to meet strict quality standards. In contrast, Japanese producers in consumer electronics target local markets more heavily and procure from Japanese small and medium-sized enterprises (SMEs) that have located in the region (as indeed do most other producers).

A similar pattern appears in the Singapore survey and census data. US firms tend to export more to the home country than Japanese firms, although it was difficult to determine whether these were mainly intrafirm or non-arm's-length transactions. This difference also turns up in the Singapore industrial-census data covering 247 firms in the electronics industry. Export orientation differs significantly by corporate nationality, with US firms being more export-oriented than their Japanese counterparts (export–total sales ratios of 90% versus 65%, respectively). Industrial electronics, such as computers and peripherals, disk drives, original equipment manufacturer (OEM), and semiconductors, have export ratios of more than 90%, whereas consumer electronics and printed circuit boards have much lower export ratios; US firms concentrate in industrial electronics and electronic components, for which export ratios are high, whereas Japanese firms concentrate in consumer electronics, for which export ratios are lower. These industrial specializations of US and Japanese affiliates in Singapore reflect the relative competitive strengths of their parent companies in the global electronics industry. Another factor reducing the export ratio of Japanese firms in Singapore is the presence of multiple Japanese affiliates, international procurement offices (IPOs), and regional headquarters (RHQs); interaffiliate exchange of components, as well as sales and procurement through IPOs and RHQs, lowers the direct exports of Japanese affiliates.

Second, trade patterns of Japanese and US firms resemble each other in ways that are clearly suggested in Table 11.2. Sales by both through market channels increase (that is, intrafirm transactions decline) as the host economy develops and matures. Market channels are used more heavily in Taiwan than in the other two host economies. Both producers sell more to the local market as the economy develops and matures; around 40% of sales by both US and Japanese firms are to the local market in Taiwan, whereas such sales are negligible in Thailand and Malaysia.

On the procurement side, a similar pattern is evident for Japanese firms, but it is less pronounced for US firms. Japanese firms procure nearly half their inputs locally in Taiwan (compared with less than 30% in Thailand and Malaysia), whereas US firms fail to show such a pattern, again probably because of the greater knowledge and technology intensity of industrial-electronics inputs. Sieh Lee and Yew note that one of the reasons US affiliates in Malaysia source within the firm from other countries is the existence of centralized purchasing arrangements and the fact that proprietary assets are embodied in these components.

In autos and T/G (Tables 11.4 and 11.5), trade patterns of US and Japanese producers are also similar. Variance occurs by location, that is, reflecting government policies and international trade rules, rather than by corporate nationality. In autos, import-substitution policies still operate in most host economies in the region. US and Japanese auto producers both sell and source locally as domestic policies dictate. Japanese producers' plentiful but inefficient branch-plant investments in Southeast Asian local markets are beginning to pay off as plans in the ASEAN Free Trade Area (AFTA) proceed to liberalize auto trade. US producers have been absent from the non-Chinese markets, more because of their differing strategic focus than anything else. In T/G, policies such as the GSP and MFA quotas are important determinants of trade patterns. In autos and T/G, both NIE and US firms in Indonesia and the Philippines export most of their production and import much of their procurement.

Table 11.3. Traded sales and procurement in the electronics industry, by corporate nationality: Guangdong, Indonesia, the Philippines, and Singapore, 1993–94. [a]

	Japanese firms		NIE firms [b]		US firms		Total sample	
Sales (%)								
China [c]								
67–100	0/5	(NA)	5/9	(NA)	1/1	(NA)	6/15	(NA)
0–66	5/5	(NA)	4/9	(NA)	0/1	(NA)	9/15	(NA)
Indonesia								
67–100	3/4	(100)	3/4	(25)	—		8/11	(55)
0–66	1/4	(0)	1/4	(75)	—		3/11	(45)
Philippines								
67–100	1/3	(0)	1/1	(0)	1/1	(0)	5/11	(0)
0–66	2/3	(100)	0/1	(100)	0/1	(100)	6/11	(100)
Singapore								
67–100	7/12	(58)	—		8/12	(67)	20/29	(52)
0–66	5/12	(42)	—		4/12	(33)	9/29	(48)
Procurement (%)								
China [c]								
67–100	3/5	(NA)	5/9	(NA)	1/1	(NA)	9/15	(NA)
0–66	2/5	(NA)	4/9	(NA)	0/1	(NA)	6/15	(NA)
Indonesia								
67–100	3/4	(75)	4/4	(75)	—		9/11	(55)
0–66	1/4	(25)	0/0	(25)	—		2/11	(45)
Philippines								
67–100	2/3	(0)	0/1	(0)	0/1	(NA)	7/11	(0)
0–66	1/3	(100)	1/1	(100)	0/1	(NA)	3/11	(100)
Singapore								
67–100	8/12	(58)	—		10/12	(17)	22/29	(31)
0–66	3/12	(42)	—		1/12	(83)	5/29	(69)

Source: Survey data as presented in Tables 2.10, 2.12, 7.6, 7.7, 8.4, 8.5, 9.9, and 9.14.
Note: NA, not available; NIE, newly industrialized economy.
[a] Cell entries report the number of firms by interval, exporting sales, or importing procurement. Numbers in parentheses are shares of intrafirm transactions for each interval reported by all interviewed firms.
[b] Hong Kong firms in Guangdong; Korean and Singaporean firms in Indonesia; Korean firms in the Philippines.
[c] *China* refers to Guangdong survey.

This analysis tends to confirm that locational factors, particularly government policies, are significant determinants of corporate trade behaviour. Analysis of variations in trade behaviour, holding corporate nationality and location constant, is possible for Japanese producers in Thailand and Indonesia (Tables 11.2–11.5). In Thailand, for example, Japanese electronics producers export most of their sales, but Japanese auto producers export almost nothing because of an import-substitution policy bias. Similarly, in Indonesia, most Japanese electronics producers export more than two-thirds of their sales, but Japanese auto and T/G producers in the same country export less than a third. Procurement data in those tables show slightly less industry variation, in that Japanese firms in Thailand imported more than half of their inputs in both the electronics and auto industries (and largely through intrafirm channels), although larger shares of auto than electronic parts were produced locally. In Indonesia, most of the inputs used by Japanese producers in both the electronics and

Table 11.4. Traded sales and procurement in the auto industry, by corporate nationality: Thailand, Malaysia, and Indonesia, 1992–93.

	Shares (%) (% intrafirm trade)					
	Japanese firms			US firms		
	Thailand	Malaysia	Indonesia	Thailand	Malaysia	Indonesia
Sales						
Local economy	98.5 (100.0)	16.5 (49.3)	>67 (>90)	NA (NA)	NA (NA)	100 (>90)
Home country	0.5 (100.0)	80.7 (100.0)	<33 (>90)	NA (NA)	NA (NA)	0 (0)
Third country	1.0 (100.0)	2.8 (0.0)	<33 (>90)	NA (NA)	NA (NA)	0 (0)
Total	100.0 (100.0)	100.0 (88.8)	NA (NA)	NA (NA)	NA (NA)	100 (>90)
Procurement						
Local economy	43.8 (74.6)	13.3 (0.0)	0 (0)	NA (NA)	NA (NA)	10–33 (67–90)
Home country	56.2 (100.0)	76.6 (40.6)	>90 (100)	NA (NA)	NA (NA)	0.0 (0.0)
Third country	0.0 (0.0)	10.1 (0.0)	0 (0)	NA (NA)	NA (NA)	67–90 (67–90)
Total	100.0 (88.8)	100.0 (31.1)	>90 (100)	NA (NA)	NA (NA)	NA (NA)

Source: Survey data as presented in Tables 5.9, 6.7, 9.10, and 9.15.
Note: NA, not available.

auto industries were imported from home through intrafirm channels. In T/G, however, inputs were largely procured locally. A more extensive comparison for US and NIE producers, holding location and nationality constant, is not possible because of their absence from one or more of the industries in the economies studied.

The procurement data, particularly in electronics, illustrate the tendency of foreign investors (regardless of corporate nationality) to exclude local producers in these investors' procurement practices, both to protect ownership advantages and to meet the high quality standards and stringent timing requirements of customers.

Official industrial-survey data also show that foreign firms in almost all countries and industries are more export oriented than local firms. The industry effect is significant in determining the degree of export orientation (export/total sales ratio). In all the countries surveyed, the electronics industry is highly export oriented, the T/G industry is slightly less so, and the auto industry is highly domestic market oriented. The Singapore census data for electronics show that export orientation is higher for industrial electronics (except communications equipment), TV sets in consumer electronics, and semiconductors and lowest in electronic components (excluding semiconductors). The Indonesian industrial survey data show that within electronics, components are more export oriented than consumer electronics as in Singapore; in T/G, garments are the most and spinning is the least export oriented.

These industry differences in export orientation are probably due to both policy and industry effects. The high export ratios in electronics reflect the globalization of production and the segmentation of production processes and products to different locations and the promotion of FDI in

Table 11.5. Traded sales and procurement in the textiles and garments industry, by corporate nationality: Guangdong, Indonesia, and the Philippines, 1993–94. [a]

	Japanese firms	NIE firms [b]	US firms	Total sample
Sales (%)				
China [c]				
67–100	—	6/15 (NA)	—	6/15 (NA)
0–66	—	9/15 (NA)	—	9/15 (NA)
Indonesia				
67–100	1/3 (0)	7/12 (42)	—	12/21 (24)
0–66	2/3 (100)	5/12 (58)	—	9/21 (76)
Philippines				
67–100	—	1/1 (0)	4/4 (0)	11/11 (0)
0–66	—	0/1 (100)	0/4 (100)	0/11 (100)
Procurement (%)				
China [c]				
67–100	—	9/15 (NA)	—	9/15 (NA)
0–66	—	6/15 (NA)	—	6/15 (NA)
Indonesia				
67–100	1/3 (0)	6/12 (25)	—	10/21 (14)
0–66	2/3 (100)	6/12 (75)	—	11/21 (86)
Philippines				
67–100	—	1/1 (0)	4/4 (0)	10/11 (0)
0–66	—	0/1 (100)	0/4 (100)	0/11 (100)

Source: Survey data as presented in Tables 7.8, 7.9, 8.6, 8.7, 9.7, 9.8, 9.12, and 9.13.

Note: NA, not available; NIE, newly industrialized economy.

[a] Cell entries report the number of firms by interval, exporting sales, or importing procurement. Numbers in parentheses are shares of intrafirm transactions for each interval reported by all interviewed firms.

[b] Hong Kong firms in Guangdong; Korean and Taiwanese firms in Indonesia; Hong Kong firms in the Philippines.

[c] China refers to Guangdong survey.

electronics in export-processing zones following the transition in trade and industrial policies from import substitution to export orientation. Within electronics, consumer electronics was established earlier and often originally targeted at the domestic market; in electronic components, export orientation declines when the components form the inputs of the local assembly industry. The high export orientation of the garments industry in some countries reflects the inflow of FDI attracted by the availability of export quotas under the MFA. The auto industries in the countries studied were all established under import-substitution programs.

Finally, although this study focused on trade, some observations on production are pertinent. Dobson's cross-border analysis in Chapter 10 shows that Japanese and US MNEs differ in the regional distribution of R&D, with US firms establishing many more R&D and design facilities than Japanese firms have. Comparisons of trade behaviour across host economies also suggested some differences in production behaviour. US affiliates behaved in uniform ways, whereas Japanese affiliates with the same MNE parent showed considerable variation in their behaviour. Some became vertically integrated in the host economy, selling as well as producing there, whereas others remained less integrated and concentrated on selling to Japan. Overall, however, Japanese affiliates, probably because of their consumer orientation, were more localized and market oriented than were US firms in industrial electronics.

Production-cost data obtained in the Taiwan survey compared firms that invested elsewhere in the region with those that did not. The investors were more efficient producers, probably because the intent of such investment was to achieve intraregional division of labour and vertical integration. No clear industry differences between chemicals and electronics were detected. But within the electronics industry, Japanese firms performed better, probably because they achieved more extensive (and therefore more efficient) division of labour. In other words, the organization of the value chain within the region enhanced the multinationals' ability to control costs.

Emerging NIE firms

An interesting and increasingly significant player in East Asian production is the Asian NIE investor. As economies have developed and matured, appreciating currencies and rising relative costs have pushed many local producers into offshore production. It is too soon to tell whether such firms will grow up to be multinationals. Firms such as Acer in Taiwan and Creative Technology and Aztech in Singapore have intentionally pursued global strategies and diversified from exclusively OEM production to brand-name differentiation. As the Acer case in Chapter 10 documented, however, the costs and risks have been very high.

Cross-border investments by Taiwanese and Hong Kong manufacturers are important in several studies in this volume. Tu's study of Taiwan illustrates how FDI became an engine of trade and integration as the outward flow of FDI into surrounding economies in the 1986–92 period was paralleled by a dramatic increase in two-way trade. Likewise, Chen and Wong discussed the migration of Hong Kong firms and industrial production to Guangdong, although their networks were confined to family members.

Malaysia, Indonesia, Thailand, and Guangdong are major recipients of NIE investments. Sieh Lee and Yew's study notes the growing importance of NIE investors as suppliers of electronics and auto components to the Malaysian market. NIE firms, mainly from Taiwan, sell more than 50% of their production to their parents, but they have strong links with local suppliers, rather than with their parents. Both kinds of transaction take place through the market because such firms are not yet large enough to establish international networks, nor are they (yet) part of international value-added chains. Hence, one of their impacts on host economies was that they played a stronger role than foreign MNEs in stimulating local sourcing and in the development of local supply chains.

Taiwanese firms in Indonesia are also SMEs whose investments are smaller than those by industrial-country MNEs. The SMEs' investments have tended to be defensive, to enable them to continue to serve foreign customers by locating closer to them to survive as relative production costs have risen at home. Thus, although these SMEs have imported from Taiwan, they have tended to move most of their proprietary assets (embodied in the owners) to Indonesia. Being too small and new to afford international networks, the SMEs develop most of their networking activities with the local economy as they attempt to localize and build up a local customer base.

The sample of NIE firms among the countries is too small to draw meaningful comparisons on the basis of corporate nationality. It is also too soon to tell whether these firms will grow beyond penetrating host-economy markets for sourcing and sales to become MNEs with proprietary assets that they then leverage in international networks. Nevertheless, they have played significant roles in promoting intraregional trade.

Production networks

The larger significance of these patterns of trade by corporate nationality is that firms in the assembly-based industries in this study, regardless of nationality, use production networks to reduce transactions costs.

Faced with intensifying competition because of deregulation, falling trade barriers, and increasing capital mobility, international firms seek production efficiencies by unbundling value-added activities previously vertically integrated within a single location or production unit. Locational factors, particularly factor endowments and government policies, determine the allocation of those activities.

Ownership factors and internalization capabilities (relying on advances in microelectronics and information technology) to coordinate production and trade of the many components to be assembled into the final product facilitate this unbundling. Parenthetically, it should be noted that in one corporation or interfirm network, production activities may be found in one or several locations, depending on comparative advantage, whereas coordination (services activities) will be found in other locations with differing comparative advantage.

Value-added activities with price sensitivity and low entry barriers (and standard technologies) will be located and relocated to sites with a comparative advantage in low-cost labour or natural resources. Services or products that embody new innovations, that are differentiated and capital or technology intensive, and that have high entry barriers will be allocated to sites with comparative advantage in skilled labour, low-cost communications, and infrastructure. Since the many intermediate goods in the assembly-based industries in this study must be shipped from where they are produced to other locations (with differing comparative advantage) — where further value is added in the form of finishing, testing, assembly, or marketing — production networks are created by these cross-border trade linkages, both within a firm and among cooperating firms.

As the former socialist economies have emerged, they have increased the diversity of locations in the region and extended the range of value-added activities possible. This lengthening of the value chain has increased the importance of MNE coordination functions — through RHQs in Hong Kong and Singapore, where good infrastructure, ample supplies of professionals and skilled labour, and financial and commercial services are located.

Around these service hubs, networking has increased. Chen and Wong note the rise of networking in Hong Kong. Hong Kong's locational advantage next to China has provided the added impetus to interfirm and intrafirm networks that link manufacturing in China with Hong Kong's service specialty. Chen and Wong note that these networking arrangements are evolving from traditional hub–spoke relationships between parents and their affiliates to spoke–spoke relationships between the Hong Kong RHQs and Chinese affiliates. In other words, authority has been decentralized in response to pressures to coordinate the diverse activities in a lengthening value chain. They also note that networking itself is evolving from intrafirm to interfirm relationships. Interfirm spoke–spoke relationships respond to the need to specialize to meet ever-stricter quality standards. As a result, affiliates (not necessarily from the same firm) cooperate with others with complementary capabilities, thereby achieving greater flexibility in adapting to rapid change.

Internationalization and changes in organizational behaviour

A major organizational change is localization of foreign firms through such practices as local sourcing and local hiring. In a number of countries, localization is required of foreign firms in terms of equity ownership, input content, and employment. These performance requirements have been liberalized recently, but local-content requirements in the auto industry are still imposed by all countries. Localization of inputs is also required to satisfy the rules of origin for trade preferences under the GSP, the ASEAN Preferential Trading Arrangement, and AFTA. Singapore has no localization requirement, but MNEs have responded to incentives to open up their supply chains to local suppliers under the Local Industry Upgrading Programme noted earlier. Malaysia's subcontracting-exchange scheme is another example. These programs may raise costs initially over what they would be if MNEs persisted with traditional intrafirm arrangements.

Asian NIE firms that have invested abroad defensively (to continue to serve their foreign customers) have been shown to be extremely adaptable (Chen 1995b). The head office usually migrates with the owner, and the enterprise relies heavily, if it survives, on local sourcing and sales. For example, Hong Kong and Taiwanese investors in the T/G industries in Singapore in the 1960s and, more recently, Taiwanese investors in Indonesia have since indigenized. The same indigenization phenomenon is not evident among Korean investors. This extensive localization may be peculiar to investors from Hong Kong and Taiwan who seek to escape political uncertainties at home.

Vintage may be a determinant of organizational change, but it can work two ways. In the case of the Asian investor, the more immature and smaller the investing firm is, the greater the initial emphasis on localization of sourcing to survive. If the firm survives and grows, it may import more and internationalize its network as it ages. It works the opposite way among MNEs, as Alburo and Gochoco-Bautista noted in the Philippines: as investments mature to the production stage, more localization occurs. Tu demonstrated for Taiwan, with his time-series observations, that intrafirm trade declines through time. This finding can be explained by his analysis, which shows that vintage is positively related to localization: the more established firms engage in more local sourcing and sales as they become more familiar with the host economy.

Intrafirm trade and FDI

Intrafirm trade is growing fast; because such trade and investment are complementary, coherence should be sought in trade and investment policies and governments should cooperate in removing obstacles to intraregional trade and investment flows.

It is well established in the literature that market imperfections and transaction costs contribute to intrafirm trade because they create incentives for the internalization of goods and services embodying firm-specific knowledge and expertise. As such, intrafirm trade is more prevalent in oligopolistic industries with proprietary technologies and capabilities that firms wish to protect from imitation. MNE decisions to internalize transactions may also be influenced by the fiscal, trade, investment, and exchange-rate policies of home governments. US tariff provisions under sections 807.00 and 806.30 of the US tariff schedule, for example, have contributed to the growth of offshore processing and intrafirm transactions.

Chen and Wong's study of Hong Kong firms provides some insights into the motivations for intrafirm versus interfirm trade. The purpose of foreign affiliates in Hong Kong is to coordinate Chinese affiliates' production and trade to increase overall MNE profitability and efficiency. MNEs pursue these goals through intrafirm channels; through interfirm arrangements, including arm's-length subcontracting and buyer-driven commodity chains; and (among large firms) through strategic alliances. Interfirm arrangements in the form of subcontracting and commodity chains were cost driven. Strategic alliances are determined largely by rapid technological change and the need to specialize; partners are found (which include competitors) to share risk and to provide market access. Chen and Wong also found that internalized intrafirm transactions are important in sourcing and exporting, especially among large firms. For Malaysia, Sieh Lee and Yew note that these transactions are intrafirm, especially within electronics firms, because of the simple but essential requirement that components embody proprietary technology. This technology is specified in product design, of course, but beyond that, intrafirm transactions help to protect it from imitation.

With respect to the relationship between intrafirm trade and regional integration, our studies of Thailand and Malaysia show that affiliates, regardless of nationality, rely heavily on intrafirm trade with parents, implying that American and European affiliates' transactions reduce intraregional trade. But this observation needs to be qualified by several factors. The first is statistical. If these affiliates in Singapore, for example, invest in other affiliates in the region, the statistical record will show Singaporean, not American or European, investments. Increasingly, however, such investments are being made. The second of these factors is the age of affiliates and the degree of industrial upgrading in the host country, as Tu's study of Taiwan suggests. He demonstrates that intrafirm sourcing by both Japanese and US firms is positively related to intraregional investment, implying that a motivation for intraregional investment is indeed to create regional production networks. Such networking may be more cost effective for affiliates in the more advanced, higher-cost economies.

NIE firms that invest offshore are a significant force for regional integration. As Chia, Tu, and Ramstetter note, NIE firms from Taiwan and Singapore, by investing offshore, promote intraregional trade in capital and intermediate products and in services, at least during the early stages of their investment. Sieh Lee and Yew's study of Malaysia, however, shows that NIE investors lack the resources to maintain networks and rely quite heavily on local markets for both sales and inputs.

Table 11.6 compares the total amount of intrafirm trade in the industries and economies included in this study. This table shows that intrafirm sales by US firms in the electronics industry tend to be between 87% and 100% in China, Malaysia, and Thailand (where assembly operations of final products for export are located) and drops to lower ratios in Singapore and Taiwan (where components are produced). Procurement tends to follow a similar pattern. Among Japanese firms,

Table 11.6. Intrafirm trade by industry: eight East Asian economies, 1993–94.

Host economy	Investor	Shares (%)			
		Japanese firms	US firms	NIE firms	All foreign firms
China	Electronics				
	Sales	31.3	99.3	29.3	NA
	Procurement	37.0	100.0	47.0	NA
	Textiles and garments				
	Sales	—	—	49.8 (Hong Kong)	NA
	Procurement	—	—	70.2 (Hong Kong)	NA
Hong Kong	Electronics				
	Sales	65.0	34.0	45.0	33.0
	Procurement	NA	NA	NA	33.0
Indonesia	Electronics				
	Sales	4/4 > 90	—	1/3 > 90	6/11 > 67
	Procurement	3/4 > 67	—	3/4 > 67	6/11 > 67
	Textiles				
	Sales	3/3 < 33	—	5/12 > 67	5/21 > 67
	Procurement	2/3 < 33	—	3/12 > 67	3/21 > 67
Malaysia	Electronics				
	Sales	58.5	87.0	34.5	74.0
	Procurement	40.5	74.3	24.2	65.8
	Autos				
	Sales	88.8	NA	0.0	83.1
	Procurement	31.1	NA	10.0	30.0
Philippines	Electronics				
	Sales	0.0	NA	0.0	50.0
	Procurement	0.0	NA	0.0	50.0
	Textiles and garments				
	Sales	—	0.0	0.0	50.0
	Procurement	—	0.0	0.0	50.0
Singapore	Electronics				
	Sales	7/12 > 67	8/12 > 67	—	15/29 > 67
	Procurement	7/12 > 67	2/12 > 67	—	9/29 > 67
Taiwan	Electronics				
	Sales	39.0	57.0	—	53.0
	Procurement	29.0	63.0	—	46.0
	Chemicals				
	Sales	28.0	100.0	—	75.0
	Procurement	30.0	81.0	—	14.0
Thailand	Electronics				
	Sales	94.8	100.0	96.0	97.4
	Procurement	81.4	100.0	61.0	92.6
	Autos				
	Sales	100.0	—	—	100.0
	Procurement	100.0	—	—	100.0

Source: Survey data as presented in Tables 2.10, 2.12, 3.6, 3.7, 5.9, 6.6, 6.7, 7.10, 7.11, 8.4–8.7, and 9.7–9.14.

Note: NA, not available; NIE, newly industrialized economy; —, no data from those firms in survey. Estimates applied to trade exclude local intrafirm transactions.

intrafirm sales and procurement ratios are lower in most economies. Singapore sample survey data show no significant difference on sales, but Japanese firms have higher procurement ratios.

Our calculation of the values of intrafirm trade, using country data on the value of trade in the electronics industry and applied to the ratios in Table 11.6, appears in Table 11.7. In total, the value of intrafirm trade, including both exports and imports, is estimated to be US$83.9 billion in 1992, or 55.5% of total electronics trade in seven economies, excluding China. As economies industrialize and trade shares accounted for by firms with vertically integrated production networks increase, the amount of intrafirm trade also increases (although total intrafirm trade in Table 11.6 does not show any particular trend by economies' levels of development). The policy implications of this estimate are a subject of the next section.

Policy lessons and implications

In this concluding section, we draw four policy implications, based on the summary in this chapter and on policy implications in the country studies.

The first implication concerns international firms' impact on regional integration. The impact is mixed, as indicated above; firms investing from within the region are more likely to contribute to intraregional trade than those investing from outside the region. But our evidence suggests that vintage plays a role. Most international firms, as they mature, aspire to global strategies; hence, intraregional production and trade tend to be organized or, at least, to be rationalized within a global rather than strictly regional division of labour.

The second implication is directly related. The close ties between the regional activities of multinationals (and those of the larger regional firms) and their global strategies have important implications for governments' roles in influencing locational advantages. In a number of countries, the domestic market is still not fully open. Firms in Thailand surveyed by Ramstetter, for example, saw the lack of transparency in import regulations as a persistent problem. Governments continue to rely on more direct interventions in the forms of fiscal incentives and performance requirements.

Most of the studies in this volume, however, have emphasized that governments should be moving toward framework policies that create new endowments, of skilled labour for example, through policy shifts from mere removal of illiteracy and supply of vocational education to the supply of education for technical and engineering labour and information technology. Sieh Lee and Yew note that Malaysia's fiscal incentives to attract FDI are easily imitated by latecomers and recommend a policy

Table 11.7. Value of intrafirm trade in the electronics industry: East Asia, 1992. [a]

Economy	Value of exports in intrafirm trade (US$ millions)	Value of imports in intrafirm trade (US$ millions)	Total intrafirm trade (US$ millions)
Hong Kong	8 518.3	7 918.7	16 437.0
Indonesia	511.2	1 059.9	1 571.1
Malaysia	9 862.7	4 542.2	14 404.9
Philippines	850.5	336.0	1 186.5
Singapore	17 848.1	11 030.9	28 879.0
Taiwan	8 230.4	3 614.7	11 845.1
Thailand	5 946.3	3 678.1	9 624.4
Total [b]	51 767.5	32 180.5	55.5 [c]

Source: Value of exports and imports as reported in the *Yearbook of World Electronics Data* (Elsevier Science Ltd 1994); intrafirm shares derived from Table 6, sales and procurement in the electronics industry.

[a] Excludes China.

[b] Value of total intrafirm trade summed across economies.

[c] Share of intrafirm trade in total electronics trade in these seven economies calculated as the ratio of total intrafirm exports and imports to the sum of total exports and imports.

shift toward framework policies to respond to the opportunities for migrating up the production hierarchy created by MNEs' production networks in the region. It has been shown elsewhere (Graham 1996) that government incentives and subsidies that attract investment from one location to another that would otherwise have taken place on the grounds of transaction costs alone represent (1) transfers from taxpayers in the country providing the subsidy to the firm and its shareholders and (2) compensation of the firm for increased costs and reduced overall efficiency.

The third policy implication relates to the high degree of intrafirm trade, as we documented above for the electronics industry. Intrafirm trade increases because of disintegration of numerous discrete value-chain activities within the firm to reduce transaction costs. The associated complementarity between FDI and trade has both positive and negative effects on host economies and on the region, however. Our case studies imply that rising intrafirm trade is a positive development in economies pursuing industrial upgrading. Production networks provide opportunities for the host economy to migrate up the value chain. Follower economies can inherit activities reallocated by firms from economies that have lost comparative advantage. Intrafirm trade has also enabled East Asian economies to embark on export manufacturing without having to undergo a lengthy and costly period of building up technological, exporting, and marketing capabilities.

Seen from the perspective of the international firm, intrafirm trade ensures greater control over both upstream suppliers and downstream markets, particularly in business environments characterized by diverse political, economic, and legal frameworks. But the use of local suppliers, as well as the transfer of technology and industrial know-how from foreign investors to local firms, has been slow because it raises transaction costs, particularly among the less-internationalized firms, including Japanese multinationals. They have been more reluctant than others to use local suppliers. Our evidence is that among MNEs, vintage is a significant factor (whereas small firms may use local suppliers because they have no alternative source of supply): the more experienced the international firm is, the more it is capable of locating and using local suppliers.

There are several implications for host governments. Because investment and trade are increasingly complementary, it is no longer logical to separate FDI and trade in domestic-policy formation. Trade-related investment measures (TRIMS) and investment-related trade measures (IRTMS) should be integrated to achieve policy coherence and effectiveness, for example. The high degree of intrafirm trade means a loss of policy sovereignty by governments, particularly with respect to transfer pricing, which must be dealt with through tax policy. Perhaps most significant, while FDI inflows represent the augmentation of domestic with foreign savings, as well as technology transfers and opportunities to migrate up the industry value chain, the negative implication is that host economies become more vulnerable to fluctuations in the world economy because of the increasing homogeneity of the region's manufacturing industrial structure (which exports final goods outside the region). When the world economy slows, as it did in 1995–96, demand for the region's consumer durables and consumer goods declines, with a cascading effect through the region's production networks.

The fourth implication is that these arguments strengthen the case for regional intergovernmental cooperation. The studies in this volume are unanimous. Governments should bow to the market forces pushing integration by removing obstacles to intraregional trade flows (Tu); they should open domestic economies to allow for greater participation in the international (global) division of labour (Alburo and Gochoco-Bautista); they should cooperate in providing favourable conditions for investment, including the freer flow of product information and accelerated preferential trading arrangements within AFTA (Sieh Lee and Yew); and they should cooperate to remove restrictions on new forms of firm cooperation, such as strategic alliances (Chen and Wong).

Agreement among Asia–Pacific Economic Cooperation (APEC) members to achieve free trade by 2020 and to adopt the APEC Nonbinding Investment Principles covering transparency, national treatment, and most-favoured-nation treatment are welcome steps in this direction. But more is needed. Host governments continue to compete for FDI inflows. They promote the entry of foreign firms and investors through the use of incentives. They screen and regulate entry and impose sectoral restrictions and performance requirements to maximize perceived benefits and minimize perceived costs of FDI. Such measures, usually administered on an ad hoc basis, lack transparency and create uneven conditions for competition among MNEs and with local firms.

Multilateral measures are under active discussion within the WTO. Such measures would encourage governments to liberalize FDI regimes and converge toward common standards on right of establishment, fair and equitable treatment, protection against nationalization, international-dispute settlement, and assurances for the repatriation of earnings and capital. Capping fiscal and financial incentives to reduce distortions should also be considered.

The interests of multinationals are directly related to progress in these areas. When regional exports slow down in response to currency appreciation or slowing external demand, as they did in 1995–96, multinationals run the risk of a hostile reaction to slower growth, blaming them for what, in reality, are cyclical fluctuations or the structural consequences of national trade and FDI policies.

In conclusion, one of the main findings of this study is that East Asia's economic integration rests not only on its rapid growth and the proximity of diverse economies but also on firms cooperating successfully with governments. Multinational and international firms augment the growth of savings, jobs, and incomes, but their objectives will not always coincide with those of host governments. It is in the interests of both players to assist in achieving self-sustaining growth, which in turn depends heavily on productivity growth.

We find production networks contribute to regional integration, but we note that this exchange of intermediate goods risks structural and cyclical vulnerability because final-goods markets, particularly at the high end, lie outside the region. We have raised the question of whether, in pursuing rapid growth in this way, East Asia's firms and governments are introducing structural vulnerability through heavy reliance on production networks and intrafirm trade in a few industries. To answer this question, further research is required to determine the destinations of exports of intermediate and final goods. Such research may help to confirm our observation that economies in the region are simultaneously becoming more regionally and globally integrated.

ACRONYMS AND ABBREVIATIONS

AFTA	ASEAN Free Trade Area
AMS	Asian operational headquarters of Matsushita Electric Industrial Co. in Singapore
ANU	Australian National University
APEC	Asia–Pacific Economic Cooperation
ASEAN	Association of Southeast Asian Nations
ATM	automated teller machine
AT&T	American Telephone & Telegraph Co.
AV	audio–video
BOI	Board of Investment [Indonesia; Thailand]
	Board of Investments [the Philippines]
CBS	Central Bureau of Statistics [Indonesia]
CBU	completely built-up
CD	compact disk
CD–ROM	compact disk – read-only memory
CEPT	Common Effective Preferential Tariff
CKD	completely knocked-down
CMOS	complementary metal-oxide semiconductor
CRT	cathode-ray tube
DRAM	dynamic random-access memory
EC	European Community
EDB	Economic Development Board [Singapore]
EPROM	electronically programable read-only memory
EPTE	Entrepôt Produksi Tujuan Ekspor [export-processing zones]
EU	European Union

FDI   foreign direct investment

GATT General Agreement on Tariffs and Trade
GCB   growth cost–benefit
GDP   gross domestic product
GERD gross expenditure on R&D
GIS   geographic information system
GNP   gross national product
GSP   Generalized System of Preferences

HP   Hewlett-Packard

IBM   International Business Machines Corp.
IC   integrated circuit
ICL   International Computers Limited
IIT   intraindustry trade
IPO   international procurement office
IRTMS investment-related trade measures
ISDN   Integrated Services Digital Network
ISIC   International Standard Industrial Classification
ITRI   Industrial Technology Research Institute [Taiwan]

JV   joint venture
JVC   Japanese Victor Corporation

KDD   Kokusai Denshin Denwa [Kokusai telephone and telegraph corporation]

LAN   local-area network
LED   light-emitting diode
LIUP   Local Industry Upgrading Programme

Mb   megabyte
MEI   Matsushita Electric Industrial Co.
MFA   Multifibre Arrangement
MFN   most-favoured nation
MITI   Ministry of Trade and Industry [Malaysia]
MNE   multinational enterprise
MOFERT Ministry of Foreign Economic Relations and Trade [China]
MPS   Material Product System

NAFTA North American Free Trade Agreement

NASDAQ	National Association of Securities Dealers Automated Quotations
NEC	Nippon Electric Company Ltd
NIE	newly industrialized economy
NUS	National University of Singapore
OCM	office and computing machinery
OECD	Organisation for Economic Co-operation and Development
OEM	original equipment manufacturer
OHQ	operational headquarters
OLI	ownership–location–internalization
PABX	Private Automated Branch Exchange
PC	personal computer
PCB	printed circuit board
PPP	purchasing power parity
R&D	research and development
RCA	revealed comparative advantage
RHQ	regional headquarters
SD	standard deviation
SEZ	special economic zone
SGS	Swiss General Surveyor
SIJORI	Singapore, Johore [in Malaysia], and Riau [in Indonesia]
SITC	Standard International Trade Classification
SME	small and medium-sized enterprise
SMT	surface-mount technology
SONIS	Sony's operational headquarters in Singapore
T/C	Tetoron/Cotton
TDB	Trade Development Board [Singapore]
T/G	textiles and garments
TI	Texas Instruments
TRIMS	trade-related investment measures
TV	television
VCR	videocassette recorder
VTR	videotape recorder
WTO	World Trade Organization

CONTRIBUTING AUTHORS

Florian A. Alburo is Professor of Economics, University of the Philippines, Diliman, Quezon City, Philippines.

Edward K.Y. Chen is President, Lingnan College, Hong Kong.

Chen Kang is Lecturer, Nanyang Business School, Nanyang Technological University, Singapore.

Chia Siow Yue was Associate Professor of Economics, Department of Economics and Statistics, National University of Singapore, until July 1996, when she became Executive Director, Institute of Southeast Asian Studies, Pasir Panjang, Singapore.

Wendy Dobson is Professor and Director, Centre for International Business, University of Toronto, Toronto, Ontario, Canada.

Maria Socorro Gochoco-Bautista is Associate Professor of Economics, University of the Philippines, Diliman, Quezon City, Philippines.

Mari Pangestu is Head, Economic Department, Center for Strategic and International Studies, Jakarta, Indonesia.

Eric D. Ramstetter is Professor, Department of Economics, Kansai University in Osaka, Osaka, Japan (on leave in 1994–95 at the National University of Singapore).

Sieh Lee Mei Ling is Dean, Division of Business Administration, and Professor, Faculty of Economics and Administration, University of Malaya, Kuala Lumpur, Malaysia.

Tu Jenn-hwa was Associate Professor of Economics, Graduate Institute of the Three People's Principles, College of Law, National Taiwan University, Taipei, Taiwan, until January 1996, when he became an elected representative to the Taiwan Parliament.

Teresa Y.C. Wong was Research Assistant, Centre for East Asian Studies, University of Hong Kong, Hong Kong, until December 1995, when she moved to Burnaby, British Columbia, Canada.

Yew Siew Yong is Lecturer, Faculty of Economics and Administration, University of Malaya, Kuala Lumpur, Malaysia.

Zhang Zhaoyong is Assistant Professor, Department of Economics and Statistics, National University of Singapore, Singapore.

BIBLIOGRAPHY

ADB (Asian Development Bank). Asian development outlook. ADB, Manila, Philippines.

Acer. n.d. Annual report. Acer, Taipei, Taiwan. Various years.

Akamatsu, K. 1962. A theory of unbalanced growth in the world economy. Weltwirtschaftliches Archiv, 86(2), 196–215.

Alburo, F.A. 1994. Intra-industry trade: the Philippines in AFTA. UP School of Economics, Quenzon City, Philippines. Discussion Paper 9402.

ANU (Australian National University). 1995. International Economic Data Bank. ANU, Canberra, ACT, Australia. Diskette and hard copy.

APEC (Asia–Pacific Economic Cooperation) Economic Committee. 1995a. 1995 APEC economic outlook. APEC, Singapore.

———— 1995b. Foreign direct investment and APEC economic integration. APEC, Singapore.

Arrow, K. 1974. The limits of organization, W.W. Norton, New York, NY, USA.

Asian Business. 1994. Hard drive to global network. Oct.

AT&T (American Telephone & Telegraph). n.d. Annual report. AT&T, New York, USA. Various years.

Bangko Sentral ng Pilipinas. n.d. Annual report. Central Bank of the Philippines, Manila, Philippines. Various years.

Bank of Thailand. 1994. Monthly bulletin. Bank of Thailand, Bangkok, Thailand. July issue.

———— 1983, 1986–94. Foreign investment data mimeos. Bank of Thailand, Bangkok, Thailand. Undated, Sep 1983; Jul 1986, 1987, 1988, 1989, 1990, 1991, 1992; Aug 1992; Apr 1993, 1994; Sep 1994.

Bartlett, C.A.; Ghosal, S. 1989. Managing across borders. Harvard University Business School Press, Boston, MA, USA.

Belassa, B. 1986. Intra-industry specialization: a cross-country analysis. European Economic Review, 30, 27–42.

Bergsten, C.F.; Horst, T.; Moran, T. 1978. American multinationals and American interests. Brookings Institution, Washington, DC, USA.

Bergsten, C.F.; Noland, M., ed. 1993a. Pacific dynamism and the international economic system. Institute for International Economics, Washington, DC, USA.

———— 1993b. Reconcilable differences? Institute for International Economics, Washington, DC, USA.

Bernard, M.; Ravenhill, J. 1995. Beyond product cycles and flying geese: regionalism, hierarchy, and the industrialization of East Asia. World Politics, 47(2), 171–209.

Bhattacharya, A.; Pangestu, M. 1993. Indonesia: public policy and transformation. In Leipziger, D., ed., Lessons from East Asia. World Bank, Washington, DC, USA.

Bhote, K.R. 1989. Strategic supply management. American Management Association, New York, NY, USA.

Biggart, N.W.; Hamilton, G.G. 1992. Reorganizing Asia: Japan's new development trajectory and the regional division of labour. Berkeley Roundtable on the International Economy, Berkeley, CA, USA.

———— 1993. On the limits of a firm-based theory to explain business networks: the Western bias of neoclassical economics. In Nohria, N.; Eccles, R., ed., Networks and organization. Harvard University Business School Press, Boston, MA, USA.

Brimble, P.J. 1993. Industrial development and productivity change in Thailand. Johns Hopkins University, Baltimore, MD, USA. PhD dissertation.

Buckley, P.J.; Casson, M. 1986. Multinationals and world trade: vertical integration and the division of labour in world industries. Allen and Unwin, Boston, MA, USA.

———— 1991. The future of the multinational enterprise. Macmillan, London, UK.

Business Times. 1991a. ATT rings in new era of product development. Business Times, 4 Feb.

———— 1991b. ATT plans to boost Japan operations. Business Times, 28 Aug.

———— 1993a. Business Times, 22 Feb.

——— 1993b. Why Motorola desperately needs the MFN renewed. Business Times, 30 Mar.

——— 1993c. Business Times, 5 Aug.

——— 1993d. Mitsubishi and AT&T in chip tie-up. Business Times, 24 Sep.

——— 1994. TI joins race to develop advanced DRAM pkg. Business Times, 18 Jul.

Casson, M. 1987. The firm and the market: studies on the multinational and the scope of the firm. MIT Press, Cambridge, MA, USA.

Caves, R.E. 1982. Multinational enterprise and economic analysis. Cambridge University Press, Cambridge, UK.

Chao, C.M. 1991. T'iao-t'iao vs k'uai-k'uai: a perennial dispute between the central and local governments in mainland China. Issues and Studies, Aug.

Chen, E.K.Y.; Drysdale, P., ed. 1995. Corporate links and foreign direct investment in Asia and the Pacific. Pacific Trade and Development–Harper Educational Publishers, Canberra, ACT, Australia.

Chen, L.I.; Chung, C. 1993. An assessment of Taiwan's indirect investment toward mainland China. Asian Economic Journal, 7(1), 41–70.

Chen, P. 1994. Foreign investment in the southern China growth triangle. In Thant, M.; Tang, M.; Kakazu, H., ed., Growth triangle in Asia. Asian Development Bank, Manila, Philippines.

Chen, T.-J. 1994. FDI by small and medium-sized enterprises from Taiwan. CIER Newsletter, 2, 2.

——— 1995a. Taiwanese investments in Malaysia. In Chen, T.-J., ed., Taiwan's small- and medium-sized firms' direct investment in Southeast Asia. Chung-Hua Institution for Economic Research, Taipei, Taiwan.

——— , ed. 1995b. Taiwan's small- and medium-sized firms' direct investment in Southeast Asia. Chung-Hua Institution for Economic Research, Taipei, Taiwan.

Chia, S.Y. 1995. Trade and foreign direct investment in East Asia. In Dobson, W.; Flatters, F., ed., Pacific trade and investment: options for the 90s. John Deutsch Institute for the Study of Economic Policy, Queen's University Press, Kingston, ON, Canada.

China Resources Trade Consultancy. n.d. Almanac of China's foreign economic relations and trade. China Resources Trade Consultancy Co., Ltd, Hong Kong. Various years.

China SSB (State Statistical Bureau). n.d. China statistical yearbook. SSB, Beijing, China. Various years.

Chong, L.M. 1993. An econometric model of China's Guangdong Province. Department of Economics and Statistics, National University of Singapore. Honours academic exercise.

Chou, T.C. 1980. American firms' employment effects and wage differences in Taiwan. Bank of Taiwan Quarterly, 31, 65–86.

Clifford, M. 1992a. Hungry for chips. Far Eastern Economic Review, 10 Sep.

——— 1992b. Labour on tap. Far Eastern Economic Review, 17 Dec.

Coase, R. 1937. The nature of the firm. Economica, 4(16), 386–405.

Coe, D.T.; Helpman, E.; Hoffmaister, A.W. 1994. North–South R&D spillovers. Canadian Institute for Advanced Research, Toronto, ON, Canada. Working Paper 41.

DBS Bank. 1994. Singapore: a base for MNCs' regional headquarters in Asia. Economic Research Department, Singapore, DBS Bank, Singapore. Briefing 43.

de Rosario, L. 1992. Wanted: a new gizmo. Far Eastern Economic Review, 12 Nov.

Dobson, W. 1993. Japan in East Asia: trading and investment strategies. Institute of Southeast Asian Studies, Singapore.

Dobson, W.; Flatters, F., ed. 1995. Pacific trade and investment: options for the 90s. John Deutsch Institute for the Study of Economic Policy, Queen's University Press, Kingston, ON, Canada.

Doherty, E.M., ed. 1995. Japanese investment in Asia. The Asia Foundation, San Fransisco, CA, USA.

Doner, R. 1995. Japanese automotive production networks in Asia. In Doherty, E., ed., Japanese investment in Asia. Asia Foundation and Berkeley Round Table on the International Economy, San Fransisco, CA, USA.

Drysdale, P.; Garnaut, R. 1993. The Pacific: an application of a general theory of economic integration. In Bergsten, C.F.; Noland, M., ed., Pacific dynamism and the international economic system. Institute for International Economics, Washington, DC, USA.

Dubashi, J. 1991. The dragon's curse. Forbes Weekly, 23 Jul.

Dunning, J.H. 1981. International production and the multinational enterprise. Allen and Unwin, London, UK.

——— 1988. The eclectic paradigm of international production: a restatemant and some possible extensions. Journal of International Business Studies, 19(1), 1–31.

————— 1993. Multinational enterprises and the global economy. Addison-Wesley Publishing Ltd, Wokingham, Surrey, UK.

Dunning, J.H.; Cantwell, J., ed. 1987. IRM directory of statistics of international investment and production. Macmillan, London, UK.

Economist, The. 1992. Asia beckons. The Economist, 30 May.

————— 1996. Tough at the top. The Economist, 6 Jan.

EDB Economic Development Board (Singapore). 1994a. Report on the census of industrial production 1992. Singapore Information Services, Singapore.

————— 1994b. Singapore electronics manufacturers directory 1993. Singapore Information Services, Singapore.

————— 1994c. Yearbook. Singapore Information Services, Singapore.

————— n.d.a. Singapore investment news. Singapore Information Services, Singapore. Various years.

————— n.d.b. Yearbook. Singapore Information Services, Singapore. Various years.

Eisenstodt, G. 1994. We are Matsushita's pupils. Forbes Weekly, 26 Sep.

Elsevier Science Ltd. 1994. Yearbook of world electronics data. Elsevier Science Ltd, Oxford, UK.

Encarnation, D.J. 1992. Rivals beyond trade. Cornell University Press, Ithaca, NY, USA.

Ernst, D.; O'Connor, D. 1992. Competing in the electronics industry: the experience of newly industrialising economies. Organisation for Economic Co-operation and Development, Paris, France.

Fallows, J. 1994. Looking at the Sun. Pantheon, New York, NY, USA.

Fan, G. 1994. The key issue in China is system renovation. Lianhe Zaobao, 28 Jul.

Federal Reserve Bank of Kansas City. 1991. Policy implications of trade and currency zones. Economic Review, 76(4).

FEER (Far Eastern Economic Review). 1993. Long spoon shortens. FEER, 8 Apr.

Flannery, R. 1993. Striking a double act. Asian Business, Nov.

Flatters, F.; Harris, R. 1995. Trade and investment: patterns and policy issues in the Asia–Pacific Rim. *In* Dobson, W.; Flatters, F., ed., Pacific trade and investment: options for the 90s. John Deutsch Institute for the Study of Economic Policy, Queen's University Press, Kingston, ON, Canada.

Fortune. 1995. The Global 500. 7 Aug.

Frankel, J.A. 1993. Is Japan creating a yen bloc in East Asia and the Pacific? *In* Frankel, J.A.; Kahler, M., ed., Regionalism and rivalry. The University of Chicago Press, Chicago, IL, USA.

Frankel, J.A.; Wei, A.S.-J.; Stein, E. 1995. APEC and other regional economic arrangements in the Pacific. *In* Dobson, W.; Flatters, F., ed., Pacific trade and investment: options for the 90s. John Deutsch Institute for the Study of Economic Policy, Queen's University Press, Kingston, ON, Canada.

Fukasaku, K. 1992. Economic regionalization and intra-industry trade: Pacific–Asian perspectives. Organisation for Economic Co-operation and Development, Paris, France. Technical Paper 53.

Gereffi, G. 1996. Commodity chains and regional divisions of labor in East Asia. Journal of Asian Business, 12(1), 75–112.

Gereffi, G.; Korzeniewicz, M., ed. 1994. Commodity chains and global competition. Praeger, Westport, CT, USA.

Gittelman, M.; Graham, E. 1994. The performance and structure of Japanese affiliates in the European Community. *In* Mason, M.; Encarnation, D., ed., Does ownership matter? Japanese multinationals in Europe. Clarendon Press, Oxford, UK.

Goldstein, C. 1990. Acer in the hole. Far Eastern Economic Review, 13 Dec.

————— 1992a. Acer trumped. Far Eastern Economic Review, 7 May.

————— 1992b. Taiwan's PC gamble. Far Eastern Economic Review, 24 Sep.

Goodman, D.S.G.; Feng, C. 1993. Guangdong: Greater Hong Kong and the new regionalist future. Asian Research Centre, Murdoch University, Perth, Western Australia, Australia. Working Paper 27.

Government of Canada. 1995. Foreign direct investment and APEC economic integration. Industry Canada, Ottawa, ON, Canada.

Government of Hong Kong. 1994. Report on the 1993 survey of regional representation by overseas companies in Hong Kong. Industry Department, Hong Kong.

————— n.d.a. Hong Kong trade statistics. Census and Statistics Department, Hong Kong. Various years.

————— n.d.b. Hong Kong yearbook. Information Services, Hong Kong. Various years.

———— n.d.c. Survey of overseas investment in Hong Kong's manufacturing industries. Industry Department, Hong Kong. Various years.

———— n.d.d. Surveys on imports from and exports to China for outward processing. Census and Statistics Department, Hong Kong. Various years.

Government of Indonesia. 1992. Survey of manufacturing industries: large and medium enterprises. Central Bureau of Statistics, Jakarta, Indonesia.

———— n.d. Monthly bulletin. Board of Investment, Jakarta, Indonesia.

Government of Japan. 1986. Kaigai jigyo katsudo kihon chosa: kaigai toshi tokei soran. No. 2. [A comprehensive survey of foreign investment statistics, 1983 survey.] Ministry of International Trade and Industry and Keibun Press, Tokyo, Japan.

———— 1989a. Kaigai jigyo katsudo kihon chosa: kaigai toshi tokei soran. No. 3. [A comprehensive survey of foreign investment statistics, 1986 survey.] Ministry of International Trade and Industry and Keibun Press, Tokyo, Japan.

———— 1989b. Small business in Japan: 1989 white paper on small and medium enterprises in Japan. Ministry of International Trade and Industry, SME Agency, Tokyo, Japan.

———— 1991. Kaigai jigyo katsudo kihon chosa: kaigai toshi tokei soran. No. 4. [A comprehensive survey of foreign investment statistics, 1989 survey.] Ministry of International Trade and Industry and Ministry of Finance Printing Bureau, Tokyo, Japan.

———— 1994a. Kaigai jigyo katsudo kihon chosa: kaigai toshi tokei soran. No. 5. [A comprehensive survey of foreign investment statistics, 1992 survey.] Ministry of International Trade and Industry and Ministry of Finance Printing Bureau, Tokyo, Japan.

———— 1994b. Zaisei kinyu geppo. Ministry of Finance Printing Bureau, Tokyo, Japan.

Government of Malaysia. 1968. Census of manufacturing industries. Department of Statistics, Kuala Lumpur, Malaysia.

———— 1973. Census of manufacturing industries. Department of Statistics, Kuala Lumpur, Malaysia.

———— n.d.a. Bank Negara annual report. Bank Negara, Kuala Lumpur, Malaysia. Various years.

———— n.d.b. Economic report. Ministry of Finance, Kuala Lumpur, Malaysia. Various years.

———— n.d.c. Financial survey of limited companies. Department of Statistics, Kuala Lumpur, Malaysia. Various years.

———— n.d.d. Monthly statistical bulletins. Bank Negara, Kuala Lumpur, Malaysia. Various issues.

———— n.d.e. Quarterly bulletins. Bank Negara, Kuala Lumpur, Malaysia. Various issues.

———— n.d.f. Surveys of manufacturing industries. Department of Statistics, Kuala Lumpur, Malaysia. Various years.

Government of Singapore. 1994. Economic survey of Singapore 1994. Ministry of Trade and Industry and Singapore Information Services, Singapore.

———— n.d.a. Foreign equity in Singapore: 1980–1989. Department of Statistics and Singapore Information Services, Singapore. Various years.

———— n.d.b. Singapore yearbook of statistics. Department of Statistics and Singapore Information Services, Singapore. Various years.

Graham, E.M. 1996. Global corporations and national governments. Institute for International Economics, Washington, DC, USA.

Graham, E.M.; Krugman, P. 1993. The surge of foreign direct investment in the 1980s. In Froot, K., ed., Foreign direct investment. The University of Chicago Press (for the National Bureau of Economic Research), Chicago, IL, USA.

Grubel, H.G.; Lloyd, P.J. 1975. Intra-industry trade: the theory and measurement of international trade in differentiated products. The MacMillan Press Ltd, London, UK.

Guangdong Statistical Bureau. n.d. Guangdong tongji nianjian. [Guangdong statistical yearbook.] Guangzhou, Guangdong, China. Various years.

Hainan Statistical Bureau. n.d. Hainan tongji nianjian. [Hainan statistical yearbook.] Zhengzhou, Hainan, China. Various years.

Hamilton, G., ed. 1991. Business networks and economic development in East and Southeast Asia. Centre of Asian Studies, University of Hong Kong, Hong Kong.

Helpman, E.; Krugman, P.R. 1985. Market structure and foreign trade. The MIT Press, Cambridge, MA, USA.

Hill, H. 1988. Foreign investment and industrialization in Indonesia. Oxford University Press, New York, NY, USA.

————— 1995. Australia's Asia–Pacific connections. *In* Dobson, W.; Flatters, F., ed., Pacific trade and investment: options for the 90s. John Deutsch Institute for the Study of Economic Policy, Queen's University Press, Kingston, ON, Canada.

Hong Kong Productivity Council. n.d. The directory of Hong Kong industries. Hong Kong Productivity Council, Hong Kong. Various years.

IMF (International Monetary Fund). 1980–93. Direction of trade statistics yearbook. IMF, Washington, DC, USA.

————— 1993. Direction of trade statistics yearbook. IMF, Washington, DC, USA.

————— 1994a. Direction of trade statistics yearbook. IMF, Washington, DC, USA.

————— 1994b. International financial statistics yearbook 1994. IMF, Washington, DC, USA.

Japanese Chamber of Commerce. 1978. Dai 7 kai Nikkeikigyo (seizogyo) no tai keizai ni tai suru kokendo chosa kekka. [The seventh survey on the activities of Japanese joint-venture manufacturing companies in Thailand.] Japanese Chamber of Commerce, Bangkok, Thailand.

————— 1981. Dai 8 kai Nikkeikigyo jittai chosa (kokendo chosa) kekka. [The eighth survey (survey of contributions) on the state of Japanese firms.] Japanese Chamber of Commerce, Bangkok, Thailand.

————— 1984. Dai 9 kai Nikkeikigyo no jittai chosa. [The ninth survey of the state of Japanese firms.] Japanese Chamber of Commerce, Bangkok, Thailand.

————— 1990. Nikkeikigyo no jittai (kokendo) chosa. [A survey of the state (contributions) of Japanese firms.] Japanese Chamber of Commerce, Bangkok, Thailand.

————— 1994. Dai 12 kai Nikkeikigyo no jittai (kokendo) chosa. [The twelfth survey of the state (contributions) of Japanese firms.] Japanese Chamber of Commerce, Bangkok, Thailand.

JETRO (Japan External Trade Organization). 1995. JETRO white paper on international trade. JETRO, Tokyo, Japan.

Jung, K.-H. 1994. From subcontractor to partner: strategic alliance involving NIC-based firms in the Asia–Pacific. Paper presented at the 2nd Conference on Economic Cooperation in the Asia–Pacific Community, Nov 1994, Seoul, South Korea.

Katseli, L.T. 1992. Foreign direct investment and trade interlinkages in the 1990s: experience and prospects of developing countries. Centre for Policy Research, London, UK. Discussion Paper 687.

Kehoe, L.; Taylor, P. 1996. Prosperity without profits. Financial Times, 10–11 Feb.

Khanthachai, N.; Tanmavad, K.; Boonsiri, T.; Nisaisook, C.; Arttanuchit, A. 1987. Technology and skills in Thailand. Institute of Southeast Asian Studies, Singapore.

Kim, H.-J.; Yoan, S.C.; Sung, J. 1994. Investment demand of the ASEAN electronics industry. Korea Institute of Economics and Technology, Seoul, Korea.

Kojima, K. 1973. A macroeconomic approach to foreign direct investment. Hitotsubashi Journal of Economics, 14(1), 1–21.

————— 1978. Direct foreign investment: a Japanese model of multinational business operations. Croom Helm, London, UK.

————— 1990. Japanese direct investment abroad. Social Science Research Institute, International Christian University, Mitaka, Tokyo, Japan. Monograph Series 1.

————— 1995. Dynamics of Japanese direct investment in East Asia. Hitotsubashi Journal of Economics, 36(2), 93–124.

Kraar, L. 1995. Acer's edge: PCs to go. Fortune, 30 Oct.

Krugman, P. 1979. A model of innovation, technology transfer and the world distribution of income. Journal of Political Economy, 253–266.

————— ed. 1986. Strategic trade policy and the new international economics. MIT Press, Cambridge, MA, USA.

————— 1995. Growing world trade: causes and consequences. Brookings Papers on Economic Activity, 1, 327–376.

Lardy, N.R. 1992. Foreign trade and economic reform in China, 1978–1990. Cambridge University Press, Cambridge, UK.

————— 1994. China in the world economy. Institute for International Economics, Washington, DC, USA.

Lawrence, R.Z. 1991. Emerging regional arrangement: building blocs or stumbling blocs? *In* R. O'Brien, ed., Finance and the international economy. Oxford University Press, Oxford, UK.

Leventhal, M.W. 1989. American entrepreneurs and their Hong Kong fit: a study of networks used by Americans starting businesses in Hong Kong's service industry. University of Hong Kong, Hong Kong. MBA thesis.

Lim, C.F. 1994–95. Global sourcing in the electronics industry. School of Postgraduate Management Studies, National University of Singapore. MBA Advanced Study Project.

Lim, L.; Pang, E.F. 1991. Foreign direct investment and industrialization in Malaysia, Singapore, Taiwan and Thailand. Organisation for Economic and Co-operative Development, Paris, France.

Lipsey, R.E. 1993. Direct foreign investment and structural change in developing Asia, Japan and the United States. *In* E. Ramstetter, ed., Foreign direct investment in Asia's developing economies and structural change in the Asia–Pacific region. Westview Press, Boulder, CO, USA.

Lipsey, R.E.; Blomström, M.; Ramstetter, E.D. 1995. International production in world output. NBER (National Bureau of Economic Research) Working Paper 5385.

Lipsey, R.E.; Weiss, M.Y. 1981. Foreign production and exports in manufacturing industries. Review of Economics and Statistics, 63(4), 488–494.

————— 1984. Foreign production and exports of individual firms. Review of Economics and Statistics, 66(2), 304–308.

Liu, T.Y., Jiang, J.C.; Chang, P.W.; Chou, Z.H.; Juang, C.Z. 1985. The impacts of Japanese firms on our national economy. Research, Development and Evaluation Commission, Executive Yuan, Taiwan.

Markusen, J.R. 1991. The theory of the multinational enterprise: a common analytical framework. *In* Ramstetter, E.D., ed., Direct foreign investment in Asia's developing economies and structural change in the Asia–Pacific region. Westview Press, Boulder, CO, USA.

Mason, M.; Encarnation, D., ed. 1994. Does ownership matter? Japanese multinationals in Europe. Clarendon Press, Oxford, UK.

MEI (Matsushita Electric Industrial Co.). n.d. Annual report. MEI, Tokyo, Japan. Various years.

MIDA (Malaysian Industrial Development Authority). n.d. Statistics on the manufacturing sector. MIDA, Kuala Lumpur, Malaysia. Various years.

MOEA (Ministry of Economic Affairs) Investment Commission. 1995a. Statistics on outward investment, ROC. Investment Commission, Taipei, Taiwan.

————— 1995b. Statistics on overseas Chinese and foreign investment. Investment Commission, Taipei, Taiwan.

Motorola, Inc. 1995. Fourth quarter report. Motorola Inc., Schaumberg, IL, USA.

————— n.d. Annual report. Motorola Inc., Schaumberg, IL, USA. Various years.

Naya, S.; Ramstetter, E.D. 1992. Direct foreign investment and trade in the Asia–Pacific region. *In* Foreign investment, trade and economic cooperation in the Asian and Pacific region. UN Economic and Social Commission for Asia and the Pacific, Bangkok, Thailand. Document E/ESCAP/1006.

Nidhiprabha, B. 1993. Monetary policy. *In* Warr, P.G., ed., The Thai economy in transition. Cambridge University Press, Hong Kong.

Orrú, M.; Biggart, N.W.; Hamilton, G.G. 1991. Organizational isomorphism in East Asia. *In* Powell, W.W.; DiMaggio, P., ed., The new institutionalism in organizational analysis. The University of Chicago Press, Chicago, IL, USA.

Ozawa, T.; Hine, S. 1993. A strategic shift from international to multinational banking: a 'macro-developmental' paradigm of Japanese banks qua multinationals. Banca Nazionale del Lavoro Quarterly Review, 186, 159–174.

Pangestu, M. 1993. Deregulation of foreign investment policy: past, present and future. Paper presented at the Conference on Economic Deregulation in Indonesia, 26–28 Apr, Jakarta, Indonesia.

————— 1995. Taiwanese investment in Indonesia. *In* Chen T.J., ed. Taiwan's small and medium sized firms' direct investment in Southeast Asia. Chung-Hua Institution for Economic Research, Taipei, Taiwan.

Pauly, P. 1995. Trade and investment options in the Pacific area: implications for international economic development. *In* Dobson, W.; Flatters, F., ed., Pacific trade and investment: options for the 90s. John Deutsch Institute for the Study of Economic Policy, Queen's University Press, Kingston, ON, Canada.

Petri, P. 1992. Platforms in the Pacific: the trade effects of direct investment in Thailand. Journal of Asian Economics, 3(2), 173–96.

———— 1993. The East Asian trading bloc: an analytical history. *In* Frankel, J.; Kahler, M., ed., Regionalism and rivalry. The University of Chicago Press, Chicago, IL, USA.

———— 1994. Trade and investment interdependence in the Pacific. Paper presented in the 21st Pacific Trade and Development Conference. Centre of Asian Studies, University of Hong Kong, Hong Kong.

———— 1995. Trade and investment interdependence in the Pacific. *In* Chen, E.K.Y.; Drysdale, P., ed., Corporate links and foreign direct investment in Asia and the Pacific. Pacific Trade and Development–Harper Educational Publishers, Canberra, ACT, Australia.

Porter, M.E. 1985. Competitive advantage: creating and sustaining superior performance. Free Press, New York, NY, USA.

———— ed. 1986. Competition in global industries. Harvard Business School Press, Boston, MA, USA.

———— 1990. The competitive advantage of nations. Free Press, New York, NY, USA.

Ramstetter, E.D. 1990. The macroeconomic effects of direct investment in Thailand: an econometric investigation. *In* Toida, M., ed., ASEAN, Ajia NIEs no Keizai Yosoku to Bunseki (II) — Heisei Gannendo ELSA Hokokusho. [Economic forecasts and analyses for ASEAN and the Asia NIEs — 1989 ELSA annual report.] Institute for Developing Economies, Tokyo, Japan.

———— 1992a. Foreign direct investment and exports of manufactures from developing economies — Part I: Economic policies. United Nations Conference on Trade and Development, Geneva, Switzerland. UNCTAD/ITD/1, GE.92-555817.

———— 1992b. Foreign direct investment and exports of manufactures from developing economies — Part II: An empirical evaluation by regions and countries. United Nations Conference on Trade and Development, Geneva, Switzerland. UNCTAD/ITD/2, GE.92-555822.

———— ed. 1993a. Foreign direct investment in Asia's developing economies and structural change in the Asia–Pacific region. Westview Press, Boulder, CO, USA.

———— 1993b. Macroeconomic trends, foreign firms, and economic policy in Thailand. *In* Toida M.; Hiratsuka, D., ed., Ajia kogyoken no keizai bunseki to yosoku (II). [Projections for Asian industrializing region (II).] Institute of Developing Economies, Tokyo, Japan.

———— 1993c. Production technology in foreign and local firms in Thai manufacturing. Graduate School of International Development, Nagoya University, Nagoya, Thailand. Discussion Paper 8.

———— 1994a. Comparisons of Japanese multinationals and other firms in Thailand's non-oil manufacturing industries. ASEAN Economic Bulletin, 11(1), 36–58.

———— 1994b. International trade, multinational firms and regional integration in Thailand. Institute for Southeast Asian Studies, Singapore.

———— 1994c. Trade dependence in foreign multinationals and local firms in Thailand's non-oil manufacturing, 1990. Mimeo.

———— 1994d. Characteristics of foreign multinationals in selected Asian host economies. Paper prepared for the 4th Convention of the East Asian Economic Association, 26–27 Aug, Taipei, Taiwan. East Asian Economic Association, Taipai, Taiwan.

———— 1995. Sectoral flows of foreign direct investment in Thailand. *In* Sectoral studies of foreign direct investment in Asia and the Pacific. Economic and Social Commission for Asia and the Pacific, United Nations, New York, NY, USA. ST/ESCAP/1501.

Ramstetter, E.D.; James, W.E. 1993. Multinationals, Japan–US economic relations, and economic policy: the uncomfortable reality. Kansai University, Osaka, Japan.

Rapp, W.V. 1995. Capturing Japan's attention. *In* Safarian, A.E.; Dobson, W., ed., Benchmarking the Canadian business presence in East Asia. The University of Toronto, Toronto, ON, Canada.

Redding, S.G.; Adler, N.J.; Doktor, R. 1987. From the Atlantic to the Pacific century: cross-cultural management reviewed. Department of Management Studies, University of Hong Kong, Hong Kong. Research Paper 1.

Redding, S.G.; Tam, S. 1991. Networks and molecular organizations: an exploratory view of Chinese firms in Hong Kong. Department of Management Studies, University of Hong Kong, Hong Kong. Departmental discussion paper.

Reuber, G. 1973. Private foreign investment in development. Organisation for Economic and Co-operation and Development, Paris, France, and Blackwell, Oxford, UK.

Riedel, J. 1975. The nature and determinants of export-oriented FDI in a developing economy: a case of Taiwan. Weltwirtschaftliches Archiv, 111(3), 505–528.

Rugman, A.M. 1980. Internalization as a general theory of foreign direct investment: a re-appraisal of the literature. Weltwirtschaftliches Archiv, 116(2).

———— 1985. Internalization is still a general theory of foreign direct investment. Weltwirtschaftliches Archiv, 121(3).

Safarian, A.E. 1993. Multinational enterprise and public policy. Edward Elgar, Aldershot, Hants, UK.

Safarian, A.E.; Dobson, W., ed. 1995. Benchmarking the Canadian business presence in East Asia. The University of Toronto, Toronto, ON, Canada.

Sahasakul, C. 1993. Fiscal policy. In Warr, P.G. ed., The Thai economy in transition. Cambridge University Press, Hong Kong.

Salleh, I.M. 1995. Foreign direct investment and technology transfer in the Malaysian electronics industry. In The new wave of foreign direct investment in Asia. Institute of Southeast Asian Studies, Singapore, and Nomura Research Institute, Tokyo, Japan.

Saxonhouse, G. 1993. Pricing strategies and trading blocs in East Asia. In Frankel, J.A.; Kahler, M., ed., Regionalism and rivalry. The University of Chicago Press, Chicago, IL, USA.

Schive, C. 1990. The foreign factor: the multinational corporation's contribution to the economic modernization of the Republic of China. Hoover Institution, Stanford University, Palo Alto, CA, USA.

Sibunruang, A.; Brimble, P. 1987. Foreign investment and export orientation: a Thai perspective. In Naya, S.; Vadakan, V.V.; Kerdpibule, U., ed., Direct foreign investment and export promotion: policies and experiences in Asia. East–West Center, Honolulu, HI, USA, and Southeast Asian Central Banks Research and Training Centre, Kuala Lumpur, Malaysia.

Sibunruang, A.; Brimble, P.; Greer, S.; Dunne, M.; Asawachintachit, D.; Harnchanpanit, K. 1991. Export-oriented industrial collaboration: a case study of Thailand. United Nations Centre on Transnational Corporations, New York, NY, USA. Mimeo.

Sieh Lee, M.L. 1992. The transformation of Malaysian business groups. In McVey, R., ed., Southeast Asian capitalists. Cornell University Press, Ithaca, NY, USA.

Singapore Economic Committee. 1986. The Singapore economy: new directions — Report of the Economic Committee. Ministry of Trade and Industry, Singapore.

Singapore Economic Planning Committee. 1991. The strategic economic plan towards a developed nation. Ministry of Trade and Industry, Singapore.

Sony Corporation. n.d. Annual report. Sony Corporation, Tokyo, Japan. Various years.

Straits Times. 1993a. ATT sets up $24M support centre for Asia–Pacific region. Straits Times, 8 Jun.

———— 1993b. ATT to invest extra $100M in IC production. Straits Times, 23 Nov.

Sung, Yun-wing. 1991. The China–Hong Kong connection: the key to China's open-door policy. Cambridge University Press, Cambridge, UK.

Tambunlertchai, S.; Ramstetter, E.D. 1991. Foreign firms in promoted industries and structural change in Thailand. In Ramstetter, E.D., ed., Direct foreign investment in Asia's developing economies and structural change in the Asia–Pacific region. Westview Press, Boulder, CO, USA.

TDB (Trade Development Board Singapore). 1992. Singapore trade statistics: imports and exports, December 1992. Singapore Information Services, Singapore.

———— 1993. Singapore electronics trade directory, 1993/94. Singapore Information Services, Singapore.

———— n.d. Singapore trade statistics: imports and exports. Singapore Information Services, Singapore. Various years.

Texas Instruments. n.d. Annual report. Texas Instruments, Houston, Texas. Various years.

Thailand NESDB (National Economic and Social Development Board). 1988. National income of Thailand: new series 1970–1987. NESDB, Bangkok, Thailand.

———— 1992. National income of Thailand: rebase series 1980–1991. NESDB, Bangkok, Thailand.

———— 1993a. Diskette with TSIC 5-digit data on total income and value added. NESDB, Bangkok, Thailand.

———— 1993b. National income of Thailand 1992. NESDB, Bangkok, Thailand.

———— 1994. National income of Thailand 1993. NESDB, Bangkok, Thailand.

Thee, K.W.; Pangestu, M. 1995. Technological capability in manufactured exports from Indonesia. *In* Ganiatsos, T. ed., Technological capability in manufactured exports in Asia. United Nations Committee on Trade and Development, Geneva, Switzerland.

Tsai, P.L. 1991. Determinants of foreign direct investment in Taiwan: an alternative approach with time-series data. World Development, 19(2–3), 275–285.

Tu, J.H. 1990. Direct foreign investment and economic growth: a case study of Taiwan. Institute of American Culture, Academia Sinica, Taipei, Taiwan.

Tu, J.H.; Schive, C. 1996. Determinants of foreign direct investment in Taiwan: a new approach and findings. UNCTC, New York, NY, USA.

Tyson, L.D.A. 1992. Who's bashing whom? Trade conflict in high-technology industries. Institute for International Economics, Washington, DC, USA.

UNCTAD (United Nations Committee on Trade and Development). 1993. World investment report 1993: transnational corporations and integrated international production. UNCTAD, Geneva, Switzerland, and New York, NY, USA.

———— 1994. World investment report 1994: transnational corporations, employment and the workplace. UNCTAD, Geneva, Switzerland, and New York, NY, USA.

———— 1995. World investment report 1995: transnational corporations and competitiveness. UNCTAD, Geneva, Switzerland, and New York, NY, USA.

———— n.d. Handbook of international trade and development statistics. UNCTAD, Geneva, Switzerland, and New York, NY, USA. Various years.

United Nations. 1993. Foreign investment and trade linkages in developing countries. United Nations Department of Economic and Social Development, New York, NY, USA.

———— n.d. International trade statistics. United Nations Statistics Department, New York, NY, USA. Various years.

USAID (United States Agency for International Development). 1992. Philippines: barriers to entry study — Final report (Vols I and II). USAID, Washington, DC, USA.

US Department of Commerce. 1981. U.S. direct investment abroad, 1977. Department of Commerce, Bureau of Economic Analysis, Washington, DC, USA.

———— 1985. U.S. direct investment abroad: 1982 benchmark survey data. Department of Commerce, Bureau of Economic Analysis, Washington, DC, USA.

———— 1986. U.S. direct investment abroad: operations of U.S. parent companies and their foreign affiliates, revised 1983 estimates. Department of Commerce, Bureau of Economic Analysis, Washington, DC, USA.

———— 1990. Survey of current business. Department of Commerce, Bureau of Economic Analysis, Washington, DC, USA.

———— 1991. U.S. direct investment abroad: operations of U.S. parent companies and their foreign affiliates, revised 1988 estimates. Department of Commerce, Bureau of Economic Analysis, Washington, DC, USA.

———— 1992. U.S. direct investment abroad: 1989 benchmark survey, final results. Department of Commerce, Bureau of Economic Analysis, Washington, DC, USA.

———— 1993. U.S. Direct investment abroad: operations of U.S. parent companies and their foreign affiliates, revised 1990 estimates. Department of Commerce, Bureau of Economic Analysis, Washington, DC, USA.

———— 1994. U.S. direct investment abroad: operations of U.S. parent companies and their foreign affiliates, preliminary 1992 estimates. Department of Commerce, Bureau of Economic Analysis, Washington, DC, USA.

Vasuprasant, P. 1994. Turning points in international labor migration: the case of Thailand. Asian and Pacific Migration Journal, 3(1), 175–202.

Vernon, R. 1966. International investment and international trade in the product cycle. Quarterly Journal of Economics, 80(2), 190–207.

———— 1972. Influence of national origins on the strategy of multinational enterprise. Revue Économique, 23(5), 547–62.

———— 1994. Multinationals and governments: key actors in the NAFTA (North American Free Trade Agreement). *In* Eden, L., ed., Multinationals in North America. The University of Calgary Press, Calgary, AB, Canada.

Warr, P.G. 1993. The Thai economy. *In* Warr, P.G., ed., The Thai economy in transition. Cambridge University Press, Hong Kong.

WEF (World Economic Forum). 1995. World competition report. WEF, Lausanne, Switzerland.

Westlake, M. 1991. Busy signals? Far Eastern Economic Review, 7 Mar.

Westney, D.E. 1994. The large Japanese industrial firm as a network organization. MIT Sloan School of Management, MIT, Cambridge, MA, USA. Mimeo.

———— 1996. The Japanese business system: key features and prospects for change. Journal of Asian Business, 12(1), 21–50.

Williamson, O.E. 1975. Markets and hierarchies, analysis and antitrust implications: a study in the economics of international organization. Free Press, New York, NY, USA.

Wong, Siu-lun. 1992. Business networks, cultural values and the state in Hong Kong and Singapore. Paper presented at the 3rd Soka University Pacific Basin Symposium, 14–16 Sep, Japan.

Wong, T.Y.C. 1994. Hong Kong's manufacturing sector: transformations and prospects. *In* Leung, B.K.P.; Wong, T.Y.C., ed., 25 years of social and economic development in Hong Kong. Centre of Asian Studies, University of Hong Kong, Hong Kong.

Wong, T.Y.C.; Kwong; K.S. 1994. The role of Hong Kong in Asia's regional economic growth and development. *In* Hong, N.S., ed., The business environment in Hong Kong. Oxford University Press, Hong Kong.

World Bank. 1990. China: macroeconomic stability and industrial growth under decentralized socialism. World Bank, Washington, DC, USA.

———— 1993. The East Asian miracle. World Bank, Washington, DC, USA.

———— 1995. Global economic prospects and the developing countries. World Bank, Washington, DC, USA.

———— 1996. World development report. World Bank, Washington, DC, USA.

Worth, F.S. 1991. Keys to Japanese success in Asia. Fortune.

WTO (World Trade Organization). 1996. International trade. WTO, Geneva, Switzerland.

Wu, R.Y.; Wang-Liang, C.F.; Chou, T.C.; Lee, T.K. 1980. American firms' investment and its effects on our national economy. Institute of American Culture, Academia Sinica, Taipei, Taiwan.

Yokota, K.; Imaoka, H. 1993. Structure of trade interdependence in Asia. *In* Ohno, K., ed., Regional integration and its impact on developing countries. Institute for Developing Economies, Tokyo, Japan.

Young, A. 1994. The tyranny of numbers: confronting the statistical realities of the East Asian growth experience. National Bureau of Economic Research, Cambridge, MA, USA. NBER Working Paper 4680.

Yuan, F. 1995. Guangdong products facing challenges. Hong Kong and Taiwan Information Daily, 1 Jun.

Yukawa, K. 1992. Economic cooperation between Guangdong and inland areas. Japan External Trade Organization, China Newsletter, 100, 9–16.

Zhu, J.J. 1992. Guangdong's economic relationships with central government and with other provinces/municipalities. *In* Maruya, T., ed., Guangdong: open door economic development strategy. Centre of Asian Studies, University of Hong Kong, and Institute of Development Economies, Tokyo, Japan.

Zhu, S.L. 1993. The development of the Guangdong economy has been accelerated by opening up to the outside world. Nanfang Ribao, 20 Jan.

INDEX

Locators followed by f indicate figures; those followed by n indicate footnotes; those followed by t indicate tables.

The Publishers

The **International Development Research Centre (IDRC)** is committed to building a sustainable and equitable world. IDRC funds developing-world researchers, thus enabling the people of the South to find their own solutions to their own problems. IDRC also maintains information networks and forges linkages that allow Canadians and their developing-world partners to benefit equally from a global sharing of knowledge. Through its actions, IDRC is helping others to help themselves.

IDRC Books publishes research results and scholarly studies on global and regional issues related to sustainable and equitable development. As a specialist in development literature, IDRC Books contributes to the body of knowledge on these issues to further the cause of global understanding and equity. IDRC publications are sold through its head office in Ottawa, Canada, as well as by IDRC's agents and distributors around the world.

The **Institute of Southeast Asian Studies (ISEAS)** was established as an autonomous organization in 1968. It is a regional research centre for scholars and other specialists concerned with modern Southeast Asia, particularly the many-faceted problems of stability and security, economic development, and political and social change.

The Institute's research programs are the Regional Economic Studies Programme (RES, including ASEAN and APEC), the Regional Strategic and Political Studies Programme (RSPS), the Regional Social and Cultural Studies Programme (RSCS), and the Indochina Programme (ICP).

The Institute is governed by a 22-member Board of Trustees comprising nominees from the Singapore government, the National University of Singapore, the various Chambers of Commerce, and professional and civic organizations. A 10-member Executive Committee oversees day-to-day operations; it is chaired by the Director, the Institute's chief academic and administrative officer.